☀ INSIGHT GUIDES
THE FRENCH RIVIERA

Discovery
CHANNEL

APA PUBLICATIONS
Part of the Langenscheidt Publishing Group

L

✻ INSIGHT GUIDE
FRENCH RIVIERA

Editor
Lesley Gordon
Art Director
Ian Spick
Picture Editor
Hilary Genin
Cartography Editor
Zoë Goodwin
Production
Kenneth Chan
Editorial Director
Brian Bell

Distribution

UK & Ireland
GeoCenter International Ltd
Meridian House, Churchill Way West
Basingstoke, Hampshire RG21 6YR
Fax: (44) 1256-817988

United States
Langenscheidt Publishers, Inc.
36–36 33rd Street, 4th Floor
Long Island City, NY 11106
Fax: (1) 718 784-0640

Australia
Universal Publishers
1 Waterloo Road
Macquarie Park, NSW 2113
Fax: (61) 2 9888 9074

New Zealand
Hema Maps New Zealand Ltd (HNZ)
Unit D, 24 Ra ORA Drive
East Tamaki, Auckland
Fax: (64) 9 273 6479

Worldwide
Apa Publications GmbH & Co.
Verlag KG (Singapore branch)
38 Joo Koon Road, Singapore 628990
Tel: (65) 6865-1600. Fax: (65) 6861-6438

Printing

Insight Print Services (Pte) Ltd
38 Joo Koon Road, Singapore 628990
Tel: (65) 6865-1600. Fax: (65) 6861-6438

©2007 Apa Publications GmbH & Co.
Verlag KG (Singapore branch)
All Rights Reserved

First Edition 1992
Fourth Edition 2007

ABOUT THIS BOOK

The first Insight Guide pioneered the use of creative full-colour photography in guidebooks in 1970. Since then, we have expanded our range to cater for our readers' need not only for reliable information about their chosen destination but also for a real understanding of that destination. Now, when the internet can supply inexhaustible (but not always reliable) facts, our books marry text and pictures to provide that much more elusive quality: knowledge. To achieve this, they rely heavily on the authority of locally based writers and photographers.

How to use this book

The book is structured to convey an understanding of the French Riviera:

◆ To understand the region today, you need to know something of its past. The first section covers its people, history and culture in lively essays written by specialists.

◆ The main Places section provides a full run-down of all the attractions worth seeing. The main places of interest are coordinated by number with full-colour maps. Margin notes provide background information and tips on special places and events.

◆ Photographic features highlight art, gardens, architecture and the glamour and glitz of the coastal area.

◆ Photographs are chosen not only to illustrate the landscape and buildings but also to convey the moods of the region and the life of its people.

◆ The Travel Tips listings section provides information on getting around, hotels and activities. Information may be located quickly by using the index printed on the back cover flap.

the Places chapters including: *Hyères and the Maures, St-Tropez and its Peninsula, St-Raphaël, Fréjus and the Argens Valley, Antibes and The Plateau de Valbonne, Cagnes, Vence and St-Paul, Cap Ferrat and The Golden Triangle, Monaco* and wrote the *Tropical Gardens* photo story.

London-based writer, editor and regular Insight contributor, **Roger Williams**, used his knowledge of the region to provide additional photo stories on architecture, *Riviera on Canvas* and *The Cult of Celebrity*. Williams also reworked *Post-War Boom* and *In Words and Pictures*.

Lyn Parry, a longtime resident of France updated *Perched Villages* and *Border Country*. **Margie Rynn** updated and extended the Travel Tips.

Caroline Radula-Scott updated *Cannes* and edited the text, while Insight Guide editors **Siân Lezard** and **Carine Tracanelli** worked tirelessly and skilfully, steering the text through the editing process.

Other contributors to previous editions whose work is still evident, include **Lisa Gerard-Sharp, Rowlinson Carter, Barry Miles, Peter Graham, Chris Peachment, Sophie Radice, Philip Sweeney, Tony Rocca** and **Mike Meade**.

The principal photography for this guide was produced by Insight regular **Gregory Wrona**. **Douglas Corrance, Catherine Karnow** and **Bill Wassman** provided additional images.

Neil Titman proofread the text and **Isobel Mclean** compiled the book index.

The contributors

This edition of *Insight Guide: French Riviera*, based on earlier editions by **Rosemary Bailey** and **Freddy Hamilton**, has been thoroughly updated by Insight Guides editor **Lesley Gordon**.

Gordon enlisted the skills of several writers and researchers including original editor **Rosemary Bailey** who lived for many years in the south of France and still has a home in the country. She revisited the Riviera history and updated chapters on: cuisine, Nice and Menton.

Paris based journalist and editor **Natasha Edwards**, is a regular contributor to Insight's French titles and also writes on travel, contemporary art and design for the *Independent* and *Condé Nast Traveller* among other publications. As the main contributor Edwards reshaped most of

CONTACTING THE EDITORS

We would appreciate it if readers would alert us to errors or outdated information by writing to:

Insight Guides, P.O. Box 7910, London SE1 1WE, England. Fax: (44) 20 7403-0290. insight@apaguide.co.uk

NO part of this book may be reproduced, stored in a retrieval system or transmitted in any form or means electronic, mechanical, photocopying, recording or otherwise, without prior written permission of *Apa Publications*. Brief text quotations with use of photographs are exempted for book review purposes only. Information has been obtained from sources believed to be reliable, but its accuracy and completeness, and the opinions based thereon, are not guaranteed.

www.insightguides.com
In North America:
www.insighttravelguides.com

Contents

Maps

Travel Tips

THE BEST OF THE FRENCH RIVIERA

Art, culture, nature, food and festivals... Here, at a glance, are our recommendations for your visit

BEST PERCHED VILLAGES

- **Eze**. Spectacular medieval fortified village with a tumultuous history of piracy. *See pages 185–6.*
- **Gourdon**. High above the Gorges-du-Loup; the castle has an Art Deco museum in. *See page 144.*
- **Mougins**. Immaculate hill village where Picasso once lived. *See pages 132–3.*
- **Peillon**. Arguably the most beautiful of all the perched villages, high up among olive and pine trees. *See pages 221–2.*
- **Ramatuelle**. Escape the crowds in St-Tropez in this chic hilltop village which has summer music and theatre festivals. *See page 89.*
- **St-Paul-de-Vence**. This village was "rediscovered" by artists in the 1920s and has art at every corner, be it at La Colombe d'Or restaurant or the Fondation Maeght. *See pages 155–8.*
- **Ste-Agnès**. Atmospheric, fragrant and historic. *See pages 224–6.*

BEST BEACHES

- **Cannes**. Palm-fringed beaches edge the famous Croisette boulevard. *See page 109.*
- **Fréjus-Plage**. Fine, sandy stretch of beach lined with cafés and restaurants, and flanked by the yacht basin of Port-Fréjus. *See page 98.*
- **Juan-les-Pins**. Beach fun under the fragrant pines. *See page 129.*
- **Le Lavandou**. Glitzy bars and busy restaurants make this popular resort a trendy nightspot, but there are also some fine, quiet beaches for the less energetic. *See pages 74–5.*
- **Opéra Plage, Nice**. A favourite with locals, it claims to be the oldest private beach in France. *See page 172.*
- **Pampelonne, St-Tropez**. Legendary beach where the international jet set flock to in the summer. *See pages 87–8.*

GOURDON

Altitude: 760 m.

Place forte Sarrazine
Eglise · Château · Fontaine

BEST FOR ART

- **Fondation Maeght, St-Paul-de-Vence.** World-class museum showcasing paintings by Chagall, Braque and Miró among others. *See pages 156, 157–8.*
- **Musée de l'Annonciade, St-Tropez.** See how Matisse and Seurat painted St-Tropez in this attractive museum. *See page 85.*

- **Musée Chagall, Nice.** Admire Chagall's flamboyant work. *See page 174.*
- **Musée Jean Cocteau, Menton.** A display of the writer's own art in a colourful converted fort. *See page 209.*
- **Musée Matisse, Nice.** Matisse bequeathed this collection to the town he lived in from 1918 to 1954. *See page 174.*
- **Musée Picasso, Antibes.** The artist spent a prolific year in this chateau. *See pages 123–5.*
- **Musée d'Art Moderne et d'Art Contemporain (MAMAC), Nice.** French and American art from the 1960s to present day. *See pages 173–4.*

OPPOSITE TOP: the Cannes coast. **OPPOSITE RIGHT:** the beach at Juan-les-Pins. **LEFT:** stained glass art by Fernand Léger. **TOP RIGHT:** Jardin Botanique du Val Rahmeh, Menton. **BELOW RIGHT:** Villa Kérylos, Beaulieu-sur-Mer.

BEST GARDENS

- **Jardin Biovès, Menton.** A fragrant citrus delight which comes alive during the town's Fête du Citron. *See page 206.*
- **Jardin Botanique du Val Rahmeh, Menton.** Luxuriant exotic fruit trees from all over the world, and indigenous Provençal species. *See pages 210, 211–12.*
- **Jardin des Colombières, Menton.** Romantic

gardens with a true Provençal allure. *See page 210.*
- **Jardin Exotique, Monaco.** Covering a steep cliff, these magnificent hanging gardens of cacti and succulents are a feast for the eyes. *See pages 194–95.*
- **Jardin Oblius Riquier, Hyères.** Tropical garden with a Moorish villa and peacocks. *See page 70.*

BEST MUSEUMS

- **Musée de l'Auto-mobiliste, Mougins.** Impressive collection of antique cars. *See page 133.*
- **Musée de la Photographie, Mougins.** A collection of photographic portraits of Picasso. *See page 133.*
- **Musée International de la Parfumerie, Grasse.** Learn all

about the perfume industry and see ornate old bottles and Marie-Antoinette's vanity case. *See pages 140–1.*
- **Musée Renoir, Cagnes-sur-Mer.** Renoir spent his latter years in the delightful Domaine des Collettes, now filled with valuable memorabilia. *See page 151.*

8

BEST RESTAURANTS

- **Alain Llorca at the Moulin des Mougins.** A "Deconstructed" take on Provençal classics. *See page 137.*
- **Auberge de la Madone, Peillon.** Wonderful Provençal cuisine with extraordinary mountain views. *See page 231.*
- **La Bastide St-Antoine, Grasse.** Gastronomic gem in an atmospheric setting of olive groves. *See page 145.*
- **La Colombe d'Or, St-Paul-de-Vence.** Legendary atmospheric restaurant once frequented by Miró, Picasso and Matisse. *See page 163.*
- **Fleur de Sel, Haut-de-Cagnes.** Inventive Provençal dishes in a stunning village setting. *See page 163.*
- **Joël Robuchon, Monte-Carlo.** Famous chef Robuchon brings his innovative and conceptual dishes to glitzy Monaco. *See page 201.*

- **La Merenda, Nice.** A Niçois institution, this tiny bistro is popular for its local cuisine. *See page 176.*
- **Leï Mouscardins, St-Tropez.** Chef Laurent Tarridec serves innovative Provençal cooking. *See page 93.*
- **La Palme d'Or, Cannes.** A Michelin two-star restaurant with imaginative gastronomic cuisine in the Hollywood-set favourite Hôtel Martinez. *See pages 116–17.*
- **Restaurant de Bacon, Antibes.** A legendary, luxury fish restaurant with views of old Antibes and a great bouillabaisse. *See page 137.*
- **Spoon Byblos, St-Tropez.** A Mediterranean version of the Paris original in the hip Byblos Hotel. *See page 93.*
- **Villa des Lys, Cannes.** Renowned chef Bruno Oger received two Michelin stars for his exquisite regional fare. *See page 117.*
- **Le Vistaero, Menton.** Avant-garde cuisine in a luxurious hotel with sea views and a botanical garden. *See page 217.*

BEST OUTDOORS

- **Gorges du Loup.** The steep gorges make for an adventurous hike past waterfalls. *See pages 143–4.*
- **Iles d'Hyères.** Luxuriant islands and formerly a centre of piracy. *See page 71.*
- **Massif de l'Estérel.** The *maquis*-covered peaks have scenic views and hiking trails. *See pages 100–2.*
- **Massif des Maures.** Hiker's paradise with abundant flora and a tortoise breeding centre. *See pages 75–8.*
- **Parc National du Mercantour.** Atmospheric national park teeming with game. *See pages 240, 242.*
- **Roya Valley.** The well-preserved valley is dotted with picturesque perched villages. The Haute Roya has more dramatic scenery, with deep gorges and waterfalls. *See pages 236–8 and 238–42.*
- **Vallée des Merveilles.** Step back in time and marvel at spectacular ancient rock carvings. *See page 240.*

ABOVE climbing in the gorges. **LEFT:** fresh food everywhere. **RIGHT:** beautiful butterflies can be seen in the tropical gardens.

BEST ARCHITECTURE

- **Cathédrale St-Michel, Sospel**. Extravagant façade flanked by Romanesque tower. *See page 235.*
- **Château de la Napoule**. Medieval castle housing an art foundation showcasing sculpture from American artist Henry Clews. *See page 102.*
- **Château de Roquebrune**. This feudal castle par excellence offers sweeping views of the coast. *See pages 214 15.*
- **Château Grimaldi, Cagnes-sur-Mer**. Old medieval tower turned Renaissance residence with a fine collection of modern art and the Musée d'Art Moderne Méditerranéen. *See pages 153–4.*
- **Cité Episcopale, Fréjus**. Medieval complex comprising a cathedral, baptistery and cloister. *See pages 98–9.*
- **Hôtel Carlton, Cannes**. The oldest and most glamourous hotel on the Croisette. *See page 111.*
- **Palais Lascaris, Nice**. Restored 17th-century mansion with a pharmacy, Genoese staircase, frescos and tapestries. *See page 169.*
- **Villa Noailles, Hyères**. Cubist jewel of concrete and glass complete with a Cubist garden; it was once frequented by Dalí and Man Ray. *See pages 68–9.*
- **Villa Ephrussi de Rothschild**. Belle Epoque villa with an exquisite collection of paintings and antiques; the highlight of a visit, however, are the stunning themed gardens. *See pages 182–3.*

ABOVE the grand Eglise St-Michel, Sospel. **LEFT:** Hôtel Carlton, Cannes. **BELOW:** traditional handblown bubble glass from Biot.

- **Villa Kérylos, Beaulieu-sur-Mer**. Mock Greek villa on the waterfront with beautifully laid-out courtyards as the highlight. *See page 184.*

BEST SHOPPING

Ceramics, Vallauris. This town's long tradition for pottery was revived by Picasso, who came here to make his own extraordinary pieces, and it is now one of France's leading pottery centres; you'll be spoilt for choice of plates and vases on rue Clémenceau. *See pages 130–1.*

Fashion. The Riviera is the place to be seen, so make sure you're looking your best by browsing the trendy shops in St-Tropez, Nice and Cannes. *See pages 81–8, 165–75, 107–15.*

Food. The Côte d'Azur is a gourmet's paradise; every town has a market selling juicy olives, fragrant herbs and heavenly sweets among a whole array of edible temptations.

Glass, Biot. After watching a glass-blower at work in the museum, you will want to buy a souvenir from one of the glass shops; look out for "bubble glass", a unique technique for which Biot is reputed. *See pages 135–6.*

Perfume, Grasse. Grasse is famous for its fragrances, which can be bought at the boutiques of the perfume factories – Fragonard, Galimard and Molinars being the most prestigious names. *See page 141.*

Wine. Visit vineyards on the lower slopes of the St-Tropez peninsula; follow the scenic route des Côtes de Provence, which is dotted with pretty *domaines* where visitors can take part in a *dégustation* before deciding what to buy. *See page 89.*

A TRICK OF THE LIGHT

The Côte d'Azur offers the classic image of a summer holiday with sunny, palm-fringed beaches and chic cafés. Beyond the sand are scenic views and cultural highlights

The French Riviera, the Côte d'Azur: the names are interchangeable but both conjure up an atmosphere of sun, sea and glamour. Generally, the Côte d'Azur refers to the whole of France's sunshine coast from Marseille to Menton, and the Riviera, which we are focusing on in this guide, to the region stretching southeastwards between Hyères and the Italian border. Along here, the exotic towns of St-Tropez, Cannes, Antibes, Nice, Monte-Carlo and Menton lie like a glittering necklace of sophistication, luxury and fun.

Admittedly, if you're not one for concrete and crowds, there are parts that have lost their edge and *je ne sais quoi*. But you don't have to travel far inland to find pretty medieval villages perched on hilltops, unspoilt mountainous countryside with a network of spectacular hikes, and the Haut-Pays in the east, where the villages close to the border are more Italian than French – appropriate, since the Italian influence is a significant aspect of the region. Nevertheless, the coast's plentiful pleasures include not only sun and sea and a hyperactive nightlife, but magnificent art and architecture, glorious perfumes and gardens, world-class yachts, casinos, film and jazz festivals, food, wine and spectacular scenery. It has also become a hub for high-tech industry and a year-round venue for business conferences.

As one of the world's most glamorous holiday destinations, the French Riviera has attracted visitors for more than two centuries, from Queen Victoria to Elton John, Picasso to Brigitte Bardot, many making it their home. The British first discovered the Riviera's health-giving climate and then the artists found how remarkable the Mediterranean light was for their work. The Americans brought the hedonistic jazz age to the coast in the 1920s and 1930s. So many writers and artists have been inspired by the Riviera, creating a rich cultural heritage that remains at its very soul.

In this guide, we have tried to be honest, to acknowledge the problems as well as exploring the pleasures, because it is these issues, as much as its traditional diversions, that make the Côte d'Azur today such a fascinating place to visit. ❏

PRECEDING PAGES: a couple enjoy sea views on the Côte d'Azur; the perched village of Peillon. **LEFT:** Cannes Old Town and harbour.

FROM CAVES TO CISTERCIANS

Early cave dwellers, Ligurians, Greeks, Romans, Saracens
and Genoese all occupied France's south coast in
succession, leaving evidence of their presence
on rocks, in ruins and in the architecture

At first glance the stretch of Mediterranean coast which we now call the
Côte d'Azur shows little evidence of a
rich and varied history among the high-rise
hotels, motorways and shopping centres. But
look a little deeper and you will uncover
many layers of history, going right back to the
earliest cave dwellers.

The first settlers

Some of the very first signs of human habita-
tion in Europe have been discovered in this
corner of France. Remains around 400,000
years old were recovered from a cave complex
near Nice harbour and can be seen in the
Musée Terra Amata *(see page 173)* built on the
site. Evidence of Cro-Magnon hunters who
lived around 40,000 years ago has been found
in caves around Grasse, and later signs of settlement can be seen at Mont Bégo in the Vallée des Merveilles in the form of Bronze Age
rock carvings, believed to have been left by
Ligurians between 1800 and 1500 BC.

Little more survives of the Ligurians, apart
from the faint remains of their forts, built of
unworked stone, and some shards of pottery
and beads. It is not until the time of the
Greeks, who set sail from Phocaea in Asia
Minor in the early 6th century BC, that we
have much knowledge of everyday life in the
region. The peaceable Phocaeans expanded
trade links throughout the Mediterranean.
Their new colony, Massalia (Marseille), soon
became the most important commercial
centre along the coast, and by the mid-4th
century BC they had founded Nikaia (Nice),

Antipolis (Antibes), Citharista (La Ciotat),
Olbia (Hyères) and Athenopolis (St-Tropez).
The Phocaeans introduced techniques for
cultivating vines and olive trees to the region.

Saracen invaders

With Roman rule from 125 BC *(see box page
19)*, hill tribesmen ventured down from their
fortified settlements to establish themselves
in towns along the coast. However, after the
fall of the Roman Empire Goths, Vandals and
Lombards ravaged the area and chaos reigned.

ABOVE: a remnant of a bygone empire.
RIGHT: Roman remains at Cimiez, Nice.

Marauders also came from the sea. The Saracens were to devastate great swathes of the Mediterranean coastline from Rhodes to Spain, and foray inland as far as the Loire river. They were Arabs originating from North Africa and the eastern Mediterranean coast, and appear to have been exceptionally violent. By about the year AD 800 they had taken power in Eze (just west of Monaco), La Turbie and Ste-Agnès, and by the 10th century occupied most of the coast.

Eventually, in 980, a concerted effort was made to drive them out by the Count of Provence, Guillaume le Libérateur, who numbered among his soldiers a Genoese named Gibellino Grimaldi, the first mention in the region of a Grimaldi, the name of Monaco's ruling house today.

It was a period of internal strife in which everybody fought with everybody else for dominance. The history of Eze in particular is a litany of violent attack and subjugation, with generations of inhabitants being murdered and pillaged, the village itself repeatedly burnt and razed to the ground. What is remarkable is the tenacity with which the village has always risen from the ashes – and today continues to flourish on the lucrative proceeds of tourism.

Neither France nor Italy was united in the way we know them today. Instead, both were

EARLY GAZETTEERS

The history of travel to the region is a story in itself; antiquarian travel books abound from the days when 18th-century visitors like Tobias Smollett came to look for antiquities or restore their health.

The writers of these books, rattling about in their horse-drawn carriages along dusty roads lit only by fireflies or moonlight, or clambering over headlands still rich with fragrant maquis in search of Roman inscriptions and rare butterflies and plants, supply us with a wealth of classical learning and acute observation about the region, both as it used to be in ancient times and as it appeared to them in their own time.

Some of the most fascinating include the Rev. Hugh Macmillan's scriptural reflections in his 1885 *The Riviera*; Edward Strasburger's *Rambles on the Riviera* (1906), with its loving detail of the long-lost flora of the region; Sir Frederick Treves's highly coloured historical anecdotes in *The Riviera of the Corniche Roads* (1923); or the altogether racier picture painted by Charles Graves in *The Riviera Revisited*, written just after World War II, and rather more concerned with the price of a good coq au vin than with anything else.

Their tales give us an excellent reference point for linking the rich history of the region with life here today.

divided into warring fiefdoms, with towns constantly at war with each other, Pisa at war with Genoa, Genoa at war with Nice, even tiny Gorbio, north of Monaco, at war with nearby Roquebrune.

The famous long-running conflict between the Guelphs and Ghibellines, defenders and enemies of the Pope, also engulfed the towns and villages of the region. Nice itself had been a constantly shifting pawn on the Mediterranean chessboard, and was frequently besieged, often by the French.

From the 14th century Nice and the surrounding region was under the protection of Savoy, ruling from Italy, and did not elect to

become part of France until 1860. The Italian influence is apparent everywhere, in architecture, place names and the Niçois dialect.

Penitents, saints and monks

Religion, of course, played a great part in the area's early history, and a wealth of religious art and architecture survives. Christ's followers are reputed to have brought Christianity to the region when they landed at Les-Stes-Maries-de-la-Mer in AD 40.

Almost every town and village has a religious festival or procession to celebrate, often revived for the benefit of tourists, but authentic nonetheless. One curious example is *La*

procession aux escargots, which takes place in Gorbio. It is in fact not a promenade of snails, but a festival celebrated by the White Penitents when all the streets and houses are illuminated by oil flames lit in a multitude of snail shells.

There are Penitents' chapels in Nice, Cannes and Sospel near the Italian border. These were lay brotherhoods that appeared in the 14th century and proliferated throughout the Midi. They were denoted by the colours of their hoods, the most important being *Pénitents Gris, Blancs* and *Noirs*, and were devoted to charitable and sacred duties.

All over the Côte d'Azur are sanctuaries and pilgrimage centres, often in high mountain reaches, and heavily festooned with votive offerings. The Knights Templar also had a presence here, and there are vestiges of their castles near Vence and La Gaude.

One of the most interesting ecclesiastical locations is the Ile St-Honorat, one of the Iles de Lérins, a group of islands near Cannes. After its foundation in the 5th century, the island's monastery was for hundreds of years the centre of Christianity in southern Europe, described as "the Iona of the South". Honorat's sister, Marguerite, started a convent on the next island, now named after her.

Honorat's holy life attracted many followers, including St Patrick, and the monastery rapidly became a centre of learning. It grew very wealthy, and eventually owned land from Grasse to Barcelona, including the village of Cannes itself. But such riches were a great temptation, and attacks by pirates and quarrels between the monks and abbots undermined the monastery. By the 17th century it had collapsed, and later the Cistercians built a new monastery there.

Damsels and pirates

The history of the region is awash with pirates, troubadours, distressed damsels, grand feats of bravery and dramatic betrayals. Even today, among the high-rises and pink villas, an old staircase, a curiously carved lintel or a Renaissance window can evoke a past both humble and heroic.   ❑

LEFT: a detail from a door on Saint-Maximin-la-Ste-Baume Basilica.

Roman Remains

The Roman occupation of Provincia (Provence) lasted from 125 BC for more than 500 years and left a considerable imprint on the landscape. Although their primary intentions were military, the Romans can in a sense be regarded as the first visitors to appreciate the pleasures of the coast, building luxurious villas, arenas, baths and temples of which substantial ruins still remain. In some cases entire towns have been excavated, and everywhere there are stones with Latin inscriptions.

In Fréjus, the amphitheatre and arena is one of the largest built in Gaul, and the aqueduct, with enormous pillars and buttresses, is almost as massive as its more famous counterpart in Nîmes. The theatre is ruined but used for atmospheric summer performances, and the restored arena is also still in use. The cathedral encloses a 5th-century baptistery and also includes late Roman walling and mosaics.

The cathedral in Vence was built on the site of a Roman temple, and throughout the town are scattered fragments of blocks with Roman inscriptions. Vallauris was founded by the Romans and was famous for its pottery even then, thanks to the quality of the red clay of the surrounding mountains.

Cimiez, high on a hill above Nice, has a splendid amphitheatre, perhaps best appreciated on a starry summer night sitting on the original seats carved from rock. You can also see the baths here, cut into a natural alcove, with fragments of paving still remaining, and evidence of latrines, with two hollowed-out lavatory seats still perched over the gully for running water. A swimming pool, which was once lined with marble, has a single reconstructed white column to indicate the original colonnade around it, and the entrance to the frigidarium is defined by its white marble thresholds - despite only fragmentary evidence you can imagine the leisure centre it once was, with attendant slaves, masseurs oil-

ing recumbent bodies, and ancient Romans relaxing and discussing the latest imperial pronouncements.

One of the most magnificent sights in the entire region is the Trophée des Alpes at La Turbie, the victory monument which still towers over its surroundings today, dwarfing the little village of the same name and providing an enduring emblem of the power and self-confidence of the Romans at that time, around 6 or 7 BC. The Via Aurelia, the main Roman road from Rome to Arles, passed through Menton, La Turbie and Cimiez, part of the route following what is now the Grande Corniche. La Turbie was the

highest point of the road, a landmark visible for miles around and an important staging-post, bustling with merchants, centurions, slaves and gossip from Rome.

Other sites in the Alpes de Haute Provence include a Roman temple in Riez, with remains of granite pillars and marble capitals, and the foundations of baths. A rock-cut inscription can be seen to the northeast of Sisteron, in a narrow ravine called the "Pierre Ecrite". It commemorates the construction of a road through the gorge, and probably dates from around AD 414–30, when the Roman Empire was in decline. ❑

RIGHT: the ruins of Trophée des Alpes, La Turbie

SHAPING THE COAST

The Riviera's mild Mediterranean winters attracted foreign visitors, from invalids and artists to distinguished royalty. Victorians flocked here for their health. The arrival of the railway simplified the journey, and by the start of the 20th century the hedonists were moving in

annes is for living, Monte-Carlo for gambling and Menton for dying – such was the Victorian popular wisdom on the Riviera. During the days of the Grand Tour, France was considered a mere antechamber to classical Rome. But in the 1850s the south of France replaced Italy as the British home from home and began to attract visitors from all over Europe.

The Côte d'Azur was first noticed as a pleasant place to visit by Tobias Smollett, the Scots doctor and writer who pioneered sea-bathing as a cure for consumption. During his stay in Nice from 1763 to 1765, Smollett enjoyed the climate but found fault with the garlicky Niçoise cuisine; however, his ill humour melted on contact with fruit sorbets. These "sorbettes, which are sold in coffee houses and places of public resort... are very agreeable to the palate," he wrote.

Escaping the northern winter

In Smollett's day, medical fashion favoured spas such as Bath and Cheltenham, but the prescription in the following century was for Riviera resorts. Until the 1870s consumption was the killer disease in Victorian Britain, and the only remedy was believed to be a warm climate. Visitors in search of health were soon followed by social climbers and pleasure-seekers. The British migrated south in autumn and north in spring. From May to September

LEFT: the winter season in Nice.
RIGHT: Lord Brougham, who "discovered" Cannes for the British in 1834.

the Riviera villas were shuttered and the resorts deserted by all but unfashionable merchants, gamblers, prostitutes and, horror of horrors, the locals.

The journey south

By the 1830s the days of corsairs and Barbary pirates were over, and the civilised world could travel freely once more. For the British upper classes this meant travelling by private carriage to the Riviera, stopping at inns along the way. In 1832 the Boyle family journeyed south in a drawing-room on wheels at a maximum speed of 55 km (34 miles) a day. Money bought only a certain degree of comfort and convenience, not speed. The journey took up to three weeks, as long as in the time of the Roman Empire.

From the 1830s steamships linked the Riviera ports, and the British often opted for the sea voyage. Despite the *fin de siècle* opulence of the later steamers, the sea route was hardly any better than the overland journey. There were many complaints about vibration and noise. In the 1880s the Rev. John Aiton complained that "the passengers are starved; English passengers are insulted by Frenchmen... and as to a Frenchman lending an English voyager a spyglass or telling him the name of an island, he would rather spit in his face".

A NECESSARY DILIGENCE

Passengers who could not afford private transport to the Riviera were forced to use the diligence, a contraption built like an overgrown hay wagon. Weighing up to 5 tons, the diligence carried 15 to 30 passengers and travelled at little more than walking pace. In 1829, one disgruntled passenger, Dr James Johnson, likened French diligences to "locomotive prisons... in which one is pressed, pounded, and, what is worse than all, poisoned with mephitic gasses and noxious exhalations from above, below and around". Passengers faced a choice between the cold, hard seat beside the driver, or the cowshed odours of the seats inside.

Taking the train

The arrival of the railway in the 1850s dramatically reduced the hardships of travel to the Riviera. Yet horse power was not rendered obsolete overnight, since key stretches of railway were not complete before 1870. Until then, carriages bridged the gaps. Diligences would be placed on a rolling platform and hitched to a train: a forerunner of the modern Motorail service. The most luxurious trains included private saloon carriages, each containing a bedroom, sitting-room, smoking-room and study.

Within 10 years of the arrival of the railway, Hyères, Cannes and Nice had large foreign colonies in the winter. Hyères was the first Riviera resort to be patronised by the British, with a solid British clientele from the 18th century, and Queen Victoria wintered there before finding a more desirable address in Nice. By the 1890s, Hyères's date palms incongruously sheltered an Anglican church, English estate agencies and public tennis courts.

The British in Nice

Compared with the privacy of Hyères, Nice was a more ostentatious resort, with British residents living in grand hotels in the public eye. Even before the arrival of the railway, Nice had a flourishing British community which, by the 1820s, was sketching and botanising its way through the mild Mediterranean winters. Visitors indulged in literary readings, *soirées musicales*, "quantities of gossip and a great deal of dressiness".

The Victorian obsession with standards and public works soon had an impact on Nice. Winter residents insisted on better roads, English plumbing, new bandstands and public parks. The British imported nurses and ladies' maids, gardeners and grocers, lawyers and estate agents, and the local labour force had to conform to quirky British requirements. Hotels advertised "drainage executed by English engineers". French hoteliers grumbled about the demands of English hygiene, the frostiness of English manners and the sibilance of English speech.

Yet British philanthropy was also grudgingly acknowledged. After the failure of the olive and citrus crops in 1821, the impoverished locals were offered employment by the

Rev. Lewis Way and Charles Whitby. Funded by British families, the scheme subsidised the building of the camin des Anges, the coastal road now known as the promenade des Anglais in Nice. Only the uncharitable questioned British motives: the promenade provided better access to the shore and effectively shielded ostentatious Victorian strollers from the hordes of beggars.

The development of a British quarter known as Newborough attracted a new wave of Victorian visitors, as did the arrival of the railway link in 1864. Then Queen Victoria set the tone, wintering in the palatial Hotel Regina in the Cimiez district of Nice from 1895.

this charming fishing village while looking for a suitable home for his invalid daughter. Brougham built several villas in Cannes and wintered there for almost 35 years. Under his patronage, the village became one of the Riviera's most British resorts and was home to over 1,000 English residents shortly after the railway reached Cannes in 1862. The atmosphere, heavy with Victorian divinity and charitable works, changed with the Prince of Wales. By the Naughty Nineties, Cannes was a cosmopolitan resort with a reputation for vice second only to Monaco's.

Baptist ministers, such as Charles Spurgeon, condemned Monaco as "the serpent in

Dens of iniquity

Regal Nice was eventually eclipsed by stylish Cannes – in British eyes, at least. Queen Victoria's son, the future Edward VII, was not alone in thinking Cannes's Cercle Nautique the most exciting club on the Côte. Still, Edward did as much to keep the *entente cordiale* as his mother. The Prince of Wales and his yacht *Britannia* were regular fixtures from 1878.

However, it was an earlier and more endearing Englishman who put Cannes on the map. In 1834, Lord Brougham "discovered"

paradise". Queen Victoria was not alone in refusing to stay in this "moral cesspool". Before the end of the century, Monaco was labelled "a sunny place for shady people", the haunt of arms dealers, courtesans and gold-diggers. But the glamour drew British gamblers such as Charles Wells, the fortune hunter who became famous as "The Man Who Broke the Bank at Monte-Carlo".

The Riviera's sanatorium

The archetypal British resort was Menton. In its heyday, in the 1890s, it was home to the largest British colony on the Continent. As the main Riviera sanatorium, the resort had at least

LEFT: veranda view of Monte Carlo.
ABOVE: the casino on the pier at Nice.

50 British doctors and several rest homes. It was quieter and cheaper than Cannes and combined a dowager-like atmosphere with a seductive setting. Menton's dullness could be attributed to Dr James Henry Bennet, an eminent Victorian doctor who came "to die in a quiet corner". Instead, his consumption was cured by "the bracing, stimulating climate". From 1859 to 1891 he promoted Menton as the ideal health resort, and his book, *Winter and Spring on the Shores of the Mediterranean*, became a European bestseller. Consumptives were told to wrap up warmly but to have as much fresh air and exercise as possible. Flannel underwear and woollen

received the Kings of Italy, Sweden, Saxe, Belgium and Bulgaria, as well as visits by Count Pushkin and Russian Grand Dukes.

Queen Victoria, travelling incognito as the Comtesse de Balmoral, arrived in such style that her identity was no secret. The royal train was hung with silk and was partly decorated with Louis XVI furnishings. Naturally, the Queen travelled with supplies of familiar foods, including Irish stew, kept lukewarm in red flannel cushions.

Homes and hotels

The royals visited not as Grand Tourists of the 18th century, explorers on a unique adventure,

clothes were obligatory, as were shoes with india-rubber soles, designed to insulate one against cold stone floors.

Royals aplenty

Beaulieu, Menton and San Remo were soon competing for the aristocratic clientele while Monte-Carlo catered exclusively to the rich and pleasure-loving. "Princes, princes, nothing but princes. If you like them, you're in the right place," French novelist Guy de Maupassant complained of Cannes in 1884. The royals were headed by Queen Victoria, the Empress of Russia and Emperor Frederick of Germany. At the turn of the 20th century, Menton alone

but as *habitués*, comfortable in their second homes. Second palaces would be a more accurate description. Queen Victoria had a huge residence in the Cimiez quarter of Nice. Menton's magnificent 18th-century Palais de Carnolès was owned by the Queen of Prussia in the 1860s and by Prince Metternich shortly afterwards. But given the difficulties of finding suitable French servants, royal visitors often preferred to spend the whole winter season in hotels.

Unsurprisingly, such hotels were known as *les palaces de la Côte d'Azur*. Among the grandest were L'Hermitage in Monte-Carlo and the Victoria Hotel on the promenade des

Anglais in Nice. Charles of Prussia stayed in the Victoria in the 1860s, while Tsarevich Alexander made it his home until his accession to the Russian throne in 1881. In Menton, the Winter Palace was favoured by oriental royals, while Grand Duchess Anastasia occupied the Riviera Palace. In the lovely *salon de musique*, a Parisian orchestra played Gregorian chants or gypsy music before Anastasia's afternoon nap.

The regal lifestyle

When the Riviera was Ours (1977), Patrick Howarth's unashamedly chauvinistic account of the region's development, argues that even foreign royals followed an English lifestyle on the Riviera. Prince Albert of Prussia regularly attended Anglican services at Christ Church in Cannes, where he made it known that he hoped the hymns would include *The Son of God Goes Forth to War*. Tea and tennis were immovable fixtures; Russian Grand Dukes wore starched white linen; Belgian and Swedish aristocrats challenged one another to polo matches.

Chauvinism aside, the royal way of life on the Riviera was not so much English as regal. Crested dice were thrown in the Monte-Carlo Casino; coroneted carriages paraded the promenade des Anglais in Nice; the *jeunesse dorée* dined on caviar, blinis and pink champagne in the Hôtel de l'Hermitage. Leopold I of Belgium was Queen Victoria's domineering uncle, but it was his son who made an indelible mark on the Riviera. As an ageing playboy, Leopold II wintered on the Riviera from the 1890s to his death in 1909. He resided at a villa on Cap Martin and filled the grounds with lush vegetation he had transplanted from the Belgian Congo.

Princess Daisy of Pless, a noted Edwardian beauty who married a German baron, described Leopold peeling grapes with "a look of cruelty on his face as if he were skinning alive all the members of the Aborigines Protection Society". Apart from orchids and palms, Leopold's main hobby was young girls. Princess Daisy describes how his lecherous pursuits were hampered by a dangling white beard and grotesquely long fingernails.

Doyenne of Riviera royalty

Empress Eugénie of France, often described as the doyenne of the Riviera royalty, also held court on Cap Martin in the 1890s. Although Spanish-born and married to a French emperor, Eugénie was an anglophile who had been educated in England. After the Empire collapsed in 1870, she left Deauville for Kent. By the 1890s her husband and son had died, and Eugénie relished her role of grande dame in exile, even managing to charm Queen Victoria. Eugénie had long been a diplomat behind the scenes and, after a dull period of suburban exile in Chislehurst in Kent, England, found the Riviera a more

LEFT: the Grand Hotel, facing the beach at Juan-les-Pins. **RIGHT:** Queen Victoria on one of her many visits.

The Blue Train

A long with the Santa Fe Superchief, the Orient Express and the Trans-Siberian Express, the Blue Train was never just a train: to travel on it from London to the Côte d'Azur in the 1920s and 1930s represented the epitome of style and fashion. It was said that for a woman to have made it in the world, she should have dined at the Ritz and Colony restaurants in New York, the Everglades Club in Palm Beach, the Ritz in Paris, Claridge's in London and the Hôtel du Cap in Antibes, sailed on the *Berengaria* and the

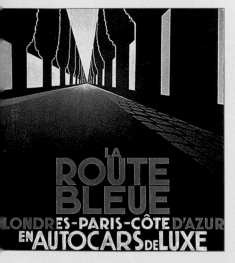

Aquitania, and, of course, travelled on the Blue Train. It was the only way to travel to the Côte d'Azur.

From the 1850s the south of France was opened up to foreign visitors as trains reduced travelling time from about three weeks by carriage to just a couple of days by train. All that was then needed was sleeping accommodation, of the type pioneered by Pullman in the United States.

The first manufacturer of sleeping cars in Europe was the Compagnie Internationale des Wagons-Lits, founded by an enterprising Belgian, Georges Nagelmackers, in 1872. Its sleeping cars became famous, and the

Calais–Nice–Rome Express, the first train to the south to be equipped with sleeping accommodation, began operating in 1883, about six months after the Orient Express. The Italian section was little used, and the train eventually became known as the Calais-Mediterranean Express. It was popularly referred to as the Blue Train after 1922, when blue-and-gold painted sleeping cars first appeared. The words "Train Bleu" were painted on the carriages only after 1949.

This luxurious palace on wheels, whose carriages each catered to only 10 passengers, would leave Calais at 1pm, arriving in Monte-Carlo at 9.30 the following morning. For early British visitors travelling south for the winter, nothing could beat the pleasurable contrast of boarding under the grey skies and smog of London and waking the next morning to the blue skies, terracotta roofs and orange trees of the Mediterranean.

It became known as the "millionaires' train", with some justification. The American James Gordon Bennett, owner of the *New York Herald* and famous for his profligacy, once, to the horror of his valet, tipped the conductor 20,000 francs. The conductor used the money to open a restaurant in Boulogne. When Charlie Chaplin came to stay with Frank Jay Gould, he arrived on the Blue Train. The Duke of Windsor had a carriage with a specially designed bathroom. When the casinos brought girls down from Maxim's in Paris, they were guaranteed return tickets on the Blue Train (to be used if they failed to snare a rich husband).

The fame of the Blue Train has been enshrined by the arts: Agatha Christie set a Hercule Poirot story on it, *The Mystery of the Blue Train*; Diaghilev directed a musical called *Le Train Bleu*, which was written by Jean Cocteau, with bathing costumes by Chanel and curtain by Picasso.

Today, the Blue Train is no more, though its name endures: Monte-Carlo Casino has a restaurant called Le Train Bleu. But it is still possible to travel in great comfort overnight through France, half-waking at dim-lit stations in the dead of night and rising to the golden sunlight glinting off the Mediterranean. ❏

LEFT: an advertising poster for the Blue Train.

satisfying stage. From her rococo-style Villa Cyrnos, Eugénie quietly advised foreign sovereigns and ministers on world politics.

From Russia with money

Before World War I, the Russian community was second only to the British in size and influence. In 1856, Alexandra Feodorovna, the widow of Tsar Nicholas I, bought Villa Acquaviva on the promenade des Anglais and forged the early Russian links with Nice.

Not that the Russians needed much encouragement. French was the language of the Russian court, and the Riviera made a restful second home, a welcome change from Russian winters and rebellious serfs. The seafront and the boulevard Tzarewitch soon became distinct Russian colonies, set at a safe distance from the English camp at Cimiez. The Russians congregated in La Ferme Russe, Russian tearooms that were run by the formidable Madame Chirikov.

The pastries provided stiff competition to the cream cakes in Perrimond-Rumpelmayer, the favourite German haunt. Below the domed winter garden of La Ferme Russe, imported Russian servants worked the samovars while their mistresses occupied themselves with discussions about upcoming charity balls or the dangers of rheumatic gout. The flamboyant green-and-gold domes of the Russian Orthodox church, built by Tsar Alexander II, remain a testament to the importance of the Russian community in the 19th century. In 1880 Grand Duchess Anastasia, Tsar Nicholas II's aunt, founded the Association Orthodoxe Russe, which looked after consumptive soldiers and students. After the Russian Revolution, the home became known as the Maison Russe and, linked to the Russian Red Cross, it still welcomes Russian émigrés.

The Russian women had a particularly high social profile on the Riviera. One grande dame was the Princess Kotschouby whose ochre Belle Epoque villa is now the Musée des Beaux-Arts in Nice. The Princess Caramachimay abandoned her troublesome Russian estates and emigrated to Cap Martin at the turn of the 20th century. Princess Anna Cher-

vachidze settled on a grand estate near by; it later sheltered a skulking Greta Garbo.

Agas and maharajahs

Non-European royals were also drawn to the Riviera, including the Princess of Siam and the Bey of Algeria. One of the most eccentric visitors was the Maharajah of Kaputhala. In 1897 he arrived at Monte-Carlo's Hôtel de Paris with a vast retinue. One servant, dressed in national costume and bedecked with gold and jewels, would stand behind the Maharajah's chair at dinner. When signalled, he sprinkled flakes of real silver on the royal curries. A later maharajah was instrumental in

opening the Martinez Hotel in Cannes in 1926 when he insisted on Louis XVI bedrooms for every one of the guests.

Sir Mohammed Shah, the Aga Khan III, was one of the few hereditary rulers whose affection for the Riviera has been echoed by his descendants. In 1908 the Aga Khan married an Italian dancer and installed her in a Middle Eastern-style villa above Monaco. Their son, Major Aly Khan, was a member of the Free French forces that helped liberate the Riviera. Aly then went on to marry Rita Hayworth, while his father competed by marrying Yvette, a "Miss France" bathing belle. The current Aga Khan lives in an Art Deco mansion in

RIGHT: the Nice shoreline in the 19th century.

Antibes where "The only unguarded exit is the chute from the swimming pool to the sea."

Us and them

Foreigners maintained a frontier mentality. The only local people they met were shopkeepers and servants; and even this problem could be circumvented by importing staff or living in hotels. Expatriates further down the social scale often ignored all other foreign residents. "You may see English, German and French families pass many weeks together in the same house, eat twice a day at the same table, and sit for hours in the same salon without even exchanging a word."

RUSSIAN ROULETTE

The Russians were enthusiastic gamblers. Princess Souvorov arrived in Monaco in 1869 with an "infallible" method. At casinos across Europe, she had made notes of every winning number in all the games she had seen. But despite thousands of files, she lost 300,000 francs in a couple of hours. Suddenly, her luck changed and she won for eight nights in succession, breaking the bank twice. To celebrate, she scandalised high society by holding a party for complete strangers. The only entry requirement was that guests should be amusing. The locals refused to let her rent a room for the party, so she bought a villa and gave it away the next day.

Such was Frederic Harrison's view of sour-faced Victorian visitors in 1887.

The Riviera was only relatively free from social restraints; in Menton cemetery, each nationality and religion was given a separate burial tier. Nor were the pleasures of the south egalitarian; the Riviera was the preserve of the rich until the Edwardian era.

In the 1840s a house in Nice could be rented for £300 a year, while in the 1880s it cost £1,200 for the winter season. In 1896, the English writer Augustus Hare commented approvingly: "Nice is a home for the millionaire and the working man. The intermediate class is not wanted. Visitors are expected to have money, and if they have to look at pounds, shillings and pence, had much better remain at home."

Victorian and Edwardian visitors were not exclusively aristocratic. "Money increases quickly," wrote Trollope in 1866, "and distances decrease." Bourgeois visitors were, however, in the minority until the 1920s.

American takeover

While the flow of royal visitors continued during the inter-war years, a new elite emerged: the American dollar kings. Dr James Bennet's *Winter and Spring on the Shores of the Mediterranean* had been published in New York in 1870 and provoked a new wave of wealthy visitors. The simple yet sophisticated pleasures of the Mediterranean appealed to jaded American tycoons. In 1898, Dr Allis, the art collector, was attracted to the unspoilt site of the Palais de Carnolès in Menton. After adding two new wings and replanting the gardens, Allis installed his priceless paintings.

James Gordon Bennett, the ostentatious proprietor of the *New York Herald*, started the *International Herald Tribune* so he could live on the Riviera. But he still found time to indulge fellow-Americans at his Beaulieu villa. As for his yacht, *Lysistrata*, even Vanderbilt was impressed. Manned by a 100-strong crew, the yacht had three decks, Turkish baths and a resident Alderney cow. The millionaire once invited Drexel, Biddle and Vanderbilt to dine at the Café Riche, his favourite restaurant in Monte-Carlo. The Americans were turned away from the terrace when the management decided that only cocktails should be served there. An outraged Bennett immediately bought the restaurant for $40,000 and sacked the manager. Then, in appreciation of the well-cooked lamb chops, Bennett promptly handed over the restaurant to Ciro, his favourite waiter, by way of a tip. The fortunate Ciro then went on to open successful restaurants all over Europe.

Easy dames

Colourful courtesans such as Mata Hari and "La Belle Otero" worked their way through the foreign ranks, although Mata Hari's spying was beyond the pale. Until 1914, courtesans had an accepted status in Riviera society. As Mata Hari, the Dutch showgirl Gertrud Zelle came to Monte-Carlo to perform "exotic dances". Her stage name, meaning "sunrise" in Malay, was matched by exotic looks that captivated the French and German Ministers of Information. One night in the Casino, an agent accused her of secreting stolen documents in her bodice. Mata Hari shot him and was excused on the grounds of self-defence.

By contrast, La Belle Otero was apolitical. At the age of 14, Carolina Otero, a Spanish gypsy, married an Italian baron and spent her honeymoon in Monaco. After her husband had lost in the Casino, she removed all the gold buttons from her dress and, as well as causing a stir, amassed a fortune on the tables. Abandoning her husband, she began a new career as a *grande horizontale*. Her voluptuous body was appreciated by Edward VII and Kaiser Wilhelm II. Caroline retired to Monaco in 1922 but her legendary figure lives on at Cannes's Carlton Hotel: the twin domes are said to have been inspired by her perfect breasts.

American eccentrics

There was a distinct change of climate after World War I. The courtesans were no more; the Russians were dead or in exile; the kings of Italy, Spain, Albania and Yugoslavia clung to their thrones; most royals were in financial straits. Only the Americans had the means to live out their fantasies. With the glamorous

new arrivals, winter was banished and the summer season launched. Writer E. Phillips Oppenheim slept aboard a yacht, which was known as the floating double bed; the women were expected to stay awake at night to deal with the mosquitoes.

There was no shortage of eccentrics on the new summer stage. Mr Neal, an American millionaire guest at the Hôtel de l'Hermitage, installed an artificial moon in his window to remind him that it was night and therefore time to go to the Casino. One of his milder whims was to invite 80 guests to a free dinner, provided that they laughed at his jokes. His peremptory method of summoning staff

consisted of firing one pistol shot for room service and two shots if he required a chambermaid for personal services.

Henry Clews, the wealthy American sculptor, was also a noted eccentric. In La Napoule, his Saracen castle, Clews recreated a medieval setting, complete with minstrel gallery and staff dressed in Provençal costume. His wife's pet peacocks were notorious, frequently straying onto the railway line where they often brought the Blue Train to a halt. As Patrick Howarth remarks, "It happened so frequently that the SNCF felt obliged to make a formal demand that the peacocks shouldn't be allowed on the line."

LEFT: the *salle de jeu*, Monte-Carlo Casino.
RIGHT: Carolina Otéro, the courtesan whose breasts inspired the domes of the Carlton Hotel in Cannes.

Writers, dancers and artists

Not for nothing were the 1920s known as *les années folles*. Even if the bodies of bankrupt gamblers were no longer immured in the Casino walls, fortunes could still be won or lost on a dropped gold button. But, amidst the wanton partying, creativity seemed to flourish. Colette, Scott Fitzgerald, Somerset Maugham, Katherine Mansfield and many others found inspiration for their writing on the Côte d'Azur, while modern art flourished in the hands of masters like Picasso and Matisse, both inspired by the art and colours of the south – it was here that they spent their most creative years *(see pages 45–8)*.

As if this were not enough, the costumes and sets were designed by Picasso and Matisse, Utrillo and De Chirico, Georges Braque and André Derain. Unsurprisingly, the ballets ran at a financial loss, but Diaghilev was not deterred: "I don't spend a sou on myself. I have very simple tastes: only the best is good enough." Diaghilev praised Isadora Duncan for breaking with classical tradition but she spurned an invitation to see the Ballets Russes: "I don't care much for acrobats." Instead, she ran up huge hotel bills at the Negresco in Nice and, before her tragic entanglement with a silk scarf, indulged her penchant for chasing young men.

In Monte-Carlo, the impresario Raoul Gunsbourg was the first to stage Wagner outside Bayreuth and, as director of the Monte-Carlo Opera, also introduced the public to works by Berlioz, Massenet and Tchaikovsky. Ravel was invited to compose for the orchestra and created the *Ballet pour Ma Fille*, based on Colette's work. But Gunsbourg's greatest coup was to convince Sergei Diaghilev and his Ballets Russes to settle in Monaco. In turn, Diaghilev persuaded the greatest composers of the age, including Debussy and Stravinsky, to write for the Ballets Russes. The company, starring Pavlova and Nijinsky, danced to such classics ⸱ *L'Après-Midi d'un Faune* and *The Firebird*.

The beautiful people

In the 1920s and 1930s the Riviera was in glamorous American hands, and American dollars poured in. F. Scott Fitzgerald enthused about "the soft-pawed night and the ghostly wash of the Mediterranean far below". Gerald and Sara Murphy, the originals for Dick and Nicole Diver in *Tender is the Night*, had discovered it some years before. After being introduced to the Riviera by Cole Porter, the couple bought Villa America on the Cap d'Antibes and there entertained the Lost Generation. Dorothy Parker, Hemingway and the Fitzgeralds needed little encouragement to sample the sea and sun.

The Goulds, along with the Murphys, entertained *le beau monde*, welcoming André Gide and Jean Giraudoux as well as members of American high society. Frank Jay Gould, heir to a railway empire, virtually created Juan-les-Pins. For Florence, his Californian wife, the Riviera was also a *coup de foudre*: she quickly opened a casino and hotel and created a neo-Gothic villa for herself. Although long treated as arrivistes, the couple exerted great influence over the Riviera for 50 years. The tasteless splendour of Juan-les-Pins is their lasting imprint.

World War II drew the curtains on old American glamour, but the Riviera has proved indulging in cocktails and caviar, John F. Kennedy admired the hotel's exotic gardens from the gigantic terrace.

The star-spangled tradition continues. The Côte d'Azur has not lost its glamour, and continues to attract the rich and famous who rent or own villas on Cap Ferrat or Cap d'Antibes. Rock stars and supermodels still flock to St-Tropez, to dine at the beach clubs or sip cocktails on quayside yachts. The grand hotels retain their legendary status and helicopters; private planes and limousines still provide luxury transport for the privileged percentage to keep the dream of caviar days alive for everyone else. ❏

irresistible to Hollywood stars. The Hôtel du Cap-Eden Roc provides the sumptuous link. Situated on the tip of the Cap d'Antibes, this gilded white palace has long been the focus of the American set, from the Murphys onwards.

A new wave brought such stars as Clark Gable, Humphrey Bogart and Rita Hayworth. At different times, John Wayne and Charlie Chaplin were entertained by the hotel's private funicular to the beach. While

LEFT: guests at the Hôtel du Cap-Eden Roc, 1929.
ABOVE: Dany Robin, Kirk Douglas, Olivia de Havilland, Edward G. Robinson and members of the 1953 Cannes Film Festival jury.

GAMBLERS ANONYMOUS

J. P. Morgan, the American steel magnate, was a notorious gambler at the Monte-Carlo Casino. On one occasion he asked if the individual limit for bets could be doubled to 20,000 francs. When the director refused, Morgan left on the spot, complaining that he wouldn't waste his time with such paltry amounts. Morgan went on to form the US Steel Corporation. Charles Schwab, the Corporation's President, was also an inveterate gambler. After tales of Schwab's profligacy reached the American press, Morgan hypocritically took him to task. Schwab's defence – "But I sin openly, not behind closed doors" – was countered with, "But that's exactly what doors are for."

ANTIBES

SA PLAGE DE JUAN-LES-PINS
SON CAP

THE POST-WAR BOOM

From the 1950s onwards, with the help of Brigitte Bardot and the Cannes Film Festival, the French Riviera became the quintessence of glamour, sun, sex, sea and sand

World War II left much of the Côte d'Azur battered and bruised, with infrastructure and industry in key cities like Marseille virtually wiped out. Road-building and new investment helped boost the economy, while festivals and new arts projects saw the area reinvented as a summer cultural capital. The first Cannes Film Festival in 1946 attracted worldwide attention, publicising the Riviera as the place to see and be seen. This was reinforced by Roger Vadim's 1956 film *And God Created Woman*, in which Brigitte Bardot's unabashed sensuality and penchant for topless sunbathing scandalised the world *(see also page 39)*.

Land of the bikini

Bardot in a bikini was an irresistible combination, but it was just one of the factors drawing people to the beaches. With the advent of post-war youth culture and paid holidays for French workers, the Côte d'Azur entered the late 20th century. It was opened up to everyone, beyond the wealthy aristocracy, who had frequented its glamorous hot spots for more than 100 years, and the show-business people and shipping tycoons who dominated the scene immediately after World War II.

The Côte d'Azur was the quintessence of glamour: sun, sand, sea and sex, with the added frisson of famous film stars who just might be sunbathing on the next *matelas*. But

with a suntan, a bikini and a pair of sunglasses, who was to know the difference anyway. Here was a whole new swinging lifestyle that was emulated by millions of people, all hoping that two weeks on the French Riviera would somehow rub off, making them richer, more beautiful or at least more suntanned. Even these days the dangers attributed to sunbathing appear to have made little impact, and sun-worshippers continue to baste themselves slowly on the sand, as if, in Françoise Sagan's words, they were "nailed to the beach by the forces of summer". Sagan's highly successful novel *Bonjour Tristesse*, published in 1954, also gave a boost to the region.

LEFT: poster for the grand Hôtel Negresco in Nice.
RIGHT: the youthful Bardot.

Fun in St-Tropez

As Roger Vadim described St-Tropez: "It was the happy mixture of old and young, wealth and class. A person with no money could live like a millionaire and a millionaire could have fun living like a bohemian."

In her autobiography, *With Fondest Regards*, Françoise Sagan captures the rapid change that took place in the formerly quiet fishing port in the late 1950s, "a village that triggers off a daydream". When Sagan arrived in 1954 with a crowd of young, wild Parisians, they were the only young, wild people there; they found a scene of timeless calm, with old village women sitting knitting in the shade and fishermen bringing home their catch.

But the very next year she describes "wild and disorderly groups of urban bathing beauties as they rush from street stall to street stall in search of a swimsuit, speedboats and the rowdy screaming and shouting of young people who roar off in unruly disarray – all for the feeble purpose of lying on the sand five hundred metres farther down the beach." Suddenly St-Tropez was the "metropolis of illicit pleasures". She concludes, nonetheless, that St-Tropez has an indestructible beauty with its tonic winds, its peaceful yellow sun, and "red-hued coastline with its intricate inlets".

PLAYING CHICKEN

An incident in Roger Vadim's autobiography typifies the period. "It was 1958. Tahiti beach in St-Tropez. One evening the sound of a Ferrari drowned out the crickets. The roar of a Mercedes 300 SL replied to the Ferrari. It was a duel." Roger Vadim and Gunther Sachs started up their cars positioned either side of a bend in the road with a huge parasol pine in the middle. Neither driver could see the other car and had to guess which way the other would turn at the tree. If they both found themselves on the same side of the tree there would be a head-on collision unless one of the drivers yielded. "It was a sort of Russian roulette with wheels," writes Vadim. He was driving the Ferrari, and the judges included Françoise Sagan, Christian and Serge Marquand and Marlon Brando.

In the second round, the two cars came face to face and a split second before they crashed Sachs lost his nerve, jerked the wheel and plunged his Mercedes into the ditch. He wasn't hurt, and the next day a crane hauled the car out. Sachs, who later became Brigitte Bardot's third husband, was very wealthy and could easily afford to cover the damage. That evening he gave a celebration dinner at the Restaurant Tahiti; an enormous dish was served which turned out to be Serge Marquand decorated with mayonnaise and gherkins.

Rampant development

Being the world's favourite holiday destination naturally took its toll. Millions flocked every summer, renting anything from exclusive *pied dans l'eau* villas to caravans, from yachts to sailing dinghies, and from *motocyclettes* to Mercedes. The property market boomed. What began as merely good investment was rapidly exploited by developers, and by the 1970s property prices were rocketing, with luxury villas in areas like La Californie and Super-Cannes commanding record prices.

What the French termed "caviarisation" began. Soon there was barely an inch of coastline left that was not built on. Vast marinas were constructed, and every fat cat from Aristotle Onassis to Donald Trump had to have a yacht as big as a ferry moored in Antibes or Monte-Carlo.

Bardot versus the mayor

Instead of mere luxury villas, huge apartment blocks rose everywhere. For a while it was a free-for-all, with ugly results. By 1980, the government had begun to crack down. Bardot also put her foot down, threatening to leave St-Tropez if the mayor went ahead with a new development scheme. She insisted that the town must decide who was the greater tourist attraction. The mayor backed down.

From then on, new building was forbidden within 100 metres (110 yds) of the sea; highrise apartment buildings were banned, and new ones limited to seven floors; nothing was to be built in designated "natural zones" of virgin woods and fields. In many areas now, new houses can only be built using traditional materials and methods.

The permanent exception to this rule is Monaco, where skyscrapers cram the tiny principality like Hong Kong or Manhattan, the most recent built on landfill, often blocking light and views from older properties. Since many of Monaco's residents are domiciled there for tax purposes, few complain.

Enduring charm

Today, within the Alpes-Maritimes *département*, 92 percent of the housing stock is located along the coast, although villages further and further inland are being enthusiastically restored. The property market remains buoyant, with an annual growth of around 15 percent a year, making it one of the fastest-growing markets in Europe.

But, despite the continued development and the inevitable problems generated, in many essential respects this charmed coastline offers to the visitor the same interest and pleasures as ever. It has a near-perfect climate, resulting from its blessed geographical position nestling between snow-crowned mountains and palm-fringed sea. The scenery remains sensational, eclipsing even the most

grotesque architectural mistakes. The same bare red porphyry rocks and glittering turquoise sea, silvery olive trees and fragrant broom greet new arrivals as they have always done. Matisse's "glaring festive light" still bathes everything in a luminescent glow he felt was so strong no one would believe such intense colours were possible.

Inland, the mountains are covered in lavender and broom, high mountain plateaux remain silent and windswept, and if the medieval villages are less desolate than they were, so much the better. The current wave of restoration has preserved many buildings which would otherwise be reduced to rubble.

LEFT: sun worshippers on the Plage de Pampelonne.
RIGHT: Roger Vadim and Jane Fonda.

The more hedonistic latter-day attractions still hold good; F. Scott Fitzgerald's "lost caviar days" endure for some. In Monte-Carlo the casinos still draw the gullible rich; the nightclubs of Juan-les-Pins continue to attract swarms of young people for whom a day on the beach, a good suntan, the latest fashion in beachwear (or even no beachwear at all), followed by a night of dancing, constitute a perfect holiday. For the gourmet francophile, the area abounds in fine restaurants and top-flight chefs, and those with cultural aspirations cannot fail to be stimulated by a huge number of museums and world-class art galleries.

A mecca for business

Whatever the challenges, the glamorous image of the French Riviera undoubtedly remains. Perhaps what is most remarkable about the region is that it has, somehow, tenaciously hung on to its image and not gone slithering downmarket, the almost invariable fate of other popular holiday destinations.

Image, after all, is what it is all about, and it is the image of the Côte d'Azur that attracts not only over nine million tourists a year but also swarms of business visitors, and entices companies to relocate here. Increasingly, the Côte d'Azur has become the centre of the European sunbelt and a high-tech paradise along the lines of California's Silicon Valley. (The Provence-Alpes-Côte d'Azur region is formally twinned with California, and the Var aims to become, somewhat dubiously, the "Florida of Europe".)

In fact, business receipts now actually exceed revenue from tourism. With an anuual turnover of around €6 billion the business sector is the most significant source of local income and creator of employment. Foreign companies play an important role, with about two-thirds of them located in Nice and the high-tech park of Sophia-Antipolis.

Business tourism is very successful, and there is a huge year-round conference trade, accounting for about a third of total hotel turnover. Companies relocate here, attracted by the climate, lifestyle and image of the Riviera, and take advantage of improved transport and communications systems – Nice is the second-largest airport in France after Paris

THE FOREIGN ELEMENT

Foreigners were largely responsible for forming the Côte d'Azur, and they are still a significant presence today. However, they – the British, American, Scandinavian, Dutch, Russian – are less and less likely to be wealthy retirees. Many work in the high-tech sector, or in tourism and support industries. They settle with their families, aided by bilingual psychiatrists and language colleges.

The English still predominate, though Americans are increasing in numbers. There are anglophone schools in Mougins, Nice and Sophia-Antipolis. Monte-Carlo's Riviera Radio can be heard from St-Tropez to the Italian border, and English bookshops exist in Cannes, Antibes,

Monaco and Valbonne. The British Association has branches in Cannes, Nice and Menton, and the Anglo-American Group of Provence indulges in Scottish dancing and Marseille cuisine. Other nationalities are also well represented – there is the Nederlands Club, the Canadian Club and the Swedish Christmas Fair.

The region has always been a second home for celebrities, and stars like Joan Collins, Ringo Starr, Michael Caine, George Michael and Elton John have now been joined by a younger generation, with the Beckhams buying a well-defended property near Bargemon in the Var. The rich and famous, after all, still need somewhere to go.

(Charles de Gaulle), with over 46 airlines now serving 90 destinations. Marseille in particular has undergone a dramatic transformation as urban renewal projects, especially around the docklands, have injected new life and much-needed employment opportunities into the city. The expansion of the harbour in Monaco has doubled the capacity of this thriving port.

Going for quality

But a "technological Eden" it is not. Despite such visionary developments, the Côte d'Azur can often look as if it is approaching its zenith. Although the tourist authorities continue to talk in traditional terms about increasing the number of visitors (from nine million to 10 million a year – and they are almost halfway there), they do concede that it is important now to focus on "quality rather than quantity".

So tourists are being encouraged to participate in the culture and activities the region has to offer, as well as the sea and the beaches, and to travel further afield, explore the (as yet) largely unspoilt hinterland, and to visit at other times of the year, out of the traditional summer season. Thus, for example, Cannes has launched a shopping festival in January, taking advantage of all the luxury shops which need high spenders to justify their existence out of season. Chic new boutique hotels have opened, spa treatments are offered, and themed holidays such as painting or cookery courses are increasingly being promoted.

Protecting the golden goose

One innovative idea is the Azur Road Show, which offers an open-top sports car with a planned route and gourmet meals along the way. For the adventurous there are new animal parks, including a wolf park in St-Martin-Vesubie in the Parc Mercantour and an animal reserve at Andon-Thorenc, not far from Grasse, which includes wild boar, chamois and a herd of bison.

There is at last some recognition that to carry on regardless would be to risk killing the golden goose. The problems of overcrowding and increasing pollution will eventually put off even the most weathered sun-worshipper.

The 1990s saw several disastrous seasons, with the Gulf War and a particularly ill-timed oil slick resulting in deserted beaches and empty restaurants. In 1992 major floods throughout the region caused severe devastation. A heatwave in 2003 caused massive forest fires, which destroyed vast areas.

Political shenanigans

The political scandals that beset the region in the last decade of the 20th century have not done much for its image either. Most infamous was Jacques Médecin, Mayor of Nice from 1965 until 1990 (and son of former mayor Jean Médecin, who ruled Nice for 38

years). He was indicted for financial corruption in 1990 and fled to Uruguay, but was finally extradited in 1994 and sent to prison. On his release, he fled again, and died in November 1998.

He was not alone; throughout the region, mayors and public officials have been indicted, and even imprisoned for corruption and underworld dealings. Hyères became known as the "Chicago of the Côte" after a series of bomb attacks and the mysterious assassination of a local official campaigning against corruption. The Mayor of Cannes was brought to trial over a casino scandal, and the Mayor of Fréjus was investigated for financial irregularities. In 2005 some feared the bad old days of Jacques Médecin had returned when officials in the office of Mayor Jacques Peyrat (a close friend of Jean-Marie Le Pen) were accused of accepting bribes to award contracts for work on Nice's new tramway system.

Politically, the region still leans strongly to the right. Although its popularity has diminished in recent years, the National Front is still a formidable presence in the region, pulling in an alarming 21 percent of the vote in the 2004 regional elections, though rather less in the European elections the following year. Riots in and around Marseille in November 2005 were triggered by racial tensions.

Forest fires and pollution

Pollution continues to be a volatile issue, and beaches now have flags to warn bathers of excess contamination. Even so, there is a general tendency to try to minimise the problem rather than tackle it fundamentally. Toxic algae in the sea are a major problem, due in part to yacht anchors damaging the seabed, and new jetties and marinas affecting currents. The algae, first detected in 1984, have multiplied at an astonishing rate, now affecting up to 10,000 hectares (24,000 acres) between Toulon and Genoa, posing a grave threat to marine life.

Forest fires are a critical concern, with more financial resources being required every year to combat them; they destroy at least 50,000 hectares (125,000 acres) of land in the region every year. While fire has always been a threat, the scale of disasters has grown because incendiary material in the forests is no longer cleared by local inhabitants. Owners of forest land are now required to clear their own grounds, and from 30 June to 30 October, the *période rouge*, no fire-kindling is permitted in high-risk zones.

Air surveillance is used to spot fires, and fire-fighting technology has become increasingly sophisticated, with water-filled planes and motorbikes equipped with hydraulic pumps. Nevertheless, forest fires in 2003 destroyed large areas around St-Tropez and Fréjus, causing seven deaths.

The traffic nightmare

Appalling traffic means the coast roads are frequently choked, and parking is a nightmare. Transport remains the key to the development of the region. A tramway system for Nice is being built, opening in 2007, though costs have soared enormously since the project began. The TGV runs as far as Nice, but the tracks from Marseille have not yet been equipped for high speeds; upgrading the line has finally been confirmed, after years of discussion over the environmental impact, but it will take 10 years or more to complete.

A relief *autoroute* further inland from the A8 is also planned, to improve communications along the crucial Barcelona–Genoa Mediterranean axis. But this, too, has run into political difficulties. Meanwhile, more low-cost flights are pouring visitors into Nice.

It remains to be seen whether the Côte d'Azur can retain its allure while exploiting it enough to survive. There are many contradictions in this richly endowed and over-exploited region of France. When a proud new villa-owner pays €1,000 for an ancient olive tree to be planted in his designer-landscaped garden, while centuries-old olive groves are being ripped up to be built on, it is time to invoke the spirit of Renoir, who bought his land at Les Collettes with the express intention of preserving the olive trees that had been growing there for hundreds of years. ❏

LEFT: forest fires cloud the sky at Pampelonne beach.

Brigitte Bardot

When the film *And God Created Woman* appeared in 1956, it made the young Brigitte Bardot a world-famous star and a sexual icon. "You are going to be the respectable married man's unattainable dream," her director-husband Roger Vadim told her. It also put St-Tropez on the map and sun-worship on every budding starlet's agenda. Today the film seems tame, but in 1956 its nudity and love scenes caused a furore, particularly in the US.

In 1957, it earned over $8 million, more than France's biggest export, the Renault Dauphine. It was Bardot's 17th film, and hers was by no means a rags-to-riches story. Her parents were well-to-do: her father was an industrialist and her mother ran a clothes boutique in Paris. At 14, Brigitte, having done some modelling, was recruited as a cover girl for *Elle*. Her parents insisted she could only be identified by her initials, BB.

Film-director Marc Allegret was developing a film-script written by a 19-year-old White Russian, Roger Vladimir Plemiannikov (known as Vadim). He asked Vadim to investigate the new *Elle* cover girl. While they made a formal visit to Brigitte's parents, the 15-year-old Brigitte and Vadim sneaked out to the balcony together. Although the screen test was a flop, the pair soon became lovers, though Vadim had to wait until she was 18 before they could marry.

Enthusiastically promoted by Vadim, Brigitte was given a number of small parts in a series of mediocre films. Her fifth film, Anatole Litvak's *Act of Love*, starring Kirk Douglas, was promoted at the 1953 Cannes Film Festival. It was the opportunity Vadim had been waiting for. A United States aircraft carrier was in Cannes entertaining the best-known film stars on deck: Gary Cooper, Lana Turner, Olivia de Havilland and Leslie Caron all posed for the cameras. But the cameramen spotted a slender girl in a raincoat who had not been invited on board. Brigitte let slip her coat to reveal a tiny little-girl outfit, tossed her

ponytail and smiled. The next day she was splashed across the front pages of newspapers around the world.

She then became an international star with a British film, *Doctor at Sea*, starring Dirk Bogarde. Young girls everywhere copied her ponytail and affected her famous pout. Her movies became more and more daring, peaking with *And God Created Woman*.

It was after this that Brigitte bought La Madrague, a large villa near St-Tropez, where she still spends part of the year. The presence of such an icon attracted other celebrities and jet-setters, and the tiny fishing port was transformed.

After three marriages and numerous love affairs, Bardot declared that she preferred animals to men and devoted herself to various animal causes. She then married Bernard d'Ormale, a leading member of the National Front, and published an autobiography that caused such a furore her son and ex-husband tried to have it suppressed.

The latest scandal burst in 2003 when she published *A Cry in the Silence*, her musings on the state of the world. Her attacks on homosexuals and Islam were so vehement that several groups started legal proceedings against her, and she was fined €35,000 for making racist comments. ❑

RIGHT: Bardot barefoot on the beach at Cannes.

Decisive Dates

***c.*400,000 BC** Human settlement on the Riviera, as confirmed by bones and tools found in a cave complex close to the harbour in Nice.
1800–600 BC Ligurians and, later, Celts occupy the region.
***c.*600 BC** Greek Phocaeans from Asia Minor found Massalia (Marseille).
6th–4th century BC The Greeks set up a trading centre at Nikaia (Nice) and build settlements at Hyères, St-Tropez, Antibes and Monaco.
118 BC Provincia (Provence), the first Gallo-Roman province, is founded.

1st century BC The Via Aurelia from Rome to Genoa is extended as far as Cimiez, Antibes, Fréjus and Arles.
49 BC After a victorious campaign against the Gauls, Julius Caesar conquers Massalia and founds Forum Julii (present-day Fréjus).
14 BC Ligurians and other tribes are defeated by Emperor Augustus.
AD 68 A Roman centurion named Torpes is beheaded by Emperor Nero for converting to Christianity. Legend has it that his body, cast to sea, comes ashore at the port now known as St-Tropez.
410 The Lérins Monastery on the Ile St-Honorat, near Cannes, is founded.

5th century Collapse of the Roman Empire. Vandals, Visigoths, Burgundians, Ostrogoths and Franks invade the coastal zones.
536 Franks take over the region.
8th century Saracens attack the coast; the first *villages perchés* are built on inaccessible inland sites in the hinterland by coastal inhabitants fleeing the pirates.

Middle Ages to Renaissance

End of 10th century The Saracens are expelled by Guillaume le Libérateur.
1032 The region becomes part of the Holy Roman Empire.
12th century Troubadour poetry reaches its heyday.
1246 Charles d'Anjou becomes Count of Provence, beginning the 235-year Angevin dynasty.
1308 A member of the Genoese Grimaldi family acquires Monaco from Genoa.
1348 The Black Death devastates the region.
1388 Nice is ceded to the Dukes of Savoy, to be ruled from Italy, on and off, until 1860.
1434–80 Reign of Good King René.
Late 15th century Artists of the Nice School, especially Louis Bréa, gain prominence.
1481 Charles du Maine hands over Provence to King Louis XI of France.
1539 French becomes the region's official language.
1543 An unsuccessful siege of Nice by joint French and Turkish forces is led by François I.
1545–98 The Wars of Religion ravage France. Protestants massacred in Provence.
1691 The French conquer Nice, but the town is handed back to Savoy in 1715 after the Spanish War of Succession.

The Revolution

1789 The French Revolution. The south joins in with enthusiasm.
1793 Nice is occupied by French government troops. A young Napoleon Bonaparte defeats troops loyal to the King at Toulon and is promoted to general. France also captures Monaco, until now an independent state ruled by the Grimaldi family.
1815 Napoleon arrives back in France after exile on Elba. Landing in Golfe-Juan near Cannes, he marches northwards to Paris through the mountains via Grasse. The present

Route Napoléon (N85) follows more or less the Emperor's itinerary. French defeat sees Nice returned to Savoy. Monaco is returned to the Grimaldi family under the Treaty of Paris.
1820 The promenade des Anglais is built in Nice.

Early Visitors

1834 Lord Brougham settles in Cannes and the French Riviera becomes the preferred winter residence of the English nobility.
1850 Arrival of the railway reduces the hardship of travel through France to the Riviera.
1860 Piedmont-Sardinia (formerly Savoy) cedes Nice (now Alpes-Maritimes) to France. Monaco sells Menton and Roquebrune to France.
1863 Monte-Carlo Casino opens its doors.
1864 The Paris-Lyon-Mediterranean railway line is extended to Nice.
1879 The Monte-Carlo Opera is opened.
1892 Artist Paul Signac discovers St Tropez.
1895 Queen Victoria has the Hotel Regina built in the Cimiez district of Nice and winters there from this year onwards.
1906 Renoir arrives to live in Cagnes.
1912 The Carlton Hotel is built in Cannes.
1913 The Romanian Henri Negresco builds the famous hotel in Nice.
1924 The American novelist Scott Fitzgerald and his wife Zelda visit the Riviera.
1925 Coco Chanel arrives and introduces the fashion for sunbathing. Colette moves to St-Tropez.
1928 Jean Médecin becomes Mayor of Nice.
1929 Monaco holds its first Grand Prix.
1934 The Prince of Wales entertains Wallis Simpson in Cannes.
1940 Italians occupy Alpes-Maritimes.
1942 Nazi troops advance into the region.
1944 The Allies land between Toulon and Esterel on 15 August.

Post-War Riviera

1946 The first Cannes Film Festival is held. Picasso sets up a studio in Antibes.
1947 The French speaking upper Roya Valley, which remained part of Italy in 1860, is handed over to France.
1956 Brigitte Bardot stars in *And God Created Woman*, filmed in St-Tropez. Prince Rainier III of

Monaco marries the Hollywood actress Grace Kelly.
1969 Sophia-Antipolis science park is founded.
1973 Picasso dies in Mougins.
1982 Princess Grace dies in a car accident.
1986 The National Front wins over 20 percent of the Côte d'Azur's vote in national elections.
1990 The Musée d'Art Moderne et d'Art Contemporain is opened in Nice. The controversial Mayor of Nice, Jacques Médecin, flees to Uruguay after charges of tax evasion.
1994 Jacques Médecin is extradited to France. Anti-corruption campaigner Yann Piat is gunned down in Hyères, which is dubbed "the Chicago of the Côte".

1998 The National Front is split by internal feuding and an extreme-right breakaway party is formed. Jacques Médecin dies.
2001 The high-speed TGV rail network reaches Marseille.
2002 France converts to the euro.
2003 Work begins on a tramway system for Nice. Thousands of hectares of forest are destroyed in fires in the Massif des Maures.
2005 Prince Rainier of Monaco dies, Prince Albert II enthroned. French voters reject the EU constitution. Racial tension triggers riots around Marseille.
2006 The planned TVG link Marseille-Toulon-Nice is confirmed. ❑

LEFT: Good King René. **RIGHT:** Prince Rainier and Princess Grace pose for the press.

IN WORDS AND PICTURES

No other coast in the world has attracted and nurtured so much creative talent. Its writers and artists set the scene for the whole of the 20th century, beguiling us with tales set in idyllic surroundings and dazzling us with images of its extraordinary light

First came the artists, next came the writers, then came the rich. From the end of the 19th century, the drift towards the sun and the sea was inexorable, as more and more curious and adventurous people were seduced by the climate and scenery evoked in words and paint. According to the American writer F. Scott Fitzgerald, the Riviera was also "a real place to rough it and escape from the world".

The Impressionists, the first generation of artists to believe in working directly outdoors, led the way. Claude Monet (1840–1926) and Auguste Renoir (1841–1919) arrived together in 1883. Monet, who was from Normandy, found the "glaring, festive" light so strong that he feared the Paris-bound critics would think his bright palette was lying, even though he toned down his colours.

Renoir's last word

Several years later, rheumatoid arthritis forced Renoir to spend the winter months in the south. Hearing that a venerable old olive grove overlooking Cagnes was to be grubbed up and built over, he saved it from the developers to use as an outdoor studio. Eventually he had a house built for himself and his large family to live in among the olives. Tourists sought him out, wanting him to paint portraits of their families. Sometimes he did. His house and studio are open to the public today *(see page 152)*.

By 1910 Renoir was wheelchair-bound, and his paintbrush had to be wedged between

rigid his fingers. Day after day he continued, in his Arcadian wonderland of light and colour, to paint naked girls bathing in shallow ponds, washed by the Mediterranean light. "I'm still making progress," he said a few days before his death, and on 3 December 1919, as an assistant arranged a still life for him, he uttered his last word, "Flowers".

Like Renoir, Pierre Bonnard (1867–1947) had grown up in Paris. In the summer of 1909, he took a villa in St-Tropez, returning most years before settling in Le Cannet, a small village on a hill now engulfed by Cannes. In 1925, shortly after marrying his model, Maria Boursin, star of many of his domestic interiors,

LEFT: Auguste Renoir painting in his garden c.1910.
RIGHT: Colette, who lived in St-Tropez.

he bought a small pink house called Le Bosquet, nestling high among the trees on the avenue Victoria. He delighted in his garden, which was filled with birds and blossoming mimosa, almond and fig, and he painted the views from his window out across the red-tiled roofs and palm trees of Le Cannet to the bay and surrounding mountains.

The strong light of the Mediterranean was perhaps best expressed by the Fauves ("Wild Beasts"), known for their vivid colours and unrefined painting technique. Raoul Dufy (1877–1953) was among them, and between 1926 and 1929, working first in Nice and Golfe-Juan, he painted panoramic beach scenes and characteristic views seen through windows, as well as producing ceramics in the pottery town of Vallauris. The archetypal Dufy view remains a patch of pure blue sea, dotted with triangular white sails with palms neatly framing the picture. "One must meditate about pleasure. Raoul Dufy is pleasure," said the great modern art *patronne* Gertrude Stein.

Convalescing on the Côte

The Riviera's climate had long been recommended as a health cure, particularly for tuberculosis. This is what brought the artist Aubrey Beardsley (1872–98) to Menton from London in 1889, where he died of the disease

at the age of 26, and it is what brought the New Zealand writer Katherine Mansfield (1888–1923) to Villa Isola Bella in the same resort in 1920. Here she wrote many of her best short stories, including *The Young Girl*, *The Stranger*, *Miss Bull*, *Passion* and *The Lady's Maid*.

In 1919 the American writer Edith Wharton (1862–1937) bought St-Claire-le-Château in Hyères, now part of Parc St-Claire, where she spent her winters, enjoying the company of her art historian friends.

The following year the English writer Ford Madox Ford (1873–1939) arrived with his partner, Stella Bowen, at St-Jean-Cap Ferrat.

After three days of freezing rain in Paris and sitting up all night in a second-class railway carriage they were astonished by the light and warmth of the south. Their villa had been lent to them by Harold Munro, the owner of the Poetry Bookshop in London, and it was on a still night while walking among the ancient olive trees in the garden that Ford conceived and began work on his masterpiece, the war tetralogy *Parade's End*.

The Jazz Age

Scott and Zelda Fitzgerald brought the Jazz Age to the Riviera and gave a name to the frivolity, hedonism and arrogance of the rich

The climate and relaxed lifestyle proved beneficial to Fitzgerald, who was able to unwind and concentrate on getting some work done on his novel *The Great Gatsby*. Zelda, however, became bored and embarked on a love affair. The following August, they returned to the Riviera, staying with Gerald Murphy and his wife Sara, rich Americans who surrounded themselves with writers and artists, such as Hemingway, Picasso, Léger and the Mistinguetts, in their Riviera home, Villa America, just below the lighthouse on Cap d'Antibes. Fitzgerald used the summer holiday villa, the scene of many a wild party, as the model for the Divers' house in his later

young people who had begun to arrive daily on the Blue Train *(see page 26)*. They had disembarked from the steamship *Aquitania* in St-Raphaël in 1924 with just $7,000 in the bank, a sum which would last no time at all in Great Neck, Long Island, but in Europe could be spun out for a much longer time. "We were going to the Old World to find a new rhythm for our lives," Fitzgerald wrote, "with a true conviction that we had left our old selves behind forever."

novel *Tender is the Night*. In 1926 Scott and Zelda settled into the Villa Paquita in Juan-les-Pins close by, which they eventually passed on to Ernest and Hadley Hemingway. The Jazz Age bypassed much of the coast. St-Tropez, for instance, was still an unspoilt fishing village in 1927 when Sidonie-Gabrielle Colette, better known as Colette *(see page 43)*, author of *Gigi* and by then acclaimed as France's greatest living writer, moved into a villa there to write *La Naissance du Jour*, set in the village.

FAR LEFT: Katherine Mansfield. **LEFT:** Ernest Hemingway. **ABOVE:** F. Scott Fitzgerald and his wife Zelda with daughter Scottie.

Henri Matisse

Henri Matisse (1869–1954) got his first taste of the Riviera in St Tropez, where he spent the summer of 1904. However, he is most closely associated with Nice, which he first visited in 1916, living at several addresses in the city before settling in Cimiez for the rest of his life. His move to Nice at the age of 48 precipitated a significant change in his work. "Most people came here for the light and the picturesque quality," he wrote. "As for me, I come from the north. What made me stay are the great coloured reflections of January, the luminosity of daylight." He first stayed at the Hôtel Beau-Rivage, which was at 107 quai des Etats Unis, an extenion of the promenade des Anglais. Here he had a full view of the sea, the beach and the full trajectory of the sun. At least nine

The following year Henriette Darricarrère, a local ballet dancer and musician, became Matisse's primary model, entering into his exotic odalisque fantasy, and he painted her dozens of times in this role.

Matisse now felt ready to become a resident, and took a large flat on place Charles-Félix in the old town. It overlooked the market and had an uninterrupted view of the sea, the promenade des Anglais curving round to the west with its elegant rows of palms and the rooftops of Old Nice.

He remained in this building until 1938, posing his models against the window or using the spacious interiors. He loved the

paintings made from this hotel room survive.

When his hotel was requisitioned for soldiers, he moved his family to the Villa des Alliés in the hills that rise steeply above the old port of Nice, on the pass over to Villefranche. Here he took to painting landscapes and watching the dawn arrive.

During the winter of 1918–19 he stayed at the Hôtel Méditerranée at 25 promenade des Anglais – now demolished. He employed an 18-year-old model, Antoinette Arnoux, who was to figure in many nude and costume paintings made at the hotel, often posing in front of the huge windows with decorative iron grilles, a palm tree silhouetted against the blue sea.

densely patterned wallpaper and introduced it into many of his paintings. To it, he added his own collection of masks, fabric hangings and mirrors, so the studio had the lush atmosphere of an oriental bazaar. The period 1927–31 was characterised by decorative odalisques in highly stylised settings.

In 1938 he moved to the Hôtel Regina in Cimiez near the present Matisse Museum, and it was here, being too disabled by arthritis to paint, that he began to work seriously at paper cut-outs. "Cutting straight into colour reminds me of the direct carving of the sculptor," he wrote. He began his cut-outs at the age of 70 and was 84 when he did the last one. He made the medium his own, creating the famous "Jazz" series, which he executed between 1943 and 1944 at the Villa Le Rêve in Vence, and his wonderful monochrome *Blue Nude* of 1952, two years before his death.

Inspired by the Riviera

The 1930s saw many intellectuals passing through the Riviera, some, like the German Thomas Mann, escaping persecution and finding unexpected inspiration in new surroundings. His neighbour in Sanary was Aldous Huxley, who wrote *Brave New World* there, and used the town as a setting for *Eyeless in Gaza*, published in 1936: "The eye was drawn first towards the west, where the pines slanted down to the sea – a blue Mediterranean bay fringed with pale bone-like rocks and cupped between high hills, green on their lower slopes with vines, grey with olive trees, then pinedark, earth-red, rock-white or rosy-brown with parched heath…"

Huxley's colleague Cyril Connolly set his first and only novel, *The Rock Pool*, further along the coast in Cagnes-sur-Mer and Juanles-Pins, while Somerset Maugham was so famous by 1926 that he was able to buy a house on Cap Ferrat from King Leopold II of Belgium for $48,500. He called it the Villa Mauresque, after its Moorish architecture, and lived there for at least six months each year until his death in 1965. It is now a smart hotel.

Post-war sunshine

Villa Mauresque was damaged during the war, when the whole coast suffered miserably. The Cannes Film Festival helped kickstart the area's revival when it opened in 1946. In 1955 Françoise Sagan gave the coast another boost with the publication of *Bonjour Tristesse*, in which Cécile, the spoilt teenage narrator, manipulates her father's love-triangle in a villa somewhere between Fréjus and Cannes.

A year later, Roger Vadim's film *And God Created Woman*, set in St-Tropez with the

unknown Brigitte Bardot, ensured that the role of star and model passed from the artist's studio to the film set *(see page 39)*.

Pablo Picasso

Pablo Picasso (1881–1973), the giant of 20th-century art, spent most of his later life on the Côte d'Azur; he moved here from Paris in 1946, unwilling to return to live in Fascist Spain. He had been coming to the coast since 1920, staying at Juan-Les-Pins and Antibes, where in August 1939 he completed one of his few large works, *Night Fishing in Antibes*. Returning to Antibes after the war, he worked in a studio in the Château Grimaldi, donating

181 drawings and paintings to the town four months later. This collection, based on the theme *La Joie de Vivre* inspired by Jacqueline Gilot with whom he was living, has remained in the Château as the Picasso Museum *(see page 125)*.

Picasso at first acquired a house in the village of Ménerbes in exchange for a still-life before moving to the ceramic town of Vallauris, where he evolved new techniques of glazing and revived the town's pottery industry. From there he moved to La Californie, an ornate mansion above Cannes, and after a brief period near Aix-en-Provence returned to Mas Notre-Dame-de-Vie overlooking Mougins,

LEFT: Thomas Mann and his wife Katia moved to France to escape the Nazis.
RIGHT: Pablo Picasso spent most of his later years on the Riviera.

surrounded by terraces of cypresses and olives and named after a nearby chapel. During his last five years he created 1,000 works of art, taking themes and working them until they were exhausted. His astonishing productivity continued until he died at Mas Notre-Dame-de-Vie on 8 April 1973.

Chagall

Another artist to head for the south of France at the end of the war was Russian-born Marc Chagall (1887–1985), who arrived with his companion Virginia Haggard and their son David from the United States where they had spent the war years. In the spring of 1949, they

Marguerite lived near Chagall, though they had not yet opened their foundation in St-Paul-de-Vence, and it was not long before Maeght was Chagall's sole dealer. Chagall married Vava Brodsky and moved to St-Paul-de-Vence, which remained his home until 28 March 1985, when he died at the age of 97.

Klein Blue

In the 1950s, Nice produced its own school of artists, the Nouveaux Réalistes: Yves Klein, Arman, Martial Raysse (all from Nice) and César (born in Marseille but settled in Nice), plus Ben Vautier from Naples and a group of associated artists. The Nouveaux Réalistes

settled in a *pension* in St-Jean-Cap Ferrat, where the light and the sight of the sea released an explosion of new ideas in the artist. Although one of the most colourful and delightful painters of the 20th century, the influence of the Riviera is less obvious in Chagall's work than in that of other artists. His great inspiration remained the Old Testament, and after seeing the chapel that Matisse had decorated in Vence, he strived to find and decorate one of his own. Many churches in the region contain examples of his mosaics, and in 1973 he completed his Musée National Messages Bibliques in Nice *(see page 174)*.

The art dealer Aimé Maeght and his wife

were united by a common appropriation of the material surfaces of contemporary life: paint tubes, trash, packaging, the contents of the industrial junk heap. Arman packed trash into transparent containers, freezing them in acrylic so they seemed set in aspic; César presented motor vehicles, compacted into neat cubes by a scrapyard.

"Although we of the School of Nice are always on vacation," wrote Yves Klein, "we are not tourists. That's the essential point. Tourists come here for vacations; we live in a land of vacations, which gives us the spirit of nonsense. We amuse ourselves without thinking of religion, art or science." Klein (1928–62) was the acknowledged leader of the movement. In 1955, when abstract painting ruled the world, Klein set up an easel on the promenade des Anglais. Gazing out to sea, he covered the canvas with blue pigment – one of his famous monochrome paintings. It was not abstract: it was real, literally just a canvas covered in blue paint. His International Klein Blue, or IKB as it is known, became his symbol, used over and over in different contexts and a fitting colour on this coast. During his brief life, Klein astonished and irritated critics and the public with his radical inventiveness, particularly with his Anthropometries, in which he coated the bodies of nude models with paint, usually IKB, and either pressed them against the canvas or gave them directions to move their limbs or crawl. Some paintings were made before a live audience, with a 20-piece orchestra.

Another French artist to court the limelight was Jean Cocteau (1889–1963), avant-garde writer, playwright and artist. He came on holiday to Villefranche in 1925 and remained associated with the town for the rest of his life, decorating the little seafront chapel, Saint-Pierre, and adding colourful figures to the ceiling of the mayor's office in Menton.

Burgess and Greene

Towards the end of his life, the English novelist Anthony Burgess (1917–93) settled in Monaco, where he was co-founder of the Princess Grace Irish Library, a centre for Irish cultural studies. "I shall die somewhere in the Mediterranean lands, with an inaccurate obituary in the *Nice-Matin*, unmourned, soon forgotten," he wrote. But he died in England, where he is mainly remembered as the author of *Earthly Powers* and *A Clockwork Orange*.

A near neighbour was Graham Greene (1904–91) in Antibes. Moving to France to "escape the braying voices of the English middle class", he lived quietly, each day leaving his modest flat at the Résidence des Fleurs and walking to the gates of the Old Town. There, at Bernard Patriarch's café, he would buy *Nice-Matin* and a copy of *The Times* and then make his way to Chez Félix for lunch. He once wrote: "Since 1959, Chez Félix was my home-

from-home. I found short stories served to me with my meal." One of these he titled *Chagrin in Three Parts*, and it reads as if he simply transcribed the conversation of the two women in the restaurant. In the dialogue, he found a way to introduce the proprietor: "But before Madame Dejoie could reply, Monsieur Félix had arrived to perform his neat surgical operation upon the fish for the *bouillabaisse…*"

Shortly before his death at the age of 86, Greene travelled to Switzerland for his health. In a letter to the Mayor of Antibes, he wrote: "I have always been very happy in Antibes. It is the only town on the Côte d'Azur where it was possible for me to live." ❑

THE CORRUPT MAYOR OF NICE

The novelist Graham Greene caused a minor sensation in 1982 when, in a booklet entitled *J'Accuse – The Dark Side of Nice*, he said Nice was "the preserve of some of the most criminal organisations in the south of France". He pointed a finger at the Mayor of Nice, Jacques Médecin, who ran the city as though it were his own preserve but strongly denied any wrongdoing. Greene, however, was vindicated after a series of revelations forced Médecin into exile in 1990. Extradited in 1994 and brought to trial, the former mayor served a short prison sentence. He disappeared again and finally died in 1998. The political fall-out was huge as Nice discovered the extent of the corruption.

LEFT: Klein's Anthropometries astonished the critics.
RIGHT: Graham Greene made Antibes his base.

THE RIVIERA ON CANVAS

**"The whole future of art is to be found in southern France,"
Van Gogh once told Gauguin.
He was right**

The story of art in the 20th century cannot be told without recognising the part played by the French Riviera. The luminescent quality of the light here, the inspirational landscapes and azure bays, drew in many of the greats of the 20th century: Dufy, Matisse, Chagall, Picasso and Renoir, to name a few. The vibrancy of the Riviera is reflected in many of their pictures, and there is a magic at work, too. "In Paris, I never draw fauns, centaurs or mythical creatures," said Picasso, "but they seem to live in this place." Here, painters became prolific and long-lasting. In his wheelchair *(pictured above)* Renoir tied paintbrushes to his arthritic hands so he could keep working, and when Matisse could no longer paint, he cut up coloured paper to make his wonderful montages.

ABOVE: nobody's seas are as blue as Raoul Dufy's, the Fauve with an eye for design and sparkling colour. The *Baie des Anges, Nice* (1929) is one of several visions of the seafront at Nice.

RIGHT: artist, playwright, filmmaker and patron of the first Cannes Film Festival, Jean Cocteau (1889–1963) had boundless talent. Picasso called him "the tail of my comet". He is seen by some as a model for Andy Warhol.

ABOVE: *Chemin Montant dans les Hautes Herbes* (1876) by Pierre-Auguste Renoir shows the romance of Provence, which had captivated him since his first visit with Monet.

THE MUSE AS MODEL AND PARTNER

Taken by Robert Capa on the beach at Golfe-Juan in 1948, this photo shows Pablo Picasso holding a parasol for Françoise Gilot, his muse and lover (who also happened to be 40 years his junior). They met in Paris during the war, and she remained with him in Vallauris until 1952. If the Riviera artists owe a debt to their landscape, they also owe a debt to their muses. Most, though not all, were partners or lovers. The string of models who posed for Matisse were paid like the maid. "His models were working partners, not sexual captives," says his biographer, Hilary Spurling, and when, at the age 70, Matisse separated from his wife Amélie and was looked after by a young model, Lydia Delectorskaya, the relationship was platonic.

Renoir's models included his wife Aline and her cousin Gabrielle Renard, who lived with the family and looked after him after his wife died. Bonnard painted his wife, Marthe, 384 times, and when she was 72 made her appear still young. Chagall frequently pictured himself and his wife Bella flying through the air to convey their marital bliss.

ABOVE: this view of Cannes was painted by Pierre Bonnard in 1947, the year of his death. He was a great colourist and used pure colour in spades, laying on both white and black, too. Matisse called Bonnard "the greatest of us all".

RIGHT: in *The Pigeons* (1957) Picasso painted the birds he kept in the third-floor studio of his villa, La Californie, overlooking the sea at Cannes. Framing views through windows and balconies was an idea that Matisse, Dufy and others explored.

RIGHT: living in St-Paul-de-Vence, Marc Chagall (1887–1985) was inspired to paint joyous biblical pictures for the museum he helped to design in Nice. He believed that the Bible was "like an echo of nature". His distinctive style combined French Cubism with Russian Expressionism plus a touch of the surreal, and his paintings are always rich and full of life.

TASTE OF THE COAST

Abundant fresh fruit and vegetables ripened by the Mediterranean sun, seafood on the doorstep, fresh herbs, locally produced wines – the cuisine of the Côte d'Azur, with its focus on simplicity and quality, is hard to beat

"**M**y accent has a touch of garlic," says the film actor Charles Blavette in his book of memoirs, *Ma Provence en Cuisine*. The remark is not surprising coming from a native of the Midi. In no other part of France are the characteristics of a regional culture so closely bound up with food.

Characters in the films of Marcel Pagnol, for example, not only put down their cultural markers by using quaint Provençal expressions and speaking with thick southern accents, but often refer to local dishes and the ritual of making them. Indeed, the lilting words for many such specialities – *bourride, bouillabaisse, ratatouille, rouille* and *ailloli*, for example – might almost have been designed so that Pagnol's favourite actors could wrap their tongues around them.

Bounty from the sea

The cuisine of the Côte d'Azur does not differ much from that of Provence, except that it is a little more fish-orientated and has the added attraction of Nice's idiosyncratic specialities. It was forged long before the Côte became a string of seaside resorts, at a time when transport was difficult and people relied on local ingredients. Its most famous – and most often traduced – dish, the fish stew bouillabaisse, often used to be cooked on the boat after the catch. Many kinds of Mediterranean fish both great and small – whose kaleidoscopic hues before cooking have

LEFT: fresh vegetables at the market in Fréjus.
RIGHT: mussels are a popular dish.

inspired more than one painter – should go into bouillabaisse, each one of them providing its own special flavour.

Soupe de poisson, or fish soup, which when properly prepared consists of more or less the same ingredients as bouillabaisse, is sieved to remove the bones and is equally filling. In *bourride*, another delicious fish stew, *ailloli (see page 54)* is used to thicken the cooking liquid at the last moment, producing a creamy and perfumed sauce to go with the pieces of fish (sometimes filleted). A popular dish on Côte d'Azur menus is fennel-flavoured grilled *loup* (sea bass), although it can often be overcooked and dry. Grilled fresh sardines with a squeeze of lemon are a better bet. On no account miss sampling that most delicately flavoured of Mediterranean fish, red mullet *(rouget)*, best cooked very simply, grilled or fried.

In the old days, it was difficult for people living in the hinterland to get hold of fresh fish, so on Fridays they tended to make dishes using salt cod *(morue)*. If salt cod sounds dreary, you will change your mind after tasting *brandade*, a rich blend of cod, olive oil, garlic and potato. Poached salt cod is often the centrepiece of a *grand ailloli* or *ailloli garni* (sometimes just called *ailloli*), a cold dish that's great on a hot summer's day.

Ailloli and garlic

Ailloli (or *aïoli*) is just a sauce, of course, but like *pistou* (of which more in a moment) it has also come to denote a whole dish. It is basically a garlic mayonnaise traditionally served with boiled salt cod, and can also be an accompaniment to cooked vegetables (potatoes, French beans, carrots, small local artichokes), *crudités* (raw vegetables cut into sticks), hard-boiled eggs and sometimes cold poached snails.

A word here about garlic. Gone, fortunately, are the days when most British people regarded garlic with distaste, and a Pelican book on herbs written in 1949 could write: "Anyone who travels in Italian buses might be forgiven for deciding never to grow this evil-smelling plant." The classier restaurants on the Côte d'Azur are careful in their use of garlic, but that is not the way it is eaten by the locals: they rub it enthusiastically into croûtons, pound it into *ailloli*, pile it into meat stews, strew it chopped on baked *tomates provençales* – indeed, in restaurants all over the world the term "*à la provençale*" or "*provençale*" tells customers to expect lashings of garlic. Garlic also goes into ratatouille, that resonant mixture of tomatoes, onions, courgettes (zucchini), peppers and aubergines (eggplant), which can range in quality from the practically inedible to the sublime.

Local produce

A dish that combines so many vegetables is symptomatic of the way the cuisine of the Côte d'Azur revels in the ingredients which the region produces best, whether they be vegetables, fruit or herbs. Local sun-gorged tomatoes taste of the sweet fruit they really are. (Surprisingly, in view of the important role they now play in the cuisine of the Côte d'Azur, tomatoes were initially viewed with suspicion and became widely used here only from the 19th century.)

Baby courgettes, with their orange-yellow flowers still attached to one end, form the basis of a subtle gratin called *tian*. The flowers alone are sometimes stuffed with a rice-based, Parmesan-flavoured mixture. Also on sale in markets and at greengrocers all along the Côte d'Azur is *mesclun* (or *mesclum*), a mixture of baby salad plants which includes all or some of the following: rocket, dandelion, lettuce (cos, oak-leaf), watercress, chicory, radicchio and chervil. *Mesclun* has been something of a success story and it is now commonly featured, if not de rigueur, on the menus of restaurants all over France.

The luscious flavour of melons from Cavaillon in nearby Provence is unrivalled. The taste of fresh figs belies their dull external appearance; startlingly complex and not too sweet, the fig is sometimes exploited in meat dishes. Most households have several pots of carefully watered basil. Aromatic rosemary, savory, fennel and thyme grow wild on the parched hillsides. The herbs and other vegetation of the *maquis* are ideal food for the sheep that graze there, hence the lamb of the Côte d'Azur is justly celebrated.

A hearty stew

Generally, though, meat does not feature prominently in local cuisine – until recent times there was little available – though *daube*, a wonderfully rich-flavoured beef stew, is a great favourite. In his book, Blavette gives a recipe for it: a large quantity of shin is put for 24 hours in a marinade of red wine, bay leaf, thyme, pepper, zest of an orange, cloves and grated nutmeg, then cooked gently for five or six hours with salt pork, a calf's foot, garlic, onions, tomatoes and pork rind. He recommends using even a very good Burgundy like a Pommard in the dish, remarking that "what you put into the casserole you'll find in your plate".

In the Niçois version of *daube*, dried *cèpes* (mushrooms) add a further distinctive flavour. All wild mushrooms, and especially *cèpes* and *sanguins* (the aptly named *Lactarius deliciosus*, or saffron milk cap), are highly prized on the Côte d'Azur.

Italian influences

Italian culinary influences are strong on the Côte d'Azur, partly as a result of considerable immigration from Italy in the early part of the 20th century. They are particularly noticeable in Menton and in Nice – though the proudly individualistic Niçois would deny it. The Comté de Nice (Nice and its surrounding area)

has been French only since 1860. Before that it was part of the Kingdom of Sardinia, which also included Savoy, Sardinia and Piedmont. From a culinary point of view, Nice straddles several cultures but has retained its own very special character.

Delicacies of Nice

The best way to get an idea of what Niçois food is all about is to stroll through the old quarter of the city, which is packed with small food stores. Cheese shops are stacked high with Parmesan and mature Gouda, as well as local cheeses like fresh *brousse* (often made from ewe's milk) and the rare *tome de Rouré*.

Tubs of capers and salted anchovies serve as a reminder that it is in Nice that the finest version of *anchoïade*, a sauce served with vegetables in the same way as *ailloli*, can be sampled (it contains not only anchovies, olive oil and garlic but capers, unlike its cousin found along the Côte to the west).

Alongside slabs of salt cod, you may see large, curiously emaciated fish that seem to be screaming (their open "jaws" are in fact the gill-bones of the beheaded fish): this is stockfish, the wind-dried cod that goes into *estocaficada*, a pungent fish stew that is Nice's proudest speciality. Shops displaying fresh pasta and gnocchi often also sell the strange

LEFT: bouillabaisse is a speciality of the region.
RIGHT: look out for luscious melons in the markets.

cuttlebone-shaped *panisses*, made from chickpea flour, deep-fried and served with salt and pepper. Chickpea flour, a peculiarity of Niçois cooking, also goes into *socca*, a very thick, tasty pancake sold in chunks by street vendors.

Other snacks that can be eaten on the move in Nice and in many resorts along the coast are *pissaladière* (a cousin of pizza consisting of black olives, cooked onions and anchovy spread on a bread dough base) and *pan bagnat* (a small round loaf cut in half and stuffed with the ingredients of *salade niçoise* – tomato, hard-boiled egg, anchovy, tuna, spring onion, cucumber and green peppers).

The wide range of Niçoise *charcuterie* can only excite admiration – your gaze may even be returned by the spectacular *porchetta*, a boned, stuffed and reconstituted roast piglet, which is sliced from the back end. Greengrocers always have a good stock of fresh basil, handfuls of which go into that truly wonderful Niçois soup, *pistou* (though *pistou* strictly refers to the paste of pounded basil, garlic and Parmesan that is usually added to the minestrone-like soup at the last minute).

Fine dining

With its wealth of top-quality ingredients, the Côte d'Azur is also renowned for its restaurants. If you want to splurge, you cannot go

WINES OF THE REGION

The wines drunk on the sunny terraces of the Riviera tend to be light and are well suited to the region's climate and cuisine. The **rosés** are a speciality, dry and light and best served well chilled to be drunk at any time of day, but particularly as an aperitif before a meal. The crisp, fruity **white** wines are an excellent accompaniment for seafood, and the lighter Provençal **reds** are superb slightly chilled in summer, partnering grilled meat and the heavier *daubes*.

The best regional wines carry an *appellation d'origine contrôlée* (AOC) label. The AOC wines in the region include Côtes de Provence, Cassis, Bellet and Bandol, and from further afield Coteaux d'Aix-en-Provence, Les Baux-de-Provence, Côtes du Luberon, Coteaux Varois and the southern Côtes du Rhône.

The largest Riviera appellation is **Côtes de Provence**, principally producing vast amounts of good-quality rosé wine, but also small quantities of white and some fine reds. **Bellet** on the edge of Nice, with just 60 hectares (150 acres) of vineyards under cultivation, produces very good white, red and rosé wines. Bandol, made in eight communes around the resort of Bandol west of Toulon, is the area's most prestigious appellation, notable for its excellent reds.

wrong. The Louis XV, in the Hôtel de Paris in Monte-Carlo, combines the peak of luxury with sublime food and towering prices. Jacques Maximin's eponymous restaurant in Vence offers similar fare in more relaxed surroundings. Le Chantecler in the Negresco Hotel in Nice has recently acquired master chef Bruno Turbot, while its former chef, Alain Llorca, has taken over the helm at the Moulin de Mougins. He is typical of a new generation of Provençal chefs who bring an original light twist to the region's delicacies. Another is Bruno Oger, of the Villa des Lys in the Hôtel Majestic in Cannes.

All these establishments offer dishes that reflect or reinterpret local culinary traditions. Problems begin to arise when it is a question of choosing restaurants in the middle or lower price ranges. Chancing one's arm with a village bistro or tiny restaurant tucked away in some Cannes or Nice backstreet may not be too hazardous. But as soon as you decide to eat on or near the beach, or in some otherwise fashionable location, an apparently honest establishment can turn out to be a tourist trap. Our advice is to consult one of the food guides such as the Michelin or the Gault-Millau (many hotels have them at reception). Otherwise, you may find yourself paying through the nose for watery, overcooked ratatouille, bouillabaisse that is little more than overpriced fish soup with a few flakes of fish in it, and a bottle of Côtes de Provence rosé that produces instant heartburn.

Taking the flavours home

To ensure that your stay leaves a pleasant taste in your mouth, it is a good idea before leaving to browse round a street market or food store and stock up with the kind of preserved or dried staples which any good kitchen requires and which are more expensive and/or of inferior quality at home. There is a wide range of olives available, the best being the tiny black Niçois olives marinated for six months in thyme and bay. These are available in jars from Alziari in Nice, a company celebrated for its smooth and subtly flavoured olive oil, unquestionably the best on the Côte d'Azur.

LEFT: a Côtes-de-Provence vineyard.
RIGHT: olive oil, a prized export.

Other possibilities include fragrant local honey, crystallised flowers from Grasse, dried *cèpes*, Parmesan cheese, anchovies in jars and maybe a bottle or two of good Côtes de Provence (Jas-d'Esclans and Château Minuty are reliable growers), or that rare and surprisingly strong port-like Niçois wine, Bellet.

But there is one widely available product which can conjure up memories of those lazy holiday meals more powerfully than any other: *tapenade*, a smooth purée of capers, black olives and anchovies with olive oil, plenty of pepper and a little thyme, which spread on warm toast or used as a stuffing for hard-boiled eggs is delicious. ❑

This detailed guide to the French Ri[viera]
towns and villages along the coas[t]
interesting places inland. [...]
cross-referenced by [...]

From the glamorous beaches of the French[...]
of its Provençal hinterland, here we expl[...]
the ancient stones of Roman ruins to the[...]
itants fully equipped with swimming pools[...]
at every aspect of this rich and complex area[...]

The contrasts are legion: the cool, clear wa[...]
ultra-chic beach clubs of St-Tropez, the glit[...]
medieval charms of its old town, Le Suque[...]
Antibes' Port Vauban and the fabulous Châ[...]
tion. Other facets include the perfumes of Gra[...]
Sophia-Antipolis, the pulsating beaches of[...]
luxury of Cap d'Antibes, the art galleries of[...]
markets of Nice and its stunning modern ar[...]
exotic gardens of Cap Ferrat, the fishermen[...]
hotels of Beaulieu, the winding streets of[...]
rococo façades of Monaco, the celebrated[...]
Roquebrune and the remote secret places in[...]

You can play boules in the village square[...]
three-star haute cuisine or a *pan bagnat* on th[...]
bent admirers or wander a lonely hillside; inv[...]
watch dolphins at play; sunbathe by the p[...]
head for the shore.

Whatever your inclination, the Côte d'Az[...]
variety of landscapes, culture and facilit[...]
satisfied. And if all you want to do is spend[...]
no beaches are better designed for the purp[...]
shaded *matelas* for the day and only rise fo[...]
rosé and *moules marinières* in the beach res[...]
ties stretch to some light exploration, this In[...]
with all the ideas you need.

PRECEDING PAGES: Val Rahmel Botanical Garden in M[...]
old town, Gourdon.
LEFT: standing room only at the beach in front of the[...]

French Riviera

0	10 km
0	10 miles

N

HYERES AND THE MASSIF DES MAURES

The western end of the Riviera caters to both sun-worshippers and nature-lovers, from the charming resort of Hyères and its unspoilt offshore islands to the wild hills of the Massif, offering dramatic views and remote villages

Hyères-les-Palmiers ❶ is one of the oldest of the Côte d'Azur resorts – it's been a winter destination for the French since the 18th century and for the British since the 19th. Tolstoy came here in 1860 to take a winter "cure", and Robert Louis Stevenson worked on *Kidnapped* (1886) in the town, claiming it was the only place which made him happy. Nowadays it is sometimes viewed as an unfashionable and slightly shabby cousin of the "real" Riviera towns of Cannes or Nice further east.

This unfair reputation has its seeds in Queen Victoria's flippant patronage of Hyères in 1892, for no sooner had hotels and palm-lined avenues been built in honour of Her Majesty and her entourage than she decided to move on to Cimiez, near Nice, rendering the town passé almost overnight. Hyères still possesses a faded charm, with a medieval old town and 19th-century new town, as well as the palm trees that have been tacked on to its name.

The medieval town centre

Before setting off on a steep climb through the medieval streets of the old town, built on the slopes of the Castéou hill, pause for a coffee under the plane trees of the place de la République. Opening on to the square is the 13th-century **Eglise St-Louis**, named after Louis IX, who recuperated here in 1254 when the now disused port of L'Ayguade was a base for returning crusaders. The calm, elegant and beautiful church is an excellent example of a happy marriage between Italian Romanesque and Provençal Gothic.

Not far from the southern end of place de la République is a 13th-century gate, **Porte Massillon**, which gives access to rue Massillon and the Vieille Ville, or old town.

LEFT: a pretty window display in La Garde-Freinet. **BELOW:** Moorish-style architecture in Hyères.

It's all smiles in Place St-Paul, Hyères old town.

Gate and street are named after the great preacher of the court of Louis XIV who was born in nearby rue Rabaton. Stalls of North African and Provençal delicacies line rue Massillon, tempting passers-by.

Further on is place Massillon, a café-filled square overlooked by the 12th-century **Tour des Templiers** (open summer Wed–Mon 10am–noon, 2–7pm, winter Wed–Sun 10am–noon, 2–5pm; free). The tower is the last remnant of a Knights Templar command post which had been set up in Hyères in the 12th century with the blessing of Charles I of Anjou after the town gained royal status.

Continuing up the hill, you come to place St-Paul, where more expansive views open up across the rooftops. Steps lead up to the **Collégiale St-Paul** (open Apr–Sept Wed–Mon 10am–noon, 4–7pm, Oct–Mar Wed–Sun 10am–noon 2–5pm; free), which has a Gothic nave and Romanesque bell tower. The walls in the entrance are crammed with a fascinating array of naive ex-voto paintings.

Avant-garde antics

From St-Paul take rue Paradis and continue up a calf-achingly steep track which snakes past the **Parc St-Bernard** (open daily), an attractive garden containing hundreds of varieties of Mediterranean flowers and plants. Above the park is the **Villa Noailles** (montée de Noailles; tel: 04 98 08 01 98; www.villanoailles-hyeres.com; open Wed–Sun 10am–noon, 2–6pm), the Cubist masterpiece of avant-garde architect Robert Mallet-Stevens (1886–1945), built for enlightened aristocratic patrons Charles and Marie-Laure de Noailles in the 1920s *(see below)*.

Originally intended to just be a simple winter residence ("a little house that is interesting to live in"), the house evolved during its construction to become a Cubist maze of concrete and glass, set within a Mediterranean park and featuring a Cubist garden.

In the 1920s and 1930s the villa was visited regularly by members of the Dada and Surrealist movements, including Buñuel, who wrote the script for *L'Age d'Or* here, Cocteau,

The Villa Noailles

After years when it had been almost forgotten, the Villa Noailles is now seen as an icon of the architectural Modern Movement. Not for architect Robert Mallet-Stevens (1886–1945) the mass-housing schemes and urbanisation projects of Le Corbusier or Perret – rather, luxurious mansions, casinos, boutiques, artists' studios, car showrooms and cruise liners. But beyond this dilettante image, Mallet-Stevens, who participated in the influential Exposition des Arts Décoratifs in Paris in 1925, emerges as one of the most distinctive figures of Modernist architecture, who best allied Modernism with the elegance of Art Deco.

When Charles and Marie-Laure de Noailles first met Mallet-Stevens in 1923, they intended to commission just a simple winter residence. Instead, the house evolved to become a vast structure with complex arrangements of terraces and balconies. To the first eight bedrooms, each with bathroom opening on to a roof terrace, completed in 1925, more bedrooms were added, along with garages, guest wing, an indoor swimming pool, gym and even a squash court. By 1932, the villa had more than 60 rooms.

Breton and Dalí – Man Ray's bizarre film *The Mysteries of the Château de Dé* was filmed here in 1929. Occupied by the Italians in 1940, then inhabited sporadically by Marie-Laure de Noailles until her death in 1970, the villa subsequently fell into near ruin, but has now been restored by the municipality and is used for interesting exhibitions of contemporary art, design, fashion and photography.

The track continues uphill to the ruins of the 13th-century **Château**. The castle's foundations sit on a Greek defence wall dating from the 4th century BC. The castle was established by the Lords of Fos and passed to Charles I in 1257. In 1662, the castle was pulled down following the Wars of Religion. Without its stronghold the importance of the town was drastically reduced in favour of Toulon.

The view from the turrets provides a strong sense of the local geography. To the east are the dark curves of the Massif des Maures, to the south the Giens peninsula and the Iles d'Hyères. The American novelist Edith Wharton fell in love with the view when she first visited Hyères in 1915. She returned after World War I and wrote that she was ravished by "views of land and sea such as were never seen before".

A newer castle

Edith Wharton is also associated with the **Castel Ste-Claire**, a 19th-century neo-Romanesque castle situated just below the castle ruins, where the writer lived between 1927 and 1937. Today it houses the headquarters of the **Parc National de Port-Cros** (tel: 04 94 12 82 30; www.portcrosparcnational.fr; *see page 71*), but you can stroll through the grounds and enjoy the views, looking over pines, cypresses and dramatic rocks to the sea. Other literary figures to visit Ste-Claire were

Henry James, H.G. Wells, Joseph Conrad, Aldous Huxley and Kenneth Clark.

Another inhabitant of old Hyères, with a tomb in the grounds of Ste-Claire, was Olivier Voitier, the 19th-century naval officer who first came across the statue of *Venus de Milo*, now in the Louvre, when on a maritime campaign in Greece.

The new town

Outside the medieval town and within the recent sprawl of apartment blocks and villas that now spreads down towards the sea and over adjacent hills, the new town laid out in the 19th century shows signs of a certain revival. Several of the white stucco houses along avenue Joseph Clotis have recently been restored.

On avenue Jean Jaurès, the shiny **Casino des Palmiers** has been restored to its former grandeur and filled with the usual array of gaming tables and one-armed bandits, and the Park Hotel on avenue de Belgique, once the town's grandest hotel, is now used for exhibitions.

Map on page 72

The Villa Nouailles, a superb example of Modernist design, is open to the public for art, design, fashion and photography exhibitions.

BELOW: the rooftops of Hyères from Place St-Paul.

Queue at the foot of La Tour-Fondue at the tip of the Giens peninsula to catch a ferry over to the Ile de Porquerolles (30 minutes).

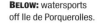

BELOW: watersports off Ile de Porquerolles.

The new town also points to the 19th-century taste for exoticism, seen in several Moorish-style buildings, such as the Villa Tunisienne (1 avenue de Beauregard) and La Mauresque (2 avenue Jean Natte), both designed by Pierre Chapoulard, who was also responsible for the neo-Gothic former Anglican church, built to serve the large number of English residents. Another Moorish villa sits amid the tropical plants, flowers, peacocks and ornamental lakes of the **Jardin Olbius Riquier** (open daily May–Sept 7.30am–8pm, Oct–Apr 7.30am–5.30pm).

Olbius refers to Hyères's ancient Greek ancestor, the maritime trading post of Olbia, founded in the 4th century BC, remains of which can be seen towards L'Almanarre at the **Site Archéologique d'Olbia** (tel: 04 94 57 98 28; www.monum.fr; open Apr–Sept 9.30am–12.30pm, 3–7pm; admission charge). Here, excavations have revealed sections of Greek fortifications, traces of Roman baths, temples and homes and remains of the medieval abbey of St-Pierre de l'Almanarre.

Hyères-Plage

For the town's beaches, marina and watersports facilities, head south of the airport and the Hippodrome (racetrack) to Hyères-Plage, with its miles of beaches on either side of the tombola – a distinctive form of isthmus formed by two spits of land – leading to the Giens peninsula. On the eastern side is **La Capte**, with a long beach and safe shallow waters, now lined by rather downmarket hotels and campsites. On the more exposed western side, the long **Plage de l'Almanarre**, a favourite beach with windsurfers and kite-surfers, and used for the heats of the windsurfing world championships each year.

Between the two lie the disused salt pans, **Salins des Pesquiers**, which were in use until 1995. Their rare brackish habitat, which still sometimes floods in winter, is now a bird reserve. At the end of the long route de Giens, the peninsula is heavily built up around the old hill village of Giens.

At the southeastern tip of the peninsula is **La Tour-Fondue ②**, a

squat fortress put up by Cardinal Richelieu, from where ferries leave regularly for the Ile de Porquerolles. At the foot of the tower, which the young Napoleon re-established as a stronghold when he was an artillery officer at Toulon, day-trippers and divers congregate for the crossing.

The Iles d'Hyères

The main reason many people come to Hyères is to visit the beautiful and densely vegetated **Iles d'Hyères**, also called the Iles d'Or, because of the mica or "fool's gold" which sparkles in the sand and rocks there.

In the 16th century, François I constructed forts on the islands and granted the right of asylum to convicts, provided they would live there and protect the islands from corsairs and pirates. However, as a result, the criminal underclass came flooding in and itself turned to piracy, rewarding the king's generosity by trying to capture one of his ships.

Troubles on the mainland have also been felt on the islands. In 1793 the British landed on Porquerolles and blew up the fort, and in August 1944 American troops came to the islands of Port-Cros and Levant to fight the Germans.

Unspoilt havens

Ile de Porquerolles ❸, named after the wild boar that once roamed there, is the largest and most popular of the islands, and was the inspiration for Robert Louis Stevenson's *Treasure Island*. It offers the most amenities for families and pleasure-craft owners, while its white sandy beaches and woods of pine, eucalyptus and myrtle remain remarkably unspoilt. Porquerolles has been protected from developers by state ownership, with a large conservation area established in 1972, as well as a working vineyard on the island's east side.

The village, also called Porquerolles, has a strong colonial flavour in the simple style of its houses and its gravel main square, laid out as a military parade ground in the 19th century, ringed by scented eucalyptus trees. The many restaurants surrounding the square offer good, inexpensive lunches. The small village church displays the Stations of the Cross carved in wood by a soldier with his penknife.

On the high point of the island above the village, the **Fort Ste-Agathe** (open May–Oct 10am–12.30pm, 1.30–5pm; admission charge) was one of the fortifications put up by François I. The two nearest beaches, the Plage d'Argent and Plage de la Courtade, are each an easy walk on either side of the village. Alternatively, hire a bike by the quay and set off with a picnic to other fine beaches on the north coast, or through the woods to the lighthouse, **Phare de Porquerolles** (tel: 04 94 58 30 78; visits by appointment) on the south, from where there are dramatic views.

The rugged, mountainous **Ile de Port-Cros ❹** (www.portcrosparc national.fr) is a national park, which

Map on page 72

TIP

The ferry company TLV (tel: 04 94 58 21 81; www.tlv-tvm.com) operates from Port d'Hyères to Port-Cros (1 hour) and Ile de Levant (1½ hours), and from la Tour-Fondue on the Presqu'ile de Giens to Porquerolles (30 mins).

BELOW: a bicycle is a popular mode of transport on Porquerolles.

It was in Le Manoir on Port-Cros that D.H. Lawrence is supposed to have met the Englishwoman whose confessional post-coital conversation inspired him to write Lady Chatterley's Lover.

has the particularity of extending both on land and under the sea. Strict rules against smoking and the lighting of fires must be observed.

The **Maison du Parc** (tel: 04 94 01 40 70; open daily, hours vary according to ferry times – *see Tip on page 71*) near the jetty has information on the island's flora and fauna and on footpaths (no cycling here). The island is named after the hollowed-out *(creux)* shape of its harbour. Birdwatchers can observe nearly 100 different species here.

Explore the island by walking through the Vallon de la Solitude to the only hotel on the island, Le Manoir. Continue to the **Fort de l'Estissac** (open May–Oct 10.30am–5.30pm; free), another fortress probably put up by Richelieu in the 17th century. It contains an exhibition about the history of the island and the park; the botanical path is overgrown with wild flowers whose scent follows you down to the sheltered beach and blue waters of La Palud.

Naturist island

Ile du Levant ➎ is a strip of barren rock 8 km (5 miles) long and less than 1.5 km (1 mile) wide. Here you

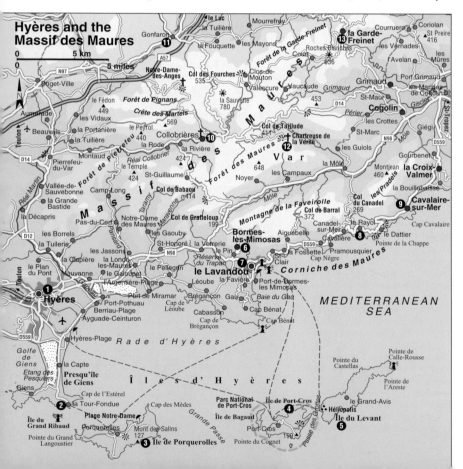

can bare all at the nudist village and beach of Héliopolis, which used to be the "Mecca of Naturism". The nudist colony was founded on the island (once inhabited by Lérins monks) in 1931 by the doctors Gaston and André Durville, who urged their patients to enjoy the physical and psychological benefits of "the childlike liberation of nakedness". Since it has become acceptable to take off your swimsuit on many beaches around the Mediterranean, the island has lost some of its risqué reputation, but is still popular with dedicated nudists. There is not much of the island to explore, as most of Levant is owned by the navy, but there is the strange sight of shopkeepers, estate agents and waiters going about their daily routine in a G-string or less.

The Corniche des Maures

Back on the mainland, the coast east of Hyères, from La Londe to Cap Bénat on the end of the next peninsula, hides a number of relatively uncrowded beaches, under the eye of the closely guarded Fort de Brégançon (a presidential summer residence). The fort cannot be visited, but the Cap itself, planted with vineyards and pine woods, has some lovely unspoilt beaches, such as the **Plage de Cabasson** (parking fee), beneath the hamlet of Cabasson; the lovely **Plage de l'Estagnol** (open Easter–Oct; parking fee) – a shallow curvy bay, bordered by pine woods where you can picnic, which belongs to the wine-producing Château de Brégançon; and the long **Plage de Pellégrin** (open Easter–Oct; parking fee), bordered with pines and sand dunes.

At the southern tip of the peninsula, **Cap Bénat** is a private domain of exclusive holiday villas, but is accessible on foot along the Sentier du Littoral (coast path), giving access to some pretty little coves.

Up on the hill inland from Cap Bénat is the old village of **Bormes-les-Mimosas** ❻, whose coral-coloured houses and steeply sloping streets, lavishly planted with mimosa and flowing bougainvillea, give a delightful flavour of Provence; although it has its inevitable share of galleries and craft shops, there is also a sense of genuine village life here.

The centre of activity is place Gambetta, where there are cafés and restaurants. From here rue Carnot winds through the old village with steep, stepped streets and covered alleyways leading off to either side. The names of the picturesque narrow streets – Roumpi-Cuou (neck-breaker) and Plaine-des-Anes (donkey's sorrow) – suggest their steepness. Look out for the painted sundial on the Eglise St-Trophime and the small **Musée d'Art et d'Histoire de Bormes** (103 rue Carnot; tel: 04 94 71 56 60; open summer Tues–Sun 10am–noon, 3.30–6.30pm, winter Tues–Sat 10am–noon, 2.30–5pm, Sun 10am–noon), in a fine 17th-century village house, that contains some terracottas by

Map on page 72

TIP

The Office National de Forêts (ONF) organises a variety of guided walks in the Maures to discover flora and fauna, prehistoric remains or hidden chapels. Information at Bormes-les-Mimosas tourist office: tel: 04 94 01 38 38; www.bormes lesmimosas.com

BELOW: the rooftops of Bormes-les-Mimosas.

TIP

Vedettes Iles d'Or (tel: 04 94 71 01 02; www. vedettesilesdor.fr) runs ferries from Le Lavandou to the Ile du Levant (35 mins; 1 hour via Port-Cros), and to Porquerolles in summer, as well as boats from La Croix-Valmer and Cavalaire. Check times – ferries are frequent in July and August, limited the rest of the year.

BELOW: Plage St-Clair at Le Lavandou.

Rodin and neo-Impressionist paintings by Bénézit and Van Rysselberghe. On the edge of the old village, the **Chapelle St-Vincent de Paule** was built in the 16th century in gratitude to Italian monk Francesco di Paolo, who was said to have delivered the village from the plague in 1481. Above the town, a road leads up to the remains of the Château des Seigneurs de Fos (private), offering magnificent views over the coast.

Le Lavandou

Bormes's beach suburb of **La Favière** is a low-rise development with a sandy beach, marina and watersports facilities, and lots of simple restaurants serving up various preparations of mussels from the Bay of Toulon. Almost adjoining it is the popular resort of **Le Lavandou ❼**. Glitzy bars and busy restaurants make this a lively place by night, although there are also a few relics of the old fishing town behind the port, and a huge general market behind the promenade on Thursday morning. (This is also the best place

for boats to Port-Cros and the Ile de Levant, *see Tip*.)

Rather than squeeze on to the long and very crowded main beach which stretches along the front of the town itself, you could take the Corniche des Maures (D559) road that winds round the coast to the quieter beaches of Le Lavandou's more attractive satellites, such as the steeply shelving little beach of **St-Clair**, which is framed by an attractive bowl of mountains; **Cavalière,** with a fine beach amid pine trees and views of the Iles d'Hyères; **Pramousquier**, one of the key spots for the Allied landings in 1944; or secluded **Cap Nègre**.

Further east, in **Canadel-sur-Mer**, a narrow road, the D27, turns away from the coast and twists steeply up into the Pradels range (follow signs to La Môle). Just when you've had enough of the stomach-churning hairpins, the road reaches the top of the ridge, where it crosses the GR51 hiking route. Here the views are quite stupendous, stretching from the St-Tropez peninsula in the east to the Ile de Porquerolles in the west.

Rayol gardens

In **Le Rayol** ❽, the next village along the coast, are the fabulous gardens of the **Domaine du Rayol** (tel: 04 98 04 44 00; www.domainedurayol.org; open daily 9.30am–5.30pm, until 7.30pm in summer; admission charge). Here different zones have been planted to reflect other places in the world that have a a similar climate to the Mediterranean, from Mexico to Chile, California to Australia, as well as the Mediterranean itself. Paris banker Alfred Courmes originally created the gardens in 1910, building the house and central pergola, and packing the grounds with exotic plants from around the world.

Now the property of the Conservatoire du Littoral, the gardens were rethought in 1989 by gardening wizard Gilles Clément, who added New Zealand, Mexican and Asiatic zones. There's an incredible variety of vegetation, from Australian blackboys and Chinese bamboo and figs to Mexican agaves, as well as spectacular views to the sea below. There's even an underwater garden, which can be visited in summer with snorkel and flippers.

Beyond Le Rayol, a rare stretch of undeveloped road will bring you to **Cavalaire-sur-Mer** ❾, a town built for the convenience of boat-owners. It has mooring for 1,200 boats, good shops and a long sandy beach. From April onwards you can catch a ferry from here to the Hyères islands or St-Tropez (*see Tip opposite*). The Wednesday-morning market on place Jean Moulin offers an abundance of regional produce: honey, olives, olive oil, *saucisson* and the local rosé wine.

Exploring the Massif

North of Bormes is the oldest range of mountains in Provence, the **Massif des Maures**. The mainly schist rock was originally part of the huge Tyrrhenian Massif, which once included Corsica and Sardinia. The name *Maures* is not an allusion to the Moors (Saracens), who occupied the area for more than a century and who were driven out in AD 973, but to the Provençal word *Mauro*, which

Map on page 72

Prickly pears blooming in the Domaine du Rayol.

BELOW: lush vegetation at the Domaine du Rayol.

BELOW: view of the
Massif des Maures.
RIGHT: a field of
lavender is a familiar
sight in the country.

describes the dark density of the
cork oak, chestnut and pine forest.

The glorious views and abundance of flowers and plants such as
yellow gorse, lavender and wild
roses are enjoyed by drivers, walkers and cyclists who use the Massif's villages to shape their route
through the mountainous forest.
Apart from the N98 which crosses
the vine-covered Vallée de la Môle
between the two principal ridges,
few roads cross the mountains, and
those that do are mostly narrow
and extremely twisty, with hair-
raising hairpin bends.

Fortunately several footpaths,
including the GR51, GR9 and
GR90 long-distance footpaths
(indicated by red-and-white-striped
markings), traverse the Maures,
making them great for walking.

Over the past few years, especially the hot summer of 2003, the
Maures have suffered from some
devastating fires, often caused by
carelessly jettisoned cigarette ends,
illicit campfires or by arson, and
leaving large tracts where only blackened tree stumps and burnt-out cars

remain. In summer, firemen are sta-
tioned at viewpoints around the Massif, and many footpaths and side
roads are closed at times of risk, especially when there are strong winds.

Capital of the Maures

The small town of **Collobrières** ⑩,
self-proclaimed capital of the
Maures and located at its centre, is
reached from Bormes by a tortuous
road over the thickly wooded Col de
Babaou. Here, locals are employed
mainly in the timber industry and in
chestnut production. In October you
can join in the chestnut harvest
(contact the tourist office; tel: 04 94
48 08 00).

The village centre is not, as you
might think, the attractive main
square with a Spanish feel, or the
main boulevard with its grand mer-
cantile houses put up by timber
barons in the 19th century, but the
extensive *bouledrome* by the Réal
Collobrier river.

A 12th-century bridge crosses the
river near by, and beside it is the
Confiserie Azuréenne, a delicious-
smelling shop and small museum

(open daily; free) dedicated to its chestnut sweets (*marrons glacés*) and purées. At the eastern end of the village is the romantic-looking ruin of the 12th-century Eglise St-Pons.

North of the village you can take an 11-km (7-mile) detour to the eccentric priory of **Notre-Dame-des-Anges**, standing at 771 metres (2,530 ft) and sharing its high point with a large communications tower. The 19th-century chapel is filled with offerings made by pilgrims who have climbed to the spot where a statue of the Virgin Mary was found by a shepherd in the 11th century. Babies' bonnets and pictures of the sick being cured cram the dark chapel, and, more strangely, two stuffed alligators hang from the ceiling.

Tortoise territory

On the northern edge of the Maures, the village of **Gonfaron** ⓫ (D39 from Collobrières, which climbs over the Col de Fourche pass, the highest section of the Maures; or direct from the A57 *autoroute* and the N97), with a large tree-lined square, is crowned by the Chapelle St-Quinis. The pretty church is dedicated to the village's patron saint, who brought Christianity to the village in the 6th century.

Outside Gonfaron is the **Village des Tortues** (quartier les Plaines; tel: 04 94 78 26 41; www.village-tortues.com; open Mar–Nov 9am–7pm; admission charge), which is a breeding centre for tortoises, with the mission to safeguard the endangered Hermann's Tortoise and re-introduce it into the Maures.

Deeper into the woods

The road east of Collobrières (the D14 towards Grimaud) is spectacular. Winding through forests of oak and chestnut, it climbs high into the heart of the Massif. Along the route there are points for cars to stop, so you can admire the breathtaking

views (or simply let a hill farmer overtake in his van). Tracks and paths are clearly marked for walkers.

About 6 km (4 miles) east of Collobrières, an even narrower and more tortuous road turns off to the south and climbs to a desolate and brooding Carthusian monastery, the **Chartreuse de la Verne** ⓬ (tel: 04 94 43 45 41; http://la.verne.tree.fr; open Wed–Mon summer 11am–6pm, winter 11am–5pm, closed Jan; admission charge), which offers a suitably isolated setting for this silent Order.

The forbidding-looking structure, built in browny-grey schist with local blue-green serpentine rock around the doors and vaults, stands on a plateau overlooking the forest, and dates mostly from the 17th and 18th centuries. Some vestiges remain from its 12th-century beginnings. Burnt and pillaged on several occasions during the Revolution, the few remaining monks fled and the monastery became state property. Restoration began in the 1970s, and since 1983 a community of nuns from the Order

Map on page 72

The view of the Massif des Maures are spectacular from the open road.

BELOW:
the Hermann tortoise is a protected species.

The pretty village of La Garde-Freinet makes a good day trip from the coast.

BELOW AND RIGHT: view of La Garde-Freinet.

of Bethlehem has lived here. The visit, which starts in the massive gatehouse, includes the cloister, the cemetery, a restored monk's cell with a private courtyard for meditation, the church, granary, bakery and oil press.

A corking village

The D14 continues to Grimaud *(see page 91)*. From here, a more substantial road leads north to **La Garde-Freinet** ⓭, the main village of the Massif and fashionable among second-home owners and expats escaping the crush on the coast.

In the 19th century, the village produced more than three-quarters of France's bottle corks. The industry has declined dramatically since then, but the cork-oaks in these hills are still harvested, and you will often see them stripped of their bark on the side of the road. The light, impermeable and elastic outer bark is cut off and sent to factories in Fréjus and further afield.

You can pick up local antiques, pottery and fresh flowers on rue St-Jacques, or browse the morning market on place Neuve (Wed and Sun) for ornaments crafted from the local cork. Look out for the exquisite jewellery made from local serpentine stone.

The Saracens were at one time credited with building the **fortress** on a high point to the northwest of the village, but it is now thought to be of a later period (12th–16th centuries). The **Conservatoire du Patrimoine** (tel: 04 94 43 08 57; open Tues–Sat; admission charge), in the same building as the tourist office on place de la Mairie, contains a model of the fort, archaeological finds from the area and displays on cork and silkworms. The tourist office also provides information on the many superb hiking routes that criss-cross the surrounding hills.

If you visit in late May or early June, try to make it on the day of the *transhumance* festival, when the village celebrates the departure of its sheep for the higher summer pastures. In this area, the shepherds still walk all the way with the flocks of sheep, often spending several days on the march. ❑

RESTAURANTS

Bormes-les-Mimosas

Lou Portaou

1 rue Cubert des Poètes.
Tel: 0494 64 86 37. Open D
daily in summer, D Wed–Sun
in winter; closed mid-Nov–
mid-Dec. €€

Delightful atmospheric
restaurant located in a
fortified medieval tower
in Bormes village.
Excellent Provençal
dishes full of colour
and flavour.

Restaurant de l'Estagnol

Parc de l'Estagnol. Tel: 04
94 64 71 11. Open L & D
Apr–Sept; closed Oct–Mar.
€€

Popular alfresco eating
under the pines just
back from the beach at
l'Estagnol. The speciali-
ties are fresh fish,
bouillabaisse and
langoustines wonder-
fully grilled on an open
wood fire.

La Tonnelle

Place Gambetta. Tel: 04
94 71 34 84. Open
L Fri–Tues, D Thur–Tues;
closed mid-Nov–mid-Dec.
€€

www.la-tonnelle-bormes.com

In a pleasant airy dining
room on the village
square, Gil Renard's
attractively presented
modern Mediterranean
cooking includes such
dishes as tuna tartare
with artichokes, or land-
sea combinations such
as lamb with anchovies.
Home-made bread and
inventive fruit-based
desserts.

Collobrières

Hôtel-Restaurant des Maures

19 boulevard Lazare Carnot.
Tel: 04 94 48 07 10. Open L
& D daily. €

A popular family-run
restaurant with tables on
the terrace spanning the
river. Sustaining rustic
fare includes a fine wild-
boar stew.

La Garde-Freinet

La Faucado

Route Nationale, boulevard
de l'Esplanade. Tel: 04 94 43
60 41. Open L & D
Wed–Mon; closed Feb. €€€

On the main road to the
south of the village, here
you'll find traditional
Provençal cuisine served
on a pleasant open-air
terrace. Specialities
include wild mushrooms
in autumn.

Hyères

Le Bistrot de Marius

1 place Massillon. Tel: 04
94 35 88 38. Open L & D
daily; closed Mon–Tues
Sep–Jun. €€

This unassuming restau-
rant specialises in local
fish dishes accompanied
by seasonal vegetables.
The soupe de poisson is
especially delicious. In
the summer, you can eat
outside in the shadow of
the Tour des Templiers.

Le Jardin de Sarradam

35 avenue de Belgique.
Tel: 04 94 65 97 53. Open L
& D daily; closed Sun D &
Mon in low season. €€

This family-run restau-
rant dishes up exquisite
Mediterranean and orien-
tal specialities, including
couscous and tajines. In
fine weather, tables are
displayed in the beautiful
garden. You can also
come for a cup of mint
tea and a puff of narguilé.

Ile de Porquerolles

Restaurant l'Olivier

Le Mas du Langoustier. Tel:
04 94 58 30 09. Open L & D;
closed mid-Oct–Apr. €€€

www.langoustier.com

Expensive, exclusive
island dining, but worth
the trip for lunch even if
you don't stay at the
hotel. Try the fish soup,
the sea bass stuffed with
olives and tomatoes and
the exquisite desserts.

Les Jardins de Bacchus

32 avenue Gambetta. Tel: 04
94 65 77 63. Open L
Tues–Fri, Sun, D Tues–Sat.
€€

www.les-jardins-de-bacchus.com

On the main street
leading up to the old
town, chef Jean-Claude
Santoni prepares classic
southern cuisine with a
cosmopolitan touch.

Le Lavandou

Les Roches

Hôtel des Roches, 1 avenue
des Trois-Dauphins, Aiguebelle. Tel: 04 94 71 05 07.
Open L & D daily. €€€

www.hotellesroches.com

The Dandine brothers
from L'Escoundudo at
Bormes-les-Mimosas
have recently taken over
the restaurant at this luxury waterside hotel, with
a chic new contemporary
decor for Mathieu Dan-
dine's modern interpreta-
tion of Provençal cuisine.

Les Tamaris "Chez Raymond"

Plage de St-Clair. Tel: 04 94
71 02 70. Open L & D.
€€€–€€€€

The most upmarket of
the fish restaurants
along the Plage de St-
Clair is renowned for its
bourride and the daily
catch. It's an old
favourite so book ahead.

Rayol-Canadel

Maurin des Maures

Boulevard du TCF. Tel: 04 94
05 60 11. Open L and D
daily. €€

www.maurin-des-maures.com

This noisy, animated
institution has lashings of
atmosphere, combining a
popular restaurant, where
you are packed elbow to
elbow down long tables,
with the local bar with
its pinball and table
football. Come for fish
dishes and Provençal
classics like daube de
bœuf and rabbit.

PRICE CATEGORIES

Prices for a three-course
meal without wine.

€ = under €25
€€ = €25–40
€€€ = over €40

St-Tropez and its Peninsula

Although crowded in August, St-Tropez still wears the crown as *the* place to see and be seen in. The action spreads around the Golfe de St-Tropez to Ste-Maxime, but in the hilltop towns of the peninsula a more calm and sophisticated atmosphere pervades

Maps:
City 82
Area 88

Few places enjoy more mythic status than **St-Tropez** ❶, which continues to draw the rich and famous from all over the world, combining as it does glamorous resort and authentic Provençal village. For all its showbiz flavour, luxurious hotels, legendary nightlife, ostentatious yachts, and sometimes outright vulgarity of the *m'as-tu vu* scene (see to be seen), St-Tropez still has a surprising charm and even a certain democracy: anyone can dress up and parade along the *quais*, and those with the right look will be able to make it past the rigorous *physionomistes* (bouncers) of Les Caves du Roy.

Crammed with between 45,000 and 60,000 daily visitors in July and August, in winter the population of St-Tropez returns to a placid and neighbourly 5,400. Though obviously not for those in search of rustic serenity, at least in summer, a visit to St-Tropez can be considerable fun if taken in the right spirit, and preferably equipped with a generous budget.

First impressions

St-Tropez's original attraction was based on the beauty of the dusky pink and ochre houses of the old town, its position on the southern curve of its large, sheltered gulf,

and the climatic conditions which enhance its clear light. Uniquely on the Riviera, St-Tropez faces north, so that the quayside cafés receive the famous golden evening light, as well as the bay's stunning sunsets.

As neither railway nor major trunk roads passed through the town due to its position on a peninsula, St-Tropez escaped the late 19th-century development of earlier resorts such as Juan-les-Pins and Cannes. Its restricted road access is now a mixed blessing – in summer,

LEFT: view over St-Tropez old town.
BELOW: narrow streets and dusky pink houses.

The tiny corps of remaining fishermen moor up at the quai Mistral and trade at the market on place aux Herbes.

traffic jams run the length of the N98 to the huge roundabout at La Foux and, sometimes, the whole way round the bay to Ste-Maxime. It's best not to take a car into town – even if you get through the jams, there's nowhere to park. Instead, use one of the car parks in Port Grimaud or Ste-Maxime and take the shuttle ferry across the bay, or cut through the back roads from Ramatuelle (the Corniche des Maures from Le Lavandou is generally less crowded than the Ste-Maxime coast road). Even those who arrive by private plane risk getting stuck in traffic, as the airstrip is out of town at La Môle in the Maures.

Early history

St-Tropez is named after Torpes, a Christian Roman centurion, steward of the Emperor Nero's palace at Pisa who, according to legend, was beheaded for his faith and cast adrift with a dog and a rooster in a boat which eventually drifted to the site of the present port. The early town was sacked and its population killed or dispersed by Saracen raiders who occupied the region in the 7th, 8th and 9th centuries.

In the 15th century, St-Tropez was ceded to a Genoese nobleman, Raphaël de Garezzio, with rights tantamount to those of a republic, and was populated by a number of Genoese families, some of whose descendants remain today. The citadel overlooking the town dates from the ensuing period of well-organised security, provided by an elected "town captain" and militia. In 1637, this militia successfully defended the town against a raiding force of 22 Spanish galleys.

By the late 19th century, St-Tropez was primarily involved in tuna fishing, shipping wines from the region to Marseille and Toulon, and making corks from the bark of the local oak trees. A handful of

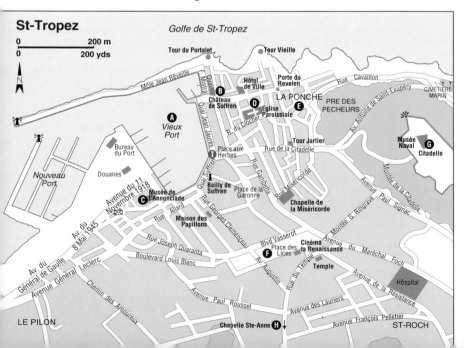

large houses outside the town had been restored or constructed by prominent individuals such as Napoleon III's minister Emile Ollivier, who retired to the Château de la Moutte, where his tomb now stands "seeking only peace, but finding delight".

The artists arrive

In 1887, the writer Guy de Maupassant arrived at St-Tropez aboard his boat *Bel Ami* and found it "a charming, simple daughter of the sea" with "sardine scales glistening like pearls on the cobblestones". It was the painter Paul Signac, however, who, sailing into the port on his yacht in 1892 and falling in love with the light, acquired a small house overlooking the Plage des Graniers and began to attract friends and painter acquaintances. Matisse, Bonnard, Camoin and Dunoyer de Segonzac.

In 1927, the celebrated novelist Colette moved to her villa La Treille Muscate. She was followed by the 1930s *beau monde*, such as the couturier Paul Poiret, the writer

Anaïs Nin, and after the interruption of World War II, when the long Pampelonne beach was used for the Allied liberation landings, by the first of the St-Germain bohemian stars, the fashionable singer Juliette Greco.

In 1955, Roger Vadim shot *And God Created Woman* in St-Tropez, with the sex kitten Brigitte Bardot wreaking havoc around the Old Port, and the floodgates of the town's modern showbusiness invasion were opened.

The *yé yé* industry – pop stars led by Johnny Hallyday and record magnate Eddie Barclay – followed the film world, and in 1969 the opening of the luxurious Hôtel Byblos marked a turning point in the transformation of the hitherto simple fishing village into a fully paid-up jet-set destination.

The St-Tropez season traditionally starts at Easter, peaks in the frenzy of the national holiday month of August and continues until the end of Les Voiles de St-Tropez, a fashionable yacht-racing week at the end of September. The

Maps:
City 82
Area 88

It was the film And God Created Woman, *released in 1956, by Brigitte Bardot's then husband, Roger Vadim, that rocketed the overtly sexy actress to stardom and put St-Tropez, where it was filmed, on the tourist map.*

BELOW: yachts jostle for space in the port.

St-Tropez Style

St-Tropez is a barometer of style for the well-heeled, a summer alternative to the catwalks of Paris or the ski slopes of Megève. Getting the measure of the St-Tropez look is deceptively complex. Informality has always been the keyword, but studied informality – this is not a place to go if you don't want to bother about what you look like. Everyone stares at everyone else all the time, and it's not always clear whether it's out of contempt or admiration.

Once chic, the shops on the quayside now cater to the tour groups. Set back from the port, however, in little shopping streets, the cream of European *prêt-à-porter* is available to those who can afford it. Hermès has a shop here, as does Louis Vuitton; Joanna sells Alexander McQueen and Dries van Noten; elsewhere boutiques offer Versace, Anna Sui, Emilio Pucci, Prada and much more.

The surprising thing is how popular St-Tropez remains with the super-rich. Like much of the Côte d'Azur, it is often seen as overcrowded and overrated, but for many people (usually the ones with the yachts and private villas) it has remained as desirable as ever. Star-spotters will not be disappointed – the likes of Robbie Williams, Naomi Campbell and Jack Nicholson still wander the streets.

The Vieux Port of St-Tropez is a good place to sit and watch the world go by.

BELOW: watching the sunset in Vieux Port.

quiet winter months are interrupted by a substantial mini-season around Christmas; many shops, restaurants and hotels close during the off-peak period.

The Vieux Port

The centre of St-Tropez is the pretty **Vieux Port Ⓐ** (old port), lined with colour-washed houses which have been faithfully restored after World War II damage, and enclosed by the long stone jetty, the Môle Jean Réveille, extending outwards from the squat, round 15th-century **Tour du Portalet**.

The quays (Suffren, Jean Jaurès and Frédéric Mistral) are lined with restaurants and fashionable cafés, notably the all-red **Sénéquier**, originally a pâtisserie and still famed for its nougat. Beside it is the more youthful **Le Gorille**, open 24 hours a day in the summer, making it *the* place to go for post-clubbing hunger pangs. Both are ideal venues for people-watching.

Behind Sénéquier is the small **place aux Herbes**, reached via an archway beside the tourist office.

Every morning except Monday, a flower, vegetable and fish market is held here.

Stern to the quay are the great yachts – futuristic white plastic-looking gin palaces or gleaming teak classics – with uniformed crews and, increasingly, non-sailing corporate charterers. The old, and adjacent new, ports welcome a wide range of craft, from vintage sailing yachts to the long, spear-head-shaped, V8-engined, offshore "cigarettes" that drone across the bay at 100 kph (60 mph).

Continuing westwards around the port is the **quai Suffren**, on which stands a bronze statue of one of St-Tropez's most illustrious adopted citizens, the Bailly de Suffren. De Suffren's late-flourishing nautical career ended with a famously successful Indian campaign in the 1780s and the command of the French navy. His name was retrospectively applied to the 10th-century square tower, the **Château de Suffren Ⓑ**, back at the eastern end of the port, just behind the quai Mistral. The tower was used, along with a similar building in Ste-

Night out in the Old Town

A St-Tropez night out might well start with a drink in the Vieux Port, watching the fading sunlight and the yachts from the red directors' chairs at Sénéquier (try to get a front-row seat), or from the eternally open Gorille where the younger set like to hang out, or at the retro-chic Bar du Port, which has a large selection of cocktails and a DJ or two. Alternatively, you'll be able to see many a beautiful person from the balcony vantage point of Le Sube. You can eat at any of these places, or you might prefer to join the boules players on place des Lices and have a meal at Le Café, a St-Trop institution, nibble on tapas at the baroque-style lounge bar Chez Maggy on rue Sibille, or sink into the low chairs at the Octave Café, a stylish piano bar on place de la Garonne.

Around midnight, queues start to form outside St-Tropez's night-clubs, led by the ever-popular Les Caves du Roy at the Hôtel Byblos, still the sort of place where George Clooney, Ivana Trump or Naomi Campbell might be spotted, followed by the classic 1960s favourite, Papagayo, and the newer, hipper VIP Room. All can be difficult to get into; dressing up and looking good will help.

Maxime, by the Knights Templar, to protect the gulf's settlements from the North African Barbary pirates whose raids plagued the region until the 15th century. It is sometimes used for art exhibitions.

Art museum

Over on the western side of the Vieux Port is the **Musée de l'Annonciade ⒞** (place Gramont; tel: 04 94 17 84 10; open Sept–June Wed–Mon 10am–noon, 2–6pm, July–Aug daily 10am–1pm, 3–7pm; admission charge), a 16th-century chapel attractively converted to house a large and excellent collection of paintings and sculptures by artists who lived or worked in the town. Partly donated by the Tropezian philanthropist Georges Grammont, the museum holds one of the most important collections of neo-Impressionist and Fauvist art outside Paris.

Signac is represented by a rotating collection of 10 watercolours and five oils, and other high points include works by Van Dongen, Matisse, Seurat, Bonnard, Dufy, Vuillard and Braque. Many of the paintings depict scenes of St-Tropez itself, and there's also an important temporary exhibition each summer.

Exploring the old town

Behind the Château de Suffren is the attractive ochre-coloured **Hôtel de Ville** (town hall). From here you can explore the lovely narrow stone streets of the **Vieille Ville** (old town), those nearer the port lined with shops and restaurants, those further back residential and surprisingly quiet and unspoilt even in August.

In the centre of the old town is St-Tropez's 18th-century neo-baroque **Eglise Paroissiale ⒟** (parish church; open daily am only), whose distinctive pink-and-yellow bell tower and typically Provençal wrought-iron belfry have become a symbol of the town. The church contains statues of Torpes, the town's patron saint, both headless and recumbent, plus menagerie, in his boat, invariably festooned with votive offerings of flowers and hearts.

The quiet, old *quartier* of **La Ponche ⒠**, reached through the 15th-century stone gate, the Porte du Revelen, was once the haunt of Tropezian fishermen. In years gone by they would beach at the **Port des Pêcheurs** and sell their catch from nearby stalls.

The narrow streets of La Ponche hold a couple of fine hotels frequented by the literati in the pre-Byblos 1950s and 1960s. Hôtel La Ponche, which has a terrace restaurant, and the similarly elegant Yaca Hotel, have both managed to update their facilities and decor with great taste, retaining the charm of the lovely old buildings.

A network of pedestrian streets lead southward to **place des Lices ⒡**, where there is a colourful market

Map on page 82

Every year on 16–18 May the people of St-Tropez take to the streets in honour of the town's patron saint. Known as the Bravades, the colourful procession involves singing, dancing and a noisy army of musket-firing men.

BELOW: a carousel provides fun at the fair.

The plane tree-shaded place des Lices serves as a terrain de boules *on non-market days. Le Café will lend a set of boules to its clientele.*

BELOW: walking on Plage de Pampelonne.

on Tuesday and Saturday mornings, offering all the best produce of Provence. Even at the height of the season, this is one of the best places to see the real St-Tropez.

Designer fashion labels and jewellers to rival any world capital are concentrated on rue Allard, rue Sibille, place de la Garonne and rue Gambetta, where you'll also find the 17th-century **Chapelle de la Miséricorde** with a blue-, green- and gold-tiled belfry. Between the quay and the square are more narrow streets lined with small boutiques, including Atelier Rondini, famed for its strappy leather Tropezian sandals.

On one of the streets, a small village house contains the **Maison des Papillons** (9 rue Etienne Berny; tel: 04 94 97 63 45; open Apr–Oct and Christmas hols Mon–Sat 2.30–6pm; admission charge), which houses a display of more than 4,500 colourful butterflies from around the world collected by the painter Dany Lartigue, the son of a famous 1920s society photographer.

The citadel

Above the 16th-century semi-ruined **Tour Jarlier**, the montée de la Citadelle climbs up to the 16th-century **Citadelle ⓖ** (tel: 04 94 97 59 43; open daily summer 10am–6pm, winter 10am–noon, 2–6pm), overlooking the bay from its grassy, pine-dotted hillock. The most important fortification between Toulon and Antibes, it has an impressive set of ramparts and bastions, and cannons looking out to sea.

The hexagonal keep houses the **Musée Naval de la Citadelle** (due to reopen after renovation in summer 2007), containing souvenirs of local hero Admiral de Suffren (who took his fleet on an odyssey around the Cape of Good Hope in 1781), model ships and diving equipment. Below the citadel, on the opposite slope of the hill from the town centre, is the **marine cemetery**, its white headstones outlined strikingly against the blue of the sea.

Excellent views of the town (and, in the other direction, of Cap Camarat) can be had from the 17th-century **Chapelle Ste-Anne ⓗ**

Plage de Pampelonne

The Plage de Pampelonne is a 5-km (3-mile) stretch of sand between Cap Pinet and Cap Camaret, bordered by bamboos, pines and vineyards. Much of the bay is taken up by "private" beach clubs, ranging from the boho bamboo shack with its beach restaurant and sun loungers to designer haunts offering cosmopolitan menus, cocktail bars, DJs and spas. Trendy spots include the veteran showbiz haunt Tahiti, the Millesim, venerable Club 55, Kon Tiki, the Nikki Beach, Voile Rouge, Nioulargo, Key West, the simpler Tropicana and fish restaurant Chez Camille. But there are also free public stretches where you can park your parasol – and the shorefront is accessible to anyone.

(closed to public), 20 minutes' walk uphill south of the town centre.

The beaches

St-Tropez itself has very limited beach areas, being centred around the port. The famous golden beaches are on either side of the town. The biggest, Plage de Pampelonne, is 5 km (3 miles) to the southeast, technically in the commune of Ramatuelle. Most of them are occupied by a series of beach "clubs" which are not really clubs at all, but concessions rented by their proprietors from the local council and offering their bars, restaurants, parasols, loungers, sometimes shops, hairdressers, and tenders to pick up customers from their offshore yachts, to anyone who is willing to pay.

This is not to deny they can seem as cliquey and exclusive as clubs, with different social sets patronising different establishments. Beach life tends to begin late morning, proceed to a leisurely lunch at the restaurant and peak during the post-prandial mid- to late-afternoon lazing time. There are also stretches of free public beach between the concessions.

The beaches actually forming part of St-Tropez are, to the west, **Bouillabaisse**, where the action centres on two concessions, upmarket La Bouillabaisse, one of the town's best restaurants, and Pearl Beach, frequented by a younger crowd; **Plage des Graniers**, a simple beach below the citadel favoured by native Tropeziens; further east, the slightly larger **Plage des Canebiers**, overlooked by Bardot's villa, La Madrague; and on the eastern edge of the peninsula, the rather crowded **Plage des Salins**. For less populated sands, head for the **Plage de la Moutte**, reached by a separate road just north of Salins.

Legendary Pampelonne

Along the 5-km (3-mile) golden sands of **Plage de Pampelonne** ❷ the popularity of the beach restaurants/concessions is subject to the flighty whims of fashion. Current favourites, from north to south, are: Tropezina; Tabou-Plage;

Maps:
City 82
Area 88

Anyone has the right to swim in the water or walk along the shorefront of any beach, private or not.

BELOW: windsurfing in the Golfe de St-Tropez.

Viticulture accounts for 40 percent of the agriculture in the region, and the peninsula is a major part of the Côtes de Provence appellation contrôlée area.

BELOW: a vineyard near St-Tropez.

Tahiti, a big, long-established showbiz favourite including a hotel, beauty salon, tennis courts, shops and helicopter landing strip; Bora Bora and the very chic Moorea; Le Liberty and Neptune, both naturist; Club 55, the oldest (founded in 1955 by the de Colmont family) and classiest, which is still a favourite with royalty and rock stars; Key West Beach; trendy young designer-style Maison Ocoa; Nioulargo-Kaï Largo, with traditional and Asian restaurants; La Plage des Jumeaux, noted for its Provençal food; the much-hyped Nikki, with a young, hip, cutting-edge crowd; La Cabane Bambou offering Thai cuisine; funky l'Esquinade; and 1970s-style all-orange Tropicana, another showbiz favourite with excellent local cooking. Amazingly enough, there is room for small stretches of public beach where you can enjoy the sands without shelling out. Right at

the furthest end, Chez Camille is a long-established and very popular fish restaurant in an old fisherman's shack.

Further round the peninsula, there is a small, attractive beach at **L'Escalet**. If you have a boat, you will have access to the beach at **Baie de Briande**, which you won't have to share with so many people.

Peninsular hill villages

Inland on the peninsula sit the beautiful hilltop villages of **Ramatuelle** and **Gassin**, their old stone centres rising above the surrounding vineyards and woodland. From here are superb views of the sea, and, on a good day, far back to the north, you can glimpse snow on the peaks of the lower Alps. In and around the villages are opulent holiday homes, and in the centres are pretty, chic, tree-shaded restaurants offering a more secluded alternative to those of St-Tropez.

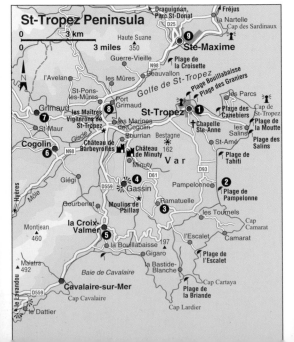

The Saracens are said to be responsible for the name of **Ramatuelle** ❸ (from *Rahmatu 'llah*, Arabic for "God's gift"), which retains two 10th-century doors in the remains of its fortifications from the Saracen occupation. Other significant episodes in the village's martial history include the unusual use of beehives hurled from the ramparts to repel a Royalist siege in 1592, and, during World War II, its role as a point of contact for the Resistance with Allied submarines, attested to by a monument near the cemetery.

A pretty, tile-roofed, flower-bedecked village of narrow, winding streets, built in a tight spiral, Ramatuelle is also noted for its lively summer festivals of jazz, classical music and, especially, theatre, all held in an open-air auditorium on the southern slope of Ramatuelle's hill.

On place de l'Ormeau, the Romanesque village church contains a 17th-century doorway carved from serpentine, the same stone as the Chartreuse de la Verne (*see page 77*). Just outside the village is a magnificent view of three ruined windmills known as the **Moulins de Paillas**.

Ramatuelle's neighbour **Gassin** ❹, about 4 km (2½ miles) to the northwest, is the more elevated of the two. It is an exquisite little town with a 16th-century church and town hall, a pretty central square planted with African lotus trees and surrounded by a warren of tiny roads and alleys, and a circular boulevard with great views over the entire gulf. Gassin's position was its early *raison d'être* – as a lookout post, it was manned from the 10th century by the Knights Templar, who did not, however, prevent a Saracen raiding party carrying off 33 of the village's inhabitants in 1394.

Fruit of the vine

The lower slopes of the peninsula are dominated by vineyards. Running through this region is the Route des Côtes de Provence, a signposted itinerary passing by some of the most important individual *domaines*, all of them open for visits and sales. Favourites just north of Gassin include the elegant Napoleon III **Château de Minuty** (tel: 04 94 56 12 09; open Easter–June Mon–Sat, July–Aug daily, Sept–Easter Mon–Fri; free) off Route D61, and the nearby **Château de Barbeyrolles** (tel: 04 94 56 33 58; open Easter–Oct Mon–Sat, Nov–Easter Mon–Fri; free).

The wine co-operative **Les Maîtres Vignerons de St-Tropez** (tel: 04 94 56 40 17; open Mon–Sat) at La Foux junction near Port Grimaud is the best place to taste local wines and pick up other regional products.

On the southern slope of the peninsula, looking across vineyards, reed beds and pine groves towards the Baie de Cavalaire, the village of **La Croix-Valmer** ❺ contains few

Map on page 88

Many Côtes de Provence wines are made in the warm coastal hinterland.

BELOW: small town Gassin.

BELOW: the village of Grimaud.

vestiges of its Roman past. Its name, however, is believed to derive from the legend that Emperor Constantine, while passing through en route to Italy, was persuaded by the vision of a cross in the sky to convert to Christianity. Mostly dating from the early 20th century, La Croix-Valmer has some striking modern buildings, including the parish church. In addition to its role as a centre for holiday homes, it is an important wine-producing centre. Down on the coast is the local beach, Plage de Gigaro.

West of St-Tropez, just before the coastal plain begins its long mutation into the hills of the Massif des Maures, sits the town of **Cogolin** ❻. This village was the headquarters of General de Lattre de Tassigny during the 1944 battle to liberate Provence. Although possessed of a pretty old centre with a 16th-century church, numerous serpentine doorways and vaulted passageways, Cogolin is also a working town. In addition to wine, it produces pottery, handwoven carpets, mouthpieces for reed instruments from the surrounding reed beds, and pipes carved from the roots of local mountain heather *(see left)*.

Foothills of the Maures

Just as the Massif de l'Estérel to the north acts as a buffer against the urbanisation of the coast between Cannes and St-Raphaël, so the great wild bulk of the **Massif des Maures** counterbalances the St-Tropez build-up. Indeed, until the seaside boom in the early 1900s, the presence of the Maures kept the coastline isolated and undeveloped for centuries.

The Maures are among the areas of the Riviera worst afflicted by brush fires, however, and long stretches of the roads which wind north through the low hills pass acres of fire-blackened, dead trunks, protruding from the thistle, thyme and broom scrub. Patrolling fire engines and lookout points are a common sight in summer.

At the point where the Massif begins to rise northwest of Cogolin is the typical fortified village of

The Birth of Port Grimaud

Port Grimaud is essentially the creation of one man, architect François Spoerry, whose idea for Port Grimaud was nurtured in the 1950s at his parents' holiday home in Cavalaire. He didn't like getting up in the night to check on their boat's mooring in a storm, so he determined to design a leisure port, with yacht-owners primarily in mind, on the model of Venice.

In 1962, Spoerry obtained a stretch of mosquito-infested marshy land by the mouth of the little river Giscle at the end of the Gulf of St-Tropez in the commune of Grimaud. It took him four years to obtain building permission for a project widely regarded as crazy.

Spoerry believed that buildings should avail themselves of local traditional materials and techniques. He therefore designed Port Grimaud with Provençal-style terracotta tiled roofs and colourful façades. Every house has a waterfront and boat mooring – later "streets" have small front gardens with lawns and trees. Movement between the 2,500 houses, two squares, 30-odd bars and restaurants and several dozen shops is on foot, via the little wood or stone-clad bridges connecting the tiny islands, or by the small electric-powered boats used as runabouts.

Grimaud ➐, flower-decorated and immaculately maintained by a population that seems to consist largely of four-wheel-drive-owning architects. The name of the village derives from that of Gibellino Grimaldi, a knight who was given lordship of the area in the 10th century as a reward for his part in the expulsion of the Saracen occupiers; the name is also that of the Monaco royal family.

Modern-day Grimaud, clustering around the ruins of its medieval castle, has a simple but impressive Romanesque church, St-Michel, once used by the Templars, after whom the lovely arcaded street near by is named. There is no shortage of chic and pretty hotels, one of the prettiest being the small, traditional Côteau Fleuri, with a flower-packed garden and wonderful views

The hike up to the castle is worth braving for even better views in all directions. The romantic ruins themselves are notable for their sharp-edged serpentine window frames, which seem to hold their own while the rest of the edifice crumbles around them.

Grimaud's scene-stealing seaside extension, **Port Grimaud ➑**, is 5 km (3 miles) to the east, at the head of the Gulf of St-Tropez. The inhabitants of the purpose-built yachting town like to ask visitors, jokingly, if they have ever visited St-Tropez – "you know, that little village across the bay". The implication of the newer resort's fame is by no means all hyperbole: it now rates as one of the most popular tourist attractions in France, averaging over a million visitors a year – not bad going for a town that did not exist before 1966.

Designed by François Spoerry against all odds *(see box opposite)*, the earliest houses went for as little as 150,000 francs. These days you would be lucky to get a studio apartment for four times that value, and the houses sell for more than €1 million. After Spoerry died in 1999 (he is buried in Port Grimaud's striking church), his house sold for €5.3 million.

An impressive achievement and in places very pretty, Port Grimaud

Map on page 88

A war memorial to honour the fallen soldiers of the allied forces.

BELOW: a view of Port Grimaud.

Map on page 88

Ste-Maxime was once protected by the monks of the Iles de Lérins, who named the port after their patron saint and put up the defensive Tour Carrée.

BELOW: sun worshippers flock to the beach at Ste-Maxime.

is ultimately a stage set. Its convenience attracts the buyers, but the multinational owners of the huge yachts moored outside the houses are absent for a large part of the year, consigning their properties to resident caretakers.

But now, after 40 or so years, the buildings are acquiring a patina of age, and cicadas chirrup in the main square, adding the quintessential Midi soundtrack to the pastiche.

Ste-Maxime

Further around the gulf, opposite St-Tropez, is **Ste-Maxime ⑨**, a prosperous and pleasant resort of over 12,000 inhabitants with a marina and pretty seafront marred only by the traffic passing along its main coast road. The centre is occupied by the massed striped parasols of the main beach, the pastel bulk of the casino, with an Art Deco bas-relief of swimming girls, and well-kept gardens of palm trees, mimosa and oleander.

Just behind the port, the old town is pedestrianised and busy in the summer; on its edge is the cool,

immaculately kept 19th-century parish church and a square 16th-century tower, the **Tour Carrée** (place de l'Eglise; tel: 04 94 96 70 30; open Wed–Sun 10am–noon, 3–6pm; admission charge), now a local history museum.

For sun-worshippers, Cherry Beach, 3 km (2 miles) east of the marina, is the chic choice, while further on, Plage des Eléphants is more affordable.

On route D25, about 10 km (6 miles) northwest of Ste-Maxime, in the foothills of the Massif des Maures, look for a sign on the right indicating the privately run **Musée du Phonographe et de la Musique Mécanique** (tel: 04 94 96 50 52; open Easter–Sept Wed–Sun 10am–noon, 3–6pm; admission charge). In a shed behind a folk-kitsch façade, one woman has collected around 400 assorted antique record players, barrel organs and other mechanical music-makers, all displayed in an amiable jumble. If you're lucky, Madame will demonstrate some of the still-working pieces. ❑

RESTAURANTS

Cogolin

Grain de Sel

6 rue du 11 Novembre. Tel: 04 94 54 46 86. Open L & D Tues–Sat. €€

Fresh seasonal bistro cooking, such as stuffed vegetables, roast lamb and fruit tarts, prepared in an open kitchen by a young haute-cuisine chef.

Gassin

La Verdoyante

866 chemin de Coste Brigade. Tel: 04 94 56 16 23. Open L & D Thur–Tues; closed mid-Nov–mid-Mar. €€–€€€

Regional cuisine in a beautiful setting, with an exceptional view of the Gulf from the terrace.

Villa Belrose

Boulevard des Crêtes la Grande Bastide. Tel: 04 94 55 97 97. Open L & D daily, July–Aug D only; closed Nov–Easter. €€€

www.villabelrose.com

Luxurious hotel-restaurant with a superb terrace overlooking the bay of St-Tropez. High-quality Mediterranean cuisine, with some unusual combinations and the option of diet dishes.

Grimaud

Café de France

Place Neuve. Tel: 04 94 43 20 05. Open L & D daily; closed Nov–Mar. €–€€

Simple Provençal food, served on a shady terrace set back from the village square.

Le Coteau Fleuri

Place des Pénitants. Tel: 04 94 43 20 17. Open L & D Wed–Mon; closed Nov–Dec. €€€

www.coteaufleuri.fr

In an 18th-century house, quietly situated in the old village. Renowned locally for its gastronomic take on regional cuisine by chef Jean-Claude Paillard.

Ramatuelle

Chez Camille

Route de la Bonne Terrasse. Tel: 04 98 12 68 98. Open L & D Wed–Sun, July–Aug D only; closed Oct–Easter. €€€

Right at the Cap Camarat end of the Plage de Pampelonne, this ancient fisherman's shack draws "le tout St-Trop" for its bouillabaisse, fish soup, lobster and grilled fish.

La Farigoulette

Rue Victor-Léon. Tel: 04 94 79 20 49. Open L & D daily, July–Aug D only. €

A simple, informal bistro located on the old rampart climb, serving grilled meats and an intensely herby daube de bœuf.

La Forge

Rue Victor-Léon. Tel: 04 94 79 25 56. Open L & D daily, Wed–Mon in low season; closed mid-Nov–mid-Feb. €€

A quietly dressy place set in a former forge

for chef Pierre Fanzio's accomplished bistro cooking.

St-Tropez

La Bouillabaisse

Plage de la Bouillabaisse. Tel: 04 94 97 54 00. Open L & D daily; closed mid-Oct–mid-May. €€

In an old fisherman's house serving excellent fresh fish on the terrace right by the beach.

Le Café

Place des Lices. Tel: 04 94 97 44 69. Open daily. €€

www.lecafe.fr

Traditional bistro with hearty fare on the site of the former Café des Arts, the original hang-out of the places des Lices boules players.

Le Girelier

Quai Jean Jaurès. Tel: 04 94 97 03 87. Open L & D Tues–Sun, July–Aug D only; closed Nov–mid-Mar. €€

Highly reputed fish cooking in the midst of the portside buzz.

Joseph

1 place de l'Hôtel de Ville. Tel: 04 94 97 01 66. Open L & D daily, Wed–Mon in low season; closed mid-Nov–mid-Dec. €€€

A trendy contemporary restaurant with two chefs and two styles of cuisine, one Provençal, the other Thai.

Leï Mouscardins

Tour du Portalet. Tel: 04 94 97 29 00. Open L & D daily, Tues–Sun out of season;

closed Mar, Nov–mid-Dec, Jan–mid Feb. €€€

Considered by many to be St-Tropez's best restaurant, chef Laurent Tarridec serves light, innovative and delicious southern cooking.

Le Petit Charron

6 rue des Charrons. Tel: 04 94 97 73 78. Open L & D daily, Tues–Sat out of season; closed first 2 weeks Aug, second 2 weeks Nov & Jan. €€

A delightfully non-hip atmosphere here, accompanied by excellent regional dishes.

Spoon Byblos

Hôtel Byblos, avenue Maréchal Foch. Tel: 04 94 56 68 20. Open D daily, Thurs–Mon out of season; closed Nov–Mar. €€€

www.byblos.com

Alain Ducasse's mix-and-match world food concept allows you to choose different sauces and accompaniments to go with your lacquered beef, seared tuna or scallop kebab. A more Mediterranean emphasis than in the Paris original, and a globetrotting wine list. Located within the ultra-fashionable Byblos Hotel.

PRICE CATEGORIES

Prices for a three-course meal without wine.

€ = under €25
€€ = €25–40
€€€ = over €40

ST-RAPHAEL, FREJUS AND THE ARGENS VALLEY

The thriving seaside resorts of St-Raphaël and Fréjus
have plenty to offer. As well as Roman remains, sandy
beaches and vibrant nightlife, they make a good base
from which to explore the hills of the Estérel, 400-year-
old villages and the vineyards of Côtes de Provence

Between glamorous St-Tropez to the west and glitzy Cannes to the east, St-Raphaël no longer enjoys the fashionable reputation it had in the 1920s, but nonetheless the area merits exploration. Neighbouring Fréjus has impressive if scattered Roman remains and an attractive medieval centre, while the Massif de l'Estérel which rises to the east offers one of the most spectacular colour shows along the Riviera, its deep-red porphyry rocks contrasting with glistening blue seas and skies. Even in summer, you can find footpaths into the hills and hidden coves to escape the crowds. The wine-growing valley of the Argens offers more tranquil days out, discovering medieval villages and spectacular views.

St-Raphaël

The earliest citizens of **St-Raphaël** came looking for sea air and relaxation. They were wealthy Romans from the important naval and military settlement of Fréjus, and they built terraced villas decorated with mosaics close enough to enjoy the restorative properties of the sea.

In the Middle Ages, the settlement was sacked by the Saracens; it was re-inhabited by monks from Marseille, placed under the protection of the Knights Templar, and

subsequently attracted a small fishing and agricultural community. In 1799 Napoleon entitled St-Raphaël to one of its rare entries in the history books by disembarking here on his return from Egypt.

In the 1860s, the celebrated Parisian journalist Alphonse Karr moved along the coast from already crowded Nice and began to invite down the advance guard of metropolitan intellectual trendsetters (including writers Dumas and Maupassant, and composers Berlioz

Map on pages 96–7

LEFT:
on the côte de l'Estérel.
BELOW:
a St-Raphaël fisherman.

A statue of the Roman general Gnaeus Julius Agricola in Fréjus. His biography detailing his part in the Roman conquests was written by Tacitus, his son-in-law.

and Gounod) who, together with wealthy English visitors, turned St-Raphaël into a fashionable resort.

Along the seafront

As you approach from the east, you pass St-Raphaël's purpose-built yacht harbour, **Port Santa Lucia**, which has 1,600 berths and a modern Palais des Congrès (conference centre). Further along, on the boulevard de Gaulle and the promenade René Coty, are the few early 20th-century hotels and shabbier apartment blocks that lend the town its air of a little Cannes. Curlicued Art Nouveau balconies look out over the tall palms lining the raised promenade.

At the end of this sweep stands the casino, built after the seafront was badly bombed in World War II, in front of the dome of the late 19th-century church of Notre-Dame-de-la-Victoire de Lépante.

The Vieux Port (old port) in front of the casino is actually late 19th

century. It is home to a small fishing fleet, pleasure craft, the occasional naval vessel and regular ferry services to Port Grimaud, Ile de Port-Cros, Ile Ste-Marguerite and St-Tropez. (Services start in April; the 50-minute trip to St-Tropez is the nicest, and in August the fastest, way of getting to the town from here.)

The fishing boats' daily catch is on sale every morning from market stalls set up alongside the quay on cours Jean Bart. This broad boulevard, with stone benches and a double row of plane trees, is the centre for strolling and café life. Entertainment is provided in high season by a panoply of itinerant street performers, fake Louis Vuitton pedlars, and, in some of the cafés, resident entertainers on Yamaha keyboards.

At its western end, marked in summer by a plastic reproduction 18th-century Venetian fairground carousel, the bustle of activity merges with that of Fréjus-Plage.

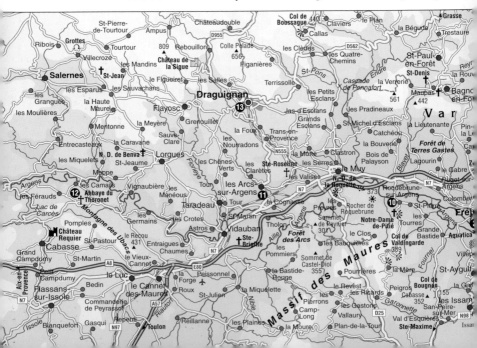

The old town

Heading away from the port, is the wood-beamed market on place Victor Hugo. Here, fruit and vegetable traders rub shoulders with traditional *charcutiers* and fishmongers. Northeast is the pretty, but minuscule and unkempt, old town, or Vieille Ville. Here, the small 12th-century, single nave **Eglise St-Pierre-des-Templiers**, built by the Knights Templar, was once used as a fortified refuge against attacks by pirates, as the military-looking watchtower suggests.

Traces of the town's Roman past are restricted to a collection of amphorae displayed in the **Musée Archéologique** (tel: 04 94 19 25 75; open Tues–Sat 9am–noon, 2–6pm; admission charge) in the former presbytery beside the church. Most have been lifted from the seabed by local diving teams. The museum also contains prehistoric material, as well as documents and photos from the town's 19th-century heyday.

In the hillside suburbs to the north and east of the town centre are the Edwardian-Provençal villas built for the early moneyed English visitors. These are concentrated particularly around the suburb of **Valescure** and its famous golf course – the fifth-oldest in France – whose perimeters feature a common Riviera phenomenon – holiday apartments for visiting golfers.

Roman metropolis

If present-day signs of St-Raphaël's medieval past are limited, and of its Roman past virtually non-existent, the reverse is true of **Fréjus** ❸. The larger town (48,000 inhabitants as opposed to St-Raphaël's 33,000) retains extensive remains from the period during which it was second only to Marseille in size and importance as a Roman military port. Fréjus was founded by Julius Caesar as a stopping place on the main route to Spain, but was rapidly

The freshest bread is just one of the delights of eating out in France.

BELOW: Eglise St-Pierre-des-Templiers.

St-Raphaël, Fréjus and the Argens Valley

MEDITERRANEAN SEA

0   5 km
0   5 miles

A two-faced bust of Hermes looking in opposite directions, excavated in 1970 and now on show in the Musée Archéologique, has become the symbol of Fréjus; you will find it on the town's logo and as a sculpture at the centre of a modern roundabout.

expanded by Augustus, and at its Roman zenith had almost as large a population as it has today.

The town's medieval centre bears an impressive testimony to its status in the early Christian world: Fréjus was a bishopric as early as 374 and remained one until 1957.

Seaside extensions

Although Fréjus lost its maritime functions in the 10th century as the sea receded, it has responded to the demands of modern tourism by acquiring two offshoots radically different in style from the old town, and both closer to St-Raphaël.

Fréjus-Plage is a 1960s and 1970s development of apartment blocks and hotels running the length of a fine, flat sandy beach bordered to the east by St-Raphaël and to the west by the new yacht basin of **Port-Fréjus**. Its attractions are by day quite simply the beach, and by night the numerous cafés, shops and stalls, which in high season stay open and busy until midnight or later, along with various nightclubs.

Port-Fréjus was built in 1989 to

provide accommodation for 10,000 people, mooring for 700 yachts and restaurants and shops. Port-Fréjus is at the mouth of the original Roman port, which was connected to a second basin inland, beside Fréjus proper, by a broad channel. Demand for more space in Port-Fréjus has prompted developers to expand away from the sea, re-excavating this same channel. Unfortunately, the waterway will not be extended to the site of the original inland port.

Just west of Port-Fréjus are two attractions popular with kids and located near the beach. **Base Nature** (tel: 04 94 51 91 10; open daily) is a former military base converted into an 80-hectare (200-acre) open-air sports centre, with mountain-bike trails, a skatepark and basketball courts, as well as a year-round indoor swimming pool. **Aquatica** (tel: 04 94 51 82 51; www.parc-aquatica.com; open June–Aug daily admission charge), on the main road to Ste-Maxime, is a water amusement park.

The medieval centre

The old central area of Fréjus has considerable charm, particularly in contrast to the brashness and the crowds of summertime St-Raphaël and Fréjus-Plage. At the centre of the old town, beside the 14th-century Hôtel de Ville (formerly the Bishop's Palace) on place Formigé, is the **Cité Episcopale**. This medieval complex includes a 12th-century, double-naved cathedral (open daily), a small stone baptistery – one of the oldest in France, dating from the 5th century – and a lovely two-storey cloister with a ceiling composed of hundreds of painted wooden tiles.

Visits to the baptistery and cloister (tel: 04 94 51 26 30; open Oct–May Tues–Sun 9am–noon, 2–5pm; June–Sept daily 9am–6.30pm; admission charge) are well worth it. The tall, sombre octagonal baptis-

BELOW: medieval cloister in the Cité Episcopale.

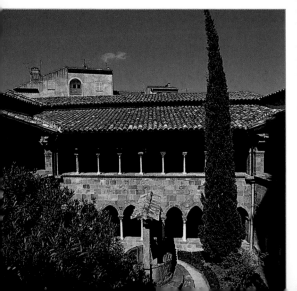

tery has separate entry and exit doors, octagonal baptismal pool and dolium for liturgical oil. The cloister, by contrast, with white marble columns, central tile-roofed well and laurel bushes, is serene and sunny. If you take the guided tour you will be shown a pair of 17th-century wooden doors (normally covered up), which are beautifully carved with gruesome scenes of a Saracen massacre.

Beside the cloister is the **Musée Archéologique** (place Calvini; tel: 04 94 52 15 78; open Tues–Sun 9.30am–12.30pm, 2–6pm, until 5pm in winter; admission charge), which displays a fine collection of Roman and early Ligurian tiles, mosaics and sculptures. Highlights include a complete mosaic floor with a leopard as its centrepiece, and a fine double-faced marble head of Hermes, discovered in 1970.

To the north along busy rue Jean Jaurès, which circles the pedestrianised medieval centre, an attractive town house contains the **Musée d'Histoire Locale** (153 rue Jean Jaurès; tel: 04 94 51 64 01; open

Tues–Sun 9.30am–12.30pm, 2–6pm, until 5pm in winter; admission charge), where displays include costumes from the *bravade* (local festival) and rooms recreating a Provençal kitchen, a shop, schoolroom, shoemaker and forge.

Just to the west of the cathedral is the triangular place Paul Albert Février, which contains the prettiest open-air restaurants, though not necessarily those with the best cuisine; nonetheless, tables can be hard to obtain by 9pm in summer. The Saturday market takes place here.

Further west is the other centre of café life, place de la Liberté. This is the best spot for coffees, afternoon beers, aperitifs and midnight café cognacs. Much later Fréjus closes down, and you head for the seafront.

Roman remains

Fréjus's major Roman remains are dispersed around the edges of the town. To the south, beside boulevard Decuers, is the base of the western citadel, the **Butte St-Antoine**, which once overlooked the inland port and is now over-

Map on pages 96–7

TIP

The Fréjus Pass gives entry to five sites in Fréjus (the Musée Archéologique, Musée d'Histoire Locale, Théâtre Romain, Amphithéâtre and Chapelle Cocteau) for €4.60 and is valid for seven days. Contact the tourist office for more information, at 325 rue Jean Jaurès, tel: 04 94 51 83 83.

LEFT: the Musée Archéologique entrance.
BELOW: place Paul Albert Février.

*Bullfighting is still a
popular sport in
Fréjus, and the high-
light of the year is the
Féria, a bullfighting
festival that takes
place in July and
August and includes
music and other
entertainment.
Contact the local
tourist office (see Tip
on page 99) for more
information.*

BELOW: the ruins of the
Roman ampitheatre.

grown with vegetation. A partly
ruined wall leads east from the Butte
to the stump of a tower, the
Lanterne d'Auguste. This structure
once held a flame marking the
entrance to the port, and at night was
the anchor point for an iron chain
across the canal which denied
access from the sea. North towards
the town centre is the **Porte d'Orée**,
a decorative arch, probably once the
entrance to the baths.

North of the centre, on avenue du
Théâtre Romain, are the enclosed
remains of the 2,500-capacity
Théâtre Romain (Roman theatre;
open Tues–Sun 9.30am–12.30pm,
2–6pm, until 5pm in winter; admission charge). It is largely destroyed,
but the low remaining section has
been renovated and is used, with
scaffolding benches, for concerts
and theatrical productions.

Northeast of the theatre are the
remains of the aqueduct, which once
supplied the whole city with water.
Large, impressive sections can be
seen on either side of avenue du XV
Corps d'Armée and within the
attractive park that surrounds the

Villa Aurélienne (tel: 04 94 52 90
49), a Palladian-style mansion
which hosts temporary art and photography exhibitions year round.

The 2nd-century AD **Arènes**
(amphitheatre; rue Henri Vadon; tel:
04 94 51 34 31; open Tues–Sun
9.30am–12.30pm, 2–6pm, until
5pm in winter; admission charge),
half resting against a grass knoll, has
suffered from centuries of looting,
and is neither as large nor as sumptuous as those at Nîmes or Arles.
The arena is often used for concerts
and, several times a year, bullfights.

Exotic outskirts

On the edge of town are two architectural curiosities from the town's
military past. Both buildings acknowledge the role of troops from
France's former colonies. The
Mosquée Missiri de Djenné (visible from the exterior only), on rue
des Combattants d'Afrique du Nord,
is a replica of the Missir Mosque in
Mali, while the Buddhist **Pagode
Hong Hien** (rue Henri Giraud; tel:
04 94 53 25 29; open summer daily
9am–7pm, winter 9am–5pm; admission charge) commemorates the
Vietnamese and Cambodian soldiers
who served the French Republic in
World War I.

Ten minutes' drive outside town
on the N7 is the small circular
chapel of **Notre-Dame-de-Jérusa-
lem ❹** (tel: 04 94 53 27 06; open
Tues–Sun 9.30am–12.30pm, 2–6pm,
until 5pm in winter; admission
charge), also known as the Cocteau
Chapel, designed by Jean Cocteau
in 1961. The beautiful cool, blue and
pastel murals inside are among the
artist-poet-filmmaker's last works.

Exploring the Estérel

The Corniche de l'Estérel or N98
coast road – and the railway line it
runs alongside, for most of the time
– provides the best introduction to
the Estérel Massif, passing beside a

succession of coves, small beaches and villages surrounded by a scarcely interrupted fringe of villas, hotels, restaurants and campsites – in July and August the traffic is heavy. Behind it the mountains are mainly accessible by footpath or forest roads. To one side rear the red porphyry peaks of the Pic de l'Ours and the Pic du Cap Roux. To the other, the sea is dotted with little islets, forming part of the same ancient rock mass.

In even the most densely touristed places, however, oases of calm subsist, surprisingly near to the beaten track. At **Boulouris** ❺, a resort of pine-shaded villas just outside St-Raphaël, the Plage d'Arène Grosse is a pleasant spot to sip an evening aperitif and watch the pin-prick shimmer of lights on the far-off St-Tropez peninsula. A seafront walk here is pretty and quiet. Gardens of umbrella pine and yucca stretch down to the path. The occasional dog races in and out of the waves.

Covering the long slope of the hillside above the wide beach of **Le Dramont** (a key landing point of the

American 7th Army in August 1944) is a development which symbolises the nadir of the rampant overbuilding of the 1970s and 1980s, but also represents its belated check. Cap Estérel, a huge concrete complex of holiday apartments, centred around a pair of stadium-sized swimming pools, was obliged to limit itself to just half its size after a regional tribunal revoked building permission, a landmark decision in an area long milked with impunity by French property companies.

To the east the former Roman port of **Agay** ❻, with a lovely deep bay shaded by pines and red cliffs, saw its heyday as a summer and winter destination in the 1930s, and remains one of the region's most laid-back resorts, with three excellent beaches. From here, the least built-up section of the Corniche winds past the rocky inlet of **Anthéor**, the resort of **Le Trayas** and small harbour and sandy beach of **La Figuerette**, from where there are several footpaths up into the hills.

The coast then gets more and more built-up, with panels announcing the

Map on pages 96–7

The Buddhist Pagode Hong Hien memorial garden.

BELOW: on the corniche de l'Estérel.

Map on pages 96–7

Gaspard de Bresse

Gaspard de Bresse – the Robin Hood of the Estérel – was a notorious brigand who terrorised travellers from his hideout, where he would lie in wait, in the Estérel during the 18th century.

His speciality was robbing tax officers and wealthy voyagers, while redistributing the booty to the poor. He was a gentleman thief who robbed without bloodshed, a prankster and a dandy, and he won over several of his female victims.

After escaping from Draguignan prison 1779 with the aid of the gaoler's daughter, he was arrested for good at an inn in La Valette du Var and eventually executed in 1781.

Looking out across the Mediterranean from a peak above La Figuerette is Notre-Dame d'Afrique, a 12-metre (40-ft) high metal copy of the famous black Virgin at Notre-Dame d'Afrique in Algiers; it is a place of pilgrimage for the French pieds noirs returned from Algeria, and a blessing ceremony is held here each May.

BELOW: view of the Massif de l'Estérel.

construction of "grand standing" apartment complexes again as resorts merge into one another in an almost continuous sprawl that joins up to Cannes. At **Théoule-sur-Mer** there is a 19th-century soap factory turned chateau, and you may spot high up above the Corniche the strange hemispherical forms of the **Palais Bulles**, Pierre Cardin's avant-garde villa, built in 1968 by experimental Finnish-born architect Antti Lovag, who rejected the use of straight lines and angles. The amphitheatre is the setting for an eclectic summer music festival.

At the eastern edge of the Massif de l'Estérel, just west of Cannes, is **La Napoule** ❼, in effect just a seafront extension of the Cannes satellite Mandelieu. La Napoule possesses three sandy beaches, a leisure port and the **Château de la Napoule** (tel: 04 93 49 95 05; www.chateau-lanapoule.com; open mid-Feb to mid-Nov daily 10am–6pm, mid-Nov to mid-Feb Sat, Sun and school hols 10am–6pm, Mon–Fri 2–6pm; admission charge), an arts foundation set in a

fancifully renovated medieval castle filled with the idiosyncratic sculptures of American artist Henry Clews. Henry and his wife Marie liked to dress in pseudo-medieval attire, and filled the castle and grounds with his strange sculptures and gargoyles.

Into the interior

The interior of the **Massif de l'Estérel** ❽ is crossed only by forestry roads, and is best explored on foot, horseback or mountain bike. Several footpaths leave from Le Trayas and La Figuerette heading up through herby *maquis* scrub, eucalyptus, mimosa, cork oak and pines up to the main peaks, the Pic d'Aurelle and Pic de l'Ours. **Mont Vinaigre**, the highest point at 618 metres (2,027 ft), can be approached via the N7.

Continuing inland, the D837 road passes through Les Adrets-de-l'Estérel, crosses the *autoroute* and shortly afterwards arrives at the **Lac de St-Cassien** ❾. This extensive man-made lake, situated south of the hill village of Montauroux, is a popular day-trip for local Varois or nearby residents of Grasse. It is still relatively wild in aspect, but heavily patronised by trout and carp fishermen, picnickers, swimmers and dinghy sailors in summer (no motor boats are allowed here), though there has been recent concern over falling water levels.

Up the Argens Valley

Back at Fréjus, the N7 heads northwest, following the valley of the River Argens through fields of flowers and vegetables, gradually climbing through vineyards and rockier olive, pine and oak groves. About 10 km (6 miles) from Fréjus a smaller road leads to the pretty village of **Roquebrune-sur-Argens** ❿. In the village centre almost every house is over 400 years old, and many are

joined by covered passageways and arcades. Vestiges of the 16th-century ramparts also remain.

Northwest of Roquebrune, in the heart of the Côtes de Provence wine region, is the small town of **Les Arcs-sur-Argens** . Here, the **Maison des Vins** (tel: 04 94 99 50 20; www.caveaucp.fr; open Apr–Oct daily, Nov–Mar Mon–Sat), beside the N7, provides copious information and free tastings of the many *crus* of the region.

The medieval village of Les Arcs, known as the **Parage**, is as lovely as any in the region. Part of the remains of the former feudal castle of the powerful Villeneuve family, destroyed after the Revolution, is now occupied by exquisitely pretty little houses and tiny olive-shaded squares, and partly by a beautiful hotel and superb restaurant, the **Logis du Guetteur** *(see page 105)*. The hotel's vine-draped terrace and shuttered bedroom windows offer stunning views over the red roofs of the town to the vineyards beyond.

Sitting in the midst of the wine *domaine* of Château Ste-Roseline northeast of Les Arcs is the **Chapelle de Ste-Roseline** (open daily 2.30–6pm; free), a former abbey of which the Romanesque chapel and cloisters remain. The chapel interior was beautifully restored by art patron Marguerite Maeght, who commissioned pieces from Marc Chagall, Diego Giacometti (brother of Alberto) and other artists to decorate the space.

The ornate baroque altarpieces, Renaissance rood-screen, huge Chagall mosaic, Giacometti sculptures and modern stained-glass together create an astonishingly harmonious synthesis. For fans of the macabre, however, the highlight is the preserved body of St Roseline, which still attracts pilgrims more than 600 years later.

Saintly Roseline, former abbess of the monastery and daughter of the powerful Count of Villeneuve, was born in 1263 in the castle at Les Arcs. One day, she was caught by her father in the act of giving away the family's possessions to the poor; when she opened her apron, the

TIP

Northeast of Les Arcs is Lorgues, a busy town with some grand 18th-century buildings and tiny medieval alleyways, which draws foodies to the restaurant of truffle king Bruno Clément *(see page 105).*

Map on pages 96–7

BELOW: Roquebrune.

Interior views of the Abbaye du Thoronet: beautiful stained-glass window (above) and the cloisters (below).

items were miraculously transformed into roses. After her death, her body failed to decompose, and is now preserved in a glass cask, along with an ornate reliquary containing her still "living" eyes.

West of Les Arcs, in the thick of the beautiful Darboussière forest, stands one of the most imposing sights in Provence: the 12th-century **Abbaye du Thoronet** (tel: 04 94 60 43 90; www.monum.fr; open Apr–Sept Mon–Sat 10am–6.30pm, Sun 10am–noon, 2–6.30pm; Oct–Mar Mon–Sat 10am–1pm, 2–5pm, Sun 10am–noon, 2–5pm; admission charge).

Thoronet is the finest of the Provençal trio of so-called "Cistercian sisters", together with the abbeys of Sénanque and Silvacane, which were all built during the 12th century to the ascetic precepts of the Cistercian Order. Only the play of light and shadow decorates the finely proportioned, simply designed chapel, cloisters and chapterhouse, all built in precisely fitting drystone blocks, without mortar. Neglected since before the French

Revolution, the abbey was saved from ruin by Prosper Mérimée (1803–70), author of *Carmen* on which Bizet's celebrated opera was based, who urged its restoration during the 1840s.

André Le Nôtre gardens

You can continue on the other side of the Argens river to the pretty village of **Entrecasteaux**, overlooking the River Bresque and dominated by an elegant 16th- to 18th-century classical **chateau** (tel: 04 94 04 43 95; guided visits usually Sun–Fri 4pm, phone for extra times in summer; admission charge). The grounds, which are now a public park, were laid out in the 17th century by André Le Nôtre, who was responsible for Louis XIV's gardens at Versailles.

North of Les Arcs is **Draguignan** , the former departmental capital and one of the biggest army bases in France. Most people simply pass by its numerous road junctions on the way to the Gorges du Châteaudouble or pretty upper Var hill villages such as Flayosc, Tourtour and Ampus. Nonetheless, beyond the outskirts of roundabouts and superstores and a ring of boulevards built under the direction of Baron Haussmann (who was Prefect of the Var before trying out his town-planning ideas on Paris) is a pleasant country town with an old centre, a good market on Wednesday and Saturday mornings and two worthwhile museums.

Housed in an old monastery, the **Musée des Arts et Traditions Populaires** (15 rue Joseph Roumanille; open Tues–Sat 9am–noon, 2–6pm, Sun 2–6pm; admission charge) has scenes recreating local life through costumes, tools, furniture and household items, while the **Musée Municipal** (tel: 04 98 10 26 85; open Mon–Sat 9am–noon, 2–6pm; free) houses a variety of art, furniture and local archaeological finds. ❏

RESTAURANTS

Les Adrets-de-l'Estérel

Auberge des Adrets
RN 7. Tel: 04 94 82 11 82.
Open l Fri–Sun, D Tues–Sat.
€€€
Refined food in this historic coaching inn in the heart of the Estérel, once frequented by highwayman Gaspard de Bresse.

Les Arcs-sur-Argens

Le Logis du Guetteur
Place Château. Tel: 04 94 99 51 10. Open L & D daily; closed 15 Feb–15 Mar. €€€
Sophisticated menu in a beautiful setting above the village. Tables on the terrace offer great views of the rooftops and surrounding vineyards.

Le Relais des Moines
Route Ste-Roseline. Tel: 04 94 47 40 93. Open L Tues–Sun, D Tues–Sat (and Sun July &Aug). €€€
In a stone farmhouse that once belonged to the counts of Villeneuve, *cuisine de terroir* (game) is revisited with finesse by young chef Sébastien Sanjou, who has worked in the southwest and in Cannes. Excellent France-wide wine list.

Lorgues

Chez Bruno
Route de Vidauban. Tel: 04 94 85 93 93. Open L & D daily; closed winter Sun D & Mon. €€€
Extremely rich menus based around truffles

and foie gras at this beautifully situated country *mas*, where charismatic Bruno Clément, the truffle king, draws the sort of clientele who helicopter in for dinner.

Montauroux

Les Fontaines d'Aragon
Quartier Narbonne. Tel: 04 94 47 71 65. Open L & D Wed–Sun. €€€
A rising name on the French culinary scene, chef Eric Maio is another protagonist of the truffle: you'll find it in everything, even ice cream. Elaborate specialities include pigeon *en cro te* stuffed with Swiss chard and pine kernels and accompanied by truffles and foie gras.

La Napoule

L'Oasis
Rue Jean-Honoré-Carle. Tel: 04 93 49 95 52. Open L & D daily; closed mid-Dec to mid-Jan. €€€
Opinions are divided on the Oasis, but there's no doubt that the grand Riviera style of chef Stéphane Raimbault still has plenty of influence on the Côte. Exemplary local produce with some Asian touches.

La Pomme d'Amour
209 avenue du 23 Août. Tel: 04 93 49 95 19. Open L Sun–Fri, D daily in summer, L & D Wed–Mon; closed 15 Nov–15 Dec. €€

Old-fashioned and rather good fish restaurant in the centre of La Napoule.

St-Raphaël

L'Arbousier
6 avenue de Valescure. Tel: 04 94 95 25 00. Open Tues pm– Sun; closed Sun in winter. €€
Using seasonal produce and regional recipes, this cosy Provençal restaurant has become a local institution for the generously served cooking of Philippe Troncy. Magnolia-shaded terrace in warm weather.

La Bouillabaisse
50 place Victor Hugo. Tel: 04 94 95 03 57. Open L & D Tues–Sun. €€€
Near the covered market, La Bouillabaisse, with checked tablecloths and ivy-covered terrace, is a

great place for bouillabaisse and paella.

Théoule-sur-Mer

L'Etoile des Mers
Miramar Beach Hotel, 47 avenue de Miramar. Tel: 04 93 75 05 05. Open L & D daily. €€
Popular panoramic dining room. The creative cooking can fall down when being too complicated, but is excellent when updating southern classics, like the *grand ailloli*, with filo-wrapped cod, whelks and vegetables.

RIGHT: lunch for two.

CANNES

One of the most glamorous resorts on the coast, Cannes is still the preferred resort of the rich and famous. But as well as the world-famous film festival and luxury hotels, there are sandy beaches, a palm-fringed seafront, narrow cobbled alleys and a market selling the best of Provençal produce

I n his 1921 book *The Twenties: From Notebooks and Diaries of the Period*, the American literary critic Edmund Wilson wrote: "Cannes: Côte d'Azur. Some gleaming town of rose and white, there where the Alps like elephants come down to kneel beside the calm and azure sea. On the sky and the water lies a hard glaring glaze of gold. The Mediterranean, level and smooth, laps the shore with a slow rise and fall of sound like the breath of a sleeper – a gentle insistent rhythm – brushing the beach with sound. The cactus clumps (aloes) like spiky octopi. The palms that stud the Croisette at Cannes with tignasse tufts and thick pineapple stems. At night the pale dark peppered with stars like the finest of silver tinsel. The last soft red streamers of the sunset faded behind the gray silhouette of the Estérel, and from the jetty I saw the green trees and the red roofs of the houses that mount the little hill to the square Saracen tower grown somber and black above the silver blue-gray water of the harbor, where the little boats were neatly moored in a fringe about the shore: above the boats was the low avenue of lindens and along between their trunks were the lights of the shops."

Cannes ❶ (www.cannes.fr) has undoubtedly changed since Edmund Wilson recorded its charms. The surprising news is that in a changing world where the character and soul of many a resort have been swept away in a tide of mass tourism, Cannes sparkles miraculously as a jewelled survivor of a bygone age.

Early visitors

Earlier, though, the place wasn't even on the map. Three roads with fishermen's houses, a tower on the hill and an inn serving bouillabaisse were all there was to Cannes before

Maps:
City 108
Area 120

LEFT: the Hôtel Carlton is one of the *grande dames* of the seafront.
BELOW: a fisherman and his dog, St-Honorat.

The ideal way to get to Cannes is by boat.

a chance incident altered its destiny late in 1834. Fatigued after six years as Lord Chancellor of Great Britain (where among other achievements he championed the abolition of slavery), Henry, Lord Brougham, resigned and set off from London with his sickly daughter Eleonore in search of a mild climate on the Riviera, where the British were already making their presence felt.

He intended to go to Nice, travelling in a six-horse berlin as far as the River Var, which then formed a formidable frontier between Provence (France) and the Kingdom of Sardinia (Italy). However, he found more than a raging torrent barring his way. Soldiers refused to let him through as cholera had broken out in Provence. They forced him to turn back, first to Antibes which displeased him, then to Cannes where an inn which had previously accommodated Victor Hugo and Pope Pius VII proved more to his liking.

Brougham was so captivated by the surrounding countryside that he bought a plot of land within a week and soon built the Villa Eleonore. It still stands, tastefully converted into flats, on avenue du Docteur Picaud.

Royal attention

So began the Anglicisation of Cannes. Other rich and influential British visitors soon followed, encouraged to find an alternative winter retreat to Nice where an "inferior class" was establishing itself, and a highly cultivated society took root. Quite literally, it seems: they even had their new villas' lawns relaid annually with turf brought from England by boat. Brougham extracted one million francs out of King Louis-Philippe – 33 times the town's municipal budget – to fund a new harbour so the boat could dock.

Royalty was not far behind. Though Queen Victoria did not dis-

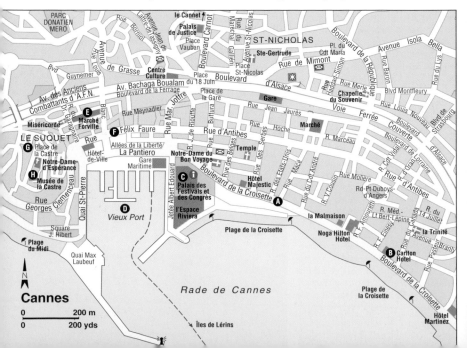

dain Nice, it was in Cannes that her sons Leopold, Duke of Albany, and Edward, Prince of Wales, discovered the more entertaining aspects of Riviera life. Poor Leopold, who was a haemophiliac, vaguely remembered for having introduced croquet to the coast, died after falling down stairs at Cannes' Cercle Nautique. Edward (later King Edward VII), on the other hand, is hugely famed for having indulged his appetite for gambling, tobacco, food and sex.

Brougham died in 1868, two years before the railway came to town and spelled the end of an idyll. A statue of him stands in the allées de la Liberté, not far from another, of Edward VII, as if emphasising the diverse roles which the British have played in the city's history.

The city today

The city is most famous now for being the home of the Cannes International Film Festival: two weeks in May when the movie world turns this resort upside down, starlets cavort topless on the sands and big deals are clinched by moguls clenching big cigars.

This is big business, and behind the scenes a huge effort goes into ensuring that the 80,000 plus people attending the festival are not disappointed. The golden sands, for instance, are raked and disinfected fastidiously every day, and the private beaches are groomed to perfection before the *beau monde* gathers for cocktails beneath pastel-coloured parasols.

Likewise the floral arrangements; the municipality grows 400,000 bedding out plants a year, and out on La Croisette they are replanted four times a year. Boughs of mauve wisteria snake around its old ochre façades in April. Gardens burst with oleander pinks in summer, and for much of the year splashes of purple and red bougainvillea adorn the city.

Heat and light

From mid-July until the end of August, Cannes is packed. The sand disappears under the press of near-naked bodies, "full" signs go up in restaurants and hotels, and the

Maps:
City 108
Area 120

One theory has it that Cannes takes its name from the Provençal cano, for the reeds in the marshes that used to surround the town. Another more probable explanation comes from the Ligurian word for high ground or peak – the original fortified settlement was on Le Suquet hill where the castle still stands.

LEFT: a rest in the shade.
BELOW: fun in the sun on La Plage du Midi.

The Cannes Film Festival

Every May for 12 days, Cannes is transformed into a mini-Hollywood, almost sinking under the weight of 80,000 visitors who come to schmooze, eat, drink and, most importantly, make deals in film. Around 4,000 are journalists and photographers, another proportion are budding and fading starlets, chancers and liggers, while the great majority are businessmen with the big American studios occupying whole floors in the four palace hotels.

The early days

The origins of the festival lie in the French distrust of the Venice Film Festival, launched by Mussolini in the 1930s. With all the prizes going to the Fascist films, France proposed retaliation with an international festival at Cannes set to begin in September 1939. However, the timing was not right. Mae West and Norma Shearer arrived on the steamship *Normandie* at the outbreak of World War II and had to sail straight home again.

So the festival had its premiere in September 1946; it started more as a film forum than a competition, as almost all the films presented received a prize. In 1951, the timing was changed to the spring, and over the next few years it was possible to fit everyone involved in the festival into a small boat and head off for an island lunch. It was also common for the jury to include illustrious members of the Académie Française – one particular member admitted that the last time he had seen a film was in 1913. A British critic records that in 1955 he was invited to a screening where he shared the auditorium with just two other men, Pablo Picasso and Jean Cocteau. Publicity for the festival escalated when Brigitte Bardot appeared at Cannes in 1955 and 1956.

As the festival gained in importance, the Marché du Film was established in 1959, showing films not in the competition to distributors and journalists. It created a unique opportunity to meet colleagues, build up future projects and do business with partners from an increasing number of countries.

Coveted prizes

An international jury, composed of a president and eight other artists in the film world, is appointed by the board of festival directors. They award the Palme d'Or to the best feature film, the highest award a film can receive outside Hollywood, which confers upon the film considerable prestige but not usually the box-office takings of an Oscar winner.

In 1993, for the first time, two Palme d'Or awards were given: one to *The Piano*, directed by Jane Campion (the first female director to win at Cannes), and the other to the Chinese film *Farewell My Concubine* by Chen Kaige. Recent Palme d'Or winners include *L'Enfant* (2005), by Jean-Pierre and Luc Dardenne, and *The Wind that Shakes the Barley* (2006), by Ken Loach. Other awards are given for best director, actor, actress and screenplay, as well the Jury Award, the Caméra d'Or for best first feature film and the Palme d'Or for best short film.

In a bid for these coveted prizes and international recognition, Cannes, for two weeks a year, incorporates the film world along with all it entails: glamour, glitz and a never-ending quest for *the* party of parties. ❏

LEFT: film director Pedro Almodovar with actresses Penelope Cruz and Carmen Maura.

thermometer soars. There is a small charge to enter most beaches, and sun-loungers cost extra.

During this period there are six evenings of festivities. Three of them celebrate important dates: Bastille Day (14 July), Assumption (15 August) and Cannes Liberation Day (24 August).

On all six evenings, crescendos of fireworks burst around La Croisette in a spectacular celebration lasting half an hour, provided free by the city council. Each show is different, involving tons of explosives launched from barges, and if you don't have your own personal yacht as a vantage point (some coming into the bay are the size of cross-Channel ferries) there are alternatives.

The beach restaurants offer superb dinners and a front-row seat under a sky that suddenly erupts in a storm of light. Or for a dress-circle view, you could retreat inland to a hill and watch the pyrotechnics while listening to the local radio.

A tour of the sights

Your first port of call to soak up the atmosphere should certainly be **La Croisette Ⓐ**, the broad boulevard that runs alongside the manicured beach. It is lined with palms and pristine flower beds tended 12 months of the year by more than 100 full-time gardeners. Despite being one of the most internationally recognised of all beachfront promenades, its Edwardian elegance has remained remarkably unsullied by adverts for fast food or tanning cream.

La Croisette is home to Cannes' four so-called palace hotels, the grandes dames of the seafront, frequented by the rich and famous, particularly during the film festival. The oldest and most glamorous is the 1912 **Carlton Hotel Ⓑ**, whose wedding-cake façade has barely changed since it was built. The pepper-pot

cupolas at each end are said to be modelled on the breasts of La Belle Otero, a famous dancer and courtesan of the period. The edifice symbolises Cannes as much as Big Ben does London, its name a synonym for comfort and grace.

Further down, at No. 73, is the **Hôtel Martinez**, built in 1929; many of its original Art Deco details, both inside and out, have been lovingly restored. Heading in the other direction, you come to the least attractive of the four, the **Noga Hilton Hotel**, at No. 50. This concrete eyesore was built in 1992 on the site of the old Palais des Festivals, where Vadim launched Brigitte Bardot in *And God Created Woman*.

Beside, and virtually swamped by, the Hilton, is **La Malmaison**, the only surviving part of the original Grand Hotel, a 19th-century forerunner of today's seafront giants. The elegant building now houses the city's most significant temporary art exhibitions (tel: 04 97 06 44 90; open Tues–Sun, times vary; admission charge). Further west, at No. 14, is the 1926 **Hôtel**

A stroll along the beachside promenade of La Croisette is a classic Riviera experience.

BELOW: La Croisette.

Tourists take a turn on the red carpet at the Palais des Festivals.

BELOW: the dazzling white hulls of vessels dwarf fishing boats.

Majestic, famous for its bar. During the festival, movie deals are struck here under the gaze of huge, *faux* sarcophagi, which evoke the kitsch but grand ambitions of Hollywood heroes such as Cecil B. DeMille.

Festivals and fish

Virtually opposite the Majestic is the vast concrete bunker of the current **Palais des Festivals** , home to the film festival since 1983 (tours by arrangement; tel: 04 92 99 84 22). On the ground outside, film stars have left a trail of hand prints in the allée des Stars. In recent years, Cannes has used its film-circuit fame to sell itself as a top venue for business conferences and other media gatherings, and the Palais is in almost constant use, hosting more than 100 events per year.

Beyond the Palais is the **Vieux Port**, where you'll see Cannes' fishing fleet tied up to a jetty parallel to quai St-Pierre, their nets piled high on deck. The fishermen are an endangered species. Dwarfing their boats are the dazzling white hulls, shining brass and polished teak of the bigger vessels sharing the little basin. Further threat to the fishing industry comes from the 150-metre (490-ft) cruise-ship quay, built here by the city to capture some of the lucrative cruise market.

For the moment, the *manja pei* (literally, "fish-eaters") still chug past the huge status symbols to bring in their catch in the early dawn, every day of the year. Strange Mediterranean fish with names like *rascasse, rouquier* or *blavier* are best enjoyed in a large bowl of bouillabaisse on the quayside.

To see the catch being sold by the fishermen's wives, head away from the port to the **Marché Forville** (food market mornings daily in summer, Tues–Sun in winter; flea market all day Mon), a covered market where *coquillages* and glistening fresh fish spill from the colourful displays. Elsewhere in the market, smallholders from the back country proudly mark their produce with the name of the village of origin instead of bothering with a sell-by date. Nobody cares; it is always dewfresh. The traders' clamorous cries and good-natured banter fill a pitch the size of a football field with their Provençal accents. On Mondays, the marketplace is transformed into an all-day flea market *(brocante)*.

Just to the east of the market is **rue Meynadier**, a pedestrian thoroughfare where local gourmands have always shopped for the best homemade pasta, the freshest cheese and the most mouth-watering delicacies its master *traiteurs* can produce. The street is also home to a number of inexpensive clothing outlets and tourist emporia, but the likes of La Ferme Savoyarde, a delicatessen at No. 20, still hold their own and tempt the taste buds of passers-by.

Prince of Cannes

They say the Duke of Windsor, when he was Prince of Wales, deliberately

gave his bodyguards the slip on one of his many visits to Cannes in the 1930s. There was panic, of course, and for hours his friends and courtiers scoured his favourite haunts. The places they searched have not changed much over the years.

They tried the restaurants of **rue Félix Faure** and the flower stalls facing them, both of which still attract locals and visitors today. They scanned the boules pitch on the nearby **allées de la Liberté** (still frequented today by diehards of the quintessentially Provençal game, except on Saturdays and Sundays when an antiques market takes over). They combed the boutiques of **rue d'Antibes** further east – still one of Cannes' most fashionable shopping streets.

Finally, someone had the wit to eschew the ritzy side of life and investigate the market and the old streets to the west. There, in the back lanes, he found the future king of England sitting in the sun outside a tiny *auberge*, eating sea urchins in *allioli*. Pleased with himself for his few hours' freedom as a commoner, the Prince looked up and said (according to local history): "Cannes is like a beautiful woman. Charming, but full of secrets."

The old town

The Prince had discovered the oldest part of town, **Le Suquet** , which still has secret alleys, passages and half-hidden *auberges* and bistros, especially on rue St-Antoine. Le Suquet's hill and moorings were used in Roman times (they named the site Canois Castrum because of the reeds and canes growing there). At the top of the hill, up steep and narrow cobbled lanes, is the **place de la Castre**, from where there are fabulous views along the shore in both directions and inland to the hill of La Californie.

Facing the place de la Castre is a 19th-century church, **Notre-Dame d'Espérance**. Behind the church are a castle and square tower dating from the 11th century and built by the monks of the Iles de Lérins to guard against Saracen attack. Also here is the 12th-century Romanesque Chapelle Ste-Anne. The castle and chapel house the **Musée de la Castre** (tel: 04 93 38 55 26; open Apr–June and Sept Tues–Sun 10am–1pm, 2–6pm, July–Aug daily 10am–7pm, Oct–Mar Tues–Sun 10am–1pm, 2–5pm; admission charge), which contains varied displays covering ethnology, Mediterranean archaeology, art of the region and a fine collection of musical instruments from around the world.

Villas in the hills

Another secret Edward must have remarked upon lies in the city's residential streets away from the seafront. Mrs Simpson took sanctuary in a villa here when the King was preparing to abdicate, and they planned to move into one of their own which they rented on a 10-year lease but never took up because of the outbreak of war.

There are several casinos in Cannes; try the tables at the Hotel Splendid (pictured above), the Hilton or the Carlton Hotel for a glamorous game of chance.

BELOW: Le Suquet.

Abbaye de Lérins was once home to thousands of monks.

BELOW: catching a boat to St-Honorat.

Now, these same houses, hiding their charms behind sentinel palms and wisteria-entwined pergolas, are a dying species. They are the last bastions of the Belle Epoque, under siege in an age when site values are appreciating faster than the properties standing upon them. No matter how sweetly they evoke the past, it counts for little with unsentimental property developers who are changing the face of Cannes remorselessly.

Another area which has succumbed to development is the old village of **Le Cannet ❷**, now effectively engulfed by the city. However, wander around and you will still find intriguing little lanes and pretty squares with 18th-century houses. The painter Pierre Bonnard lived here, in the Villa du Bosquet, from 1939 until his death in 1947. Place Bellevue is worth a visit for its great view of the bay and good-value restaurants. Originally, Cannes formed part of the commune of Le Cannet, and the little village still insists on the definite article prefixed to its name. The village's musical evenings are a big draw in summer.

Havens of the super-rich

Skirting the skies above Cannes, sumptuous summer palaces glitter like golden eggs. Here, in the wealthy enclave of **Super-Cannes ❸** there is a hidden lane, the **Corniche du Paradis Terrestre**, the road to Heaven on Earth, which hardly figures on some maps. The bumpy corniche has one of the best views of the city of stars. And it is precisely to deter hoi polloi that the road has been left unpaved.

Much of the wealth up here is Arabian and royal. If you can possibly afford to live here or in next-door **La Californie ❹** you have to think big. Twin marble palaces built here in the early 1980s for two brother princelings were not occupied for a single night before they were demolished and resurrected as apartments in classic Palladian style, for sale at over £3 million each, including individual swimming pools. Disgracefully, there was but one, shared, helipad.

The islands

Every day, boats leave quai Laubeuf – in front of the Sofitel in the Vieux Port – for the short trip across to the **Iles de Lérins**; these peaceful, traffic-free islands make a pleasant contrast to the buzz and glitz of the city.

Ste-Marguerite ❺, the larger of the two islands, is the more touristy, but if you head away from the crowded port you will find quiet paths through the woods and rocky inlets for bathing.

Near the port is the 17th-century **Fort-Royal**, identified as the prison of the mythical Man in the Iron Mask, made famous by Alexandre Dumas. The fort houses the **Musée de la Mer** (tel: 04 93 38 55 26; open Tues–Sun 10.30am–1.15pm, 2.15–5.45pm, Oct–Mar until 4.45pm; admission charge), which has artefacts salvaged from

nearby wrecks, including a 1st-century Roman ship and a 10th-century Arab vessel.

Monastic seclusion

St-Honorat , just 400 metres (1,300 ft) wide and mainly covered by parasol pines, eucalyptus trees and cypresses, is more secluded. The island has an impressive ecclesiastical history, starting with the monastery originally founded by St Honorat in the 5th century.

For hundreds of years, the **Abbaye de Lérins** was a centre of religious life for the whole of southern Europe, and was so powerful that it owned larges swathes of the land along the Mediterranean coast, including the town of Cannes itself. At one time 3,700 monks lived on the island, and the monastery was responsible for the training of many important bishops, including Ireland's St Patrick.

But its abundant wealth meant it was subject to constant raids from pirates, as well as papal corruption, and its decline was inevitable. In 1869 it was bought by the Cistercians, who then built a new monastery on the site of the old one.

The **monastery** and **church** can be visited (tel: 04 92 99 54 00; open daily; July–Sept guided visits only; admission charge, free in low season), but the island is the private domain of the monks, who grow grapes and will sell you their Lérina liqueur. The 11th-century tower of the earlier fortified monastery can be seen, and of the seven chapels originally scattered across the island, the **Chapelle de la Trinité** at the eastern end still celebrates Mass (call the abbey for times). There is just one snack bar, La Tonnelle, open in the summer, so bring your own picnic.

St-Honorat is one of the Riviera's last secluded hideaways. Out here on a summer's day only the distant jet stream of planes approaching Nice airport reminds you that the centuries have marched on. It is a small price to pay, because a sound as old as time, that of the cicadas, reasserts itself to convince you that here you have indeed found that rare and elusive prize: a little corner of Heaven on Earth. ❑

Map on page 120

TIP

Boats run all year from Cannes to the Iles de Lérins. Trans Côte d'Azur (www.transcote-azur.com) and Compagnie Estérel-Chanteclair run services to Ile Ste-Marguerite; Planaria runs services to Ile St-Honorat. In summer there are additional services to Monaco, St-Tropez, the Corniche d'Or (the Estérel), San Remo and the Ile de Porquerolles.

BELOW: view of Abbaye de Lérins.

RESTAURANTS, BARS & CAFÉS

Restaurants

Les 3 Portes
16 rue des Frères Pradignac. Tel: 04 93 38 91 70. Open daily D only in season, Sat pm, Sun & Mon out of season. €€–€€€
www.3portes.com
Fashionable food for the fashionable set – white, minimalist decor, original dishes of local seasonal produce with a light, exotic touch.

38 Le Restaurant
Hôtel Gray d'Albion, 38 rue des Serbes. Tel: 04 92 99 79 60. Open L & D Tues–Sat. €€–€€€
Le Royal Gray reopened in January 2006 with a new name and new modern look. Still with master chef Alain Roy at the helm, the restaurant

offers "world" cuisine laced with Provence. And there is a lunch menu for €19 to appeal to a wider clientele. Dinner menus start at €38.

Astoux et Brun
27 rue Félix Faure. Tel: 04 93 39 21 87. Food served all day daily. €€
www.astouxbrun.com
At this brasserie overlooking the old port, it's not the decor that counts but the huge platters of excellent shellfish. The home made fish soup is made with rockfish from the Cannes coastal area.

Au Bec Fin
12 rue du 24 août. Tel: 04 93 38 35 86. Open L & D Tues–Sun, L Mon in summer. €–€€
Busy restaurant serving up hearty meals using

fresh local ingredients. Extensive menu that changes regularly with good daily specials, too.

Aux Bons Enfants
80 rue Meynadier. Open L & D Mon–Sat; closed Sat pm out of season. €
Right by the Marché Forville, this small family-run restaurant offers home regional cooking with fresh produce from the market. Friendly atmosphere. It is popular but has no telephone, so you have to pop in to reserve a table before you do anything else. No credit cards or cheques.

Le Bouchon d'Objectif
10 rue Constantine. Tel: 04 93 99 21 76. Open L & D Tues–Sun; closed Sun pm out of season. €–€€
Friendly and intimate bistro dishing up country-style food with a sophisticated edge. Pretty terrace and popular with locals. Photographic exhibition changes monthly.

La Cave
9 boulevard de la République. Tel: 04 93 99 79 87. Open L & D Mon–Fri, D only Sat. €€
A lively, typically French bistro with mirrors and posters on the walls and leather *banquettes* for a more intimate experience. An open kitchen serves up a variety of classic French dishes, with specialities

of the day written up on a blackboard.

Le Caveau 30
45 rue Félix Faure. Tel: 04 93 39 06 33. Open L & D daily. €–€€
A large brasserie reminiscent of the 1930s with outdoor seating on the shady square in front. A wide choice of dishes with seafood dominating. Try the seafood platter and the *pot-au-feu* "from the sea".

Le Comptoir des Vins
13 boulevard de la République. Tel: 04 93 68 13 26. Open L & D Mon–Sat. €€
A small, atmospheric bistro at the back of a wine shop. Dishes served on wooden boards complement the wines sold, and you can try several by the glass. The menu includes a wide range of charcuterie and cheeses, as well as vegetarian dishes.

Mantel
22 rue St-Antoine. Tel: 04 93 39 13 10. Open L & D daily, D only Thur. €€–€€€
A small romantic restaurant in Le Suquet serving delicious dishes with an exotic flair and a touch of Italian. Excellent fixed-price menus. Reservations imperative.

La Mère Besson
13 rue des Frères Pradignac. Tel: 04 93 39 59 24. Open L & D Mon–Sat. €€
Good home-cooked Provençal meals, with a different menu for every

day of the week, not far from La Croisette. Seating available outside.

La Palme d'Or
Hôtel Martinez, 73 La Croisette. Tel: 04 92 98 74 14. Open L & D Tues–Sat; closed Jan & Feb. €€€€
A Michelin two-star restaurant in one of Cannes' palace hotels with a view of the bay and the Iles de Lérins. Imaginative gastronomic cuisine with a taste of the Mediterranean.

La Piazza
9 place Bernard Cornut-Gentille. Tel: 04 92 98 60 80. Open L & D. €
This often busy establishment dishes up exquisite home-made pasta, risottos and pizzas. There's a choice of nearly 40 pasta sauces.

Relais des Semailles
9 rue St-Antoine. Tel: 04 93 39 22 32. Open L Tues–Fri, D Mon–Sat; closed 4–23 Dec. €–€€
Tucked into the labyrinth of Le Suquet, this popular restaurant has been serving quality traditional fare for more than 20 years.

La Pizza
3 quai St-Pierre. Tel: 04 93 39 22 56. Open L daily. €
Wood-fired pizzas served up in a restaurant seating nearly 400 over two floors. No reservations, and at the busiest times waits can be up to 30 minutes. But it's worth it.

Le Restaurant Arménien
82 La Croisette. Tel: 04 93 94 00 58. Open D Mon–Sat, L Sun; closed Mon out of season. €€€
www.lerestaurantarmenien.com
A massive choice of Armenian dishes on one menu of the day, including 20 mezes, 15 dishes of the day and five desserts. There's also plenty of choice for vegetarians.

Lou Souleou
16 boulevard Jean-Hibert. Tel: 04 93 39 85 55. Open L & D daily; closed D Mon & Wed out of season. €€
Tucked away behind the Vieux Port with marvellous views, this restaurant offers steaming bowls of mussels and a whole array of other fresh and flavourful Mediterranean fish dishes.

Villa des Lys
Hôtel Majestic Barrière, 10 La Croisette. Tel: 04 92 98 77 00. Open D Tues–Sat; closed 14 Nov–30 Dec. €€€€
Bruno Oger is one of France's renowned chefs, and he has earned this restaurant two Michelin stars serving top-quality regional food with an emphasis on seafood.

Bars & Cafés

Bar Le 4U
6 rue des Frères Pradignac. Tel: 04 93 39 71 21. Open 6pm–2.30am daily.
www.bar4u.com
A popular large bar frequented by a regular clientele. Sophisticated decor and a large lit-up circular bar gives a good pre-club ambience. DJ music.

Caffé Roma
1 square Merimée. Tel: 04 93 38 05 04. Open daily.
Opposite the Palais des Festivals, the terrace at Caffé Roma is a good spot for people-watching over an espresso or cocktail or two. A reasonably priced menu is offered, too. €€

Cannolie
32 rue des Serbes. Tel: 04 93 38 72 79. Open Mon–Sat 9.30am–6.30pm.
A delicatessen with tables among the shelves groaning with gourmet delights. Try their savoury tarts and salads or splash out and go for the caviar. A good selection of wines are on offer too.

Le Loft
13 rue du Docteur Monod. Tel: 04 93 39 40 39. Open nightly 10.30pm–2.30am. An expensive night out but plenty of good music at this lounge bar. The restaurant downstairs serves Thai food and cocktails from 7.30pm.

Pause Café
39 rue Hoche. Tel: 04 93 39 83 03. Open daily, closed Sat & Sun evenings. Upmarket with an intimate ambience, this café offers a wide range of coffees from around the world and speciality teas, along with ice cream and cakes.

PRICE CATEGORIES
Prices for a three-course meal without wine.
€ = under €25
€€ = €25–€40
€€€ = over €40

LEFT: fashionable places to eat in Cannes.
RIGHT: at the bar in the Hôtel Martinez.

THE CULT OF CELEBRITY

The luminous quality of the light continues to draw artists to the Côte d'Azur, though these days they're more likely to be media artists and celebrities

You don't have to be rich to visit the Côte d'Azur, but it helps if you are beautiful, or at the very least cool. Here millionaires find their ideal retreats, movie stars are among their peers and even the rattiest-looking little dog is pampered. The star turn, of course, is the Cannes Film Festival in May, still the most presitigious event in the industry, but there is also the annual television festival in Monaco, a country which has the highest concentration of millionaires on the planet. In fact, the summer season is crammed with events to be seen at, from the Monaco Grand Prix to various yacht races, not to mention the Porsche parade in St-Tropez, the resort where you are likely to recognise more famous faces per square metre than anywhere else in the world.

There is a snobbery attached to all this showing off, of course, and it's important to know the right places to go and be seen. As the old ditty says:

Menton's dowdy. Monte's brass.
Nice is rowdy. Cannes is class!

ABOVE: bagged! French actress Melanie Doutey chooses the wrong moment to try to switch off her phone before entering Cannes' Palais des Festivals.
LEFT: Les Caves du Roy in the Byblos Hotel, St-Tropez, is the glitziest disco and obviously *the* place to be seen. Entrance is free, if you can make it past the all-powerful doormen.

BELOW: Hôtel du Cap-Eden Roc, on the tip of Cap d'Antibes in Millionaires' Bay, featured in F. Scott Fitzgerald's *Tender is the Night*. Still the choice of A-list film stars, it's about as good as it gets.

BELOW: Nicolette Sheridan of *Desperate Housewives* at the annual Festival de Télévision de Monte-Carlo. Prince Albert II gives the winner in each category a "Golden Nymph", a copy of a statue by Monégasque sculptor François-Joseph Bosio (1768–1845). The original is in the Louvre in Paris.

RUSSIAN, RICH AND ON THE RISE

Le Grand Bleu, pictured here in Monte-Carlo, is the largest and most expensive private yacht in the world. It was built for Roman Abramovich at a cost of £90 million. The Russian millionaire is no stranger to the Riviera. His own portfolio of properties includes a £10 million villa in St-Tropez and Le Croe in Cap d'Antibes, once home to the Duke and Duchess of Windsor. The Russians have been coming to the Riviera since the time of the Tsars, but since capitalism returned to the country they have been bringing their new riches by the boatload. Among the first wave was Boris Berevovsky, who in 1996–7 purchased two of the most prestigious mansions on Cap d'Antibes, La Garoupe and neighbouring Clocher, with a 17-hectare (43-acre) park, for 20 million euros. Granted political asylum in the UK in 2003 after falling out with Putin (he had been Boris Yeltsin's security adviser), Berevovsky has been accused of being the head of the Russian mafia, and allegations of money-laundering led police to raid the villas in 2006.

For Russians, like so many others, the Côte d'Azur is the place for wealth to be flaunted. At the Millionaires' Fair held in Cannes in 2006 one Russian paid £1.2 million for a watch. And when billionaire Andrey Melnichenko married Alexandra Koktovic, a former Miss Yugoslavia, in Cannes the previous year, he had a Russian chapel dismantled and shipped to his Riviera estate for the occasion and asked Christina Aguilera to the wedding, paying her £2 million to sing just three songs.

BELOW: in Cannes, richest of all the French Riviera resorts, poodle collars glitter with diamonds and millionaires mingle on the boulevard de la Croisette. Here, £30 for a padded lounger on a private beach, £11,500 for a suite in a palace hotel, and £15,000 for a day's yacht hire are all mere bagatelles.

ABOVE: a couple of model tourists in St-Tropez – isn't that Naomi Campbell? Who's her friend? Star-spotting is the favourite pastime in the Var's best-known resort. It's even more popular than *pétanque*. On the beach you might see Paris and Nicky Hilton, the Beckhams, Bono or Bruce Willis. Or you might sit at a café in the old port, Sénéquier or Le Gorille, to encourage the celebrities as they stroll modestly past pretending to be real human beings.

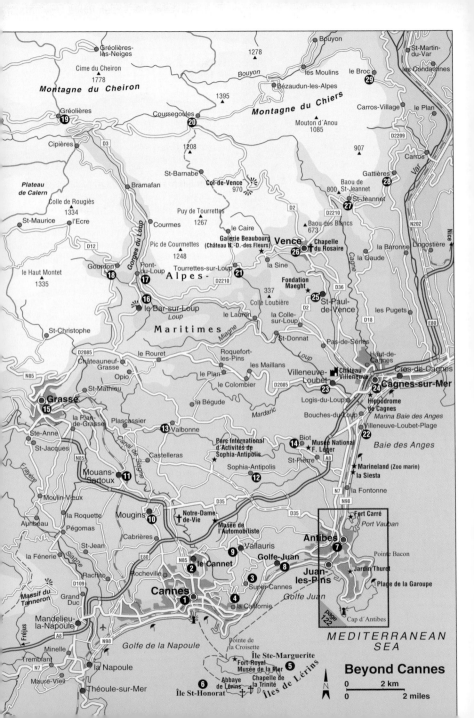

Beyond Cannes

Gréolières-les-Neiges
Cime du Cheiron
1778
Montagne du Cheiron
Gréolières **19**
Cipières
Plateau de Calern
Colle de Rougiès 1334
l'Ecre
St-Maurice
le Haut Montet 1335

Bouyon
1278
les Moulins   le Broc
Bouyon   **29**
Bézaudun-les-Alpes
1395
Montagne du Chiers   Carros-Village   le Plan
Courségoules   Mouton d'Anou 1085   D2209
20   907   Carros   Var
1208   Gattières **28**   St-Martin-du-Var   les Condamines
St-Barnabé   Baou de St-Jeannet 800   St-Jeannet **27**   Lingostière   Nice
Col-de-Vence 970   Baou des Blancs 673   N202

Puy de Tourrettes 1267
Courmes
Pic de Courmettes 1248
Gourdon **18**
Pont-du-Loup **17**
16
le Bar-sur-Loup
Loup
St-Christophe

le Caire
Galerie Beaubourg (Château N.-D.-des Fleurs)   Vence **26**   Chapelle du Rosaire
Tourrettes-sur-Loup **21**   la Sine   la Baronne   la Gaube
Alpes-   D2210   Cagne   les Pugets
Maritimes   Colle Loubière   337   Fondation Maeght **25**   St-Paul-de-Vence   D18   E80
le Lauron   la Colle-sur-Loup   D2   St-Donnat   Pas-de-Sènes   Haut-de-Cagnes
Magne   Roquefort-les-Pins   Château Villeneuve   Cros-de-Cagnes

le Rouret
Châteauneuf-Grasse
Opio   St-Mathieu
N85
Grasse 15
la Plan-de-Grasse
Plascassier
Ste-Anne
St-Jacques   N85
Castelleras
Moulin-Vieux
Mouans-Sartoux **11**
la Roquette   Mougins **10**
Auribeau   Pégomas   Cabrières
St-Jean   E80
la Fénerie   Rachito   N85   Rocheville
Massif du Tanneron   D109   Grand Duc
Mandelieu-la-Napoule   A8   N98
Fréjus   Minelle
Tremblant   N7
Maure-Vieil   la Napoule
Théoule-sur-Mer

les Maillans   le Plan   le Colombier   D2085   Villeneuve-Loubet **23**   **24** Cagnes-sur-Mer
la Bégude   Logis-du-Loup   Hippodrome de Cagnes   Villeneuve-Loubet-Plage
Mardaric   Bouches-du-Loup   *Marina Baie des Anges*
Valbonne **13**   *Baie des Anges*
Parc International d'Activités de Sophia-Antipolis   Biot   **22**
Sophia-Antipolis **12**   **14** Musée National F. Léger   Marineland (Zoo marin)   la Siesta
St-Pierre   A8   N7
N98   la Fontonne
D35   D35   Fort Carré   *Port Vauban*
Notre-Dame-de-Vie   Musée de l'Automobiliste   **Antibes 7**
Vallauris **9**   Pointe Bacon
le Cannet **2**   Golfe-Juan   **8**   Jardin Thuret
3   Juan-les-Pins   Plage de la Garoupe
Super-Cannes   **page 122**
Cannes 1   **4**   la Californie   *Golfe Juan*   Cap d'Antibes
Grand Duc   **5**
Golfe de la Napoule   Pointe de la Croisette
Île Ste-Marguerite   *MEDITERRANEAN SEA*
Fort-Royal Musée de la Mer
Chapelle de la Trinité
6   Abbaye de Lérins   *Îles de Lérins*   **Beyond Cannes**
Île St-Honorat   N
0   2 km
0   2 miles

ANTIBES AND THE
PLATEAU DE VALBONNE

The historic port of Antibes contrasts with the luxurious villas and tropical vegetation of the Cap d'Antibes and the indulgent party town of Juan-les-Pins, renowned for its clubs and casinos. You'll also find modern art   Picasso lived here – and historic villages

t is on the Cap d'Antibes and its satellite Juan-les-Pins that the Riviera as a summer destination can be truly said to have begun. Here the art of sunbathing and sport of water-skiing were born, and the Hôtel du Cap-Eden Roc opened for the first time throughout the summer in 1923. A hot spot with American expatriates in the 1920s and 1930s and immortalised by F. Scott Fitzgerald, the jazz age is still reflected in the prestigious summer jazz festival at Juan-les-Pins.

Although it is sometimes hard to imagine the beaches as they were as you sit in a traffic jam in the middle of Juan-les-Pins, it is still possible to discover its special charms and sample its undoubted luxuries.

It must be said, however, that its real pleasures remain reserved for the rich, with their *pieds dans l'eau* villas, hotels and private beaches, from which they can contemplate the sea, forgetting the milling crowds outside. The coast itself is nearly always crowded, and venturing onto a public beach should be done with people-watching firmly a priority.

Inland, on the Plateau de Valbonne, the popular towns of Vallauris and Biot also draw visitors to their craft workshops and glass factories. Here, within just a few miles of the coast, the roads are much quieter, and one

can seek respite in the charming towns such as Valbonne, Mougins and Mouans-Sartoux. The plateau is very well known for its flower production, in particular roses, carnations and anemones.

Year-round yachting

Antibes ❼ itself is surprisingly untouristy; its venerable history gives it a gravitas that is undeterred by waves of tourism, and the Vieille Ville (old town) offers many instructive sights.

Map on page 120

BELOW:
Plage de la Garoupe at Cap d'Antibes.

TIP

Antibes' morning
market (Tues–Sun) in
cours Masséna,
crowded with locals
buying top-quality
seasonal produce,
including flowers, local
olives, cheeses and
abundant vegetables,
is the place to come
for a taste of provincial
life, away from the
tourist hot spots.

BELOW: shopping in
the busy old town.

Ultimately, Antibes is a yachting town, with the massive **Port Vauban** the true centre of Mediterranean yachting. Its inner harbour is home to several hundred vessels, and the outer port shelters some of the world's most prestigious yachts on a wide *quai* known as "millionaires' row". The presence of these yachts, and the considerable crew – including a large British expat community that has spawned some British pubs – and services required to support them, means that Antibes functions all year round, and is not as limited to seasonal visitors as are other parts of the coast. Graham Greene, who was a longtime resident, preferred Antibes in the winter, writing about it in his novel *May We Borrow Your Husband?*

Overlooking Port Vauban from a rocky promontory to the north is the imposing mass of the 16th-century **Fort Carré** (guided visits every 30

mins, Tues–Sun 10am–6pm, 4.30pm in winter; admission charge), a bastion built by Henri II, where Napoleon was imprisoned in 1794.

Across the bay from Nice

The main area of interest in Antibes is quite small, so you would be well advised to park in one of the multistorey car parks as soon as you enter the town. A good free map is available from the Maison du Tourisme on **place Général de Gaulle**, in what was once the Grand Hôtel and home of the municipal casino.

Antibes began life as the Greek city of Antipolis, "the town opposite," facing the earlier settlement of Nice. The Greeks held only a narrow stretch between the sea and the present cours Masséna; it was a narrow enclosure filled with warehouses and only one gate, entered opposite the present **Hôtel de Ville** on the cours Masséna at the rue Pardisse. The

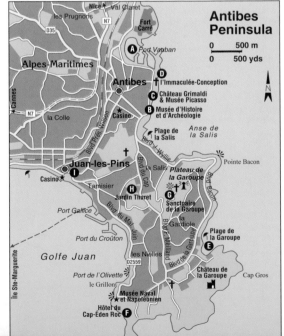

settlement traded with the Ligurian tribes along the coast but did not allow them to enter the city, so all dealing took place outside the city walls; the excellent **covered market** (open Tues–Sun mornings, daily in July and Aug) is still located on the cours Masséna at roughly the same spot. The Romans, in their turn, built an important city at Antibes.

Antibes was a keystone in French naval strategy against the Comté of Nice, facing it across the Baie des Anges, and powerful Genoa further east. Sacked twice by Emperor Charles V in the 16th century, Kings Henri II and Henri III added new fortifications, including the Fort Carré to the north of the harbour.

In 1680, Louis XIV brought in his brilliant military engineer Vauban to give the town the impressive set of star-shaped ramparts and bastions that line the shore, using stone from the ruins of the Roman town, which withstood sieges in 1707 and 1746.

No longer in the front line after the reunification of Nice with France and unable to expand behind its walls, Vauban's ramparts were demolished in 1898 except those which constituted the sea wall; today, the promenade Amiral de Grasse runs along the ramparts, beginning at the **Bastion St-André** in the south. The bastion now houses the excellent **Musée d'Histoire et d'Archéologie B** (tel: 04 92 90 54 35; open June–Sept Tues–Sun 10am–6pm; admission charge), comprising two huge barrel-vaulted rooms with a well-organised display of Greek, Etruscan and Roman pottery and exquisite examples of Roman glass. The remains include a large collection of amphorae, stacked as if in the hold of a Roman galley.

Picasso's studio

The original Roman camp was built on the ruins of the Greek acropolis, on a terrace overlooking the sea. In the 12th century, the **Château Grimaldi C** was built on the same site (now place Mariejol). Many of the Romanesque features remain, including arched windows and the square tower which dominates the old town, though the building was reconstructed in the 16th century.

Map on page 122

At the Château-Musée-Grimaldi are paintings of the Montparnasse cabaret singer Susy Solidor by artists such as Cocteau.

BELOW: the old town.

Picasso Country

Pablo Picasso's love affair with the Riviera first began in 1920 when he spent the summer at Juan-les-Pins. The beach inspired him to create a series of monumental neoclassical nudes. Here, on the coast, was the same intense light and warm Mediterranean lifestyle as his native Spain. Picasso (1881–1973) responded to the clear silhouettes of the mountains, the hard shadows and bright luminous colours.

He continued to come for the summers, returning to his Paris studio for the winter. In 1923, he painted harlequins in Cap d'Antibes; in the summer of 1924, he created a series of large still-lifes at Juan-les-Pins and spent most of 1926 and 1927 working chiefly on etchings. In 1939, he had been working on a major painting, *Night Fishing at Antibes*, when World War II broke out and he returned to Paris.

After the war, he moved to the Riviera for good, going first to Antibes with his companion Françoise Gilot, whom he met in 1943, where he was given the keys to the Château Grimaldi to use as a studio.

Picasso country is a very small area, a few square miles between Antibes and Cannes, though he moved constantly around it. He and

Gilot lived at the Villa Pour Toi, facing the fishermen's harbour at Golfe-Juan, in 1946, and in the following year, he acquired his first property in the south in Vallauris, called La Galloise: a "small, rather ugly house", as Gilot described it.

In Vallauris, Picasso began his experiments with ceramics, single-handedly reviving the town's fortunes. And it was here, between April and June 1954, that he produced his famous series of more than 30 drawings and paintings of Sylvette David, a young English girl who worked next door to his studio on the rue de Fournas. Her long neck, thick blonde hair held high in a pony-tail, straight nose and sloping shoulders created a fashionable, much copied style *à la Picasso*.

After Picasso's relationship with Gilot ended, he lived alone at La Galloise. The break-up, however, released a flood of energy, resulting in the 80-odd drawings made between 1953 and 1954 of the artist and his model, the old artist always in the act of creation, painting the young model.

Picasso then began living with Jacqueline Roque, whom he married in 1958. In 1955, he had moved to La Californie, a large, ornate mansion overlooking Cannes. The space inspired him to invent the term *paysages d'intérieur* for the series of interiors he painted, driven by an urge to fill the echoing rooms.

After a spell between 1958 and 1961 living near Aix-en-Provence, he returned to the Riviera to Mas Notre-Dame-de-Vie, a farmhouse on a hill overlooking Mougins, where he stayed until his death at 91 on 8 April 1973.

Picasso remained prolific to the end. During his last five years, he created over 1,000 works of art. His Riviera period was perhaps his most obsessional; he would take a theme or a medium and work at it until it was spent.

Today, Picasso is a constant presence on the Côte d'Azur: a major museum in Antibes *(see page 125)*; an exhibition of photographs in Mougins *(see page 131)*; ceramics in Vallauris, *War and Peace* at the château and the sculpture of *L'Homme à l'Agneau* in the town centre *(see page 131)*. Sometimes it seems as if every town or village is after some connection with the master. ❏

LEFT: Pablo Picasso in 1948.

Some of the tiny inner doorways have very attractive carvings.

The chateau is now home to the **Musée Picasso** (closed until end 2007 for renovation; tel: 04 92 90 54 20) and contains a remarkable, unified collection of more than 50 works Picasso executed here in 1946, when he was offered the keys to the chateau to use as a studio.

He painted solidly for five months, revitalised after spending the war years restricted to his Paris studio. The light and intense colour of the south were immediately incorporated into his work in a series of drawings and paintings of fish, sea urchins, goats, stars and the seashore. He was captivated by the antiquity of the Mediterranean.

Standing on the terrace of the ancient castle, the site of a Greek acropolis, a Roman *castrum*, the residence of the Bishops of Antiboul and the 16th-century Grimaldis, he invented a mythological cast of characters to inhabit his work: a faun, often playing the double flute of antiquity, a bearded centaur (undoubtedly himself) and a beautiful nymph (Françoise Gilot). The paintings and drawings eventually resulted in a major work, *La Joie de Vivre*, which symbolised his entire stay in the chateau.

Local muse

The fishermen provided another source of inspiration, as they had done before the war in his huge painting *Night Fishing at Antibes*. Some of these, such as *Man Gulping Sea Urchins*, are on canvas, and X-rays have revealed that Picasso, holding the keys of the chateau, had raided the storerooms and painted over what he regarded as mediocre 19th-century paintings. It was also here that Picasso painted the *Antipolis Suite*, a series of highly stylised, pared-down nudes, often reclining.

Picasso left virtually everything to the museum in which his works were created. On display are 27 paintings, 44 drawings, two sculptures, 50 engravings (mostly from the Vollard Suite) and 75 original ceramics – a major collection and the first permanent collection devoted to the work of a living artist. It is supported by works

Picasso was not the only world-class artist working at the Château Grimaldi; the French-Russian painter Nicolas de Staël also painted here in the early 1950s, before committing suicide in Antibes in 1955. One of the largest collections of his work can be seen at the Musée Picasso. On the terrace is also a series of sculptures by Germaine Richier, César and Miró.

BELOW: view of Antibes old town.

of tribute by other artists, as well as photographs and documentation.

Sights of the old town

North of the chateau is the cathedral, the **Eglise de l'Immaculée-Conception** . The square Romanesque bell tower is a converted 12th-century watchtower, but only the east end remains of the original 12th-century building, as the west end was rebuilt in the 17th century. The 1710 doors are worth closer scrutiny.

On avenue Tournelli is the unusual **Musée de la Carte Postale** (tel: 04 93 34 24 88; open Tues–Sun 2–6pm; admission charge), which has hundreds of vintage postcards. A guided tour (available in English) includes demonstrations of cards that move, turn and even play music.

The ramparts continue past the cathedral to the Vieux Port. Below is the small **Plage de la Gravette**, a sheltered sandy beach, separated from the Vieux Port by the quai H. Rambaud. From the ramparts there is a gateway to the **rue Aubernon**, which leads to place Audibert, where there is a small flea market.

A few streets to the south, place Nationale is home to the **Musée Peynet et du Dessin Humoristique** (tel: 04 92 90 54 30; open June–Sept Tues–Sun 10am–6pm, Oct–May Tues–Sun 10am–noon, 2–6pm; admission charge), dedicated to Raymond Peynet, whose delightful, somewhat coy drawings – notably *Les Amoureux* (the lovers) – have made him a cult figure. There are also drawings by other newspaper cartoonists. In this square and in many of the narrow streets leading to the cathedral, there are lots of restaurants, so this is a popular place to stop for lunch after the Saturday markets (arrive soon after midday to be sure of a table).

Entertainment

If you like your entertainment loud and on tap, head just north of Antibes. On the seafront, **La Siesta** (route du Bord de Mer; tel: 04 93 33 31 31; www.lasiesta.fr) is a huge beachside nightclub and restaurant complex, with an open-air disco in summer and a lounge bar, Flamingo

TIP

The tourist office in Antibes is a mine of useful information: Maison du Tourisme, 11 place Général de Gaulle, tel: 04 92 90 53 00; www.antibes juanlespins.com

RIGHT: sailing is a popular activity in Antibes.

Yacht-Watching

Riviera harbours are open to anyone wishing for a closer look at the lifestyles of the rich and famous, and at Port Vauban, the outer port, built to shelter Adnan Khashoggi's 83-metre (270-ft) *Nabila* (now under new ownership with a new name), is home to some of the world's most prestigious megayachts. These are fully crewed private vessels over 36 metres (120 ft) long, often berthed in the wide quay known as "millionaires' row". Here you can walk along wondering at the enormity of these vessels and guessing a yacht's owner by its name. Some are not much smaller than a cross-Channel ferry, which has the capacity to carry hundreds of passengers.

To join the yacht set, a second-hand 18-metre (60-ft) yacht can set you back about £1.5 million. For more speed or cabin space you will have to part with around £4 million. Today, yachts worth more than £25 million are quite common; the annual upkeep tots up to about 10 percent of the boat's value. For the "budget-conscious", chartering a four-cabin yacht at £3,000 a day could be an alternative.

Sailing may be an overstated term for the activities of many yachts, as they seem to spend more time hosting parties quayside than at sea.

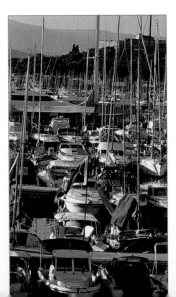

restaurant and casino open all year.

Across the railway line, almost in Biot, is the extremely popular marine theme park, **Marineland** (www. marineland.fr; open Feb–Dec daily 10am–7pm; admission charge), which combines crowd-pulling attractions with a more serious purpose as a marine-breeding and research institute. It includes penguins, seals, a shark tunnel, mangrove swamp and piranha pool, although the highlight is the afternoon whale and dolphin shows. On the same site are **Aquasplash** (open June–Sept; admission charge), an aquatic fun park, crazy golf and the cowboy-themed **La Petite Ferme du Far West** (open daily; admission charge), where there are baby farm animals for children to bottle-feed, goats to milk and pony rides.

The hedonists' peninsula

Cap d'Antibes is still very much the preserve of those fortunate enough to have villas here, but as a result it has retained much of its charm. South of Antibes, the **Plage de la Salis** is a public beach with golden sand stretching from the Pointe de l'Ilet down to the Port de la Salis. Although not large, it is the only sandy beach this side of the Cap apart from the diminutive but famous **Plage de la Garoupe E** just beyond Pointe Bacon.

It is so small that it is more of a reference to a beach than anything else. Scott Fitzgerald's description of the "bright tan prayer rug of a beach" is most accurate – a fairly moth-eaten rug at that. Had Gerald Murphy, American millionaire and original model for Fitzgerald's hero Dick Driver in *Tender is the Night*, known the fate of his quiet little cove he may have been more inclined to cover it up with rocks than painstakingly remove all the seaweed, as he did in the 1920s, while his villa – Villa America – was being remodelled. Today, wooden sundecks on stilts extend the beach out over the rocks, with beachclubs charging for the use of a lounger.

One of the first visitors from the Hôtel du Cap Eden Roc to the Murphys' villa, set in a large garden, was Rudolph Valentino.

Maps on pages 120/122

"There was no one in Juan-les-Pins this summer except Zelda and myself, the Valentinos, Murphys, Mistinguett, Rex Ingram, Dos Passos, Alice Terry, the Maclieshes, Charlie Khan, Marguerite Namara, Etienne de Beaumont, E. Phillips Oppenheim, Mannes the violinist... in short, it was a perfect place to get away from everything and everyone. It was marvellous."
– F. SCOTT FITZGERALD

BELOW: the famous Plage de la Garoupe.

TIP

Held each July since 1960 in the Pinède Gould, Jazz à Juan is one of the world's leading jazz festivals and the place to catch first-rate names in American jazz, blues and fusion, such as B.B. King, Dizzy Gillespie, Wayne Shorter and Keith Jarrett, in a stunning setting against the Mediterranean Sea. Recently established Jazz Révélations is a smaller festival in April seeking out new discoveries. www.antibes-juanlespins.com

BELOW: on the pier at Juan-les-Pins.

From Garoupe you can walk out to the rocks at **Cap Gros**, following the cliff path. Further around the Cap, one aristocratic villa that can be visited is the **Villa Eilen Roc** in avenue Mrs L.D. Beaumont (tel: 04 93 67 74 33; open Sept–June: house Wed 9am–noon, 1.30–5pm, gardens Tues–Wed 9.30am–5pm; free), designed in 1875 by Charles Garnier, who designed the opera houses in Paris and Monte-Carlo. The palm tree-filled gardens provide the stage for the Musiques au Cœur classical music festival in July. Across the bay is the **Pointe de l'Ilette**, the southernmost point of the Cap, with spectacular rocks and a lighthouse sweeping the night sea.

Exclusive hideaway

The coast between here and the **Musée Naval et Napoléonien** (Batterie de Graillon, boulevard Kennedy; tel: 04 93 61 45 32; open June–Sept Tues–Sat 10am–6pm, Oct–May 10am–noon, 2–6pm; admission charge), which contains model ships and Napoleon memorabilia, is taken up by the grounds of

the **Hôtel du Cap-Eden Roc** ❶, the most glamorous hotel on the Riviera, popular today with top celebrities visiting Cannes. It is expensive, of course, but can be visited for a meal, drinks or a day at the pool. (Be warned, though, that there is a hefty charge for using the pool and renting a lounger.) The tiny wooden bungalows at the water's edge are the most coveted part of the hotel, where celebrities can relax in total privacy during the day, far from the prying cameras of the paparazzi.

The hotel was originally built by the founder of *Le Figaro* newspaper, supposedly as a home for impoverished artists and musicians, but in 1863 was taken over by Russian princes who transformed it into a hotel. In 1914 its luxurious annexe, the Eden Roc, was added perched on the rocks. It was one of the first luxury hotels on the Riviera, inspiring certain scenes in Fitzgerald's *Tender is the Night*, where it is called the Hôtel des Etrangers. The Murphys stayed here in 1923 and persuaded the owner to open the hotel during the summer, thus launching the Riviera summer season.

Sipping an Americano cocktail on the 1930s-style terrace with its elegant white railings and yellow cushions, watching the yellow buoys bobbing about in the sea below, is the height of luxury, as is swimming in the organic, shaped pool cut into the rocks (where eccentric Zelda Fitzgerald used to dive). It is as good a way as any to appreciate the enduring allure of the Côte d'Azur.

Votive offerings

Dominating the skyline of the Cap is the **Phare de la Garoupe**. The lighthouse itself is fairly new, since the retreating Germans dynamited the old one in 1944. The chapel next to it, the **Sanctuaire de la Garoupe** ❷, however, is old, with two naves, one 13th- and one 16th-century. Despite its set-

ting amid luxury villas, it is still used by the local people and feels like a small village church. For centuries, seafarers have left votive offerings in the church, which now resembles a trendy junk shop of naive paintings, drawings and medals. Low on the wall to the right of the entrance is an extraordinary drawing of a wrecked car, smoking in a ditch; its owners are praying for their survival but unfortunately for their future prospects they are kneeling right in the middle of the road. In front of the chapel is a viewing platform; from here you can see as far as Cap St-Erasmo in Italy to the east and St-Tropez to the west.

Not far from the chapel and lighthouse, and a fairly easy walk from the public beaches of Antibes or the casino end of the Plage de Juan-les-Pins, is the **Jardin Thuret**  (41 boulevard du Cap; open summer Mon–Fri 8am–6pm, winter Mon–Fri 8.30am–5.30pm; free), which has a collection of exotic trees and plants, many introduced to the region. Right next door is the Villa Thenard, where Grand-Duke Nicholas of Russia died in 1929.

Back up the D2559 towards Juan-les-Pins, there is a marina at Port Gallice and the tiniest of sandy beaches reaching out to the Port du Croûton. The sheltered sandy beaches of **Juan-les-Pins** ❶ itself reach almost this far down the Cap and stretch the full length of the town, providing plenty of space for a frenetic beach life of intensive sunbathing and shoreline promenading – the palpable pleasures which for many visitors fulfil their expectations of the Côte d'Azur.

This is also the place for nightlife, with a casino, throbbing nightclubs and people-watching pavement cafés. F. Scott and Zelda Fitzgerald rented the Villa St-Louis here in 1926, later rebuilt as the Hôtel Belles-Rives. In July, the annual jazz festival *(see Tip opposite)*, with a prestigious line-up of international artists, is held under the shady pine trees of the seaside Pinède Gould.

Golfe-Juan

Between Juan-les-Pins and Cannes is **Golfe-Juan** ❽. The bay of the same name is famous for Napoleon's ill-fated return from exile on Elba, when he landed here on 1 March 1815 – an event commemorated in costume re-enactment each year on the first weekend in March. He apparently met the Prince of Monaco on his way to reclaim his own throne after the Revolution and said to him, "Monsieur, we are in the same business." Napoleon headed north with his troops through the rough terrain of the Alps to Paris. His path, via Grasse, Castellane, Digne and Sisteron, on what is roughly the N85, is now known as the **route Napoléon**.

On the way into Golfe-Juan there was once a strip of 1930s villas, jammed between the railway and the coast road to Antibes, facing the beach. Now predatory tower cranes menace the buildings, and the old villas near the port are being torn

Maps on
pages
120/122

The Hôtel du Cap-Eden Roc accepts new guests on recommendation.

BELOW: at the beach, Golfe-Juan.

TIP

Napoleon's landing on the beach at Golfe-Juan on 1 May 1815 following his escape from the island of Elba is re-enacted in period costume each year on the first weekend in March. http://napoleon-golfe-juan.fr or www.vallauris-golfe-juan.fr

BELOW: potter at work in Vallauris.

down, their gardens uprooted. In their place is a row of high-rise apartment blocks which will eventually stretch all the way to Juan-les-Pins.

The long beach, however, remains the same, bordered with an elegant line of palms, golden sand banned to dogs, and with a seductive Cap d'Antibes shimmering across the bay.

The part of the old fishermen's port at Golfe-Juan that faces the enclosed harbour has not changed much, either; the traffic on the coast road has always been busy, and the fact that the old port is cut off from the main town by the railway tracks has preserved it.

After the war, Picasso and his lover Françoise Gilot *(see page 124)* lived in a villa overlooking the boats. It was on the beach at Golfe-Juan that Picasso met Susanne and Georges Ramié, who were the owners of the Madoura pottery in Vallauris, an event which was to transform the fortunes of the inland town.

An inland resort

Vallauris ❾ itself is less than three built-up kilometres (2 miles) from Golfe-Juan and the coast, and resembles a seaside town with rest homes, private hospitals and a tourist strip, except in this case, the souvenirs are pots. Vallauris has always been a potters' town, a tradition begun by the Romans and continued by Italian potters from Grasse.

A centre for everyday cooking pots for a long time, Vallauris became associated with art pottery by the pioneering Massier family in the late 19th century, who began experimenting with some extravagant new Art Nouveau forms and decorative finishes, such as an iridescent lustre glaze that was developed by Clément Massier.

Competition from mass-manufactured cooking wares saw the town's fortunes decline drastically until Picasso began patronising the Madoura pottery workshop. His output was prodigious; 2,000 pieces in the first year which required a whole team of people to prepare and fire. The pottery was permitted to make limited edition copies of his plates and vases, which it still does, and his presence attracted other artists, including Marc Chagall.

Today, Vallauris is one of France's largest pottery centres, and virtually the whole of the rue Clémenceau, from the museum to the edge of town, is lined with pottery shops. Behind them are the kilns and workshops that produce the pottery, which are open to the public when in operation (though not at weekends). Although much of the pottery produced is cheap tourist ware, there is still a handful of reputable potters.

Galerie Madoura (open Mon–Fri), on avenue Suzanne et Georges Ramié, still has the licence to produce some of Picasso's designs and is the best place to shop for high-quality, though expensive, pots. The town continues to promote contemporary pottery by inviting two contemporary designers to work with local potters each year (Jasper Morrison, Ronan Bouroullec, Patrick Jouin) and through its ceramics Biennale (even years).

Picasso's chapel

The **Château de Vallauris** (tel: 04 93 64 71 83; www.musee-picasso-vallauris.fr; open Wed–Mon 10am–noon, 2–6pm, 5pm in winter; admission charge), a largely Renaissance building constructed over an earlier priory, houses three museums, including the chapel decorated by Picasso. It is entered through a courtyard shaded by a huge lime tree, where there is a 1985 Riopelle mosaic on the wall.

Rebuilt in the 16th century, it has a round pepperpot tower at each end and a splendid Renaissance staircase. Of the priory, only the Romanesque chapel has survived intact. It has a fine barrel-vaulted ceiling and round arches.

In 1952, at the request of the town, Picasso decorated it with a huge composition called *War and Peace*, an ode to peace, painted in his studio on hardboard panels which would bend to follow the curve of the vault. It is by no means Picasso's best work, and is not improved by the fact that he neglected to prime his surface, so the dull brown of the hardboard shows through the large fields of white paint and scrubbed brushwork; a third panel depicts figures of the four continents around a dove of peace. Some

Map on page 120

TIP

The Biennale Internationale de Céramique Contemporaine (http://biennale.vallauris.free.fr) at Vallauris (next in 2008) features shows at several venues in town by leading potters from around the world, reflecting different trends in modern art pottery and ceramic design.

BELOW:
Picasso's *l'Homme à l'Agneau* in Vallauris.

BELOW: the chapel of Notre-Dame-de-Vie, near Mougins.

of the pottery made by Picasso is exhibited in the **Musée de la Céramique** (same hours), which traces the town's pottery heritage from early domestic wares via some spectacular works by the Massier dynasty to modern art pottery. A third museum, the **Musée Magnelli** (same hours) contains paintings by Italian-born abstract painter Alberto Magnelli (1888–1971).

Just outside the chateau stands Picasso's bronze of a man holding a sheep, which he presented to the town in 1949. The Atelier Fournas, the old perfume warehouse where Picasso had his studio (95 avenue Pablo Picasso) is now run as a bed and breakfast.

Around Mougins

Picasso connections abound elsewhere in the area. If you head inland from Vallauris, picking up the D35 to Mougins, you should make a short detour to the small chapel of **Notre-Dame-de-Vie** on the way, near the celebrated restaurant Moulin de Mougins *(see page 137)*, made famous by Roger Vergé and

now in the capable hands of Alain Llorca. The 17th-century chapel has an outdoor porch and is on a beautiful site overlooking Mougins. The area is popular for walking, and nearby is an entrance to l'Etang de Fontmerle, a small lake that borders the Parc Départemental de la Valmasque. In summer, the lake is covered with enormous lotus blossoms and is the home of more than 60 species of migrating birds.

Picasso spent the last 12 years of his life, until his death in 1973, in the neighbouring Villa Notre-Dame-de-Vie. It remains extremely well protected, not open to the public or visible from the road, like most of the expensive villas in the area. The house was a former *mas* (farmhouse), which was converted before World War II into a luxurious villa by Benjamin Guinness.

Mougins ❿ is rather too pristine an example of a southern hill village. Spotless renovated buildings, many now housing restaurants or art-and-craft galleries, climb up in a spiral around a little hill giving the village a picturesque but decidedly ersatz

feel, that has surely lost the avant-garde edge of the days when Picasso and Picabia were among the famous artists who settled here; instead, its cluster of restaurants and cafés make it a popular gastronomic excursion from Cannes.

The site of Mougins has been occupied since Roman times, and during the Middle Ages was owned by the monks of Ile St-Honorat (*see page 115*). All that remains of the original ramparts is a 15th-century fortified gate, the Porte Sarrazine. The church, l'Eglise St-Jacques-le-Majeur, was begun in the 11th century and has been heavily restored throughout the years.

At the **Musée de la Photographie** (tel: 04 93 75 85 67; open July–Sept daily, Oct & June Wed–Sun; free), round the corner on rue de l'Eglise, there is an excellent collection of 20th-century classics, including many photos of Picasso.

Southeast of the village, at a motorway service area on the A8, is the **Musée de l'Automobiliste** (tel: 04 93 69 27 80; open Dec–Mar Tues–Sun, Apr–Oct daily; admis-

sion charge), a snazzy glass-and-concrete structure housing the vintage car collection of Adrien Maeght, son of the founders of the Fondation Maeght (*see page 156*), which takes in everything from German military vehicles to vintage Bugattis and Formula One racing cars.

Concrete art

North of Mougins, virtually merging into the southern sprawl of Grasse on the N85, is **Mouans-Sartoux ⓫**. The village was reconstructed in the late 15th century on a grid plan like nearby Valbonne, with five streets in each direction and space for a pretty square in front of the church.

The main reason to visit is the **Espace de l'Art Concret** (tel: 04 93 75 71 50; http://art.concret.free.fr; open Sept–June Tues–Sun 11am–6pm, July–Aug daily 11am–7pm; admission charge) at the Château de Mouans, which was built in the early 16th century by Jean de Grasse. It is one of the most interesting modern art museums in the south of France, founded in

Map on page 120

Local colour in the village of Mougins.

BELOW: an art gallery in Mougins.

In the town square, a popular meeting place.

BELOW: the Provençal pastiche of Sophia-Antipolis.

1990 by artist Gottfried Honegger and Sybil Albers, widow of Josef Albers, to exhibit their collection of *art concret* – the geometrical, minimalist aspect of abstract art.

Inside the solid, triangular fortified chateau with three round towers (echoed in the art centre's logo), interesting temporary exhibitions are staged, while a new, appropriately minimalist, lime-green modern building, designed by Swiss architects Gigon & Guyer, is used for well-focused, changing displays from the permanent collection of more than 150 artists, such as Josef Albers, Gottfried Honegger and Aurélie Nemours, as well as younger artists, such as Adrien Scheiss and Laurent Saksik, who keep up the minimalist tradition.

Next to the car park is a small chapel with a naive carved tympanum over the door depicting an engaging Nativity scene with church, shepherds and dozens of sheep. In the chateau's old stables, the small **Musée Reflets d'un Monde Rural** (open summer daily, winter Tues–Sun) reflects Mouans-Sartoux's rural past as a centre of silkworm rearing, and olive and flower cultivation.

Silicon new town

To the east, **Sophia-Antipolis** ⑫ – or, to give its full name, Parc International d'Activités de Valbonne Sophia-Antipolis – covers an enormous area of the Valbonne plain – over 2,300 hectares (5,700 acres).

The development, which accommodates scores of high-tech companies, is much more than just a green-site technical park. It also includes miles and miles of new roads, plus housing, shopping, schools and research institutes, many of them in futuristic buildings – horizontal cylinders, mirrored pyramids and the like.

Sophia-Antipolis continues to expand and develop, and its success reflects the region's determination to become the Silicon Valley of southern Europe. However, the sight of eager young American executives jogging along the landscaped roads still has an inescapably bizarre quality.

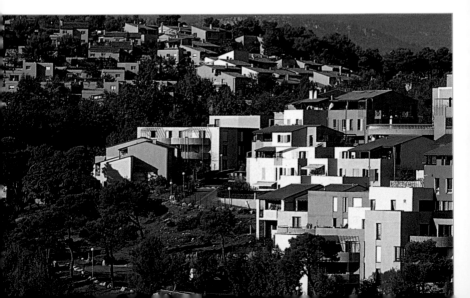

Valbonne and Opio

The first thing that strikes you about **Valbonne** ⑱ is its plan. There is no medieval meandering here: rather, like Sophia-Antopolis, this was a planned settlement, though from an earlier age. The town was laid out in the 16th century by the Lérins monks, on a strict geometrical grid four blocks wide and 10 blocks long, with a gateway on each side and lovely arcaded square in the centre.

The church, built on the river bank just outside the grid, began life as part of an abbey founded by the Chalais Order, who built it in the shape of a Latin cross. The abbey was taken over by the Lérins, and the present building finally became the parish church. Sadly, the building has been very badly restored. The adjoining convent is also being restored by the commune.

The road between Valbonne and Opio, to the northwest, passes through pleasant green and shady woodland, shielding an abundance of luxury villas and hotels. **Opio** itself is a bijou village, well maintained with painstakingly restored houses and neatly trimmed hedges. Here, you can visit the Roger Michel olive oil mill, where (Nov–Feb) you can see the olive-pressing in operation, and buy a variety of olive oil-based products *(see Tip)*.

Glassblowers and Léger

On your way back to the coast, head for the ancient town of **Biot** ⑭. Although tourists are encouraged to visit its potteries and glass-making ateliers, parking provision is poor, and you would be well advised to park instead at the foot of the hill near La Verrerie de Biot, one of the glass factories for which the town is famous, and walk up the hill to the 16th-century Port des Tines. Alternatively, in summer, park at the Centre Culturel and take the shuttle bus, which also tours the town.

Like Vallauris, Biot was long known for its potteries – the speciality here being sturdy clay storage jars. Since 1956, however, it has been more associated with glass, with the creation of the **Verrerie de Biot** (chemin des Courbes; tel: 04 93 65 03 00; www.verreriebiot.com)

Map on page 120

TIP

The Moulin de la Brague at Opio has been run by the Michel family for over 150 years. Although water power has now been replaced by electricity, traditional methods are still used to make high-quality olive oil from the tiny purple *caillette* or "olive de Nice". Open Mon–Sat except 15–30 Oct; tel: 04 93 77 23 03; www.moulin-opio.com

BELOW AND RIGHT: watch master glassblowers create Biot's famous bubble glass.

Map on page 120

An abstract work of painted glass by Joseph Fernand Henri Léger.

BELOW: in the town square, Biot.

famed for its "bubble glass", a unique technique that create swirls of bubbles in clear or iridescently coloured blown glass. You can watch the master glassblowers at work in the factory located at the foot of the village; adjoining it are a shop and showroom, small glass museum and the Galerie Internationale de Verre, exhibiting the work of international art glassmakers.

Potteries and glass shops, along with cafés, tourist information and a small **local history museum** (tel: 04 93 65 54 54; open Wed–Sun; admission charge) are concentrated on rue St-Sébastien, but it is a pity if that is all you get to see. The rue de Mitan has a number of fine examples of medieval shops, and the entire quarter has a charm that is missing from some of the more popular hill towns.

In the centre of Biot is the place des Arcades, an oblong plaza built on the site of the Roman forum, with two long 13th- and 14th-century arcades on either side. The church, built between 1470 and 1655 on the foundations of a Romanesque church, stands at the east end of the square and, owing to the slope of the ground, has a flight of 20 steps, leading down into the nave. The old cemetery, just a few streets to the north, is also well worth a visit.

Not far from the Verrerie de Biot, at the foot of the town is the **Musée National Fernand Léger** (tel: 04 92 91 50 30; www.musee-fernandleger .fr; due to reopen Jan 2007; open July–Sept Wed–Mon 10.30am–6pm, Oct–June 10am–12.30pm, 2pm– 5.30pm; admission charge), dedicated to the artist Fernand Léger (1881– 1955) and conceived by his widow Nadia. They had moved to Biot not long before his death.

Announced by a vast ceramic tile mural over the entrance, the museum contains more than 300 paintings, tapestries, stained glass and ceramics, executed between 1905 and 1955. Several more paintings have been loaned to the museum by the Centre Pompidou in Paris to give an overview of his personal interpretation of Cubism and his socially committed works that reflected the machine age and industry. ❏

RESTAURANTS

Antibes & Juan-les-Pins

Restaurant de Bacon
Boulevard de Bacon, Cap d'Antibes. Tel: 04 93 61 50 02. Open L Wed–Sun, D Tues–Sun; closed Nov–Feb. €€€
www.restaurantdebacon.com
A legendary luxury fish restaurant founded in 1950 with views from Cap d'Antibes across the bay to the ramparts of old Antibes. Go for the catch of the day, grilled or *en papillote* and paid for by weight, or splurge on the renowned bouillabaisse.

Les Pêcheurs
10 Boulevard Maréchal-Juin, Juan-les-Pins. Tel: 04 92 93 13 30. Open July–Aug D Wed–Mon, Sept–June L & D Thur–Mon. €€€
www.lespecheurs-lecap.com
Under the same ownership as the Juana Hotel, this new waterside restaurant complex has rejuvenated the Juan-les-Pins scene with its stylish contemporary decor in teak and brushed aluminium and the acclaimed modern cooking of chef Francis Chauveau. The complex includes a private sandy beach, casual beach restaurant La Plage and bar-club Le Cap.

Taverne du Safranier
1 place du Safranier, Antibes. Tel: 04 93 34 80 50. €€
This animated bistro on a square in the Vieille

Ville is very popular with arty locals. Specialities include marinated sardines, ravioli and fresh fish. Be sure to finish with the gigantic chocolate profiterole.

Les Vieux Murs
25 promenade Amiral de Grasse, Antibes. Tel: 04 93 34 06 73. Open L Wed–Sun, D Tues–Sun. €€€
www.lesvieuxmurs.com
This long-standing Antibes address with vaulted dining rooms looking out over the ramparts has recently changed hands and gained a stylish new decor and cocktail bar. New chef Thierry Grattorola has kept up the culinary reputation with his good southern cooking, such as whole baked fish or Nice-style hare with gnocchi.

Biot

Galerie des Arcades
16 place des Arcades. Tel: 04 93 65 01 04. Open L Tues–Sun, D Tues–Sat; closed Nov. €€
A popular village inn on Biot's main square which doubles as an art gallery. Provençal cuisine is served in the small dining room or under the medieval arcades.

Les Terraillers
11 route du Chemin Neuf. Tel: 04 93 65 01 59. Open L & D Fri–Tues; closed mid-Oct–Nov. €€€
A blend of creative innovation and French

classics in an elegant restaurant in the vaulted room of an old pottery outside the village. Attractive terrace.

Golfe-Juan

Restaurant Tétou
Avenue des Frères Roustan. Tel: 04 93 63 71 16. Open L & D Thurs–Tues; closed Nov–Feb. €€€
On the beach and considered the best place for bouillabaisse. No credit cards.

Mougins

Alain Llorca Moulin de Mougins
Avenue Notre-Dame-de-Vie. Tel: 04 93 75 78 24. Open L & D Tues–Sun. €€€
www.moulin-mougins.com
Alain Llorca, formerly of the Negresco in Nice, has stamped his own style on the legendary restaurant created by Roger Vergé. Llorca puts an adventurous "deconstructed" take on dishes from Provence and the Mediterranean. Try the weekly changing "déjeuner de soleil" lunch menu, or the "ronde de tapas"; 2007 should see a new decor and open kitchen.

Le Bistrot de Mougins
Place du Village. Tel: 04 93 75 78 34. Open L & D Thur–Tues; closed Dec. €€
Set in a beautiful vaulted stone cellar, serving excellent traditional Provençal cuisine.

Brasserie de la Méditerranée
Place de la Mairie. Tel: 04 93 90 03 47. Open L daily, D Mon–Sat. €€
www.restaurantlamediterranee.com
A casual-chic restaurant on the village square with traditional brasserie decor and an appealing choice of southern favourites.

Le Mas Candille
Boulevard Clément Rebuffel. Tel: 04 92 28 43 43. Open L & D daily; closed Jan. €€€
www.lemascandille.com
Chef Serge Gouloumes brings his own touches to attractive modern Provençal cooking. There's an informal poolside restaurant in July and August.

Valbonne

Lou Cigalon – Alain Parodi
4 Boulevard Carnot. Tel: 04 93 12 27 07. Open L & D Tues–Sat. €€€
Self-taught chef Alain Parodi is one of the discoveries of the Côte d'Azur, conjuring up a well-balanced personal interpretation of regional cuisine from a tiny kitchen. Superb-value weekday lunch menu.

PRICE CATEGORIES
Prices for a three-course meal without wine.
€ = under €25
€€ = €25–€40
€€€ = over €40

GRASSE AND THE LOUP VALLEY

Known as a perfume centre for over 400 years, Grasse
has a fine medieval quarter and stunning views of
the countryside all around. Near by are the
perched villages of the Gorges du Loup,
set amid dramatic rocky outcrops

The ancient town of **Grasse** ⓱
is an excellent place to appreciate the acute contrast between the Côte d'Azur and its
bucolic hinterland. The town is set on
a fabulous site, cradled by sheltering
hills and surrounded by flowers, and
with splendid views all the way to the
sea. Beneath its palm-fronded terraces, elegant pink villas decorate the
hillside, sloping gently down to the
highly populated valley below, thick
with executive housing and high-tech
parks. Here, the desired synthesis of
modern technology with the peace
and beauty of the countryside seems
entirely possible.

Beyond Grasse are craggy mountains terraced with lavender, meandering river gorges and the medieval
villages of Provence. Within only a
few miles, spectacular drives and
walks are possible. The Gorges du
Loup, in particular, make a wonderful excursion, leading you rapidly
into an altogether more elevated
universe of Alpine pastures and
mountain mists.

Grasse is the centre of the perfume industry, and for most of the
year the air is laden with fragrance:
golden mimosa flowers in March; in
early summer there are acres of roses
waiting to be picked and lavender to
be processed; in autumn the heavy
perfume of jasmine hangs in the air.

These days, Grasse concentrates
on processing raw materials from
other countries, but it is still possible
to see vast mountains of rose petals,
vats of jonquils and spadefuls of violets and orange blossom waiting to be
processed each morning.

Map
on page
120

A little history

The town has a venerable past.
Between 1138 and 1227 it was a
free city, allied to Pisa and Genoa
and governed by a consulate, like
the Italian republics. It became a

LEFT: climbing the
gorges outside Grasse.
BELOW: lavender for
the perfume makers.

Carved statue representing the perfumer's art, outside the Perfumerie Fragonard.

RIGHT: flowers from the market.

bishopric in 1243 and remained so until 1791, thus becoming a focal point for local power. Its most famous cleric was the 15th-century Bishop Isnard de Grasse, who was head of the monastery of the Iles de Lérins.

The town was annexed by the Counts of Provence until 1481, when Provence was united with France. Grasse continued to trade with Italy, importing animal skins and selling linen and leather goods.

Grasse leather was of very high quality, characterised by its greenish hue, caused by treating it with myrtle leaves. In the 16th century, the fashion for perfumed gloves (masking, along with pomanders and handkerchiefs, the undesirable smell of the populace) was introduced by Catherine de' Medici. This encouraged the perfume industry in Grasse, but it was not until the 18th century that tanning and perfumery began to develop as separate trades.

The place du Cours

Grasse is a very satisfying town to visit. There is much of historic interest to see, and perfumeries abound,

but tourism has not taken over completely. Despite the usual souvenir shops selling bags of Provençal lavender, the town still has a working feel to it, and shops on the main square continue to sell everyday items to local residents.

In the architecture of Grasse the influence of the Italian Renaissance is clear. It is to Genoa that the city is indebted for its austere medieval façades, its Renaissance staircases and its houses sitting on arcades.

The town walls were not demolished until the mid-19th century, so the buildings crammed within the walls were extended vertically. The majority are six storeys high, even in the narrowest of alleys, many of which are insalubrious medieval tunnels. The southern part of the old town houses many Algerians, bringing a lively street life and Arab music to the lanes and squares.

The **place du Cours** is a good place to begin a tour of Grasse. Here, a bevy of museums flanks a charming terraced garden full of fountains and waterfalls. The **Musée International de la Par-**

How Perfume is Made

The flowers must be picked early, when the oil is most concentrated, and delivered immediately. It takes huge quantities of blooms to produce the tiniest amounts of perfume: about 4,000 kg (8,800lb) to produce 1 kg (2lb) of "essential oil".

There are a number of different methods used to extract the "absolutes" or "essential oils", which the perfumer then combines to create a fragrance. The oldest method is steam distillation, which is now used mainly for orange blossom. Water and flowers are boiled in a still, and the essential oil floats to the top. Another ancient method still used today is *enfleurage*. Here the flowers are layered with a semi-solid mixture of lard, spread over glass sheets and stacked in wooden tiers. When the fat is thoroughly impregnated with the perfume, the scent is separated out by washing the lard with alcohol. A more modern method involves immersion of the raw material in a volatile solvent. Only the perfume, colour and natural wax dissolve, and after distillation and wax-separation, you are left with a final concentrate called the "absolute".

In creating a fragrance, a perfumer is rather like a musician, using different "chords" of scent to blend together in harmony.

Map on page 120

fumerie, housed in an elegant 18th-century mansion, covers the entire history of the industry, including exquisite perfume bottles and Marie-Antoinette's travelling case. Best of all is the greenhouse garden of Mediterranean and subtropical perfumed plants. The museum is closed for renovations until 2007, but part of the collection can be seen at the Musée d'Art et d'Histoire de Provence *(see below)*.

Down boulevard Fragonard is the 18th-century **Parfumerie Fragonard** (tel: 04 93 36 44 65; open daily; free), a traditional perfume factory. Opposite it is the **Villa-Musée Fragonard** (tel: 04 97 05 58 00; open June–Sept daily, Oct–May Wed–Mon; admission charge).

This 17th-century villa was where artist Jean-Honoré Fragonard, who was born in Grasse, lived with his family for some years before the Revolution. The house contains drawings and etchings, and two self-portraits by Fragonard, as well as copies of the famous panels made for the Comtesse du Barry which are now in the Frick Collection in New York. The building is surrounded by a charming formal garden.

More museums

Heading in the other direction from place du Cours you quickly reach the **Musée Provençal du Costume et du Bijou** (tel:04 93 36 91 42; open Feb–Oct daily, Nov–Jan Mon–Sat; free), the Fragonard family's personal collection of 18th- and 19th-century jewellery and traditional costume, from festive peasant dresses to frilly aristocratic frocks.

On a nearby street, Rue Mirabeau, are two town houses that belonged to the Clapiers de Cabris family, one 17th-century and the other, now the **Musée d'Art et d'Histoire de Provence** (tel: 04 97 05 58 00; open June–Sept daily, Oct–May Wed–Mon; admission

charge), built in 1771. This museum has a good collection of regional crafts, including ceramics and furniture, and a library of Provençal documents.

North of the place du Cours is the **Musée de la Marine** (tel: 04 93 40 11 11; open July–Aug daily, Sept–June, Mon–Fri; admission charge), the beautiful 18th-century former town house of the Pontèves family. The museum commemorates the life and career of Admiral de Grasse (1722–88), who was born locally in Le Bar and played a decisive role in the American War of Independence at the Battle of Yorktown, Virginia, the final battle of the campaign against the British. The museum contains flags and memorabilia, and has a delightful garden with neatly trimmed hedges surrounding roses and small lemon trees, and a pair of cannons captured from the British.

Exploring the streets

To the north is the **place aux Aires**, long and narrow, with shady trees and an 18th-century fountain facing the Hôtel Isnard, which has a slightly

Fragonard is one of the major perfume makers of Grasse.

BELOW: perfume is big business in Grasse.

The perfect way to travel around the town square.

incongruous portico of pillars supporting a balcony. The square dates from the 14th century, but the row of arcaded buildings which are its pride and joy are wealthy family town houses from the 16th and 17th centuries, mostly six storeys with shutters and washing hanging from the windows, giving an Italian feel to the scene. A market is held in the square most mornings except Monday.

Turning south, down the narrow steps of the rue des Fabreries, you encounter the remains of a 14th-century mansion on the corner of the rue de l'Oratoire. The first two floors are rusticated in the Italian Renaissance style, and there is a fine two-arched window on the third floor, below which runs the line of corbels for a missing balcony. You could be in Florence.

As you continue along the rue de l'Oratoire, you reach the **Eglise de l'Oratoire**, which dates from the 14th century, although the bright yellow ochre paintwork on the walls makes the building look much more recent. Everywhere you walk, there is evidence of great age in the buildings, with blocks of stone and fragments of arches peeking through the now flaking rendering.

Head for place Jean Jaurès and turn right down the very narrow and rather creepy rue Répitrel to the **rue Mougins-Roquefort**, where a 14th-century double round-arched window survives. It has Italian Renaissance corbels and, like many of these buildings, was obviously originally arched on the ground floor. Further down, close to the cathedral, is a 13th-century house.

The cathedral

The **place du Petit Puy** is the centre of the medieval town. Facing the square is the cathedral of **Notre-Dame-du-Puy**. It has a very high nave with a ribbed vault supported by four enormous 12th-century pillars, scarred and worn, evidence of the burning of the building in 1795 when it was transformed into a forage store. View the nave from the west door, looking straight down to the altar. It was altered considerably in the 13th century and remodelled in the 17th century. The classic Ital-

BELOW: the nave of the cathedral of Notre-Dame-du-Puy in Grasse.

ian Romanesque façade now has a double staircase by Vauban, architect of the ramparts of Antibes; it was a failed attempt to give this crude and powerful building a touch of 17th-century elegance.

The interior features some interesting works: a rare religious painting by Fragonard, *The Washing of the Feet* (1754), in the south transept, and three works by Rubens on the south wall of the nave: *The Crown of Thorns*, *The Crucifixion* and *St Helen in Exaltation of the Holy Cross*, painted in Rome in 1601. There is also a triptych attributed to Louis Bréa, and some interesting reliquaries and church treasure.

Outside there is a good view of the south transept from the place St-Martin. A tunnel leads through to the place Godeau, where the **Bishop's Palace** forms the other side of a small square. Arrow slits in the palace are aimed straight at the north doorway of the church. The Palace (now serving as the Hôtel de Ville) once had an elegant three-arched loggia in the Italian manner, but this was mostly infilled in later years, leaving only the passage through from the place Godeau. The ensemble is completed by a tall 10th-century square tower in red tufa.

To the east of the Bishop's Palace, on the place du 24 Août, is a solitary clock tower, the remains of the 13th-century consulate (law courts).

The Gorges du Loup

Around Grasse are a number of interesting villages, especially if you head northeast towards the Gorges du Loup. At **Le Bar-sur-Loup** , a pair of cannons, captured by Admiral François de Grasse from the British, stand either side of the 16th-century chateau on place F. Pault. De Grasse was in this castle, and Rue Yorktown is named after his famous battle *(see page 141)*. Le Bar is a centre for walking, and itin-

(see page 141)

eraries are available from the tourist office located in the strange *donjon* in the middle of the village. The Gothic church has been extensively remodelled, but has fine door panels by Jacotin Bellot. There is also an extraordinary 15th-century painting of *La Danse Macabre* (The Dance of Death) in the nave.

About 4 km (2 miles) further down the D2210, tucked into a dramatic corner of the Gorges du Loup, is the **Confiserie Florian** (tel: 04 93 59 32 91; open daily; free). Specialising in delicious regional concoctions such as glazed fruits, chocolate-covered oranges and lemons and crystallised violets, this renowned confectionery makes for an interesting break from the twists and turns of the gorges. Free guided visits (available in English) take you past bubbling vats of sugar syrup, copper cauldrons of crushed fruits and huge platters of sugar-coated violets. The visit ends, of course, in the shop, where you can sample sweets while stocking up on glazed tangerines and rose-petal confit.

Pont-du-Loup , at the south

The Gorges du Loup are the most accessible of many dramatic gorges running down to the coast.

BELOW: the Gorges du Loup is a great centre for outdoors activities.

The village of Gourdon, perched on a rocky cliff, is on the edge of the Gorges du Loup.

BELOW: Tourettes-sur-Loup.

end of the Gorges du Loup, is like an Alpine village with palm trees. The village is framed by mountains on either side with spectacular views, making it a good place for walking tours. It is dominated by the remains of a railway viaduct, blown up by the Germans in 1944 and never repaired; great ruined monoliths rise hundreds of feet over the houses and trees.

Gourdon , high above Pont-du-Loup and one of the most dramatic *villages perchés* of them all, is still relatively inaccessible, though the road to it is an easy ride in comparison with the steep mountain track the peasant with his mule used in centuries past. The approach gives a stunning view of the village, with its sheer drop of several thousand feet below the chateau walls.

Today only the chateau's living quarters have survived and, where the tower once was, a formal French garden is now laid out, providing an almost surreal contrast between the neatly trimmed low hedges and topiary and the wild backdrop of the surrounding mountains. The castle has a

museum (tel: 04 93 09 68 02; open for guided visits June–Sept daily, Oct–May Wed–Mon; admission charge), which contains some very interesting (and valuable) armour: suits of plate armour, chain mail, broadswords, rifles and various types of ordnance. All the rooms have huge fireplaces, even the private chapel, certainly necessary because Gourdon is a cold and rugged place for much of the year. On the upper floor is a small museum dedicated to Art Deco furniture and artefacts (visits by appointment only).

The Gorges du Loup themselves are glorious and terrifying by turns. The road tunnels through the rock and sweeps past magnificent waterfalls, occasionally offering views down to the rushing river far below. The footpaths along the gorge are well maintained, with steps cut in the steeper parts.

Skiing near the sea

Beyond are the Clues (gorges) de Haute Provence, a barren, remote region which comes into its own in the winter skiing season. **Gréolières** to the west is on an Alpine slope, remote and quiet, the hillsides dotted with violets and spring flowers. Eighteen km (11 miles) beyond is **Gréolières-les-Neiges**, the nearest ski resort to the Mediterranean.

Turning east instead you will come to **Coursegoules** , a pretty town of muted terracotta stone nestling protectively against the bare rock of the mountain side, surrounded by sheep pastures and tinkling bells. There is a considerable amount of new building here – basic apartments, not tourist villas – and a lively school housed in a beautifully restored old building. Remote as it may seem, Coursegoules is only 16 km (10 miles) from Vence, and the excellence of the roads means local people can commute to the coast.

A mountain village

An alternative route from Le Bar follows the D2210 to **Tourrettes-sur-Loup** ㉑, clinging to the rock between two deep ravines. To the west of the village are great expanses of sheer rock, and at the cliff edge are troglodyte houses carved from the living rock. Today Tourrettes is an important centre for violet production, supplying Grasse perfumeries.

The village is in an ideal defensive position and began life occupied by Ligurian tribes. In 262 BC, the Romans established an observation post here: "Turres Altae", which was corrupted into "Tourrettes".

The Romans left in AD 476, after which the village suffered the same series of invasions and massacres that befell its neighbours. The Saracens were responsible for fortifying the site. In 1387 Tourrettes came into the hands of the Villeneuve family, where it remained until the French Revolution, when the Villeneuves fled, never to return. The Black Death, the Wars of Religion and the Revolution all took their

toll, and by 1944 the population had shrunk to 850. Today the revitalisation of the area has resulted in a population of nearly 4,000.

The old village is quite amazingly crooked, with no two windows alike or a straight line anywhere, and the twisting streets feel completely enclosed until a cool, dim alley unexpectedly emerges on to a wind-blown mountain panorama. The horseshoe-shaped Grand' Rue is lined with art galleries and craft shops but is not too commercialised, and there are medieval shops, now converted into pretty private houses, and numerous interesting doorways still survive.

In the centre of the village stands a very formal Hôtel de Ville with an 11th-century watchtower, and a pleasant courtyard with a tinkling fountain. The 11th-century church has been rebuilt on and off from the mid-16th until the 18th century, and has a simple stylised *Virgin and Child* over the front door. To the north of the village is the Chapelle St-Jean, which contains recent naive wall paintings. ❏

The game of boules or pétanque is a laid-back provençal sport. Previously a male-only pursuit it is now played by men and women, young and old.

RESTAURANTS

Map on page 120

Le Bar-sur-Loup

La Jarrerie
Route de Grasse. Tel: 04 93 42 92 92. Closed Jan. €€
Offers a traditional and elegant atmosphere and good cuisine, plus an atmospheric setting in a former monastery.

Cabris

Auberge du Petit Prince
15 rue Frédéric Mistral. Tel: 04 93 60 63 14. Closed Dec–mid Jan, Tues and Wed. €€
A country inn serving

good food and offering an attractive terrace.

Coursegoules

L'Escaou
Tel: 04 93 59 11 28. €–€€
Restaurant in this mountain village, serving rustic Provençal cuisine with superb views from its terrace.

Grasse

La Bastide St-Antoine
48 avenue Henri Dunant. Tel: 04 93 70 94 94. €€€
Hard to find but well worth the search, this

establishment set in an old olive grove outside Grasse is popular for its wonderful gourmet menu, specialising in truffles and mushrooms.

La Voûte
3 rue de Thouron. Tel: 04 93 36 11 43. Open L & D daily. €
Provençal specialities cooked in the oven fire in this beautiful two-tiered vaulted dining room, hence its name. Friendly and convivial atmosphere in the heart of Grasse. Small outdoor terrace.

Tourrettes-sur-Loup

Les Bacchanales
21 Grand'Rue. Tel: 04 93 24 19 19. €€
Contemporary Provençal cuisine in a bistro setting.

Chez Grand'Mère
Place Mirabeau. Tel: 04 93 59 33 34. €
Very popular for North African specialities and meats grilled on the open fire. Reservations recommended.

● ● ● ● ● ● ● ● ● ● ● ● ●
Prices for a three-course meal without wine.
€€€ €40 and over, €€
€25–40, € under €25.

TROPICAL GARDENS

The Riviera's mild climate and abundant sunlight has made it a paradise for an outstanding range of flora

All sorts of tropical and subtropical plants have been naturalised in the Riviera region – not just cultivated in gardens and public parks, but also growing wild, like the mimosa trees that thrive in the Estérel hills, and the eucalyptus in the forests of the Maures.

The Belle Epoque was the golden age of Riviera gardens. Most of these exotic edens were created between the 1890s and the 1920s, many of them by the foreigners who came to winter in the region. Almost as varied as the plants they contain were the people who created them: English aristocrats and colonels, American writers, Russian princesses, landscape designers, architects and artists, explorers, botanists and other scientists. Some gardens were created for scientific purposes, others provided luxuriant backdrops to go with their exuberant *palazzi* and avant-garde villas.

These green-fingered eccentrics introduced countless new species to the native Mediterranean flora of herbs, parasol pines, olive trees and cork oaks, ranging from the agaves and date palms of desert regions to the dank ferns, banana trees and purple bougainvillea of the tropics. Against the formal restraint of traditional French gardens with their gravel paths and neatly trimmed hedges, these places were often flamboyantly exotic creations bursting with colour.

LEFT: the Serre de la Madone, Menton. The romantic gardens of the Serre de la Madone were designed in the 1920s by Lawrence Johnston, creator of the garden at Hidcote Manor in England. Water is a big feature in this garden, laid out with geometrical pools and Italianate terraces, fountains and classical statues that create different perspectives and environments for irises, acanthus, camellias, water plants, toxic daturas and other flora from all over the globe.

LEFT: Jardin Exotique, Eze. A prickly feast of cacti and strangely shaped succulents sprouts up among the sun-baked ruins of Eze's castle mound, laid out in stone terraces, with spectacular views to the sea hundreds of metres below, and dotted by terracotta nudes by sculptor Jean-Philippe Richard.

BELOW: Domaine du Rayol, Le Rayol. Perched on the clifftop, these fabulous gardens were originally planted in 1910 by Paris banker Alfred Courmes, who packed the grounds with exotic plants from all over the world. The grounds are arranged in climatic zones ranging from arid desert to tropical jungle. Gullies, bowers and secret paths are dotted about this jungle, punctuated by dramatic vistas and seaside drops. There's even an underwater garden, which can be visited with snorkel and flippers.

GARDEN TRAILS

❶ The Route des Parcs et Jardins du Var (www.tourismevar.com) follows a 325-km (200-mile) loop between Saint-Zacharie in the Sainte-Baume Massif to Hyères, taking in tiny hill-village gardens, herb and scent gardens, historic chateau gardens and the arty gardens of Hyères, as well as some of the *département*'s best nurseries.

❷ The Route des Jardins de la Riviera follows the Alpes-Maritimes coast between Mandelieu-La Napoule and Menton, visiting gardens, villas and grand hotels of the Belle Epoque, including the famous Villa Ephrussi, the gardens of Menton and smaller treasures, such as Villa Eilen Roc in Antibes and the garden of actor-playwright Sacha Guitry at Cap d'Ail.

❸ The Route du Mimosa (www.bormeslesmimosas.com) traces the fragrant yellow puffballs *(main picture)* across the Var and Alpes-Maritimes *départements*, between Bormes-les-Mimosas and the perfumeries of Grasse. At its best during the flowering season (December to March), the route suggests gardens and nurseries to visit, including the national collection of mimosa at Pepinière Gérard Cavatone in Bormes and the Massif de Tannéron near Mandelieu, where wild and cultivated trees make up the largest mimosa forest in Europe.

❹ Undisputed garden capital of the coast is Menton, famed for its lemons and reputed to have the mildest climate of all. As well as the Jardin des Agrumes, the Jardin du Val Rahmeh, the Serre de la Madone and the lovely olive groves of the Parc du Pian, other gardens can be visited through the Maison du Patrimoine de Menton (tel: 04 92 10 97 10).

ABOVE: Jardins d'Ephrussi Rothschild, Cap Ferrat.
A succession of themed gardens created by Béatrice Ephrussi, daughter of Baron Alphonse de Rothschild and wife of wealthy banker Maurice Ephrussi, on the crest of Cap Ferrat. At the top is a small classical gazebo, the Temple d'Amour, from where she could watch her 30 gardeners as they worked, dressed in berets with red pompons. Around a central formal French garden with a pool and musical gardens, the seven themed gardens evoke not just different climates and vegetation but different historic eras and moods, from the melancholy of Gothic ruins, poetry of Italian Renaissance terraces and Spanish grottoes to the calm of Japanese shinto shrines.

BELOW: the Jardin Botanique du Val Rahmeh, Menton.
Over 700 species grow in profusion on a hilly site around a 1920s villa. A winding trail leads between medicinal plants, towering palms, dank tropical ferns, forests of bamboo and exotic cocoa, avocado, banana, guava and citrus trees, tea bushes and spice trees.

CAGNES, VENCE AND THE VAR VALLEY

Built-up and brash along the coast it may be, but you don't have to go far to discover the pretty little historic hill towns and villages inland, much loved by artists such as Renoir and Matisse. In these parts, you can lunch high up on a terrace and see for miles and miles

The ribbon development west of Nice has been victim to some of the worst of the "*bétonisation*" (concreting-up) on the Riviera, but the brash coastal strip conceals a hinterland of historic hill towns, including Haut-de-Cagnes, St-Paul-de-Vence and Vence. This area long had a strategic importance when the River Var marked the frontier between Provence and the Comté de Nice, and today impressive chateaux and fortifications are combined with some impressive monuments of modern art.

The N98 highway that runs along this stretch of coast resembles a Hollywood-style strip of neon lights, hoardings, petrol stations, downmarket hotels and the huge Cap 3000 shopping complex of St-Laurent-du-Var. The view is dominated in all directions by the **Marina Baie des Anges** at **Villeneuve-Loubet-Plage ㉒**. Today, this long-reviled piece of 1960s architecture has become a sort of landmark, and indeed the sweeping pyramidal complex with stepped-back garden roof terraces, flats, shops, cafés and yacht marina now seems infinitely preferable to much of the uncontrolled mediocre concrete sprawl that has gone on around it. Ask at the tourist office (tel: 04 92 02 66 16) about guided visits.

Birthplace of Escoffier

As with much of the Riviera, only a few fishermen actually lived on the coast itself. The old medieval village of **Villeneuve-Loubet ㉓** stands 3 km (2 miles) further inland up the wooded Loup Valley, on a hill safe from the risk of invading pirates. Surprisingly, it still has an authentic feel to its steep narrow lanes and lived-in ancient buildings, which have resisted gentrification. They huddle at the foot of the Renaissance **chateau**, which saw its

LEFT: a stroll through the old town, Haut-de-Cagnes. **BELOW:** taking a break at Villeneuve-Loubet-Plage.

moment of glory when King François I and his court spent three weeks here in 1538, prior to the signing of the Treaty of Nice with Emperor Charles V.

The chateau, restored in the 19th century, is private property but is now open for guided tours (reserve at the office de tourisme, tel: 04 92 02 66 16; open July–Aug Wed, Sun, Sept–June two Sun per month; admission charge). The path round the chateau walls offers a good view out over the Baie des Anges.

One of Villeneuve's most famous sons is remembered at the **Fondation Auguste Escoffier** (also known as the **Musée de l'Art Culinaire**), housed in the great chef's birthplace, a short way up the hill from the main square (tel: 04 93 20 80 51; www.fondation-escoffier.org; open Dec–Oct Sun–Fri 2–6pm, 7pm in summer; admission charge). Exhibits include an old Provençal kitchen with gleaming copperware and kitchen utensils; some of Escoffier's own inventions, including a device for making breadcrumbs; a roomful of mouthwatering old menus; some

Masterchef of the late 19th-century, Auguste Escoffier invented the peach melba in 1893 for the Australian soprano Dame Nellie Melba when she came to stay at the Savoy Hotel in London, where he was in charge of the kitchen.

BELOW: fishermen on the water at Cros-de-Cagnes.
RIGHT: a colourful rooftop.

wildly imaginative examples of sugar work, including a haywain and a model of a Loire chateau; Escoffier's own handwritten recipe book and, touchingly, the master's last toque (tall, white chef's hat).

Escoffier (1846–1935) brought French cuisine to Britain when he was director of kitchens at the new Savoy Hotel from 1890–99 and for the following 23 years at the Carlton Hotel, both in London. He was awarded the French Légion d'Honneur in 1920 in recognition for his service to French cuisine abroad. If your visit to the culinary museum has given you an appetite, there are a couple of excellent pâtisseries in the square below.

Three towns in one

Surrounded by a tangle of highway intersections, east of Villeneuve-Loubet is **Cagnes-sur-Mer** ㉔, which is divided into three very distinct parts. By the sea is the unremarkable modern seaside resort of **Cros-de-Cagnes**, which has grown up around the remnants of a former fishing village, with a long pebbly

beach, hemmed in by the coast road and railway line and uncomfortably close to the noise of Nice airport.

Cagnes long depended on agriculture for its economic survival, notably olives, vines and flowers. But in the 19th century, fishermen from Menton settled along this coast, and the little fishermen's village grew up around the church of St-Pierre, the patron saint of fishermen. In its heyday in the 1920s there were some 100 fishing boats here. Today, Cros-de-Cagnes is more turned towards tourism and watersports, and there are only a dozen or so fishing boats left, which sell their catch to local restaurants or direct to customers at the Halle aux Poissons (Tues–Sun mornings).

You'll also find the Riviera's main racecourse, the **Hippodrome de Cagnes** here, used for trotting, flat-racing and steeplechasing, roughly where the monks of Lérins *(see page 115)* had founded an abbey in the 5th century.

Further inland (and not on the coast as its name implies) is the modern town of Cagnes-sur-Mer,

with shops, a supermarket, public park and a good covered market (mornings only). On an adjacent hill, Renoir's house, Les Collettes, stands in its lovely grounds. Now the atmospheric **Musée Renoir** (chemin des Collettes; tel: 04 92 02 47 30; www.cagnes-tourisme.com; open May–Sept Wed–Mon 10am–noon, 2–6pm, Oct–Apr Wed–Mon 10am–noon, 2–5pm; closed 2 weeks in Nov; admission charge), this is where the Impressionist artist lived from 1908 until his death in 1919 *(see page 152)*.

Up above is the bijou historic hill town of **Haut-de-Cagnes**, crowned by an imposing chateau, with fine views and steep narrow streets containing numerous restaurants popular with holidaymakers, as well as with the Niçois for an evening out.

A stroll in the old town

The steep, winding streets and tiny square of Haut-de-Cagnes are as carefully tended by the town's inhabitants as their own homes. Terracotta pots of jasmine and geraniums flower against a backdrop of fig

Map on page 120

You'll see the colourful Provençal print, called indiennes, *in hotels and restaurants throughout the region.*

BELOW: the historic hill town of Haut-de-Cagnes.

Renoir at Les Collettes

Pierre-Auguste Renoir (1841–1919) first visited the south in 1881, discovering L'Estaque, near Marseille, with Cézanne, and staying at the Cézanne family house, the Jas du Bouffon, on the outskirts of Aix-en-Provence. In 1883 he toured the Riviera with Monet between Marseille and Genoa, but it was after 1900, when suffering from rheumatism, that he finally left for good the damp of the Ile-de-France and the vibrant city life of Paris, which had nurtured his most famous paintings, for the warmth of the south.

He stayed first at Cannes, then at Le Cannet until, in 1903, he discovered Cagnes-sur-Mer and moved into the Hôtel de la Poste. In 1907 he bought the Domaine des Collettes, an old farm, surrounded by a centuries-old olive grove, and had a house and studio built there, making sure it was equipped with all the modern comforts, including a telephone (one of the first in the area). He lived there from 1908 until his death in 1919, and was visited by a whole generation of new artists including Bonnard, Modigliani and Matisse, who was often a guest at Les Collettes.

Renoir complained that he found the southern light too bright – perhaps one reason for the extremely high tonality and powerful reds of his late paintings. By 1910 he could no longer walk, neither was he able to move his fingers, but he continued to paint with his brush strapped to his hand, and his work still reflected a positive attitude to life. He loved the female form, and turned more and more to sculpture. In 1913, he enlisted the help of the young sculptor Richard Guino, who had been introduced to him by the art dealer Amboise Vollard, and produced a number of bronzes, directing Guino as his hands.

The house is still preserved pretty much as when he lived there, including the salon and dining room with a fireplace and several pieces of furniture designed by the artist himself. Several paintings by Renoir include a sketch for his late version of *Les Grandes Baigneuses* in which he roughed in the form with cross-hatch pencil work over the paint; a view of the farm at Les Collettes and a delightful small study of *Coco Reading Claude*, along with paintings by some of the other artists, such as Albert André, who came to stay, and photos on the stairway by Willy Mayvald. Several of his small bronze sculptures are also dotted around the house, including the *Blacksmith* and the serene figure of *Maternity*.

In the small studio is his palette, a square of white ceramic, wiped clean after use so that he could see the pure colour as it would look on a white canvas. Not for Renoir the heavily encrusted kidney-shaped wooden palette of the stereotypical artist. In the large studio is his wheelchair, easel and some of the hats and costumes that his models – including the maids and his youngest son Claude (Coco) – were required to dress up in. Even the bathroom is on view, with a wonderful tub and, low on the wall next to the bidet, a small ceramic tile of a nude, probably by his son Claude. While you're there, be sure to visit the gardens too, complete with old farm buildings, ancient olive grove and terraces of orange trees, rose bushes and agaves. ❏

LEFT: Musée Renoir at Cagnes.

Map on page 120

trees and wisteria that overhang from roof gardens, while the traditional kitchen gardens serried beneath the ramparts are still zealously cultivated.

Steps to the left of the montée de la Bourgade, a street lined with restaurants, lead to the rue du Portis Long. This lane follows the inside of the ramparts through a long barrel vault past the ground floors and basements of the buildings. It provides a pleasantly cool walk in the heat of summer. You can also stroll along the outside of the ramparts; just go out through one of the medieval gateways.

Cagnes has many 15th- and 16th-century houses and a number of Renaissance houses with arcades near the castle. The oldest building here is the **Chapelle Notre-Dame-de-la-Protection** (information from tourist office, tel: 04 93 20 61 64; open Sun pm), a 14th-century structure on the edge of the town, erected as protection against plague and pestilence. It contains some beautiful 1530 frescos and has a large open sided porch offering a wide view south over Cagnes-sur-Mer to the Mediterranean and Nice airport.

Château Grimaldi

At the very top of the town and with an impressive crenellated tower, the **Château-Musée Grimaldi** (tel: 04 92 02 47 30; www.cagnes-tourisme. com; open May–Sept Wed–Mon 10am–noon, 2–6pm, Oct–Apr Wed–Mon 10am–noon, 2–5pm, closed 2 weeks in Nov; admission charge) began life as a simple medieval watchtower, built by Rainier Grimaldi in around 1300, before it was turned into a fine Renaissance residence by Baron Jean-Henri Grimaldi in the 1620s.

The castle is flanked by two squares. The place du Château is filled with cafés and restaurants, and to the north looks out over distant and frequently snow-covered mountains. A medieval archway takes you through to the place Grimaldi and the entrance to the chateau where an arcaded central courtyard with an impressive stairway, leading to the galleried loggia, shows the transition from medieval watchtower to

Stained glass window in Eglise du St-Pierre, Haut-de-Cagnes.

LEFT: ceiling detail in Château Grimaldi.
BELOW: Chapelle Notre-Dame-de-la-Protection interior.

The streets are lined with pretty flower displays in spring and summer.

Renaissance palace. A series of rooms on the ground floor recount the history of the olive tree and its importance to the region, and include a collection of old olive presses, terracotta storage jars and other implements. The chateau's grand reception rooms were on the first floor, and the highlight of the chateau is the *salle d'apparât*, which has an elaborate sculpted stucco fireplace and a frescoed ceiling with a vertiginous *trompe l'œil* vault. The dramatic central scene depicts the *Fall of Phaethon*, with horse and chariot tumbling from the sky, painted by the Genoese artist Giulio Benso Pietra between 1620 and 1624.

Portraits of a chanteuse

Housed in the former boudoir of the Marquise de Grimaldi, the **Donation Suzy Solidor** is an unusual collection of modern art that is definitely worth a look. In the 1930s, cabaret singer Suzy Solidor ran a famous nightclub in Paris called *La Vie Parisienne*. A thoroughly modern woman with the signature bobbed hair, she moved in artistic circles and had the brilliant idea of having her many friends paint her. In all, she had 224 portraits painted, of which 47 are on display here.

It is fascinating to see the same subject approached in so many different ways: Foujita surrounded an oriental-looking Suzy and her dog with gold-leaf panels; Van Dongen painted her in a sailor suit; Lydis treated her as a Vargas pin-up.

There's an odd, rapidly executed Picabia; drawings by Raoul Dufy and Jean Cocteau; and the jewel of the collection, a typically strange Tamara de Lempicka nude of her with a Cubist cityscape background.

The **Musée d'Art Moderne Méditerranéen** on the top floor is dedicated to quite a mixed bag of artists who have worked on the Côte d'Azur, many of them working in Cagnes itself. Above, a staircase leads up to a viewing terrace on the top of the tower.

St-Paul-de-Vence

On the way between Cagnes and Vence is the small but perfectly fortified town **St-Paul-de-Vence** ㉕,

now one of the region's main tourist spots and besieged day by day by coach parties. If you drive straight to Vence in the high season, you will have ample opportunity to examine St-Paul's fortifications from the traffic jam which usually extends all the way down the D36.

After parking your car outside the town, the Café de la Place, just by the main (north) gate, provides a good vantage point for watching a game of boules with a coffee and for spying on the rich and famous going in to eat at the celebrated restaurant **La Colombe d'Or**.

Artists' haven

During the 19th century, the village of St-Paul went into decline, and it was not until the 1920s that it was "discovered" by a group of artists, which included Bonnard, Modigliani, Soutine and Signac, who used to gather in a café that later became La Colombe d'Or.

They paid for meals and rooms with their paintings and sculptures, and the Roux family proprietors assembled a now priceless collection of art. The dining-room walls are adorned with works by Picasso, Braque, Miró and Matisse, and the garden wall features a huge, brilliantly coloured Léger mosaic. There is a Calder mobile and a Braque mosaic dove by the swimming pool, plus works by Dufy, Chagall, César and more at every turn.

The ring of sturdy ramparts, built in 1536 by François I, remains unbroken. A walk round them gives a good view of the surrounding countryside studded with dark cypresses and azure swimming pools. Glimpses of bougainvillea-filled gardens and treasured terraces hint at an insider's life beyond the stout wooden doors that are visible from the street.

A cannon captured at the Battle of Cérisoles in 1544 defends the north gate, the 14th-century Porte Royale or Porte de Vence, where a machicolated 13th-century tower houses the tourist centre. The gate opens straight on to rue Grande, a narrow crooked street which runs the full length of the village, lined with a pretty much non-stop array of sou-

Map on page 120

At the old town gate in medieval St-Paul-de-Vence.

BELOW:
the fortified town of St-Paul-de-Vence.

The Fondation Maeght

Pine woods on a hill next to the historic walled town of St-Paul-de-Vence are perhaps not the likeliest place to find a world-class museum of modern art, yet it is here in a building and sculpture park beautifully integrated with the landscape that you will find the Fondation Maeght. While the galleries are frequently rehung, with an important temporary exhibition every summer, you'll always find Braques, Mirós, Giacomettis and Chagalls on display, and some works – ceramic fountains by Miró, a pool by Braque, a mosaic by Chagall – are integrated into the design of the building itself, built in concrete and pink brick by Catalan architect Josep-Lluis Sert, who had been introduced to the Maeghts by Miró.

The tiny chapel, which contains Georges Braque's beautiful *White Bird on a Mauve Background* (1962), a delicate stained-glass panel set high above the altar, was also built by Sert. It was actually the first building on the site, erected in memory of the second son of the founders of the museum, Aimé and Marguerite Maeght. Aimé came from Nîmes, where he had studied engraving, and he met Marguerite in Cannes. They married and set up a successful electrical-goods business. Marguerite, indeed, had such an instinct for business that she once said of herself, "If I were cast up naked on a desert island, I'd make money." In 1930, they set up a printing business in Cannes followed by an art gallery six years later. Aimé did some engraving for artists who wanted books of their work. Prints and publications remain an important part of today's Galerie Maeght in Paris, set up in 1945.

After World War II, Aimé got to know the artist Pierre Bonnard through his printing work. Because Marguerite's father ran a grocery business, they were able to exchange scarce wartime provisions for artworks. Bonnard then introduced his new friends to Henri Matisse in Vence, another artist in need of groceries. The Maeghts soon got to know other people in the art world of the south, particularly Marc Chagall and Joan Miró.

Within 10 years, the Maeghts had risen to great prominence in the art world, their Paris gallery representing, among others, the work of Matisse, Miró, Giacometti, Chagall, Calder, Kandinsky and Braque.

The chapel the Maeghts built in memory of their son, Bernard, evolved into the foundation in 1964. Maeght was an art dealer who did something no art dealer had ever done before: he created a museum in his own name, paid for entirely by himself and filled with art from his own extensive stock. At the inauguration, André Malraux, the Minister of Cultural Affairs, said: "Here something has been attempted which has never been attempted before: to create, instinctively and lovingly, the universe in which modern art might find both its place and the other world once called supernatural."

After the deaths of his parents – Marguerite (1977) and Aimé (1981) – Adrien (b. 1930), already big in the publishing world, took over the helm of the Fondation Maeght, where he still presides over one of the most important collections of modern art in Europe and a vast library of art books. ❏

LEFT: the sculpture park at the Fondation Maeght.

venir shops and art-and-craft galleries. It passes place de la Grande-Fontaine, which has a pretty urn-shaped fountain. At the far end, the Porte de Nice leads to the cemetery, just outside the ramparts, where Marc Chagall is buried.

Many of the the 16th- and 17th-century houses bear coats of arms and are now "artists'" ateliers. Some of the medieval shops survive, usually as private homes; look out for a wide arch, beneath which is a doorway and an adjoining window. The window has a large marble sill which used to be the shop counter – it is a direct descendant of the Roman shop.

Sights in St-Paul

At the fountain a side street leads up to the **Collégiale de la Conversion de St-Paul**, which was begun in the 12th century and has an 18th-century bell tower. Among its treasures is a painting of St Catherine of Alexandria attributed to Tintoretto, at the end of the north aisle. Also displayed is a 13th-century enamel Virgin and Child and a silver reliquary said to hold St George's shoulder blade.

Across from the church, the old castle keep now contains the town hall and the **Musée d'Histoire de St-Paul** (tel: 04 93 32 41 13; open daily; admission charge), which presents local history in tableaux of wax figures – more endearing than it sounds. Much more interesting, however, is its exhibition of photographs of celebrities taken in St-Paul: Greta Garbo, Sophia Loren, Yul Brynner, Burt Lancaster, Jean-Paul Sartre and Simone de Beauvoir and many others enjoyed holidays here. Beside it, the Chapelle des Pénitents Blancs hosts summer concerts.

There are further riches close by; within easy walking distance of the village is the **Fondation Maeght** (montée des Trious, St-Paul-de-Vence; tel: 04 93 32 81 63; www.fondation-maeght.com; open daily July–Sept 10am–7pm, Oct–June 10am–12.30pm, 2.30–6pm; admission charge), a world-class museum of modern art, with works by Miró, Giacometti, Braque, Chagall, Calder

The Fondation Maeght includes indoor and outdoor exhibits.

BELOW: the work of Marc Chagall at the Fondation Maeght.

and many others in and around a building designed by Catalan architect José Luis Sert *(see page 156)*.

Inland to Vence

For all its illustrious historic past and artistic heritage, **Vence** , a short drive up the D2, retains far more of the feel of a real lived-in town than tourist-besieged St-Paul, with excellent food shops, a daily food market (mornings only) and pleasant leafy squares. Surrounded by rose farms and orange groves, which are sheltered by mountains to the north, its gentle climate has made it popular, especially with invalids – D.H. Lawrence died here in 1930 after coming to the town for his tuberculosis – and has resulted in property development scarring the surrounding hillsides.

Vence old town is the place to visit for original artwork and crafts; there are excellent food shops and a market too.

Vence has a chequered history. It was occupied by the Phoenicians and the Gauls. The Romans named it Ventium and made it an important religious centre when the town converted to Christianity early on, a change usually attributed to St Trophime. The first bishopric was founded here in AD 374, and the town quickly grew to become an important regional centre. The Lombards ravaged the region at the fall of the Roman Empire, and they were followed by the equally destructive Saracens.

Much of the history of Vence has been the conflict between the power of the bishops and that of the Villeneuves, because the lords of Villeneuve-Loubet shared seigneurial rights over the town with the Church. Vence won a great victory in the Wars of Religion against the Huguenots, but it suffered horribly from an outbreak of the plague that hit the town in 1572.

With the eruption of the French Revolution in 1789, Bishop Pisani was forced to flee the country and the see was never restored. Vence drifted into a steady decline so that by the beginning of the 20th century it was half-deserted, with many houses in ruins. But, today, tourism and sunbelt industries have transformed Vence into a bustling centre of more than 17,000 people, with an urban sprawl surrounding the surprisingly well-preserved old town.

BELOW: Vence old town at sunset.

Ramparts and ancient gates

Before you reach the old town, you pass through the place du Grand-Jardin and place du Frêne where there is a huge ash tree, which was planted in 1538. The medieval centre of Vence is very picturesque, and once you get away from the souvenir sellers, the lanes and alleyways are little changed from previous centuries – except that many of the lanes on the northeast side of the old town now have light and air where they end at the town ramparts; the walls have been cut down to waist height to reveal a mountain view instead of a prison-like wall.

The ramparts were built in the 13th and 14th centuries, and once had a broad walk running along the

Map on page 120

top. Vence has retained its town gates: the 13th-century Porte du Signadour incorporated into a defensive tower; the round arched Porte d'Orient pierced through in the 18th century (the date of 1592 refers to a battle during the Wars of Religion); the 14th-century Portail Levis, which once possessed a portcullis and opens on to rue de la Coste, one of the oldest lanes in the town; Le Pontis, built in 1863; and, most impressive of all, the **Portail du Peyra** built by Good King René in the 15th century and defended by a sturdy square tower.

In the 17th century, the **Château de Villeneuve-Fondation Emile Hugues** (tel: 04 93 58 15 78; www.museedevence.com; open Tues-Sun 10am–12.30pm, 2–6pm, closed between exhibitions; admission charge) was added to the side of the Portail du Peyra as the baronial residence of the powerful Villeneuve family. The building has been well restored and is now used for high-quality temporary exhibitions of modern and contemporary art.

The entrance through Portail du Peyra leads past a small fountain to the place du Peyra, which has a grand and ancient chestnut tree shading the cafés. Place Godeau, named after the famous 17th-century poet-bishop Antoine Godeau, who was a renowned wit and founder member of the Académie Française, lies outside the cathedral and was once the cemetery. Today, it is a pleasant place to stop for a drink. There is a granite Roman column in the centre of the square and some fine old houses around it.

Vence's old cathedral

The former **cathedral** is entered from place Clémenceau, the old Roman forum, where a flea market is held every Wednesday. The cathedral was built between the 12th and 15th centuries on the site of a Roman temple adapted for Christian use in the 5th century.

Buried in its outside walls along the passage Cahours are reused Roman slabs bearing inscriptions, one to the goddess Cybele and the ceremony of the Taurobolium, in which a bull was sacrificed to the gods, and another to Lucius

Little girls cool off in the fountain in place du Peyra, Vence, the location of a daily market.

LEFT: beehive-shaped bories.

Mysterious Dwellings

Dotting the arid back country of Provence and the Riviera are mysterious beehive-shaped huts called *bories*. No one knows exactly when they were first built, but some have been dated back to the Bronze Age. Seemingly primitive, these drystone constructions, made of concentric layers of flat, unmortared chunks of limestone, are in fact quite complex and extremely difficult to reproduce. Each flat stone was carefully chosen and placed according to some ancient calculation that allowed them to survive for centuries without so much as a dab of cement or a carved joint.

Bories have served as everything from shepherds' shelters, to bread ovens, to cramped living quarters, according to the needs of the epoch. Though *bories* have been documented since Roman times, most of those that remain, such as those around the Baou de Saint-Jeannet, date from the last three or four centuries. As recently as the 18th century, they were still being built using the same materials and techniques as were practised some 3,000 years ago. In use until the 19th century, today the *bories* serve as reminders of the ancient roots of this rugged region.

BELOW: Matisse's Chapelle du Rosaire (1947–51).

Veludius Valerianus, decurion of Vence, and his wife Vibia.

The cathedral consists of a nave with four aisles. The roof is carried on immense square pillars, lacking in ornament. The two side aisles were roofed over in the 15th century by a wide gallery which looks down into the nave through a row of arches, built to accommodate an enlarged congregation. Either side are two more aisles, where the chapels are located: one, which is said to contain the body of St Véran who died in 492, uses a carved Roman sarcophagus as both tomb and altar. Other Roman figures can be found in the walls, one in the pillar before the chapel of St Véran.

In 1499, at the same time as the roofing of the aisles, a tribune was added at the west end, housing the choir on a gallery high above the door. This contains the 51 famous wooden choir stalls imaginatively carved by Jacotin Bellot of Grasse, who began work on them in 1455 and finished them 25 years later. He carved animals and plants and recorded the everyday life of the

people and clergy, sometimes not at all reverently.

The cathedral also has a wonderfully carved wooden door taken from the destroyed *prévôté* or chapter house. In the baptistery, there is a mosaic designed by Marc Chagall in 1979 of Moses in the bulrushes.

Matisse's chapel

On the outskirts of Vence on the road towards St-Jeannet is another religious edifice that must not be missed by anyone interested in modern art. The **Chapelle du Rosaire** (468 avenue Henri Matisse; tel: 04 93 58 03 26; open Mon, Wed, Sat 2–5.30pm, Tues, Thur 10–11.30am, 2–5.30pm; admission charge) was designed by Henri Matisse between 1947 and 1951. The elderly Matisse had moved to the Villa le Rêve in Vence during World War II, to avoid the risk of bombs in Nice. After having been nursed back from ill health by the Dominican nuns, he was encouraged to decorate the chapel by the young Sister Jacques-Marie.

Although Matisse was not religious, his work at the chapel can be

seen as the artist's late spiritual masterpiece. The simple white chapel with tall narrow windows and ultramarine-and-white tiled roof, topped by a spindly wrought-iron cross, provides a beautifully calm and pure setting for Matisse's decoration. On three walls black-and-white line drawings on white tiles, depicting St Dominic, the Virgin and Child and the Stations of the Cross with the minimum of strokes, are typical of Matisse's extraordinary mastery of fluid line. The only colour in the white interior is brought by the blue-and-yellow stained-glass windows – a leaf motif representing the tree of life – which create dappled reflections over the walls.

On the minimalist stone altar is an equally simple and emotive tiny bronze crucifix, while the confessional door is an assemblage of wooden shapes painted white, echoing the traditional perforated doors in medieval churches. In an adjacent room, you can see the numerous preparatory sketches that Matisse made and the colourful priest's copes that he also designed.

Up the Var Valley

From Vence, the road to the northeast climbs to **St-Jeannet ㉗**, towered over by the great **Baou de St-Jeannet** (*baou* is Provençal for rock), which has inspired many a painter, among them Poussin, Fragonard, Renoir and Chagall. The village nestles on a terrace at the foot of the Baou. In some lights it looks no more than a natural outcrop of the rock; at other times the rock itself looks like a craggy chateau.

St-Jeannet is still known for its grapes and wine, but today most visitors come for its excellent rock-climbing and hiking. The face of the Baou offers 5,000 metres (16,400 ft) of rock-climbing possibilities, with another 4,000 metres (13,000 ft) on the southeastern slope. There is also a network of hiking trails, some of which pass remains of Celtic camps and ancient stone shepherds' huts (known as *bories, see page 159*).

St-Jeannet is a village of quiet courtyards, arched doorways and sloping lanes of stone steps. On a pleasant square with a fountain is the **Chapelle St-Bernadin**, built in 1666

Map on page 120

The sturdy clocktower in Vence.

BELOW: the craggy outcrop of Baou de St-Jeannet.

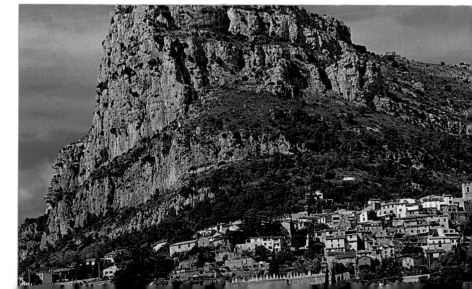

Map
on page
120

TIP

For more information
on the excellent
hiking trails and rock-
climbing around St-
Jeannet, contact the
tourist office, tel: 04
93 24 73 83.

BELOW: negotiating a
bend near St-Jeannet.
RIGHT:
market day in the hills.

and lit by only three stained-glass windows. Behind the church is a wonderful panorama from a small platform partly covered by an old archway with thick beams. Looking down at the houses below, it is amazing to see how the narrow terraces accommodate carefully tended *potagers* (kitchen gardens), parked cars and even swimming pools.

St-Jeannet has a number of fine restaurants, making it a good place to stop for lunch – before, or better still, after a climb. There is a path to the top of Baou St-Jeannet which starts from the Auberge St-Jeannet and takes about an hour each way. You will be rewarded with a spectacular view of the French and Italian Alps when you reach the viewing platform at the top.

Industrial development

Gattières ❷❽, further along the D2210, is a working perched village with steep streets filled with washing lines and barking dogs. The ancient buildings are there but are covered in pebble-dash or rendering, making it an interesting contrast to many other self-consciously picturesque villages with similar architecture.

South of St-Jeannet, on the D18, is **La Gaude**, a small, lively village built high above the River Cagne; it is the nearest village to the massive IBM Research and Study Centre on the D118 to St-Laurent. When Breuer's IBM centre was built it was highly praised for harmonising with the landscape – as well as two giant Y-shaped blocks supported by concrete pillars are able to. Now the area has become heavily built up with more industry, and the IBM architecture no longer stands out as being so modern or interesting.

Le Broc ❷❾ is another classic perched village, this time high on a rock overlooking the River Var. The view from here is extraordinary because the scale of human intervention on the landscape comes as a shock; the Var has been straightened out like a canal in a gigantic feat of engineering, taming it and binding it with freeways and industrial zones along either side. Quite a contrast to most other rural views. ❑

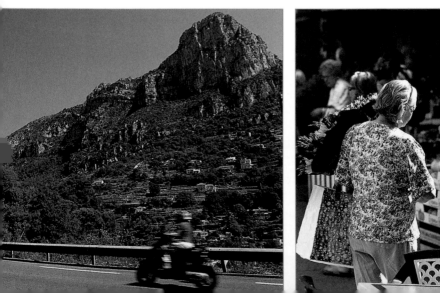

RESTAURANTS & CAFÉS

Restaurants

Haut-de-Cagnes

Le Cagnard
Rue de Pontis-Long. Tel: 04
93 20 73 21. Open L Fri–
Wed, D daily mid-Dec–
mid-Nov. €€€
www.le-cagnard.com
In an ancient fortified
building, chef Jean-Yves
Johany presents elegant
southern-inflected classic
cooking, such as foie gras
pigeon, Sisteron lamb with
petits farcis, and sea
bream with artichokes.

Entre Cour et Jardin
102 montée de la Bourgade.
Tel: 04 93 20 72 27. Open
L & D Wed–Sun. €€
http://entrecouretjardin.oreste.net
Friendly restaurant in a
little village street with
art exhibitions in the
courtyard twice a year
and a cosy vaulted cellar.

Fleur de Sel
85 montée de la Bourgade.
Tel: 04 93 20 33 33. Open
L & D Fri–Tues, D Thur.
€€–€€€
Inventive Provençal-
inspired cuisine at very
reasonable prices,
served in a delightful
village setting.

St-Jeannet

Hôtel Le St-Barbe
Place St-Barbe. Tel: 04 93 24
94 38. Open L & D Wed–Mon
mid-Dec–mid Nov. €–€€
Italian-influenced
cooking is offered at this
rustic auberge where you

dine on the terrace while
enjoying panoramic views.

St-Paul-de-Vence

La Colombe d'Or
1 place du Général de
Gaulle. Tel: 04 93 32 80 02.
Open L & D daily; closed
Nov–Christmas. €€€
www.la-colombe-dor.com
The legendary Colombe
d'Or was once
frequented by penniless
artists who persuaded
the original owner, Paul
Roux, to accept their
paintings in payment for
meals and board. Still
owned by the same
family, works by Miró,
Picasso, Modigliani,
Matisse and Chagall can
now be viewed by guests
of the hotel and
restaurant. The terrace
is arguably the most
beautiful in the region,
though this is a place
to come to for the
atmosphere and the jet-
set clientele as much as
the classic cuisine.

Vence

La Farigoulette
15 rue Henri Isnard. Tel:
04 93 58 01 27. Open
L Thur–Mon, D Mon,
Thur–Sat; closed winter
school hols. €€
Haute cuisine-trained
Patrick Bruot puts his
own adventurous spin on
Provençal cooking at this
attractive restaurant with
a lovely outside terrace.

**Table d'Amis Jacques
Maximin**
689 chemin de la Gaude.
Tel: 04 93 58 90 75. Open
L Sun in July and Aug,
D Wed–Sun, daily in July
and Aug; closed mid-Nov–
mid-Dec. €€€
www.tabledamis.com
Legendary chef Jacques
Maximin is a Riviera
personality. After making
his name with nouvelle
cuisine at the Negresco
in Nice and Pré Catalan
in Paris, he opened his
own fashionable yet
more relaxed restaurant
in this comfortable
bourgeois house with
lovely gardens on the
outskirts of Vence. Here
he goes back to his rural
routes and brings his
creative talents to the
first-rate local produce.

Café/Bar

St-Paul-de-Vence

Café de la Place
Place du Général de Gaulle.
Open daily. €
This simple café, bar
and tabac is as much an
institution in its own way
as the Colombe d'Or
opposite. Sit on the
terrace to watch the
boules players and lunch
on steak and chips,
salad or hearty plats du
jour such as lou fassum
(stuffed cabbage).

PRICE CATEGORIES

Prices for a three-course
meal without wine:
€ = under €25
€€ = €25–40
€€€ = over €40

RIGHT: try a Provençal wine with dinner.

NICE

France's fifth-largest city and the capital of the Côte d'Azur, Nice has been enchanting visitors since the 18th century. With its perfect climate, Italian inheritance, world-class museums and lively markets, the city lives up to its name

Nice is a wonderful city, as sophisticated as any in France, with a lively southern quality that makes it unique. Once known as the winter capital of the world, it ranks as one of the most important Côte d'Azur beach resorts – but it would be wasted on a simple seaside holiday. Fringed by a pebbly beach curving around the Baie des Anges, Nice pleases most when the sea and sun simply enhance some of the best art and culture, food and wine the Riviera has to offer.

It doesn't feel like a tourist town and yet its development was due largely to foreign visitors, especially the British, who spotted its potential for raising northern spirits two centuries ago. Thus it combines a Provençal heart with a welcoming *joie de vivre*, a wealth of museums with enough gardens, fountains and palm trees to raise life alfresco to an art form.

The city of **Nice ❶** has officially been part of France only since 1860. Before that it had closer ties with Italy. Local jokers, however, like to dispute even this, saying that for 62 years, up to 1990, Nice was the personal fiefdom of the Médecin men – first Jean, then his son Jacques – both of whom ruled as mayor and left indelible marks. Jacques ("Jacou") was loved by the Niçois,

and when he died in 1998, they turned out in their thousands for his funeral, despite the fact he had been indicted for tax evasion and corruption in 1990 and fled to Uruguay.

His downfall closed just another chapter in the city's see-saw history of changing management which began in 350 BC with the Greeks, who named it after the goddess Nike ("she who brings victory"), and variously saw in power Romans, Counts of Provence, Dukes of Savoy and Kings of Sardinia. As a

Maps:
City 166
Area 180

LEFT: around the coast at Nice.
BELOW: a Nice Carnival float reflects the city's *joie de vivre*.

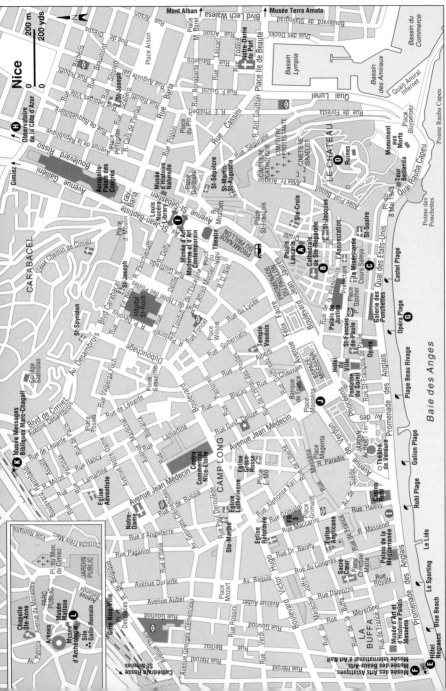

Map on page 166

tug-of-love child, the "Maid of Provence" certainly had a turbulent upbringing, and was a ward of the Italian court for most of 500 years.

Today, Nice is essentially French, but its character and temperament remain Italian, with constant reminders that the frontier is still just 32 km (20 miles) away. However, it is rightly proud of its own language, *Nissard*, its own surrounding "county" of the Alpes-Maritimes and its cuisine, which goes much further than just a famous salad.

It is now a unique city of Western, medieval and oriental influences, a provincial metropolis that is the richest, most attractive tourist centre outside Paris. Nice is France's fifth-largest city and has the country's second-largest airport. It has also become a business and cultural centre to be reckoned with. Business tourism is increasingly important, and recent developments, chic new hotels and the new tramway (scheduled to open during 2007) reflect an increasing awareness of its potential.

A French Bournemouth

It was the British who invented the name "Riviera". They laid the foundations for its present-day capital and were certainly in no doubt about its being the brightest jewel in the river of towns sparkling all the way from Cannes to Monte-Carlo.

A thriving English colony subsequently developed. Well-heeled British aristocrats and retired army officers zealously set about turning Nice into a kind of sanitised Bournemouth, with hotels called Westminster and West End in a sector they named Newborough.

Indeed, it is an English clergyman, the Rev. Lewis Way, whom we must thank for the promenade des Anglais, the road running along the seafront of the Baie des Anges. He was a skilled missionary with remarkable powers of persuasion, who talked his flock into providing construction work for men thrown out of work by a severe frost which killed the area's olive groves and orange trees in 1821.

By 1887, when poet Stephen Liégeard first named the coastline the Côte d'Azur, Nice had already expanded to the size of Cannes today, and was regularly attracting over 25,000 winter visitors, mainly by train. There were shops selling trinkets made of olive wood inscribed with the words "Nice", and *"Je reviendrai"* – forerunners of today's "Nice is Nice" T-shirts and *"J'aime la Côte d'Azur"* bumper stickers.

The old town

The promenade du Paillon, the central green artery of parks and gardens, separates the oldest part of the city to the east from the newer part. Signposted either as **Vieille Ville** or Le Vieux Nice, the old town has to be the pièce de résistance: a cracked basin of russet, yellow, pink and beige earth tones. You are now

An architectural detail above the old town gate.

BELOW: Le Vieux Nice in russet and yellow.

Matisse in Nice

Matisse was inspired by many places in the south of France, and spent sojourns painting in Collioure and St-Tropez as well as travelling to Algeria, Morocco and Tahiti. But it is in Nice that his presence is felt most strongly, and which finally became his home. "What made me stay was the great coloured reflections of January, the luminosity of the days," he declared.

He first went there in 1917, staying in the Hôtel Beau Rivage (which then had a seafront façade), painting the sea and the great sweeping bay of the promenade des Anglais fringed with palm trees. He often visited the ageing Renoir at his villa, Les Collettes in Cagnes a few miles along the coast, drawing inspiration from the older painter's determination to paint despite the infirmity of arthritis. In Nice, Matisse moved his family into a small apartment at 105 quai du Midi, then to a small house on Mont Boron from where he could watch the dawn each morning. Here his daughter Marguerite posed for him on the balcony overlooking the sea.

After returning to Paris and the north of France at the end of World War I, he came back to Nice, to the light and colour he craved, staying several times in the Hôtel de la Méditerranée on the promenade des Anglais and settling into a pattern of winter seasons, often spent alone, painting models in exotic sensual interiors. He took an apartment on place Charles Félix in the old town, where he filled the studio with props and costumes, the Moorish screens and rugs that would appear in his paintings for decades to come.

With his wife Amélie, he moved to a bigger apartment on the place Charles Félix, with superb views from balconies on two sides, where he painted his famous odalisques, framed by shuttered windows and flowers, capturing forever the voluptuous ease of the Riviera. Apart from a long trip to Tahiti, and visits to Paris and America, where he was working on *The Dance*, he spent the rest of his life in Nice. He was sustained by visits from his long-suffering family, swimming and canoeing, and a succession of devoted models, who despite their sensuous poses, were never lovers. The most important model was Lydia, a Russian refugee who became his devoted secretary, ultimately precipitating a permanent rift with Madame Matisse.

At the beginning of World War II, Matisse moved to Cimiez, buying two large apartments in the vast empty Regina Hotel, which he filled with tapestries, screens and sculptures, a jungle of plants, and his growing collection of birds, where he continued to paint, make sculptures, etchings and finally paper cut-outs, "drawing with scissors". He spent part of the war years in Vence in the Villa le Rêve where he designed the chapel which is the most moving monument to his memory. But it represented no last-minute conversion. "Why not a brothel, Matisse?" asked Picasso. "Because nobody asked me, Picasso."

At age 79, he moved back to Cimiez, where he died in 1954, his walls completely covered in cut-outs of flowers, birds, acrobats and dancers.

The Matisse Museum, a beautiful 17th-century Italianate villa in Cimiez, houses Matisse's works from every period, as well as the vases, shell furniture and Moroccan wall-hangings *(see page 174).* ❏

LEFT: the Matisse Museum.

entering the Painted City, where the municipality has breathed new life into the 13th century. In the maze of tall, narrow streets, butchers, bakers and spice merchants now rub shoulders with nightclubs, art galleries and internet cafés.

There is always a bustle about the place. For all its medieval seductions, scaffolding is a perpetual hazard, and ladders and buckets of paint are winched away with bewildering urgency in a society more at ease with the Midi spirit of *farniente* (doing nothing). Look up and admire façades adorned with *trompe l'œils* and frescos, especially at the so-called Adam and Eve house in rue de la Poissonnerie; the *Pistone* building in rue du Marché; No. 27 rue Benoît Bunico; and in rue Pairolière, where the Maison de la Treille (the house with a climbing vine) was the inspiration for one of Raoul Dufy's pictures.

The showpiece is the **Palais Lascaris** (15 rue Droite, tel: 04 93 62 05 54; open Wed–Mon 10am–6pm; free), a 17th-century mansion now restored as an elegant museum, complete with pharmacy and a splendid open staircase in the Genoese style, frescoed ceilings, Flemish tapestries and rococo silver inlaid doors. On the top floor is a small exhibition of local life, crafts, embroidery and traditional pottery.

Rue Droite, so named not because it is straight but for the fact that it directly connected the two main gates of the old city, is now where many young French artists have their ateliers, following their forebears who made an impressive contribution to the history of art. Le Vieux Nice first produced a school of primitive painters in the 15th and 16th centuries; it was home to the Van Loos in the 17th; Rodin worked here in the 19th and it has given its name to the modern Ecole de Nice centred around Yves Klein, Arman and César.

The streets become darker and narrower the further in you go, with intriguing scents and smells coming from the doorways. As you advance through the labyrinth, look at the lintels, some of which are inscribed with dates and incantations; *interna meliora* – "Better things inside" – hangs over a former brothel on rue de la Place Vieille.

Place St-François, a few streets to the north of the Palais, is where the morning fish market unravels every day (except Mon). René-Socca on **rue Miralheti** is the place to sample classic street food such as *socca*, a chickpea pancake not found anywhere else in France.

On place Rossetti is the painted façade (1650) of the **Cathédrale de Ste-Réparate** , dedicated to the city's patron saint. Admire the bell tower and roof of coloured tiles and look out for baroque music concerts. The square in front is also the best spot for a coffee or an ice cream – try the home-made ices at Fennocchio (classic flavours as well as acquired tastes such as tomato-basil, violet and Nutella).

Map on page 166

The 18th-century place Garibaldi, on the northern edge of Vieux Nice, is close to the church of St-Martin-St-Augustin, where Italian revolutionary Giuseppe Garibaldi (1807–1882) was baptised. He is buried in Le Château cemetery.

BELOW: the interior of Cathédrale de Ste-Réparate.

The cannon shot heard at midday in Nice was the idea of an Englishman, Sir Thomas Coventry, who had become so irritated by irregular mealtimes, he paid for a cannon to be shot regularly at noon from Le Château hill.

Continuing on towards the sea you reach the **Palais de Justice**, inaugurated in 1892, the city's impressive law courts. The newly renovated square on which it stands has a market on Saturday mornings selling books and pottery. Near by is the one-time palace of the Sardinian kings, now housing the Préfecture.

The markets

The promenade between the old town and the sea is known as the **cours Saleya** ⊙, the site of Nice's main markets: fruit and vegetables every morning except Monday, and a vibrant flower market (Tues–Sat 6am–5.30pm, Sun until 1pm). This is the best place to take the pulse of Nice, a complete antidote to the pace of life on the other side of the Paillon. On Mondays a large flea market sells a bountiful variety of antique furniture, china and linen.

The performance is never-ending, though it changes dramatically with the firing of a midday cannon. To the sound of flapping pigeon wings, the scenery is transformed miraculously as gangs of sweepers armed with brooms and high-pressure hoses clean up the market. Chairs and tables come out. Hardly a piece of ground is left unoccupied as the stage is set for a bravura performance of Niçois life.

From his third-floor apartment in the big yellow house at the end of the cours (No. 1; it has snarling faces of plaster lions protruding from it), Matisse painted those iconic pictures of the blue sea, the palm trees and the houses with green shutters.

Through the archway to the quai des Etats-Unis you will find the **Galerie de la Marine and Galerie des Ponchettes** (77 quai des Etats-Unis; tel: 04 93 62 37 11; open Tues–Sat 10am–6pm; free) in two rows of low white buildings, originally used by the fishermen, then converted into galleries for local artists and inaugurated by a Matisse exhibition in 1950.

Le Château

At the eastern end of the quai des Etats-Unis is a lift that can take you to the top of the hill called **Le**

Map on page 166

Château . But don't go looking for the chateau; it is just a trick of the tongue. One has not existed since the illegitimate son of James II razed it in 1706 on the orders of Louis XIV, thus sealing the fate of a citadel that was more than 2,000 years old. At the top of the 90-metre (300-ft) hill are gardens, a splendid baroque cemetery, playgrounds and a couple of discreet snack bars, but best of all are the panoramic views.

A seaside promenade

The **promenade des Anglais**, the coastal road that was used by about 100 English families and their carriages after it was built in the 1820s, has today become one of the most clogged thoroughfares in France. It is a six-lane highway, 5 km (3 miles) long, on which only the aggressive survive – you need to be alert. Watch your window, too, if you stop at the lights in summer: resplendent with proud palms and pretty flower beds, the Prom (even the French call it that) has an automatic watering system and the sprinklers are liable to turn your car into a jacuzzi if your reflexes aren't sharp enough. One Sunday a month traffic is banished, and the Prom is reserved for walkers, roller skaters, cyclists and horse-drawn carriages. Poodles permitted, if not de rigueur.

Today's scene on the promenade des Anglais is very different from its 19th-century counterpart. When Henri Negresco's palace first opened its doors in 1913 they faced north: 150 years after Tobias Smollett introduced sea-bathing here, it still had not dawned on anyone that the future of tourism lay in hotels with their fronts, not their backs, to the sea.

The famed **Hôtel Negresco** remains the crown of the Promenade. It is a national monument where visiting heads of state still occupy entire floors, and the flamboyance of the exterior is only eclipsed by the jewels within. This was where F. Scott Fitzgerald stayed, and although you won't find a "diamond as big as the Ritz", you can see a crystal chandelier by Baccarat with 16,309 stones and weighing more than a tonne, designed originally for the Tsar of Russia.

Isadora Duncan, the notorious American dancer, was staying at the Hotel Negresco when she had her fatal accident in 1927. The long, flowing scarf she was wearing caught in the wheel of her Bugatti car and broke her neck.

BELOW: the elegant Hôtel Negresco on the promenade des Anglais.

Also worth noting further east along the Promenade are the **Palais de la Méditerranée**, a famously crumbling 1920s hotel and casino recently reborn as a luxury hotel, with a splendid Art Deco façade, and the **Casino Ruhl**, which continues to delight gamblers every night.

Museums by the Prom

There are several museums in this area of town: behind the Hôtel Negresco, at 65 rue de France, is the **Musée d'Art et d'Histoire Palais Masséna** (scheduled to reopen during 2007 after several years of refurbishment; tel: 04 93 88 11 34), housed in a splendid Italianate villa built in 1898. Exhibitions on the city's history span from Napoleon Bonaparte's Empire to the late 19th century, laid out in 23 rooms over three floors. The 19th-century garden surrounding the villa is also being completely rejuvenated.

Further west towards Nice airport is the **Musée des Arts Asiatiques**  (405 promenade des Anglais; tel: 04 92 29 37 00; www.arts-asiatiques. com; open Wed–Mon 10am–6pm, Oct–Apr until 5pm; admission charge). Located on a lake within the huge botanical garden of Parc Floral Phoenix, the museum is a sleek glass-and-metal structure with a small collection of rare pieces, including 4,000-year-old Chinese jade artefacts. You can participate in a tea ceremony in the tea pavilion (for reservations call: 04 92 29 37 02).

Heading back towards the city centre you'll find the sugar-pink Château Ste-Hélène and the **Musée International d'Art Naïf** (avenue Val Marie; tel: 04 93 71 78 33; open Wed–Mon 10am–6pm; admission charge). Formerly the home of perfume magnate René Coty, it has a fascinating collection of 1,000 works from 27 countries.

Musée des Beaux-Arts (33 avenue des Baumettes; tel: 04 92 15 28 28; www.musees-beaux-arts-nice.org; open Tues–Sun 10am–6pm; admission charge), a Belle Epoque villa built for Russian royalty mainly devoted to 19th-century painting, with some early 20th-century highlights from Van Dongen, Dufy, Bonnard, Kisling and Signac.

On the Baie des Anges

The locals' sunny disposition is no doubt helped by the proximity of the **beaches**. The 5 km (3 miles) of curving seafront may be disappointingly pebbly, but the beaches are clean, like the sea, and run right through the heart of town. For a quick dip, there is nothing wrong with the public beaches (with their free showers), but various private establishments offer excellent facilities at half the price charged down the coast at Cannes.

One favourite is **Opéra Plage** , which claims to be the oldest in France, run by the same family since 1906, just a towel's shake from the old Opera House.

Traffic barrelling down the sea front vanishes into a tunnel in front

Architect Jean-Michel Wilmotte redesigned all the blue chairs on the promenade des Anglais. The old chairs have become a huge sculpture by Arman filling a floor-to-ceiling window in the Museum of Modern Art.

BELOW:
art exhibits at Musée des Beaux-Arts.

of the Opera House and emerges at the **port**, a long-neglected side of Nice which, with quays lined with terracotta and ochre buildings, bobbing yachts and excellent restaurants, is the epitome of the Mediterranean harbour.

For a city whose history depends so much on the sea, the port is disappointingly bereft of attractions, its main attribute being the bathing rocks on its eastern edge from which you can see the Corsican ferry glide by. Just beyond the port is the **Musée Terra Amata** (25 boulevard Carnot; tel: 04 93 55 59 93; open Tues–Sun 10am–6pm; admission charge), an archaeological museum built on the site where human and animal remains from around 400,000 years ago were discovered. Sights include a prehistoric cave and a human footprint in limestone.

A view of the new town

For the best overview of what is not really a very complicated city you should have a car and drive east, up to the ruined fort of **Mont Alban**, approached through 140 hectares (345 acres) of municipal forest on Mont Boron, a good place for picnics. Mont Gros to the north is the site of the **Observatoire de la Côte d'Azur** (tel: 04 92 00 31 12; www.obs-nice.fr; guided visits Wed and Sat 2.45pm; botanical tours of the surrounding gardens and groves of olive trees Wed 9.45am), built by Charles Garnier and Gustave Eiffel.

From a distance it is easy to see how the city has evolved in three different parts, with the **River Paillon** in the middle. Don't bother searching for the river on a map; it is only a trickle, and the entire river bed has been covered over with a promenade, roads, parks and hanging gardens hiding a bus terminus and car park. This is the site of the **Acropolis** convention centre, decorated inside and out with the work of contemporary artists.

Here also is the **Musée d'Art Moderne et d'Art Contemporain** (MAMAC; promenade des Arts; tel: 04 97 13 42 01; www.mamac-nice.org; open Tues–Sun 10am–6pm; admission charge), a pet project of former mayor Jacques Médecin. The museum concentrates on French and American art from the 1960s to the present and attracts topnotch temporary exhibitions.

Highlights include some iconic pieces of Pop Art and a room devoted to local hero Yves Klein. Look out for Arman's sliced violins and Klein's blue-painted nude models. The most recent addition, which enlivens the exterior, is a donation of 170 gloriously colourful sculptures by Nikki de St Phalle.

To the north of the promenade des Arts is the stunning new **Louis Nucéra library**, dominated by the *Tête Carrée*, a monumental square head designed by Sacha Sosno, containing 300,000 volumes.

At the southern end of the Paillon is **place Masséna** , the modern

Map on page 166

TIP

For the hub of Niçois avant-garde, visit **Villa Arson** (20 avenue Stephen Liégeard; tel: 04 92 07 73 73; www.villa-arson.org; open Wed–Mon 2–6pm, June–Sept until 7pm; free), a 17th-century villa set in large gardens, with an art centre, art school and café.

BELOW: the Acropolis Convention Centre.

The Museum of Modern and Contemporary Art (MAMAC) has an important collection of French and American Art from the 1960s on. Le Relève (16 bis rue Delille) is a bar and restaurant conveniently located for the museum, with good music and art exhibitions.

RIGHT: Nice is a party town in February.

heart of the city, with its neoclassical red colonnades. This is the new town, with shops, hotels and a pedestrian zone housing smart designer boutiques. **Avenue Jean Médecin**, a wide thoroughfare lined with plane trees to the north of place Masséna, is the main business and shopping street. Beyond place Masséna, the **Jardin Albert I** is a refreshing oasis of fountains looking across to the sea.

Cimiez, a Roman enclave

On a hill north of the city, the suburb of **Cimiez** is most easily reached from the boulevard de Cimiez. Here, the Romans built their Cemenelum to compete with rival Greek Nikaïa down the road. It is noted for its Roman ruins, including baths and an amphitheatre that is a venue for the Nice Jazz Festival *(see below)*.

Before you climb the hill, don't miss the **Musée National Messages Bibliques Marc-Chagall** (avenue du Docteur Ménard; tel: 04 93 53 87 20; www.musee-chagall.fr; open Wed–Mon 10am–5pm; admission charge), specially designed with

mosaics and stained glass by the artist. It houses Chagall's masterpiece, the *Messages Bibliques,* and is the biggest collection of his work.

At the top of the hill is the **Musée d'Archéologie** (160 avenue des Arènes; tel: 04 93 81 59 57; open Wed–Mon 10am–6pm; admission charge), which displays finds from the Roman town, including ceramics, coins, jewellery and tools. Here, too, is the very popular **Musée Matisse** at No. 164 (tel: 04 93 81 08 08; www.musee-matisse-nice. org; open Wed–Mon 10am–6pm; admission charge). Both Matisse and fellow artist Raoul Dufy are buried in the nearby Franciscan cemetery, with its peaceful cloister of orange trees, Bréa altarpieces in the church and a touching museum of Franciscan life.

Once-fashionable Cimiez still has intimations of empire. The crowned heads of Europe – Britain, Sweden, Denmark, Portugal, Belgium and the entire Russian imperial family – once wintered up here in nine "palais-hôtels" modelled on the formidable Regina Palace, inaug-

Carnaval de Nice and the Jazz Festival

Nice celebrates Mardi Gras with the largest pre-Lent carnival in France (www.nicecarnaval.com), culminating in a spectacular explosion of fireworks above the Baie des Anges. For two weeks around Shrove Tuesday huge papier-mâché floats proceed through the town amid confetti battles, bands and throngs of spectators. Highlights include the *bataille des fleurs*, when thousands and thousands of fresh flowers are tossed into the crowds, and the ceremonial burning of *Sa Majesté Carnaval*, the carnival king, on the promenade des Anglais at the end of the festival.

Set in the vast Jardins de Cimiez, Nice's prestigious jazz festival features three separate stages – including a dramatic 4,000-seat Roman amphitheatre – where an eclectic mix of international musicians perform for eight days in July. The atmosphere is a cross between a Gallic Woodstock and a musical fair: families arrive en masse with pushchairs, Grandma and the dog and spread picnics under the century-old olive trees. For information on the festival log on to www.nicejazzfest.com or contact the tourist office *(see page 277)* or www.nicetourisme.com.

urated by Queen Victoria in 1897, who included in her vast retinue an entire battalion of Bengal lancers.

In the western suburbs, on avenue Nicolas II, you can find startling evidence of the once thriving Russian colony in the form of the **Cathédrale St-Nicolas** (open daily 9am–noon, 2.30–5pm, June–Sept until 6pm), the finest Russian Orthodox church outside the motherland. Its five green-and-gold onion domes pleased Tsar Nicholas II himself. Services are in Russian.

A gutsy city

Nice might miss its castle, but not much else. Despite being top dog in the holiday league, with nearly four million visitors a year, and having a comparatively small resident population of around 350,000, it hasn't allowed its character and ambience to be subsumed into soulless skyscrapers. Pretty villas hide among the olives and parasol pines on the hills overlooking the bay. Tunnels of plane trees line the main streets, which lead to shaded squares and fountained gardens, ideal for life alfresco.

In the centre, the *fin de siècle* glory of the buildings, all of uniform height and rococo charm, sings to you in friezes, frescos and domed *arpeggios*. The city really has a human scale.

It is a real gutsy town, with its own gutsy wine (Bellet, whose vines were planted by the Phoenicians who founded Marseille), a commercial life based on more than just its flower industry and a cultural richness second only to Paris. It is also surprisingly efficient and clean, equipped with automatic loos and spotless bus shelters. Wardens guard against vandalism in its 300 hectares (740 acres) of public greenery, and hundreds of gardeners start work at 5am daily.

And for all its classic Mediterranean laissez-faire, Nice has developed into a highly modern city with state-of-the-art facilities: the Acropolis conference centre, with a 2,500 seat auditorium; the Arenas business zone opposite the airport, and Nikaïa, an 8,000-seat concert hall, opened by Elton John, who has a villa east of the city on Mont Boron. ❑

Maps:
City 166
Area 180

Roman remains at Cimiez, part of the archaeological park known as Les Arènes north of the city.

BELOW: well-entrenched on the seafront.

RESTAURANTS, CAFÉS & BARS

Local cuisine in Nice is a creative mix of French and Italian, with many authentic Niçois dishes. Restaurants can be superb and expensive, but there are many cheaper places and a great tradition of street food. Local delicacies include *pissaladière*, a pizza with onions, anchovies and black olives; *pistou*, vegetable soup with basil; *ratatouille*, vegetable stew; *beignets de fleurs de courgette*, stuffed courgette flowers, the ubiquitous *pan-bagnat*, a large roll stuffed with *salade Niçoise* and *socca*, chickpea pancakes, served at beach cafés *(see page 56)*.

Restaurants

L'Ane Rouge
7 quai des Deux Emmanuel. Tel: 04 93 89 49 63. Open L & D; closed Wed, Thurs midday & Feb. €€€
www.anerougenice.com
A classic seafood restaurant overlooking the port, where they add value to lobster in highly imaginative ways. Try the stuffed courgette flowers with langoustine or the superb *bourride*, a creamy soup of dried cod. Friendly staff.

Les Epicuriens
6 place Wilson. Tel: 04 93 80 85 00. Open L & D; closed Sat midday, Sun & Aug. €€€
Smart bistro, with terrace for sunny days, serves Niçoise specialities with a sophisticated twist and is much favoured for lunch by chic locals.

L'Escalinada
22 rue Pairolière. Tel: 04 93 62 11 71. Open L & D; closed Sat & Sun eve. €€
Long-established family restaurant in the old town serving authentic Niçois cuisine; try their home-made pasta, ravioli and gnocchi, stuffed squid and slow-cooked *daubes*.

Le Grand Balcon
10 rue St-François-de-Paule. Tel: 04 93 62 60 74. Open L & D; closed Sat & Sun midday. €€€
Cosy, with velvet drapes, Renaissance paintings and the ambience of an English library with low tables and comfy sofas. Exotic dishes include wild sea bass risotto, lemon risotto and cod and coconut curry.

Jouni-Atelier du Goût
60 boulevard Franck-Pillat. Tel: 04 97 08 14 80. Open L & D daily. €€€
Finnish chef Jouni Tormanen, with experience of both Ducasse at Louis XV and the legendary Spanish restaurant El Bulli, brings an original twist to Mediterranean cuisine, in the restaurant's new location on the harbour.

La Merenda
4 rue Terrasse. No phone. Open L & D Mon–Fri. €€
A tiny bistro with the most celebrated Niçois specialities in town, (stuffed sardines and stockfish particularly recommended) but opening hours are limited, it's cash only and there's no phone so you have to go in person to book.

La Part des Anges
17 rue Gubernatis. Tel: 04 93 62 69 80. Open Br, L & D Mon–Sat; closes at 8pm Mon–Thurs. €
Wine cellar and restaurant offering a selection of local and vintage French wines served with Niçois specialities to complement the wine. Drink by the glass or order a bottle for dinner at the *cave* price.

La Petite Maison
11 rue St-François-de-Paule. Tel: 04 93 92 59 59. Open L & D Mon–Sat. €€–€€€
Fashionable restaurant with a clientele of footballers and models, its motto is "*tous célèbres ici*", so don't expect a quiet night. Try dishes with an original twist like sea bass cooked in crust of salt and tuna *au poivre*.

Restaurant du Gésu
1 place du Gésu, Nice. Tel: 04 93 62 26 46. Open L & D Mon–Sat; closed mid-Dec–mid-Jan. €
Petit farcis, grilled red peppers, ravioli and pizzas are among the rustic fare served at this busy budget joint in Vieux Nice, though you come here for the raucous atmosphere more than the rather heavy

cooking. The ceiling draped with football scarves from all over the world matches the young international clientele.

La Table Alziari

4 rue François Zanin. Tel: 04 93 80 34 03. Open L & D Tues–Sat. €–€€

Simple bistro in the heart of the old town, established by the same family that sells Nice's best olive oil (the original shop is on rue St-François-de-Paule), serves a limited range of Niçois classics from stuffed vegetables and sardines to rich, meaty *daubes*.

L'Univers – Christian Plumail

54 boulevard Jean Jaurès. Tel: 04 93 62 32 22. Open L & D; closed Sat & Mon midday, Sun. €€€

Classy brasserie full of modern artworks serves *nouvelle* Mediterranean dishes like squid carpaccio and artichoke with parmesan.

La Zucca Magica

4 bis quai Papacino. Tel: 04 93 56 25 27. Open L & D Tues–Sat. €

Marco Folicaldo is the Italian chef of this vegetarian restaurant in the old port, his face as friendly, round and jolly as his signature pumpkins. The fresh menu announced daily – there is no choice – offers vegetables with pasta, grains, good olive oil and Italian cheeses.

Cafés

Café des Fleurs

13 cours Saleya. Tel 04 93 62 31 33. Open L daily. €

Traditional bar with zinc counter and wooden tables inside, terrace outside for coffee, tea and selection of beers.

Café Le Nôtre

1 promenade des Anglais. Tel: 04 93 88 13 90. Open Br & L daily. €€

Originally a celebrated pâtisserie, Café Le Nôtre has now opened its doors in Nice in a convenient location with a terrace on the Prom, for high quality and stylish snacks, coffees, teas and tisanes, breakfasts and full meals. Not to mention cakes, pastries and ice creams to die for.

La Cantine de Lulu

26 rue Alberti. Tel: 04 93 62 15 33. Open Mon–Fri, closed Mon pm & Aug. €

Friendly, unpretentious café with an open kitchen serving Niçois classics like courgette-flower fritters, mesclun salad and *pissaladière*, stockfish and *daube de boeuf*. First Friday each month features a *grand ailloli* – garlic dip served with vegetables.

Chez René Socca

2 rue Miralheti. Tel: 04 93 92 05 73. Open L & D Tues–Sun; closed three weeks in Jan. €

Popular local place for *socca*, self-service with basic wooden tables inside and out.

Fenocchio

2 place Rosetti. Tel: 04 93 80 72 52. Open daily; closed Nov–Feb. €

Wonderful outside café on a square perfect for people-watching; famous for the best and most original selection of Italian ice cream in Nice.

Grand Café de Turin

5 place Garibaldi. Tel: 04 93 62 29 52. Open Br, L & D daily. €€

Big, bustling brasserie – is the best place for seafood, from a simple plate of oysters to an entire plateau of every kind of crustacean imaginable. Service is brisk, the clientele seriously focused on eating – a truly French experience.

Le Safari

1 cours Saleya. Tel: 04 93 80 18 44. Open L & D daily €€

A big terrace café with Mediterranean blue shutters; try deep, rich calamari daube or *bagna cauda*, a hot anchovy dip with raw vegetables.

Bars

Le Comptoir

20 rue St-François-de-Paule. Tel: 04 93 92 08 80. Open L & D daily June–Sept, Mon–Sat Oct–May. €€

A 1930s-style Art Deco bar and restaurant perfect for late-night dining.

La Relève

16 bis rue Delille. Tel: 04 93 92 38 34. Open L & D, L only Mon & Tues; closed Sun. €

Centrally located bar and restaurant, convenient for MAMAC art museum, with good music and art exhibitions.

PRICE CATEGORIES

Prices for a three-course meal without wine.

€ = under €25
€€ = €25–€40
€€€ = over €40

LEFT: try a terrace café for people-watching.
RIGHT: seafood on place P. Gautier.

CAP FERRAT AND THE GOLDEN TRIANGLE

Exclusive estates and villas cling to Cap Ferrat, a legacy of the Belle Epoque, when the rich and famous came to stay. Celebrities are still drawn to this mountainous part of the Côte d'Azur, where the scenic Basse Corniche links up medieval Villefranche with the refined, old-world town of Beaulieu and the perched village of Eze

For a touch of the Riviera's Belle Epoque glamour, it is perhaps best to go along the coast just east of Nice, to the area known as the **Corne d'Or** – Golden Horn or Golden Triangle – which includes Cap Ferrat, Beaulieu and Villefranche. Here the mountains descend almost into the sea; bougainvillea-covered stucco villas cling to cliffsides, while bare, sparsely vegetated limestone peaks tower above.

Although, rather like the rest of the Côte d'Azur, the coast has become increasingly built up with apartment blocks and villas, this area still retains an area of exclusivity, with the period mansions, luxuriant gardens and keep-out signs of secluded Cap Ferrat and some beaches that remain accessible only from the coastal footpath. Every view is dominated by the mountains, giving it a grandeur that would be impossible to spoil – though thankfully, apart from in Monaco, no one has really tried.

The corniches

Three famous corniche roads between Nice and Menton snake one above the other around the mountain side. Along the clifftop, the spectacular **Grande Corniche** (the top road) was built by Napoleon and follows the old Roman road, the Via Aurelia, to Italy. Cut into the rocks beneath it, the **Moyenne Corniche** (the middle road) is the most recently built of the three scenic routes. The **Basse Corniche** (the lower road), which hugs the coast, was built in the 18th century. It emerges from Nice's port, then winds its way around the Cap de Nice and the fanciful villas of Mont Boron, offering more lovely views across Villefranche Bay to the high ridge of Cap Ferrat. This, too, is a spectacular road, but it is often jammed with traffic.

LEFT: ochre-washed houses in Villefranche.
BELOW: Villa Kerylos in Beaulieu-sur-Mer.

On the Monday before Shrove Tuesday, colourful flower-decked pointu fishing boats fill the harbour at Villefranche-sur-Mer for the annual Combat Naval Fleuri, a festival going back more than a century.

A medieval town

Despite its proximity to Nice and the fact that the US Navy used it as a base until France withdrew from NATO's integrated military command in 1966, **Villefranche-sur-Mer** ❷ retains a certain genuine fishing-port charm. The town was founded in the 13th century as a *ville franche* or customs-free port by Charles II of Anjou, and in the 14th century, as part of the Comté de Nice, became the main port of the Counts of Savoy, offering them a valuable outlet to the sea. In 1538, Emperor Charles V stayed here while negotiating the Treaty of Nice with François I. British and American ships still use its harbour, which is one of the deepest in the world.

The town itself has retained a homogeneous, medieval character. The old streets, citadel and port are well restored but not bijou. Along the old Port de la Santé fishing harbour, the houses have a cheerful, faded air, each façade a different colour, ranging from terracotta and ochre to rose and magnolia; the shutters are painted half a dozen shades of green, and the row of fish restaurants and cafés provide a popular evening out for the Niçois.

At the end of quai Courbet stands the tiny 14th-century **Chapelle St-Pierre** (open summer Tues–Sun 10am–noon, 4–8pm, winter Tues–Sun 10am–noon, 2–6pm; admission charge), also known as the "Cocteau Chapel", with a candy-coloured façade. In 1956, while staying at the Hôtel Welcome near by, the Surrealist poet, artist and film maker Jean Cocteau (1889–1963) painted the interior with fishing scenes and episodes from the life of St Peter.

The huge 16th-century stone **Citadelle de St-Elme** dominates the waterfront and still looks impregnable, though the deep dry moat is now used as a car park. It was built in 1557 by Duke Philibert of Savoy,

The Corniches

along with the fort on Mont Alban above, to protect this strategic harbour, which had previously been besieged by Frederick Barbarossa, an ally of François I, and the Turkish fleet in 1543.

The citadel is like an enormous quarry, with sheer walls set at an angle for greater stability and tiny watchtowers and viaducts crossing on slender pylons. Within the walls are housed the town hall, the chapel of St-Elme, a conference centre and a couple of museums.

The **Musée Goetz-Boumeester** has a collection of about 100 minor works by Picasso, Picabia and Miró among others, as well as engravings and paintings by Henri Goetz and his wife Christine Boumeester, displayed in the former navy barracks.

The sculptor Antoniucci Volti was a resident of Villefranche, and the **Musée Volti** has a good collection of his monumental smooth figurative sculptures, most of them female, some of which are displayed outside in the main courtyard of the citadel (tel: 04 93 76 33 27; both museums open summer Wed–Mon

10am–noon, 2.30–6.45pm, Sun pm only, winter Wed–Mon 9am–noon, 2–5.30pm, Sun pm only; free).

Italianate architecture

The Italianate Vieille Ville (old town) climbs up the hill behind the Port de la Santé, dominated by the tall campanile of the 18th-century baroque **Eglise St-Michel** at the top. Many of the houses are built on the Italian model, with large arched loggias on the ground floor, most of which have subsequently been filled in. The area around the church features the steepest, most winding streets and twisted houses.

The town seems to specialise in *trompe l'œil* wall paintings, usually of windows, often with cats in them. There is a good window with a cat on the **place de la République**, a charming little square with a large shady pine tree in the centre and houses dating from the 17th and 18th centuries. The chapel on rue de l'Eglise is entirely painted with a *faux* Pisan Romanesque façade, which has what seems to be a genuine Pisan-style doorway dated 1590.

Map on page 180

TIP

Every Sunday, a flea market is held at Villefranche-sur-Mer on place Amélie Pollonais by the Port de la Santé.

BELOW: the bay of Villefranche from Cap Ferrat.

The main street of the old town is the **rue du Poilu**, which leads to the tiny place du Conseil, from which there is a good view of the harbour and Cap Ferrat. The picturesque 13th-century **rue Obscure** starts here. Steps lead down to an arched passage that has changed little since it was built; the street is almost entirely composed of covered passageways, which the inhabitants could reach from back doors or intersecting streets and squares. This was the place people came for shelter when the town was attacked.

Home to a Rothschild

The luxuriantly vegetated headland of **Cap Ferrat** ❸ is a rare part of the Riviera that still has its sense of exclusivity (the turning off the Basse Corniche is marked, significantly, by a shop offering electronic surveillance systems and 24-hour personal security). The 10-km (6-mile) stretch of road that runs right round the Cap offers glimpses of luxurious villas and magnificent gardens, all hidden behind high hedges, impenetrable gates and guard-dog signs.

The narrowest part of the peninsula is dominated by the **Villa Ephrussi de Rothschild** (tel: 04 93 01 33 09; www.culture-espaces.com; open Feb–Oct daily 10am–6pm, Jul–Aug 10am–7pm, Nov–Jan Mon–Fri 2–6pm, Sat, Sun and school hols 10am–6pm; admission charge), a prime example of how the other half used to live. Seven hectares (17 acres) of gardens spread right along the crest of the Cap with wonderful panoramic views on all sides.

The pink-and-white Belle Epoque villa was built between 1905 and 1912 to house the personal art collection of the Baroness Ephrussi de Rothschild. A daughter of rich banker Baron Alphonse de Rothschild, she married another wealthy banker, Maurice Ephrussi, and didn't hesitate to have potential items for her collection delivered to Beaulieu station for her inspection. The villa is laid out around a Venetian Gothic-style covered central courtyard and hung with medieval and Renaissance works of art, including a painting by Carpaccio. A succession of panelled rooms is furnished with a magnifi-

BELOW: Villa Ephrussi de Rothschild.

cent variety of mainly 18th-century furniture, precious Sèvres and Vincennes porcelain, tapestries, carpets and paintings. Some rooms can be seen only on guided tours.

The highlight, however, is the series of themed gardens outside, evoking different climates and epochs, where spiky cacti and palms meet ancient roses. A meandering promenade leads through a French formal garden with musical fountains; a Japanese garden with brushed gravel and little shrines; exotic cacti; Provençal flora; an Italian Renaissance garden with a horseshoe stairway; and the romantic lapidary garden with ivy-covered fragments of Gothic architecture and medieval statuary.

Leopold and Willy

Cap Ferrat has the reputation of having the most pleasant climate on the Riviera, and it was for this reason that Leopold II, King of Belgium, bought a large estate here. His merciless exploitation of the Congo helped to finance his excesses, such as the large park, Les Cèdres, laid out on the peninsula. In its grounds he built a palace for himself and three houses, one for each of his mistresses.

With so many mistresses, Leopold became concerned that he might die without absolution, so in 1906 (three years before his death) he built another house nearby for his confessor Monseigneur Charmeton. In 1926 W. Somerset Maugham bought this house and its 3 hectares (7 acres) of terraced land, calling it the Villa Mauresque after its Moorish style.

Leopold also established a lush exotic garden, which is now the site of the small, family-run **Zooparc du Cap Ferrat** (tel: 04 93 76 07 60; www.zoocapferrat.com; open daily 9.30am–7pm, winter 5.30pm), where crocodiles, zebras, lemurs, gibbons and wild cats live amid its pools, palm trees, islands and waterfalls. Other additions include a panther canyon and a nocturnal environment for rats and bats.

The Windsors arrive

In 1938 the Duke and Duchess of Windsor arrived on the Riviera, adding even more cachet to the

Map on page 180

A view over the Cap Ferrat peninsula, with its luxury villas and pebbly beaches.

BELOW: La Radiana, a villa built for one of the mistresses of Leopold II.

TIP

The best way to get a glimpse of the exclusive villas of Cap Ferrat is to walk along the Sentier du Littoral (coast path), which follows the old Sentier des Douaniers, once used by customs officers. The 6-km (4-mile) footpath runs from the marina at St-Jean-Cap-Ferrat around the headland to the small beach, Plage de Passable.

BELOW:
inside Villa Kérylos.

already exclusive Cap Ferrat scene. They rented Sir Pomeroy Burton's villa, where the Duke dug the garden and the Duchess kept house.

Soon the Cap was home to industrialists such as Singer, the sewing-machine magnate, and a host of stars and celebrities, like Charlie Chaplin, Edith Piaf, David Niven and Otto Preminger. More recent residents have included the Rolling Stones, who lived here as tax exiles, U2's Bono and Elton John.

Despite the predominance of private estates, a great deal of the natural beauty of the peninsula, which includes some of the oldest olive trees in France, can still be seen along the coastal footpath *(see Tip)*.

The small village of **St-Jean-Cap-Ferrat ❹** itself consists of little more than a beautiful yacht harbour, once home to fishing boats, lined with a few old houses and cafés and some smart fish restaurants, with a small residential area extending up the hillside. There is a one-way system in and out of the village, and parking is often difficult. On the very tip of the Cap is the exclusive

and fashionable **Grand Hôtel du Cap Ferrat**. The hotel and its gorgeous spill-over pool are set in wonderful gardens at the water's edge.

Faded grandeur

East of the Cap is **Beaulieu-sur-Mer ❺**, a town with an air of old-world refinement and a couple of lavish palace hotels, where the Russian and British gentry wintered at the beginning of the 20th century. This is grand dowager country, and beach clothes anywhere other than the beach are still rather frowned upon. It always seems to be warm in Beaulieu, which claims (along with Cap Ferrat and Menton) to have the best climate on the coast, protected from the north wind by a great rock face. Hence its popularity as a retirement town, with many elegant rest homes and genteel hotels surrounded by softly waving palm trees, neatly clipped hedges and carefully weeded gardens. It is quietly stylish if a little old-fashioned.

The **promenade Maurice Rouvier** extends along the seafront all the way from Beaulieu to St-Jean-Cap-Ferrat, past villas and hotels with lush gardens. In the town, the walk goes through formal flower gardens flanked by park seats looking out to Fourmis Bay. The 11th-century Romanesque chapel near the old port is one of the few remaining indications of the town's long history. It has a fine round apse and round arches.

A Greek-style villa

From the Villa Ephrussi's gardens you can look down at the **Villa Kérylos** (tel: 04 93 01 01 44; www.villa-kerylos.com; open Feb–Oct daily 10am–6pm, Jul–Aug 10am–7pm, Nov–Jan Mon–Fri 2–6pm, Sat, Sun and school hols 10am–6pm; admission charge) on the bay below at Beaulieu. Built on the water's edge for wealthy German scholar Theodor Reinach in 1902–8 by architect

Emmanuel Pontremoli, the villa has the colder, more academic style of the erudite scholar. It is not a faithful reproduction of any one ancient Greek villa, but the idealised composite pastiche of what the perfect villa should be, based on the villas of the 2nd century BC on the Greek island of Delos. Nonetheless, it's an interesting place to visit for its harmony of proportions, its courtyards and copies of antique statues, frescos, mosaics and antique furniture.

Eze – perched on a rock

Further along the Basse Corniche, the commune of Eze has built a resort on the seafront of its land called **Eze-Bord-de-Mer**, with a private beach and a Club Nautique.

The medieval village of **Eze ❻** itself is situated at the top of a 429-metre (1,400-ft) hill and is accessible by car from the Moyenne Corniche or by foot (allow well over an hour if walking) up the narrow path from the coast. Built on sheer rock, the fortified medieval village is possibly the most *perché* of all the perched villages, with two gate-

Map on page 180

ways, steep lanes, tiny twisting alleys and crooked steps.

Eze has been on the brink of total destruction on a number of occasions, and its beleaguered past reflects the history of the region very well. For some of its history it has been nothing but a charred, empty ruin, at other times it has risen to become a great power.

Eze began as a Ligurian settlement and was later fortified by the Phoenicians, then developed by the Romans, who established a harbour in the bay below. After the Romans came the Lombards, who in AD 578 murdered the inhabitants and burnt the town to the ground. The Lombards held Eze until 740, when the Saracens appeared, enslaving any inhabitants they could capture and murdering the rest. It was they who built the first castle here.

Eze was one of the last strongholds of the Saracens; they were not driven from Provence until 980 and they razed the town when they left. After the Saracens, Eze was taken and retaken over and over, first by the Guelphs, then by the Ghibellines,

The ancient art of falconry is exhibited at a Medieval Festival in Eze.

BELOW: Eze, a classic *village perché.*

Map
on page
180

*The path up to the
medieval village of
Eze is known as the
Chemin Frederich
Nietzsche, after the
German philosopher
who composed the
third part of* Thus
Spake Zarathustra
*while climbing the
path from his
lodgings, near the
railway station at
Eze-Bord-de-Mer, in
the winter of 1883.*

BELOW: a medieval
re-enactment in Eze.

then by the House of Anjou and the Counts of Provence. In the 14th century, it was finally bought by Amadeus of Savoy, whose family retained control until the entire area was ceded to France in 1860.

During the Middle Ages, Eze became a centre of piracy. A particularly nasty massacre took place in 1543 when the French army of François I, aided by the Turkish fleet under the command of the corsair Barbarossa, launched an attack. Street by street the inhabitants were slaughtered and the town looted.

A new Eze slowly grew from the ruins but was struck again, this time by the 1887 earthquake which did more damage to the town and split what remained of the town walls. The village was abandoned and by the 1920s was more or less empty.

Exploring Eze

Today, there is little left of the castle at the top of the village. Its ruins are surrounded by the **Jardin Exotique** (open daily; admission charge), a fine collection of succulents and cacti laid out in terraces, dotted with terracotta sculptures of nudes. Below the garden the amber-coloured **Eglise Notre-Dame de l'Assomption**, which has an ornate baroque interior, was built in 1765, replacing the previous village church. No less than 18 sun motifs signify the presence of God, and also perhaps the cult of Isis – according to popular legend, Eze gets its name from Isis, goddess of life and eternity, to whom the Phocaeans had erected a temple on the site of the village.

The **Chapelle des Pénitents Blancs** on the place du Planet is worth popping into for its unusual 1258 Catalan crucifix with Christ smiling. The **rue du Barri** climbs up steps, tunnels under houses and meanders over them. Wonderful features can be seen at every turn: a cluster of medieval chimneys here, a Romanesque window or tiny rooftop garden there. Some of the houses are still dilapidated, but the majority have been well restored.

With few residents remaining and no cars allowed in the village itself, Eze is more like an open-air museum, most of it given over to craft and souvenir shops, galleries and restaurants; it is packed with tourists by day but much quieter by night.

Cap d'Ail

After Eze-Bord-de-Mer, the next resort before Monaco is the secluded **Cap d'Ail**, a luxury retreat of private villas and hotels, where the Lumière brothers, the Tsarina and actor-playwright Sacha Guitry built themselves villas in luxuriant gardens. The **Jardins Sacha Guitry** are now a public park. Look out for **Plage la Mala**, a deservedly popular beach with both sand and pebbles, accessible only by steps down from the coast path which winds round the Cap from Plage du Marquet next to the harbour. ❑

RESTAURANTS

Restaurants

Beaulieu-sur-Mer

African Queen
Port de Plaisance. Tel: 04 93 01 10 85. Open L & D daily. €€
A busy, trendy address by the marina. Good brasserie-style fare includes fish soup, pizzas, shellfish platters, seafood pasta and grilled steaks.

La Réserve de Beaulieu
5 boulevard du Général Leclerc. Tel: 04 93 01 00 01. Open L & D daily mid-Dec–Oct. €€€ www.reserve-beaulieu.com
Luxury classic Provençal cuisine served in the elegant Renaissance-inspired setting of a grandiose palace hotel, with prices to match. Lovely sea views and an emphasis on fish dishes. Closed for lunch from June to September when there is a simpler Mediterranean poolside restaurant.

Eze

Château de la Chèvre d'Or
Rue du Barri. Tel: 04 92 10 66 61. Open L & D daily; closed mid-Nov–Feb. €€€ www.chevredor.com
Luxurious dining experience with spectacular views. Chef Philippe Labbé prepares elaborate concoctions combining a roll call of fine ingredients, such as foie gras, wild turbot, sole and truffles, with the local touches of herbs, blettes and rare tomatoes. The gastronomic restaurant is joined by the more traditional Le Grill du Château and the summer lunchtime terrace restaurant Les Remparts.

Château Eza
Tel: 04 93 41 12 24. Open L & D daily. €€€ www.chateaueza.com
The former residence of Prince William of Sweden, suspended high above the sea, offers a series of charming private dining balconies. Attractively presented Franco-Italian cuisine.

Loumiri
Avenue du Jardin Exotique. Tel: 04 93 41 16 42. Open L & D daily, winter Thur–Tues. €
The affordable option is this simple stone bistro at the entrance to the village. Come here for salads, *plats du jour* and traditional regional dishes such as *petits farcis*.

St-Jean-Cap-Ferrat

Le Provençal
2 avenue Denis-Semeria. Tel: 04 93 76 03 97. Open L & D daily, winter L daily, D Fri–Sun; closed Nov. €€€
In an attractive setting perched above the port of St-Jean, Jean-Jacques Jouteaux offers a brilliant repertoire of Provence-inspired dishes. Expensive, but the lunch menu is a good introduction to his style.

La Voile d'Or
Port de Plaisance, 7 avenue Jean-Mermoz. Tel: 04 93 01 13 13. Open L & D daily Easter to mid-Oct. €€€
The cuisine has been rejuvenated at this Cap Ferrat classic in the expert hands of chef Georges Pélissier. He has worked at several of the Côte d'Azur's most prestigious hotel restaurants, including the Byblos and the Juana. An idyllic setting overlooking the picturesque harbour.

Villefranche-sur-Mer

L'Echalote
7 rue de l'Eglise. Tel: 04 93 01 71 11. Open D only Mon–Sat. €€
This cosy bistro on a steep, narrow street in the old town is very popular with locals. Good regional cooking that changes with the seasons.

La Mère Germaine
9 quai Courbet. Tel: 04 93 01 71 39. Open L & D daily Christmas to mid-Nov. €€€ www.meregermaine.com
Founded in 1938, the most famous of the string of restaurants along the fishing harbour (Jean Cocteau was a regular) is reputed for its fine-quality, if pricey, fish and shellfish, including grilled fish and bouillabaisse.

Beach restaurants

Private beach restaurants sometimes offer surprisingly good waterside dining, along with sun-loungers, a range of watersports and cocktails – at a price, of course.

Restaurant La Paloma
Paloma Beach, Cap Ferrat. Tel: 04 93 01 64 71. Open L & D daily May–Sept. €€€
A casual place for grilled fish, pizzas and salads at lunchtime, more romantic for candlelit dinners. A launch can pick you up from your yacht. Great sea views.

L'Eden
Plage la Mala, Cap d'Ail. Tel: 04 93 78 17 06. Open L & D daily May–Sept, except when it is raining. €
www.edenplage.com
This beach restaurant serves traditional French cooking surrounded by a Bali-style tropical decor on the idyllic Plage la Mala. It can be reached only by boat or on foot down the steps from the coastal path.

PRICE CATEGORIES

Prices for a three course meal without wine.
€ = under €25
€€ = €25–40
€€€ = over €40

MONACO

Money is essential but good taste is optional in the tiny principality of Monaco, whose capital Monte-Carlo has earned the monicker Manhattan-sur-Mer. Gambling, yachting, motor-racing and a glittering social life is what makes this surreal state tick

Monaco has to be the most surreal place on the Riviera: a mini state with a maxi number of police and millionaires. A tiny territory of 2 km (1¼ miles) square (making it the smallest state in Europe after the Vatican) comprising a cluster of glitzy skyscrapers crammed in behind a backdrop of mountains, a mix of modernity, unrivalled vulgarity and Belle Époque splendour. Like it or loathe it – and most people feel one way or the other, it's not the sort of place that will leave you indifferent – Monaco undoubtedly exercises a fascination.

Taking aim at the rich

The fiercest critic of **Monaco** was the New Zealand writer Katherine Mansfield, who labelled it "*Real Hell*, the cleanest, most polished place I've ever seen". She preferred her home in sleepy Menton down the coast to this "procession of pimps, governesses in thread gloves… old hags, ancient men, stiff and greyish, panting on the climb, rich fat capitalists".

Today, the "rich fat capitalists" are now quite sleek through working out at Monte-Carlo Golf Club. And Monaco has an idyllic, natural setting, glamorous residents, Americanised culture and international cuisine. But Monaco is different;

society runs like clockwork: toytown guards seem to be everywhere; and multilingual signs tell visitors not to walk around "bare-chested or barefoot".

"To live in Monaco, all you need is good taste and a lot of money," proclaims the principality's *Society* magazine. Money is essential, but good taste is not. In short, everything – except perhaps Monégasque citizenship – is available at a price. The writer Anthony Burgess, who was a long-term resident, once called

LEFT:
the glitzy city of Monaco at night.
BELOW: a Monte Carlo status symbol.

Maps:
City 195
Area 180

Princess Grace, former American film star Grace Kelly, who married Prince Rainier in 1956 and died in a car crash in 1982, is buried in the cathedral cemetery, along with numerous other members of the Rainier dynasty.

RIGHT: Prince Albert and guests at the Monte Carlo Television Festival.

Monaco "the most uncultivated community I've ever come across".

A new Grimaldi

In 2005 Prince Albert II succeeded to the throne (*see below*), crowned during three days of celebration which coincided with the *Fête Nationale* on 19 November. He succeeded his father Prince Rainier III, who had died that April after 56 years as head of state. Albert is the latest in the Grimaldi dynasty which has been running the principality since 1297, when François Grimaldi sneaked in disguised as a Franciscan monk and seized the fortress that had been built up on Le Rocher by the Genoese. In 1612, Honoré II took the title of Prince, which was subsequently recognised by France.

Although temporarily annexed by France from 1789 to 1814 during the French Revolution and under Napoleon – when the Prince was put in prison and the palace temporarily used as a hospital – Monaco's independence was formally recognised by France in 1861. However, its territories of Menton and Roquebrune

had opted to become French – thus depriving Monaco of its principal income from citrus cultivation.

The reigning Prince Charles III had the bright idea of establishing a casino in the new district he had created, called Monte-Carlo, as an alternative source of revenue, but it was businessman François Blanc who turned it into a profitable venture, founding the Société des Bains de Mer (SBM) in 1863 to run the casino (which it still does, along with most of Monaco's luxury hotels).

Since 1911, when the Prince relinquished absolute power, the Principality has officially been a constitutional monarchy, with a Minister of State, who heads a cabinet of four ministers and a legislature of 24, elected by Monégasque citizens. However, in practice the Prince remains hugely powerful.

Until 2002, the Minister of State was always a French citizen chosen from a list of civil servants proposed by the French government, but he can now be either French or Monégasque, chosen by the Prince and approved by the French government. The Princi-

Albert II – the Last Prince?

Prince Albert succeeded to Monaco's throne after his father Rainier III died in April 2005. The coronation of Albert II, mostly known for his sporting achievements (a member of Monaco's Olympic bobsleigh team) and succession of glamorous female companions, including Claudia Schiffer, Naomi Campbell and Brooke Shields, posed the question of whether he was planning a new style of monarchy. His father had done much to transform the Monaco economy in his 56-year reign, but his councillors had all aged with him. However, 48-year-old Prince Albert has already begun the creation of a younger team of ministers and advisers, is actively engaged against climate change and for sustainable development – and one year on, female staff were being allowed to wear trousers for the first time. As to the important question of an heir to the throne, Albert remains a bachelor with no direct heir (although he has now recognised not one but two illegitimate children, ending years of speculation that he might be gay), and his sister Princess Caroline, married to Prince Ernst of Hanover, her third husband, is currently second in line.

pality's relationship with republican France is not always an easy one: in 1962 President Charles de Gaulle, trying to stop French citizens settling in Monaco to avoid paying French taxes, sealed off Monaco's borders until Rainier conceded the issue. More recently, an official report criticised Monaco for money laundering.

Money to burn

Residents have the highest per capita income in the world. For its size, Monaco has arguably the greatest number of banks in the world. Its status as a tax haven has led to Monaco's claim to hold $25 billion in deposits, 60 percent belonging to non-residents. In fact, out of a population of 32,000, only 7,000 residents are Monégasque citizens. The rest are primarily French, Italian, British and German – and many of the 40,000 people who work in Monaco to serve all its tax exiles, gamblers and holidaymakers don't actually live in the state itself but commute in from more affordable lodgings on either side.

This pocket handkerchief of a country could fit neatly into New York's Central Park. Monaco's critics call it a princely theme park where fairy-tale lifestyles are shrewdly sold. The principality's tourist board boasts *"Monaco – un rêve, une réalité"*.

Writer Jeffrey Robinson criticises the nonchalant vulgarity of the Monaco jet set: "On a grand yacht, a Chinese waitress lays a buffet for 20 guests who will shortly be leaving on a two-hour cruise to nowhere, burning €6,000 worth of gasoline in the process."

Sea, skyscrapers and mountains form concentric circles around the headland that is Monaco. A dramatic looming crag, the Tête de Chien, is the backdrop to Monaco-Ville, the medieval quarter built on Le Rocher. The Rock is flanked by two harbours, the artificial Port de Fontvieille to the west and the original Port de Monaco in the Condamine district to the east; and east of here lie Monte-Carlo, a skyscraper-studded hill dubbed "Manhattan-sur-Mer" or alternatively "Las Vegas-Plage", and its beach extension, Larvotto.

Maps:
City 195
Area 180

The Prince's French Carabinieri are hand picked, the Constitution does not allow the use of guards from Monaco.

BELOW: skyscrapers cling to the hills.

The statue of François Grimaldi (see page 190) at the palace shows him disguised a monk with a sword hidden beneath his cloak.

BELOW: the changing of the guard at the Palais Princier.

Princely sights

Sitting at the top of Le Rocher is the **Palais Princier** (place du Palais; tel: 377-93 25 18 31; www.palais.mc; open June–Sept daily 9.30am–6pm, Oct 10am–5pm; admission charge), the official winter residence of the Grimaldis. The walk, linking the port to the palace, leads through medieval gateways. Until 1863, the gates to the old town were closed at night, much to the annoyance of sociable Monégasques. The final arch, La Rampe Major, opens on to place du Palais, known as *placa d'u Palaci* in Monégasque, a Provençal-Genoese dialect. The square is dotted with cannons, some given by Louis XIV to the Grimaldi dynasty.

The salmon-pink palace was pale yellow until it was redesigned by Princess Grace, the Hollywood star wife of Rainier III. When a red-and-white diamond-spangled banner is flying, the Prince is in residence and the palace is closed to the public. Visitors who arrive at 11.55am will see the changing of the guard, a daily ceremony performed by the Prince's French *carabinieri*. The Constitution forbids the use of Monégasque guards, a precaution designed to prevent a coup d'état. Depending upon the season, the *carabinieri* are dressed in winter blue-and-red-striped uniforms or in dazzling white.

The State Apartments are sumptuous recreations of palatial 17th- and 18th-century decor. The Cour d'Honneur, an Italianate quadrangle, forms the backdrop for concerts. However, the most appealing room is the Chambre d'York, where the Duke of York, George III's brother, died. He was on his way to visit a mistress in Genoa when he was taken ill off Monaco. Here, reported Horace Walpole, "The poor Duke of York has ended his silly, good-humoured, troublesome career in a piteous manner". Still, he managed to choose a bedchamber with a frescoed ceiling, Venetian furniture and a lovely gilt-encrusted, canopied bed.

Opening on to the square in another wing of the palace is the **Musée des Souvenirs Napoléoniens** (tel: 377-93 25 18 31; open June–Sept daily 9.30am–6pm, Oct–11

Nov daily 10am–pm, midDec–May Tues–Sun 10.30am–noon, 2–4.30pm; admission charge), a collection of memorabilia and documents from the French Second Empire, as well as an exhibition of documents from Monaco's past.

A lighter take on Monaco history can be found in the Vieille Ville at the **Historial des Princes de Monaco** (27 rue Basses; tel: 377-93 30 39 05; open daily Mar–Sept 10am–6pm, Oct–Feb 11am–5pm; admission charge), a wax museum with scenes featuring the Grimaldis since the 13th century.

Monaco-Ville

From the palace, a stroll through the old quarter leads to the cathedral and exotic gardens. This area is a labyrinth of covered passageways, tiny squares, fountains and tangerine-coloured façades. Rue Basse has several old porticoed houses with carved lintels and vaulted cellars. But in the height of summer it is hard to appreciate the architecture, since the quarter is given over to tawdry tourist trinkets, including Princess Caroline T-shirts and Princess Stephanie's albums.

The **Cathédrale** dominates a rocky spur, like the figurehead of a boat. The clinical white building was built in 1884 on the site of a medieval church. Designed in neo-Romanesque style with Byzantine flourishes, it is at once majestic and oppressive. The greatest treasures lie in the Chapelle des Princes, the Grimaldi burial chamber. Princess Grace's tomb is near by, adorned with fresh pink roses; Prince Rainier was buried alongside her in April 2005. Above is a series of lovely paintings, including the St Nicolas altarpiece by Louis Bréa, the great Niçois artist.

Near by, the **Musée de la Chapelle de la Visitation** (place de la Visitation, tel: 377-93 50 07 00; open Tues–Sun 10am–4pm; admission charge) houses a collection of baroque paintings, including works by Rubens, Zurbarán and Ribera.

Goldfish and sharks

Just outside the cathedral, the lush **Jardins St-Martin** descend to the

Legend has it that a woman wronged by Rainier I put a curse on the Grimaldi line, denying them lasting happiness. Certainly some misfortune has befallen the family, the worst being Rainier III's wife Grace Kelly's fatal car accident in 1982.

BELOW: a fountain in Monaco-Ville.

BELOW:
many visitors to Monaco arrive by sea, on luxurious yachts.

sea. Tiers of Aleppo pines and yellow agaves wind around the headland. The manicured and neatly labelled gardens are dotted with 18th-century turrets and medieval fortifications, along with bossy signs forbidding the feeding of goldfish and cats. In fact, the goldfish are fat enough already, and the teams of uniformed gardeners are a definite cat deterrent. Visitors who tend to stop too often are virtually taken in for questioning.

From here, the avenue St-Martin leads up to the **Musée Océanographique** (tel: 377-93 15 36 00; open daily Oct–Mar 10am–6pm, Apr–June and Sept 9.30am–7pm, Jul–Aug 9.30am–7.30pm; admission charge) founded in 1910 by Prince Albert I. Known as the Navigator Prince, Albert is the best-loved of the previous sovereigns. He dedicated his life to the oceans, and this "temple of the sea" is his memorial. The undoubted star is the aquarium, a surreal home to some weird and wonderful species, such as the secretive crabs called *dromies,* which hide in sponges clutched in

their back legs – *Bernard l'Hermite* travels with a sea anemone permanently lodged on his back; the noble female octopus waits weeks for her eggs to hatch on her tentacles, and as soon as her offspring are born, she dies, exhausted.

One of the most startling sights is not a fish at all but a section of live coral reef taken from the waters off Djibouti. Children are drawn to the huge tank of catsharks and black-tip reef sharks, which constantly circle a wrecked boat alive with yellow-and-blue surgeon fish.

Elsewhere, a new tank shimmers with the colours of rare tropical fish. It is a sobering thought that every morning the aquarium occupants devour over 4,000 kg (8,800 lb) of mussels, sardines, seafood cocktail and spinach.

Hanging gardens

From Monaco-Ville a short bus journey or steep walk leads to the equally surreal environment of the **Jardin Exotique** (boulevard du Jardin Exotique; tel: 377-93 30 33 65; open daily 15 May–15 Sept 9am–7pm, 16 Sept–14 May 9am–6pm or dusk; admission charge), a feast of spiky cacti and odd-looking succulents, growing on perilous terraces set just below the Moyenne Corniche. A former mayor of Monaco likened them to the Hanging Gardens of Babylon, exotic praise for gardens on this latitude. Naturally, it is Monaco's balmy climate that fosters plants normally found in Madagascar or Southern California.

Landscaping the cliffs was a mammoth feat of engineering, taking 20 years to complete. The result is breathtaking: tiered gardens are interlinked by high footbridges and canopies of vegetation; secluded spots are formed by pergolas and arbours; an ornamental pond is enclosed by jungle-like greenery. To

Map
below

weed the gardens, specialists have to be suspended in parachute harnesses over the cliff.

Amongst the 8,000 species of plants are Mexican yuccas, Peruvian monster candles and Moroccan euphorbia that grow up to 15 metres (50 ft) high. Prickly pears, red aloes and downy-leafed elephant ears climb up the rocky vaults. The most striking plant is the Mexican echinocactus: it resembles a spiky hedgehog and is better known as "mother-in-law's pillows".

At the foot of the Jardin Exotique is a series of strange caves known as the **Grottes de l'Observatoire**. A precarious descent through the garden is followed by slippery steps leading down to the bottom of the caves. All around are stalagmites and stalactites, ice-blue pools and natural sculptures. The majestic Grande Salle resembles the inside of a cathedral, with Romanesque pillars and baptismal fonts. The galleries are impressive for their silence, broken only by the faint dripping of water. Prehistoric finds from here and other caves in the region are displayed in the adjacent **Musée d'Anthropologie Préhistorique** (entrance for both included with Jardin Exotique).

Builder Prince

Between Monaco-Ville and Monte-Carlo is the port-side business area known as **La Condamine ⓔ**. The railway brought prosperity, but lemon groves were supplanted by villas and now skyscrapers. Not for nothing was Rainier III known as the Builder Prince. Princess Grace complained that one couldn't sunbathe on the beach after 3pm because of long shadows cast by the skyscrapers. But now no one claims responsibility for the Californian-style patios, hexagonal skyscrapers and a disfigured skyline.

The last major project, completed in 2002, is an enormous floating

Spiky Echinocactus grusonii *cling to the terraces and hill landscape of the Jardin Exotique.*

Monaco

0 — 200 m
0 — 200 yds

Ice-cream sundaes all round at the Café de Paris.

BELOW: the glittering Port of Monaco.

jetty built in Port de Monaco to accommodate giant cruise ships. It weighs 160,000 tonnes and is 352 metres (1,150 ft) long, and can harbour three cruise ships at the same time. The semi-floating jetty was towed in across the Mediterranean from Algeciras in Spain.

La Condamine faces the **Port de Monaco**, which is striking enough, particularly if filled with cruise liners. From the golden years of the 1950s onwards, Aristotle Onassis's boat *Christina* was moored here and often welcomed Princess Grace aboard. The 1960s and 1970s saw the jet set take to water, with or without Greek shipping tycoons. Further work began in 2006 on a new quay to enable more large yachts and cruise ships to dock here.

Fontvieille

From outside the palace, there are fine views over the **Port de Fontvieille ⑦**, a hugely successful development. Built on 30 hectares (74 acres) of reclaimed land, it combines high-rises with Provençal colours. Here you'll also find the

Roseraie Princess Grace ⑥ (Princess Grace rose garden), laid out with 4,000 rose bushes planted amid Mediterranean pine and olive trees, palms, a lake and a collection of modern sculpture. The **Stade Louis II** (3 avenue des Castelans; tel: 377-92 05 40 11; guided visits, except during sporting events, Mon, Tues, Thur, Fri 9.30am, 11am, 2.30pm, 4pm; admission charge) near by is home to Monaco's football team and an Olympic-sized pool.

Just back from the port on the Terrasses de Fontvieille is a cluster of museums: the **Collection de Voitures Anciennes** (tel: 377-92 05 28 56; open daily 10am–6pm; admission charge), containing the late Prince Rainier's collection of vintage cars and carriages; the **Musée des Timbres et des Monnaies** (Stamp and Coin museum; tel: 377-93 15 41 50; open daily Oct–June 10am–5pm, July–Sept 10am–6pm; admission charge), a collection of Monaco-issued stamps (much prized by collectors and tourists), plus coins, banknotes and medals, issued by the state since

1640; the **Musée Naval** (tel: 377-92 05 28 48; www.musee-naval.mc; open daily 10am–6pm; admission charge), a collection of ship models and other nautical items; as well as the **Jardin Animalier** (tel: 377-93 25 18 31; www.palais.mc; open daily Oct–Feb 10am–noon, 2–5pm, Mar–May 10am–noon, 2–6pm, June–Sept 9am–noon, 2–7pm; admission charge), a small zoo.

In the 1970s, Prince Rainier realised that he had to expand Monaco's economic base, so he created Fontvieille's business quarter for light industry, focusing on perfumes and electronics. These industries now produce around one-third of state revenue, while value-added tax provides about 50 percent and, contrary to popular belief, gambling brings in less than 5 percent. As Prince Rainier once put it: "Nowadays, we probably have as many gardeners as croupiers."

Monte-Carlo

However, it is the district of Monte-Carlo that has given Monaco its glamorous image. In the right company, and with the right income, **Monte-Carlo** is still a name to conjure with. Nevertheless, the only magical area is the place du Casino and the square Beaumarchais. As well as the Casino and the Salle Garnier, this golden square contains the Hôtel de Paris, the Café de Paris and the Hôtel Hermitage, haunts worth visiting for their architecture as well as their atmosphere. Until the building of the place du Casino, the plateau de Spéluges was generally known as a "desert riddled with insalubrious caves".

The **Hôtel de Paris** has a delightful setting, overlooking the lush Casino gardens, the Café de Paris and the sea. Built in 1864, this inspirational hotel was designed with unbridled extravagance and borrows from an earlier rococo style.

Exquisite details include the rotunda with a fan-shaped portico, the curvaceous cupolas and the façades decorated with bare-breasted figureheads. The interior is equally captivating, with caryatids adorning the reception rooms, and the lavishly gilded Louis XV restaurant, which is presided over by the famous superchef turned gastronomic entrepreneur Alain Ducasse.

In 1943 the Hôtel de Paris was occupied by the Gestapo. In theory, Monaco was neutral, but Rainier's grandfather supported the Vichy regime. Goering and Himmler used the principality as a place for laundering war spoils. The hotel manager feared for his finest wines and cognacs, so he concealed them in a crypt at the bottom of the cellar. The other bottles were drunk, but his cache remained intact. It is still the deepest hotel wine cellar in the world, with a "champagne alley" containing bottles dating back to 1805.

Edwardian grandeur

Situated on the far corner of the square, the **Café de Paris** was once

Map on page 195

TIP

If you want to blow your budget, go shopping on the avenue des Beaux-Arts at such luxury boutiques as Cartier, Bulgari and Ribolzi.

BELOW: welcome to the grand Hôtel de Paris.

The door manager at the Casino de Monaco is no mere doorman but someone whose main attribute has to be a photographic memory for matching faces to gambling history. The most famous of these "physiognomists" was Monsieur le Broq, who claimed to have memorised over 60,000 faces.

an equally glamorous location. It was built in 1865 but acquired an Art Deco interior in the 1920s. The overall effect is seaside Edwardian, with a delicious-looking peaches-and-cream façade adorned with a fan-shaped portico. Floral mosaics and stained-glass designs lend sophistication to the interior where, as well as the restaurant, there are also gaming rooms decked out with a racing-car-themed decor.

However, the Café's greatest claim to fame is linked to the womaniser Edward VII. Legend has it that the crêpe Suzette was invented here as a face-saving exercise when a special dessert being prepared for the King accidentally caught fire. Edward's companion was Suzette, and the *flambé* was christened crêpe Suzette in her honour.

The Casino

Crowning the square above the sea is the exuberant Belle Epoque **Casino** ❶ (place du Casino; tel: 377-92 16 20 00; over-18s only, ID required; open Mon–Fri 2pm until late, Sat, Sun noon until late; admis-

sion charge). The Casino was created by Prince Charles III, who established this whole new district (Mount Charles) on the plateau de Spéluges, which was then a wasteland. The Prince wanted a world stage for Monaco arts and, having lost Monégasque territory to France, also needed to generate new revenue. Inspired by the success of aristocratic tourism in Baden Baden, he realised that good health and gambling were a winning combination.

Early attempts were unsuccessful, but the Casino's luck changed when the adventurer François Blanc bought the concession and founded the Société des Bains de Mer (SBM). He was helped by the arrival of the railway in 1886 and by his European gambling monopoly. Business was booming in the Belle Epoque.

Occasionally, lucky gamblers would "break the bank". If so, the coffers were ostentatiously refilled, as Blanc shrewdly realised, "One winner always attracts a crowd of losers."

Today, the Casino retains much of its old glamour and strict rules. A sign forbids ministers of religion or

Faîtes Vos Jeux

Although Monaco now has several casinos and gaming rooms, the extravagant Belle Epoque Casino de Monaco in the centre of Monte-Carlo remains the big draw. This is where serious gamblers play for high stakes in the *salons privés*, and tourists try their luck at the slot machines.

Games include roulette, craps, blackjack, baccarat and *chemin de fer*. Spectators eddy from table to table, and sound is reduced to low murmurs and sliding chips. No one drinks; gambling is the only addiction. The *salons privés* are only private in so far as there is an admission charge. That said, stakes are much higher, and non-gamblers are discouraged by the door manager's penetrating gaze. The Casino's main "bank" can also be made to vanish down a trapdoor in the event of a hold-up.

In the *salons privés* there is a high ratio of croupiers to clients. The croupiers are Las Vegas-trained, highly paid and form the most powerful lobby in Monaco. John Addington Symonds had little good to say of the breed in 1866: "The croupiers are either fat, sensual cormorants or sallow, lean-cheeked vultures, or suspicious foxes."

Monégasques to enter the *salles de jeux*. If the Grimaldis attend an opera in the Casino's Salle Garnier, they have to enter through a side door.

The Salle Garnier

The **Salle Garnier**, inside the Casino building, is used for opera and ballet and designed, like the Palais Garnier opera house in Paris, by architect Charles Garnier. The Salle Garnier was added to the casino building in 1879, to provide musical entertainment for gamblers staying in Monte-Carlo and bring cultural kudos to the city state. It was inaugurated by Sarah Bernhardt.

Reopened after two years of painstaking restoration work in 2005, the theatre is a feast of coloured marble, mosaics, sculptures, painted ceilings and glittering chandeliers. It has a prestigious history, with first rate singers and adventurous programming: many operas have been premiered here, including the staged version of Berlioz's *La Damnation de Faust*, while Diaghilev's acclaimed Ballets Russes performed here regularly

from 1911 to 1914 and 1920 to 1924.

Along the seafront below the Casino, accessible by a series of lifts, the **Musée National Automates et Poupées** (Museum of Automata and Dolls; 17 avenue Princesse Grace; tel: 377-93 30 91 26; open daily Easter–Sept 10am–6.30pm, Oct–Easter 10am–12.15pm, 2.30–6.30pm; admission charge) is housed in a pretty stucco villa also designed by Charles Garnier. The museum is home to more than 400 dolls, an impressive collection of 18th- and 19th-century dolls' houses and various automata.

Almost opposite is a modern **Japanese garden**, with a symbolic landscape and shinto shrines, and the angular, glass-sided **Grimaldi Forum** (10 avenue Princesse Grace; tel: 377-99 99 20 00; www.grimaldi-forum.com), used for congresses, art exhibitions, concerts and dance.

Near here, future plans include a new terrace to be built on *pilotis* (stilts) over the sea, which will eventually be the setting for the Musée des Beaux-Arts, currently putting on shows at various temporary sites.

An exterior view of the opera house, which has been carefully restored.

BELOW: the facade of the Monte-Carlo Casino.

Map on page 195

TIP

Around 3,000 tickets for the Monaco Grand Prix are sold each year. Residents rent out their terraces overlooking the track, and advertise in the *International Herald Tribune* and *Nice Monaco Matin* newspapers. Visit www.acm.mc and www.visitmonaco.com for more information.

BELOW: the Monaco Grand Prix.

Continuing east along the seafront will bring you to **Larvotto**, which has public and private beaches, bars and restaurants and the prestigious Monte-Carlo Sporting Club.

Monte-Carlo or bust...

The Red Cross Gala is the society event of the year, an occasion for the richest society ladies to flaunt their jewels. It is held at **Le Sporting Monte-Carlo** (Sporting Club), which is not a sports club at all. According to Prince Albert, a bobsleigh champion, "to be a good Monégasque, you have to be sporty".

The major event is, of course, the **Monaco Grand Prix** (www.acm.mc). This dangerous circuit involves 78 laps around the port, the Hôtel Hermitage and the place du Casino. The timing is perfect: it takes place immediately after the Cannes Film Festival in May, so there are still plenty of stars around. Stirling Moss, who won three times, loved the atmosphere: "When I was racing, I'll never forget looking at a beautiful young girl with pale lip-

stick who was always sitting in front of Oscar's bar. Every time I passed, I blew her a kiss. This sort of thing is only possible in Monaco."

Every other year (the next one will take place in 2008), the **Grand Prix du Monaco Historique** is held a few days before the Grand Prix itself, using the same race track. Over two days – the first is a practice day – seven categories of classic racing car, dating from pre-1947, pit their tenacity against each other.

In January, the **Monte-Carlo Car Rally** kicks off the season, when rally drivers race 1,582 km (983 miles) back to Monte-Carlo. In spring, the **Monte-Carlo Tennis Open** takes place, and then there are festivals devoted to circus, cinema and contemporary dance, and prizes awarded to contemporary art, literature and music.

During the season, evening is the time for dazzling displays of wealth. Stretch limos ferry bronzed and bejewelled celebrities between the Hôtel de Paris, the Casino and Jimmy'z, Monte-Carlo's glitziest nightspot. ❑

RESTAURANTS & BARS

Bar et Bœuf

Le Sporting Monte-Carlo, avenue Princesse Grace, Monte-Carlo. Tel: 377-98 06 71 71. Open D only mid-May–late Sept. €€€
www.sportingmontecarlo.com
Ducasse's fashionable summer restaurant over-looks Jimmy'z and the sea at the *très chic* Sporting Club. The concept is centred on just two ingredients, *bar* (sea bass) and *bœuf* (beef), with dishes that vary from sea bass with a Provençal-style vegetable *tian* to carpaccios and Asian wok cooking.

Le Café de Paris

Place du Casino, Monte-Carlo. Tel: 377-92 16 20 20. Open L & D daily. €€
Completely renovated in 1920s style, the place where the crêpe Suzette was supposedly invented by accident for Edward VII (and named after one of his mistresses) deserves to be visited as one of the sights of Monte-Carlo. Classic brasserie food and great people-watching from the terrace.

Joël Robuchon Monte-Carlo

Hôtel Métropole, 4 avenue de la Madone, Monte-Carlo. Tel: 977-93 15 15 15. Open L & D daily. €€€
www.metropole.com
After Paris, Robuchon has brought his

contemporary global tapas concept to Monte-Carlo in the hands of chef Christophe Cusset; with a succession of inventive lit-tle dishes and sometimes daring combinations of flavours, although there is also a conventional rotis-serie menu.

Louis XV

Hôtel de Paris, place du Casino, Monte-Carlo. Tel: 377-98 06 88 64. Open L & D Thur–Mon (plus Wed D in summer); closed Dec and 2 weeks in Mar. €€€
www.alain-ducasse.com
The flagship of the Ducasse empire, in the hands of Franck Cerruti, a native of Nice, serves lavish seasonal Mediterranean cuisine in the palatial dining room of the Hôtel de Paris. Smart dress required.

Maya Bay

Roccabella, 24 avenue Princesse Grace. Tel: 377-97 70 74 67.
Open L & D Tues–Sat. €€€
A slick modern restaurant and lounge bar with an Asiatic decor (Buddha statue, exotic woods) and fusion food.

Polpetta

2 rue Paradis, Monte-Carlo. Tel: 377-93 50 67 84. Open L & D Mar–Jan Sun, Mon, Wed-Fri, D only Sat. €€
Once frequented by Frank Sinatra, this bistro offers hearty Italian food, which is

among the best value for money in Monaco.

St-Benoît

10 avenue de la Costa. Tel: 377-93 25 02 34. Open L & D Tues–Sat, L only Sun. €€€
A favourite with locals, with views over the marina and the Espace Grimaldi. The emphasis is on fish and shellfish.

Tip Top

11 avenue des Spélugues, Monte-Carlo. Tel: 377-93 95 50 69 13. Open (till dawn) L & D Mon–Sat, D only Sun. €€
A busy convivial bistro and café frequented by an enormously eclectic crowd, ranging from local office workers to Albert II and scores of Formula 1 drivers, as photos on the walls reveal. The special-ity is steak with match-

stick chips, but they'll also do you a pizza in the dead of night.

Zebra Square

10 avenue Princesse Grace, Monte-Carlo. Tel: 377-99 99 25 50. Open L & D. €€€
www.zebrasquare.com.
A very fashionable brasserie and lounge bar which has branches in Paris and Moscow. It has a stylish rooftop terrace in the Grimaldi Forum conference and exhibition centre. DJs late at night.

PRICE CATEGORIES

Prices for a three-course dinner per person without wine.

€ = under €25
€€ = €25–40
€€€ = over €40

RIGHT: moules et frites.

FANTASY LAND

Many of the spectacular buildings of the Riviera reflect the fantasy world that their wealthy creators wanted to live in

Château Grimaldi in Antibes *(above)* shows the rich medieval heritage of this coast of lordly princes, Saracens and pirates. It is part of the romance that has attracted wealthy visitors who have been able to act out their dreams here. The Monaco royal family are Grimaldis, and their own fairy-tale palace was the Hollywood dream of the actress Grace Kelly, who married into it. In the 1920s the rich and sociable American artist Gerald Murphy, whose motto was "Living well is the best revenge", and his wife Sara built Villa America on the Garoupe beach. It had 14 bedrooms and the first rooftop sun deck on the Riviera. More spectacularly, Béatrice de Rothschild, wife of a Russian banker, Maurice Ephrussi, built villa Ephrussi de Rothschild, inspired by his cousin, Fanny Khan, who had married Theodor Reinach, creator of Villa Kérylos, a Greek fantasy.

With a plentiful supply of money and artists it was hard for them to go wrong. But the artists, too, found great settings for their work.

ABOVE: Villa Kérylos *(see page 184)* was built in 1902–8 for the French archaeologist Theodor Reinach to resemble a 2nd-century BC villa from Delos, incorporating all modern comforts. Reinach's guests had to dress in Greek *peplos* and dine lying on couches.

BELOW: Beatrice Ephrussi de Rothschild had this Venetian-style villa built *(see page 182)* and held parties mimicking the court of Marie Antoinette at Versailles. Exotic plants and animals filled the garden.

LEFT: in Cimiez, the original Roman settlement in Nice, a highly original folly with *trompe l'œil* façades was built among the ancient ruins in the Genoese style for the Consul of Nice, Jean-Baptiste Gubernatis, and completed by his grandson in 1685. Now the Villa Arènes, it houses the Matisse Museum *(see page 174)*.

ABOVE: The ruined 14th-century Château de la Napoule *(see page 102)* was bought and restored in 1918 by the eccentric American sculptor Henry Clews, who had a fanatical hatred of anything modern. Living in a complete fantasy world, he and his wife Marie loved dressing up in medieval costumes, which they designed for their servants as well as themselves. Their menagerie included pigeons with musical pipes attached to their wings.

TYPICAL FARMHOUSES

For many visitors the *mas*, or farmhouse, of southern France embodies the ideal country style. These sturdy, squat buildings are designed to be cool in summer and easy to heat in winter; their stone walls are thick and their windows small, shuttered and absent on the north side in places where the mistral wind is strong. Terracotta tiles cover the floors both upstairs and down, and the paintwork is often a lavender blue. They have hardly changed in design since Roman times and their tiles, once made using clay moulded over the tilers' thighs, are just the same. This shape is used not just on farmhouses, but on every domestic building in the region, keeping towns harmonious. Planning laws continue to insist all new houses have these terracotta roofs, pitched at a lowly 30 degrees, so the weight of the tiles keeps pressing downwards. Other embellishments typical of the region include ironwork wind vanes and spires. A farmhouse complex may include stables, lofts, cellars and dovecotes, and even an ice house built of stone and insulated with hay.

LEFT: The fishermen's chapel St-Pierre in Villefranche had a make-over by Jean Cocteau in 1957, using local masons and ceramicists. Inside, his imaginative frescos depict Christ with the local fishermen.

RIGHT: Fondation Maeght *(see page 156)* by the Catalan architect Josep-Lluis Sert is an exemplary Modernist building and a highly successful gallery space. Sert had designed Miró's Mallorca studio, which the Maeghts saw and liked.

MENTON

Sheltered by mountains and only a stone's throw from Italy, Menton claims to have the best climate in France – its beautiful floral gardens and abundance of citrus trees on the hillsides bear witness to this. Near by is the medieval castle village of Roquebrune

"**N**owhere else have I felt such complete happiness," declared Franz Liszt of **Menton** . Sheltered by mountains, the town basks in an enchanted setting with 300 days of sun a year. In this tropical greenhouse, Mexican and North African vegetation flourishes in a climate at least 2°C (4°F) warmer than in Nice. The French weather report never shows Menton, points out one local resident rather smugly, "It would be too demoralising for everyone else!"

But in the 19th century Menton's attraction was as a winter sanatorium rather than as a hothouse. Royal visitors such as Queen Victoria and her son Edward VII helped Menton acquire a reputation as the most aristocratic and anglophile of all the Riviera resorts.

Nowadays, the dowager-like image has softened: Menton is cosy rather than genteel, anglophile rather than aristocratic. The Italian border is just a mile away, and, certainly, the presence of Italian executives and holidaymakers has revived the town. This has been boosted by Menton joining with Ventimiglia, its closest Italian neighbour, in 1993, as the European Union's first joint urban community, combining frontier posts and each town's municipal and business activities.

Foreign history

Originally Genoese, Menton became part of the Principality of Monaco in 1346 and by and large remained a Grimaldi possession until 1860. However, the Grimaldis astutely placed Menton under the protection of the rising political powers. In succession, Menton became a Spanish, French and Sardinian protectorate. In 1848 Menton rebelled against high Monégasque taxes on oil and fruit. Along with neighbouring Roquebrune, the town declared itself

Maps:
City 206
Area 180

LEFT:
a view over Menton old town.
BELOW:
a local fisherman.

As many as 120 tonnes of lemons are used during the two-week-long Fête du Citron in February. They are moulded into all sorts of shapes, as well as being juiced and iced for refreshments. For details, contact: www.feteducitron.com

a republic, but this was short-lived, and in 1861 Monaco sold both towns to France. This coincided with the beginning of Grand Tourism, and Menton was one of the first health resorts to benefit, thanks to publicity generated by Dr James Henry Bennet. The English doctor promoted Menton's mild climate as perfect for invalids, and as a result British and Germans flocked here for the winter.

Oranges and lemons

Set just behind the seafront, the sweetly scented **Jardin Biovès** Ⓐ is a natural introduction to flowery Menton, with its lush pink borders, serried ranks of palms and citrus trees, and the lemon trees decorated with fairy lights. Boughs of Seville oranges and sweet Genoese mandarins intermingle with the Mentonnais lemon, the town's trademark. This oval-shaped lemon, introduced in the 14th century, is noted for its gorgeous scent and un-

acidic flavour. The Mentonnais boast that it keeps for months longer than its common Portuguese rival. During the February Fête du Citron *(see margin)* the park looks good enough to eat.

Overlooking the park is the splendid **Palais de l'Europe**, once the city's grand casino and now home to the helpful **tourist office** and a contemporary art gallery on the ground floor. The present casino, facing out on to the seafront, is a staid affair, reduced to seaside cabaret, sedate *thés dansants* and low-key gambling.

As if in disapproval, St John's Anglican church, an incongruous Victorian brick building, turns its back on the casino. The church provides retired British expatriates with spiritual counselling, fêtes and library books.

On the promenade

In the afternoon, elderly visitors congregate on the **promenade du**

Soleil B to enjoy the sea views. Along the seafront are vestiges of Belle Epoque villas and charmingly dilapidated pastel-coloured hotels. Many of the finest villas have been converted into chic flats or homes for retired French civil servants. Below the promenade younger sun-seekers stretch out on rocks or on pocket handkerchiefs of sand.

Near by, ladies sip afternoon tea in seaside *salons de thé*. Yet, in keeping with the changing times, the cafés cater to both ends of the social scale, serving anything from chilled Chablis and bouillabaisse to hot dogs and Coke. In general, however, Menton's sea views tend to be more memorable than its cuisine.

Menton's old town

At the eastern end of the promenade, the Belle Epoque quarter merges into **Vieux Menton**, the pedestrianised old town. The **Marché Couvert C** (open every morning) provides a quirky link between the two quarters. The market, topped by a decorative clock tower, is adorned with comical sculpted faces. The profusion of lemons, figs and artichokes is a match for the market's green, yellow and brown ceramics.

Rue des Marins, beside the market, is still the centre for Menton's small but thriving fish trade. As the only medieval guild to have survived on the Riviera, it retains a symbolic importance in local eyes. The trade, passed from father to son, is based on small fry such as sardines and anchovies. In spring, anchovies are attracted to Menton's warm waters, and by May the season is well under way. May is also the traditional time for salting and storing the fish. Sardines, still fished from February to April, are eaten fried with lemon or in a spicy *omelette de poutines*.

Beside the Marché Couvert is the place du Marché, with its fragrant flower stalls doing a brisk trade in young lemon trees and cacti. Close by is the **place aux Herbes D**, an attractive arcaded square of chestnut trees, surrounding a fountain and statue, best appreciated from an outdoor café.

Map on page 206

TIP

The Service du Patrimoine (Heritage Service) offers professional guided tours of Menton in English throughout the year. For more information log on to www.menton.fr or tel: 04 92 10 33 66.

BELOW. cool down with an ice cream on the promenade du Soleil.

Riding along the seafront on the promenade du Soleil.

The oldest quarter

Seen from the old fishing harbour, Vieux Menton is stacked on the hillside, framed by rugged mountains and shimmering reflections. From here, the towers of the church, the **Basilique St-Michel Archange** (tel: 04 92 10 97 10; open daily 10am–midday, 3–5.15pm, closed Sat and Sun am; free) and two nearby chapels appear inseparable. From quai Bonaparte, steep steps lead to the parvis St-Michel, the church square, paved with a grey-and-white pebble mosaic of the Grimaldi coat of arms, and up to the pink and ochre basilica, flanked by two towers.

The first stone for the church was laid in 1619, but building didn't start in earnest until 1639; its baroque façade was added in 1819. Inside are several heavily restored chapels which were damaged in an earthquake here in 1887.

The parvis St-Michel is the setting for Menton's celebrated August Festival of Chamber Music. This sunken square has excellent acoustics, framed by the basilica and its neighbouring chapel yet open to the sea on one side. The unexpected blend of intimacy and sea views has also made it a sought-after film set.

In the adjacent square stands the apricot-tinged **Chapelle de l'Immaculée Conception** , built in 1687 for the Pénitents Blancs, a lay confraternity who sought to return to a simpler faith. The 1887 earthquake damaged the church, but after being restored in 1987 it is now the city's pride and joy. Depending on taste, the baroque interior is either garish or exuberant. The pièce de résistance is the ceiling representing Heaven, a Mediterranean paradise with golden figures and blue skies.

This medieval quarter is the oldest part of town. It is also the poorest, populated by Algerian and Moroccan immigrants as well as Mentonnais craftsmen. Renovation has yet to make much impact on this warren of vaulted brick and cobbled streets. Blind alleys end with tiny houses adorned with drying peppers.

Cocteau's local legacy

The bastion on the seafront was originally a fort, built in 1636, when

Menton's Spanish rulers feared a French attack. It now houses the **Musée Jean Cocteau ⑤** (tel: 04 93 57 72 30; open Wed–Mon; admission charge), in homage to the painter and poet who once lived in the town. Cocteau himself oversaw the restoration of the fort, designing the mosaic flooring and the bright tiling on the four turrets. He donated numerous works to the museum but sadly did not live to see the opening in 1967.

The ground floor, formerly the arms store, contains brilliantly coloured abstractions, powerful self-portraits and *Judith and Holofernes*, Cocteau's first tapestry. Matisse loved it, praising this depiction of seduction, murder and flight as *"la seule vraie tapisserie contemporaine"*. Cocteau dabbled in tapestry, ceramics, photography and sculpture, as well as painting. Throughout the museum are examples of his beautifully crafted jars influenced by Greek, Hellenic and Etruscan designs. The upper floor, once the guards' room, still contains its original vaulted ceiling and brick oven.

The highlight is the *Innamorati* collection, a series of love paintings inspired by the lives of Provençal fisher-folk.

Cocteau fans will head inland to the **Hôtel de Ville ⑪** to see the **Salle des Mariages** (tel. 04 92 10 50 00; open Mon–Fri; admission charge), designed by the artist in the 1950s. Cocteau's touch is evident in the Spanish chairs, the mock panther-skin carpet and the lamps shaped like prickly pears.

As for the murals, Cocteau's inspiration was the Riviera style at the turn of the 20th century, "a mood redolent of Art Nouveau villas decorated with swirling seaweed, irises and flowing hair".

On the wall above the official's desk, Cocteau depicts the engaged couple trying to read the future in each other's eyes. The mural is full of Provençal symbols, from the sun and swirling sea to the woman's Mentonnais straw hat and her fiancé's fisherman's cap. Cocteau's aim was to "create a theatrical setting… to offset the officialdom of a civil ceremony". He succeeds, bring-

Map on page 206

The Cocteau-decorated Salle des Mariages in the Menton Hôtel de Ville is a popular place for a wedding, particularly favoured by the Japanese.

BELOW: the mildest climate in the Med.

Menton's Gardens

Menton has long been famous for its gardens, ever since foreign residents, especially the English, took advantage of the climate and began surrounding their villas with large pleasure gardens planted with exotic palms, cacti and rare tropical blooms. Several can be visited, and others are in the course of careful restoration. In Garavan, almost on the border with Italy, is the **Villa Maria Serena** *(see page 212)*, reputed to have the mildest climate in France, a treasure trove of terraces of rare palms, grasses and cacti, ravishing against the backdrop of the sea.

The **Jardin Botanique du Val Rahmeh** was laid out by the English and is now the Mediterranean arm of the Natural History Museum. The variety of plants is amazing; Japanese cane bamboos and African succulents compete with Australian eucalyptus and Brazilian bougainvillea; Arabian date trees and Canary palms dwarf Mexican yucca and Iranian pistachios. Fruit trees include lemons, mandarins, bananas, oranges, figs and dates. Indigenous Provençal species also feature; sweet-smelling myrtle, rosemary and thyme flourish, as do evergreen lentisks, drooping lilies and a riot of roses.

On the far side of the Parc du Pian is avenue Blasco Ibáñez, named after the Spanish novelist who lived in exile here. Shunning the military dictatorship in Spain, Blasco Ibáñez settled on the Riviera in 1923. His villa, **Fontana Rosa**, is a piece of self-indulgence, heralded by ceramic portraits of Balzac, Cervantes and Dickens on the gateway. Surrounding the villa is the Spaniard's **Jardin des Romanciers** (currently being restored), a further tribute to his favourite novelists. The grounds, planted with cypress and Mediterranean shrubs, reflect a pastiche of classical and Art Deco styles.

To the north of Fontana Rosa and high above the town is the **Jardin des Colombières** (for information on visits contact the Heritage Service, tel: 04 92 10 97 10), arguably the most romantic gardens on the Riviera. The writer and artist Ferdinand Bac longed for an authentic Mediterranean garden, planted with Provençal herbs, box borders and clumps of yews. The shaded terraces are punctuated by ornamental pools, fountains, classical urns, baroque statues and giant black cypresses. A Moorish-style pavilion contains Bac's tomb.

But if the gardens are Italianate, the exuberant villa defies description. Decorated by Bac in 1926, it borrows freely from Hellenic, Roman and oriental traditions.

One of Menton's most special gardens is the **Serre de la Madone** (74 route de Gorbio; tel: 04 93 57 73 90; open Tues–Sun, Apr–Oct 10am–6pm, Dec–Mar 10am–5pm, closed Nov), created by Lawrence Johnston, who also designed the famous English garden at Hidcote Manor in Gloucestershire. In 1924 he selected a plot of land well protected from the sea winds. He spent the next 30 years travelling the world collecting plants for his garden, a romantic mingling of natural paths punctuated by carefully designed orangery, pools, parterres and pergolas. Cherished plants include an elephant's foot tree, rare camellias and Chinese peonies. The gardens, which had been badly neglected, are being restored by the Conservatoire du Littoral, and provide an exotic ambience for cultural and musical events.   ❑

LEFT: the Serre de la Madone.

Map on page 206

ing wonder and an epic dimension to a dreary registry office. Cocteau watched his adopted son get married in this very room.

Menton's Cocteau connection has recently been enhanced with a major donation from art collector Séverin Wunderman of 1,440 works by Jean Cocteau, spanning his entire career. These include drawings, ceramics, designs for the Salle des Mariages, and works by Cocteau's contemporaries Modigliani, De Chirico, Fougita, Magritte, Man Ray and Andy Warhol. A new museum is planned to house the collection, hopefully to open in 2008.

North of the Hôtel de Ville is the **Musée de Préhistoire Régionale** (rue Lorédan-Larchey; tel: 04 93 35 84 64; Wed–Mon 10am–6pm; free). Here you can see evidence of prehistoric life on the Riviera, and a section dedicated to local history has a reconstruction of a 19th-century kitchen and bedroom.

Foreign graves

From Menton it is a pleasant stroll round the bay to **Garavan**, a chic garden suburb with the most exotic vegetation in France. At the turn of the 20th century, Garavan was in its heyday, a haunt for high society. Glamorous villas with matching landscaped gardens were de rigueur. Today, despite the encroaching high-rise developments, Belle Epoque villas and Art Deco follies still survive.

The high inland road to Garavan is more appealing than the seafront route. From the basilica, climb the winding rue du Vieux-Château to the **Cimetière du Vieux-Château** ❶ (open daily; free) on the hill. The Italianate cemetery, built over the ancient citadel, spans four terraces, each devoted to a different faith. The tone is set by a smiling marble angel which looks set to soar over the Vieille Ville. The cemetery is noted for its foreign graves, a cosmopoli-

tan cast list of 19th-century celebrities who stayed longer than intended. Cats sun themselves on Prince Youssoupov's tomb, unafraid of Rasputin's murderer.

The **place du Cimetière**, just outside the cemetery walls, is a popular place for expatriate picnics and meeting friends. In the distance are signs for *Frontière*, proof if it were needed that the wooded headland beyond is, indeed, Italy.

Tropical flora

From the square, the **boulevard de Garavan** leads past terraced gardens and villas hugging the coast. Rooftop villas are draped with mimosa, bougainvillea, lentisks and giant cacti. No. 13, a Belle Epoque mansion built into the old city walls, is surrounded by olive and lemon groves. Next door is an Art Deco villa with magnificent views of the old port.

Several public paths lead down through lemon groves to the Garavan seafront. One such path, Sentier Villa Noël, takes you to the **Jardin Botanique du Val Rahmeh** ❶ (tel:

Buried in the Cimetière du Vieux-Château are Aubrey Beardsley, the young British illustrator, and William Webb Ellis, the "inventor" of the game of rugby.

BELOW: the Cimetière du Vieux-Château.

Lily at the Serre de la Madone park. Many of the tropical plants in Menton flower in winter because they are from the southern hemisphere.

BELOW: Palais Carnolès, home to the Musée des Beaux-Arts.

04 93 35 86 72; open Wed–Mon 10am–12.30pm, 2–6.30pm; closes 5pm Oct–Apr; admission charge), Menton's most successful park *(see page 210)*.

Near by is the **Parc du Pian K**, Garavan's public park. It was once part of a Spanish estate but is now a wild olive grove. This variety of olive, *le cailletier*, has been grown here for over 2,000 years, and stands out for its stocky trunk and succulent black olives, with a distinctive flavour. Some of the gnarled specimens in the Parc du Pian are hundreds of years old. By day, the grove makes a perfect place for a picnic, and on summer nights it is an open-air stage with wonderful views.

A steep walk on rue Ferdinand Bac leads to the **Jardin des Colombières L**, another spectacular garden *(see page 210)*.

A writer's home

From the park, steps cut down to the the boulevard de Garavan, and a right turn leads to **avenue Katherine Mansfield**, the New Zealand writer's retreat. The street is lined with Belle Epoque villas, from the stuccoed La Favorite to Chrisoleina, a turreted folly. Before Garavan railway station, a sign indicates Mansfield's **Villa Isola Bella M**, a rather disappointingly small, lemon-coloured villa with a disfigured view. Despite suffering from tuberculosis, Katherine wrote some of her best work here. She found Menton liberating, "a heavenly place" with life centred on "my pale yellow house with its mimosa in a slightly deeper hue". Soon after moving into the villa, Katherine wrote: "When I die you will find Isola Bella in poker work on my heart."

Just before the Italian border is **Villa Maria Serena** (21 promenade Reine-Astrid; tel: 04 92 41 76 76), whose garden should certainly be included on a tour *(see page 210)*.

Palais Carnolès

Back in the centre of Menton, a brisk walk west along the seafront leads to Carnolès. This dull suburb is worth visiting for one sight alone, the **Palais Carnolès N** (tel: 04 93 35 49 71; open Wed–Mon; free). Once a

Grimaldi summer home, the villa now houses Menton's **Musée des Beaux-Arts**. The pink-and-white palace is encircled by parasol pines and 50 different varieties of citrus trees. The museum's strengths lie in the Italian Quattrocento works, 16th-century portraits and modern Riviera landscapes. Louis Bréa, often called "Provence's Fra Angelico", is the only home-grown star of the period. The soft and spiritual *Virgin and Child* shows his delicate touch.

The ground floor displays a rotating collection of modern art, including Kisling's *Paysage à St-Tropez* and Sutherland's *La Fontaine*, which is a glowing composition of fountain and leaves.

Monastic views

A short drive north of Menton leads to the **Monastère de l'Annonciade** (visits arranged at tourist office; tel: 04 92 41 76 76) and arguably the loveliest views from Menton. By car, take the avenue de Sospel and turn left into the route de l'Annonciade. Alternatively, walk along the chemin du Rosaire, a steep but delightful walk which, until 1936, was the only way of reaching the monastery. The path winds uphill through pine trees and spiky yellow agaves; small shrines represent the Stations of the Cross.

The path and the monastery were created by Isabelle de Monaco after her miraculous cure from leprosy. Apart from an interruption during the Revolution, a Franciscan community has lived here ever since. Inside the chapel is a bizarre collection of votive offerings, from boats and crutches to a Zeppelin fragment and a strip of parachute from the 1991 Gulf War. The monastery is perched among cypress and olive groves. From its terrace of swaying eucalyptus trees there are coastal views towards Italy, Corsica and Cap Martin.

A fortified village

A few kilometres west of Carnolès lies **Roquebrune-Cap Martin**, a historic commune sandwiched between Menton and Monaco. In the 1840s, the medieval village of **Roquebrune** was practically deserted, and the

**Maps:
City 206
Area 180**

"The air smells of faint far tangerines, with just a touch of nutmeg. On my table there are cornflowers and jonquils with rosemary twigs..."
– KATHERINE MANSFIELD
MENTON ,
31 JANUARY 1920

BELOW: poster art at the Musée des Beaux-Arts.

The attractive town of Ventimiglia just across the Italian border from Menton is a popular hop for locals, thanks to its vast food and general goods market, every Friday.

wooded headland of Cap Martin was the preserve of sheep and cows. Before the end of the century, however, Cap Martin had been discovered by richer flocks, from Queen Victoria to Empress Eugénie. Villas sprang up among the olive groves, and Cap Martin remains the preserve of the rich today.

From Roquebrune railway station on the coast it is a short drive or an arduous climb to the medieval village. Steep staircases with vertiginous views lead up the reddish-brown cliff. The distinction between castle and village only evolved in the 15th century. Before then, the whole of Roquebrune was a *castellum*, a fortified 10th-century settlement which is unique in France.

The path finally emerges in rue de l'Eglise, beside the parish church of **Ste-Marguerite**. Originally Romanesque, it was heavily restored in the 18th century. Despite being overpriced, overcrowded and over-restored, Roquebrune remains a magical place. The apricot houses, chiselled out of the rock, overhang tiny squares and blind alleys. Narrow passageways burrow through a labyrinth of vaulted archways.

Château de Roquebrune

The geranium-covered walls present a misleadingly decorative picture. This ancient *castellum* was supremely functional. Its battlements commanded views of Mont Agel, Monaco and the coast; there were only two entrances, both heavily guarded. If invaders broke through the defences, they were quickly backed into cul-de-sacs and bombarded with boulders. As the oldest castle in France, Roquebrune was the prototype feudal chateau for centuries to come.

Roquebrune was built by the Count of Ventimiglia as a means of keeping the Saracens at bay. After a long struggle between the Genoese and the Counts of Provence, Roquebrune became a Grimaldi possession and remained so for five centuries. The grim **Château** (place Ingram; tel: 04 93 35 07 22; open daily 10am–6pm, July and Aug until 7.30pm; admission charge), is largely 13th century, although it was

Map
on page
180

heavily restored in the 20th century by Sir William Ingram. The locals were outraged when the Englishman added a mock medieval *tour anglaise*. The battlements offer magnificent views of the coast.

Rue Grimaldi, the main street, is marred by cute gentrification and craft shops, but the eccentricity and friendliness of the traders sets Roquebrune apart. An artist with an atelier readily discusses local history or produces photos of himself dressed as a Roman centurion. Ever since 1467, when the Virgin saved the town from the plague, 500 Roquebrunois have re-enacted scenes from the Passion every August. A sculptor carves angels and virgins out of olive wood, boasting about his discovery of "*le plus vieil homme de l'Europe*" in a local cave. Roquebrune is, indeed, riddled with prehistoric remains, especially in the famous caves, the Grottes du Vallonet.

Before leaving, stroll down rue Grimaldi to **place des Deux Frères**, named after the square's twin crags. In 1890, the square came into being when a huge outcrop was split to create an access road. The result was a success, and is a welcome release from the slightly claustrophobic feeling of Roquebrune.

Walking to Cap Martin

From the village, it is a pleasant, leisurely downhill stroll to **Cap Martin** and the coast. The prettiest route leads along chemin Souta Riba, a narrow, vaulted path edging round the outside of the village. Views through firs and pines reveal privatised Roman statuary in discreet villas. Soon after Souta Riba joins the chemin de Menton there is a huge gnarled **olive tree** *(see Tip, right)*. Further on are a couple of chapels, the dilapidated St-Roch and the rural de la Pausa, which was built in 1462 as a plague offering. Faded frescos of olive groves and angels cover the walls.

By the time the path reaches avenue du Danemark, suburbia is under way. On avenue Paul Doumer the Roman **Monument de Lumone** is a redeeming feature. These arches and mosaics are all that remain of a Roman settlement on the cape.

TIP

Roquebrune has two popular landmarks: the first is the castle, the second, to be found along the steep footpath that runs down to the lower town, is the wonderfully gnarled Olivier Millénnaire, an ancient olive tree that is probably even older than its name (1,000-year old olive tree) claims.

BELOW: at the beach in Cap Martin.

Map on page 180

"Italy is close at hand, you feel it in the air. Small streets with high narrow houses; a carriage can hardly drive through. Before reaching the old town and on departing, the main road is bordered with oleanders, cactus and palms."

– GUSTAVE FLAUBERT, *VOYAGE EN ITALIE ET EN SUISSE*, 1845

Although its olive and lemon groves have receded, Cap Martin is still lusher and less spoilt than Cap Ferrat. However, none of Cap Martin's Belle Epoque villas is open to the public, and most bask in smug celebrity. Name-droppers have a field day on Cap Martin. Fragrant Coco Chanel wafted in to entertain German officers during the war. Empress Eugénie liked to play the grande dame here, but presumably Greta Garbo didn't come for the company alone. Churchill and Le Corbusier came for the painter's light. Empress Sissy of Austria wintered here after a bad case of fin de siècle blues. W. B. Yeats came here and died.

Le Corbusier's path

The highlight of the cape is the **promenade Le Corbusier**, a lovely coastal path running west to Monaco and southeast around the cape. The path crosses an olive grove and then hugs the shore. Willows, sea pines and white rocks typify this stretch of coast. The walk towards Monaco passes the Modernist architect's beach house, just before the **Pointe de Cabbé** (tel: 04 93 35 62 87, open by appointment only, Tues and Fri 10am). Though tiny, the little wooden cabin is remarkable, designed for functionality down to the last detail, with beds, tables and shelves neatly tucked together. Clever mirrored shutters reflect a sublime sea view.

Close by is the **Etoile de Mer**, once a café, now a private house, where the camping units were also designed by Le Corbusier. Just below is No. 1027, the house of designer Eileen Grey, the first to build on this site. Her house is a superb example of Modernist architecture that respects the organic nature of the place. It has been sadly neglected, but there are now plans to restore it and develop the entire location as a tribute to Modernism.

Le Corbusier died of a heart attack while swimming in the sea here in 1965, but had the foresight to design a splendid memorial to himself in Roquebrune cemetery. Cynics label this a supremely Cap-Martin gesture. ❑

BELOW: a coastal view.

RESTAURANTS & CAFÉS

Restaurants

Eating establishments around the market are a good place to sample the local fish dishes, including stockfish spiced with garlic and white wine before being flambéed in cognac. A typical accompaniment to fish is *fleurs farcies*, courgette (zucchini) flowers that have been stuffed with cheese, tomatoes and garlic.

Le Braïjade Méridiounale
66 rue Longue. Tel: 04 93 35 65 65. Open L & D Sept–June, D only July–Aug; closed Wed. €€
Favoured local restaurant in the old town which offers Mentonnais specialities such as *bagna cauda* (hot anchovy dip with vegetables) and fish with *allioli*.

Le Louvre
Hôtel Les Ambassadeurs, 3 rue Partouneaux. Tel: 04 93 28 75 75. Open L & D daily. €€€
This classic Belle Epoque hotel in the centre of town has been recently renovated with an elegant airy terrace for dining. Food is stylish, light Mediterranean; try sea bass marinated with lemon, basil and avocado, or saffron bouillabaisse.

Pistou
9 quai Gordon Bennett. Tel: 04 93 57 45 89. Open L & D daily; closed Sun pm & Mon. €€
Overlooking the port, this popular fish restaurant with sea-view terrace serves a variety of seafood and paella, and is especially recommended for the bouillabaisse.

Riaumont
Hôtel Aiglon, 7 avenue. de la Madone. Tel: 04 93 57 55 55. Open L & D daily. €€€
Delightful old villa with a shady terrace, surrounded by a garden of banana palms, for classic French cuisine.

La Traverse
Place de la Mairie. Tel: 04 93 28 54 75. Open L & D Wed–Mon; closed Tues. €€
A small Italian family restaurant serving excellent pizzas with home-baked thin crust, pasta and house specialities such as beef fillet with rocket, parmesan and tomatoes.

Le Virginia
175 promenade du Soleil. Tel: 04 93 57 46 30. Open L & D daily; closed Mon Sept–June. €€
Comfortable restaurant on promenade between Roquebrune and Menton with wonderful sea views and shaded terrace, for classic French cuisine, especially scallops, sole, grilled meat and pizzas.

Le Vistaero
Hôtel Vista Palace, Roquebrune-Cap Martin. Tel: 04 92 10 40 20. Open D daily; closed Feb. €€€
Luxurious modern hotel, with superb sea views and botanical garden, has a restaurant presided over by young chef Olivier Streiff who offers the latest avant-garde cuisine: risotto of black cherries and parmesan, pork breast caramelised with eucalyptus, mousse of rhubarb, elderflowers and gorgonzola... you get the idea.

Cafés

Café du Centre
41 avenue Félix Faure. Tel: 04 93 28 34 09. Open L & D; closed Mon Sept–June. €

Grand café and large arcaded terrace for coffee, tea, drinks and light meals such as omelettes, grills and salads.

Café La Cigale, Salon de Thé
27 avenue. Varnot. Tel: 04 93 35 74 66. Open daily 8am–8pm; closed Tues. €
Menton's most celebrated pâtisserie, offering coffee, ice creams, gateaux and chocolate galore. Outdoor terrace.

PRICE CATEGORIES

Prices for a three-course dinner per person without wine:

€ = under €25
€€ = €25–40
€€€ = over €40

RIGHT: the brilliant light makes eating out special.

THE PERCHED VILLAGES

Deep in the countryside, not far from the fast-paced
cities of Nice and Monte-Carlo, in the foothills of
the Southern Alps lie tranquil medieval villages
perched on craggy hilltops and slopes,
where time seems to stand still

Perched villages, or *villages
perchés*, were built on hilltops
around a fortified chateau in
the early Middle Ages as safe
havens from a series of invaders
coming from the coast, such as the
Saracens, and the hinterland. These
craggy outposts were picked for
their good, often 360-degree vantage points, and the settlements, surrounded by solid ramparts, were
built in the local stone to blend
securely into the landscape. Many
of the villages have been restored.

A number of the perched villages,
such as Ste-Agnès, Gorbio and Peillon, are only a few miles inland, providing a stark and welcome contrast
to the urbanised coast. Even villages
further into the mountains, such as
Utelle, Lantosque or Lucéram, can
easily be visited in a day, since the
roads are good, if often steep, and
rarely busy.

However, it can be particularly
pleasant to find a hotel and stay
overnight in these beautiful mountains, to appreciate fully the pristine
air and star-studded night skies, and
to wake up to a deep silence broken
only by cow bells. Spring, when the
flowers are at their most beautiful,
is perhaps the best time to enjoy
such unspoilt regions, but during the
summer they can provide a cool,
refreshing break from the coast.

Above Nice

The perched village of **Falicon** ❶ is
close to Nice and well worth a visit.
It was the setting for Jules
Romains's novel *La Douceur de la
Vie,* and was also where Queen Victoria liked to stroll and take her
afternoon tea while staying in Nice
– an event commemorated by a
restaurant called Au Thé de la
Reine. The old village is very small,
filled with covered passages and
twisting lanes, and is characterised
by a series of picturesque *placettes*

LEFT: the perched
village of Peille.
BELOW:
a stroll through town.

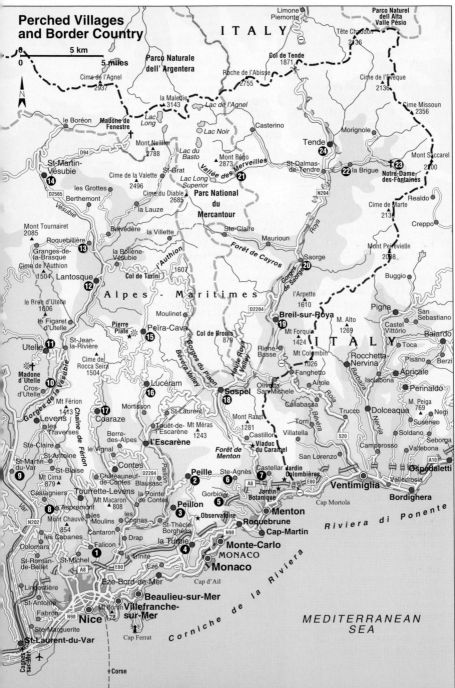

Perched Villages and Border Country

ITALY

Parco Naturel dell'Alta Valle Pésio

Limone Piemonte

Tête Chaddon 2136

0   5 km
0   5 miles

N

Cima de l'Agnel 2937

Parco Naturale dell' Argentera

Col de Tende 1871

Roche de l'Abisse 2755

Cime de l'Évêque 2136

Cime Missoun 2356

la Maledie 3143

Lac de l'Agnel

le Boréon

Madone de Fenestre †

Lac Long

Lac Noir

Casterino

Morignole

Tende **24**

Mont Saccarel 2100

Mont Neillier 2788

D94

Lac du Basto

Mont Bégo 2873

Notre-Dame des-Fontaines **23**

St-Martin-Vésubie

14

Cime de la Valette 2496

St-Grat

les Grottes

Berthemont

D2565

Cime du Diable 2685

la Lauze

Lac Long Superior

Vallée des Merveilles

St-Dalmas-de-Tende

la Brigue **22**

Realdo

Creppo

Parc National du Mercantour

N204

Cime de Marte 2136

Mont Tournairet 2085

Belvédère

la Villette

Ste-Claire

Maurioun

Saorge

Mont Pelevielle 2098

Buggio

Roquebillière **13**

la Bollène-Vésubie

Forêt de Cayros

Gorges de Saorge

Pigna

San Sebastiano

Granges-de-la-Brasque

Cima de l'Authion 1504

Lantosque **12**

Col de Turini

l'Authion 1607

Alpes - Maritimes

Saorge **20**

l'Arpette 1610

Castel Vittório

Balardo

le Bren d'Utelle 1606

le Figaret d'Utelle

Pierre Plate ☆

Peïra-Cava

Moulinet

Col de Brouis 879

D2204

Breil-sur-Roya **19**

M. Alto 1269

Rocchetta-Nervina

Toca

Pisano

Berzi

Utelle **11**

St-Jean-la-Rivière

Gorges du Piaon

Mont Forquin 1424

Riene Basse

I T A L Y

Aprícale

Madone d'Utelle

Cime de Rocca Seira 1504

Lucéram **16**

Mont Colombin 1026

Fanghetto

Barbaira

Isolabona

Perinaldo

Cros-d'Utelle

Mt Férion 1413

Sospel **18**

Olivetta San Michele

Aïrole

Dolceacqua

M. Peiga 769

Mortisson

St-Laurent

Collabassa

Roja

Torri

Trucco

Soldano

Negi

Susegno

Levens

les Traverses

Coaraze **17**

Mt Méras 1243

Mont Razet 1281

Villatella

Seborga

Valfebona

Berre-des-Alpes

Touët-de-l'Escarène

Castillon

S20

Camporosso

Ste-Claire

St-Antoine

le Vignal

Forêt de Menton

Viaduc du Caramel

San Lorenzo

A10

St-Martin-du-Var **9**

Mt Cima 879

Contes

Châteauneuf-de-Contes

Castellar

Jardin Colombières

Ventimiglia

Ospedaletti

Vallecrosia

Castagniers

la Pointe de Contes

Peille **2**

Ste-Agnès

7

E80

Bordighera

Tourrette-Levens

D2204

Blausasc

Gorbio

6

A8

Jardin Botanique

Cap Mortola

Aspremont **8**

Mt Macaron 808

Peillon **3**

5

Menton

Riviera di Ponente

N202

Mont Chauve 854

les Moulins

les Cougnas

● Observatoire

Roquebrune

Cap-Martin

Cantaron

St-Thècle Borghéas

la Turbie **4**

Monte-Carlo

Olomars

St-Roman-de-Bellet

St-Michel

A8

E80

Drap

la Trinité

Èze

MONACO

Monaco

Corniche de la Riviera

Lingostière

Èze-Bord-de-Mer

Cap d'Ail

St-Antoine

Fabron

N98

Mt Boron

Nice

Beaulieu-sur-Mer

Villefranche-sur-Mer

MEDITERRANEAN SEA

Ste-Marguerite

St-Laurent-du-Var

Cagnes-sur-Mer ✈

Cap Ferrat

✝ Corse

(little squares), one of which has a rare perpendicular staircase leading to a raised front door. The baroque church dates from 1624.

Northeast of Nice and Falicon are two superb examples of *villages perchés*, Peille and Peillon, in the valley of the Paillon river; these ancient craggy places rise up impossibly elevated above the valley floor, just about escaping the tangle of Nice's industrial suburbs.

It is surprising that **Peille ❷** is not better-known. It is a large, almost completely medieval village, with two old quarters dating as far back as the 11th century, and has a wonderful variety of features and views. There are car parks at either end of the village.

Don't miss the place André Laugier, where there is a pair of 13th-century doors, one Romanesque, one Gothic, and a pair of matching Gothic windows. Behind this is the place du Mont Agel, surrounded by very old houses, with a Gothic fountain in the centre. The rue Lascaris leaves the square through the loggia of the ancient palais, and out to a viewing platform. From here, a short path leads to the cemetery and the war memorial. The view extends all the way to Cap d'Antibes.

All the streets leading from place du Mont Agel are worth exploring: rue du Moulins has double round-arched windows, probably 15th-century; rue de La Turbie leads under an arch to a charming square housing a small **museum** of local history (open Sat and Sun pm only; free).

The finest feature is the large **Eglise Ste-Marie**, set at the head of the village and created from two adjoining chapels, the oldest being 12th-century. Two buttresses span the road, and a slender Romanesque bell tower dominates the village. A picture to the right of the altar shows Peille in the 16th century.

On the side of Montée St-Bernard next to the church are the ruins of a 14th-century castle, part of the original fortifications of the town which were mostly pulled down during the Revolution. A very old part of the village lies directly below the castle, across the main road, consisting of very steep stone stairs and covered alleys. The Hôtel de Ville on place Carnot is housed in an 18th-century chapel, which has an interesting domed roof.

Dizzy heights

Nearby **Peillon ❸** is regarded as one of the most beautiful of all the perched villages. Approaching from the main road, it seems impossible to believe that 3 km (2 miles) will be enough to reach its dizzy heights among the olives and pines. As the French memorably put it, "*Peillon marque l'extrémité du monde habité*." Its charm is in the entire ensemble, the fantastic position, the winding main "street", which would be better described as a staircase, and the superb views from the top.

As you enter the village from the

Map on page 220

Heading west out of Nice, along the route de Bellet, the terraced vineyards on the hills of Bellet soon come into view. This is the tiny and rather fashionable wine district of Bellet, one of the smallest appellations in France. Bellet wine is very hard to find outside Nice.

BELOW:
a typical hill town.

TIP

You can take a 90-minute walk along a lovely wooded ridge to Peille from Peillon. A footpath also leads from Peillon to La Turbie.

small square shaded by plane trees, there is a fragment of an old archway to the left. There is also a tower of white stone, which is very clean and well restored.

A number of houses have open top floors in the Renaissance manner. The narrow streets have very steep stone steps through vaulted tunnels and sometimes as many as four front doors leading from someone else's basement. On the edge of the village the **Chapelle des Pénitents Blancs** contains 15th-century frescos attributed to Jean Canavesio. They can be glimpsed through a grille on the door.

A Roman relic

La Turbie ❹, high above Monte-Carlo, is one of the most magnificent sights of the region. The name La Turbie comes from the Latin *tropaea* (trophy), and it is named after the **Trophée des Alpes** (tel: 04 93 41 20 84; open mid-Sept to mid-May Tues–Sun, mid-May to mid-Sept daily; admission charge;), a huge Roman monument erected to commemorate the conquest by Augustus

of the 45 Alpine tribes who had been attacking Roman Gaul. Augustus, the first of the Roman emperors, led the campaigns in 15 and 14 BC. The Trophée was built between 13 and 5 BC, probably using the enslaved Alpine tribesmen as labour.

The structure was originally 50 metres (165 ft) high, and even now, 35 metres (115 ft) are still standing after 2,000 years. It consists of a large rectangular base supporting a cylindrical core of 24 huge Doric columns, some of which remain, their load-bearing supports now visible. The columns once supported a masonry tower, surmounted by a stepped cone roof, topped with a giant statue of Emperor Augustus as the conquering general.

There is a nine-line inscription framed by two winged victories on the front face, the longest intact Roman inscription to come down to us from antiquity. From the 7th to 10th centuries its upper parts were used as a watchtower against barbarian raids, and parts of its masonry were reused in ramparts to stave off the Saracens.

BELOW: wander through the narrow old streets.
RIGHT: Trophée des Alps, La Turbie.

The trophy crumbles

In the Middle Ages, the Lérins monks destroyed its pagan statues. In the wars between the Guelphs and the Ghibellines during the 12th and 13th centuries, the villagers took refuge in its passages and stairways. In 1706, it was partially destroyed because of its strategic location, and, later, Louis XIV ordered the destruction of the "castle", not wishing any fortification to fall into the hands of the Dukes of Savoy. The ruins became a quarry, and most of the town of La Turbie is built from the very stones which gave it its name. Only one other similar trophy is known, that of Trajan at Adam Klissi in Romania, making this of particular interest.

The monument is set in a lovely clifftop park, ideal for picnics. There is also a fine museum, displaying the many pieces which have been unearthed from the ruins, with a large-scale model of how it originally looked. From the cliff is a spectacular view over the Mediterranean and to Monte-Carlo below. Yachts and speedboats go about their business, and tiny cars crawl along the winding roads, but on the days when Formula One racing cars are in Monte-Carlo for the Grand Prix, the throaty roar is deafening, even 450 metres (1,500 ft) up.

The town itself is small, built in a quarter-circle with two surviving town gates, one of which is best seen from the gardens of the Trophée, and many old buildings from the 11th and 13th centuries, particularly lining what used to be the Roman Via Julia. The baroque 18th-century church is built from stones taken from the Trophée and has attractive bands of coloured tiles on its cupola. La Turbie is utterly charming, with a wealth of architectural details embedded in its ochre walls and vaulted arcades, and its narrow cobbled streets dominated by the vast monument.

Up in the mist

Just north of Roquebrune and Menton is a group of hill villages which are just far enough from the bustling coast to have escaped the crowds. It helps that the villages lie at the end

Map on page 220

Man's best friend out for a walk in a hilltop village.

BELOW: medieval walls and doorways in La Turbie.

of tortuous roads and are literally hidden in mists. Not for nothing are the residents of Gorbio and Ste-Agnès referred to as *les nébuleux*, the mist-dwellers.

Gorbio ❺ sits high on a hill looking out to the Mediterranean, amongst the olives which provided its livelihood until the 19th century; from then on its inhabitants turned to tourism for an income, catering to the growing numbers of visitors from Menton. It is famous for its narrow arched streets, and for its snail procession in June, *la procession aux escargots*, which is not actually a promenade of snails, but a festival celebrated by the White Penitents, when the streets are illuminated by oil flames lit in a multitude of snail shells.

Although close to Menton, **Ste-Agnès** ❻ belongs to medieval Provence, a landscape at once Mediterranean and mountainous. As a quaint *village perché*, Ste-Agnès is the most attractive in the area. Its eagerness to send visitors away with souvenirs rather than memories is the only jarring note.

En route to Ste-Agnès, the familiar olive and lemon groves merge into Provençal *maquis*. As the land climbs to 700 metres (2,300 ft), the olives disappear; sturdy juniper, pine and fir trees jut over the crags. By Ste-Agnès the mists and the temperatures fall, particularly in the early morning. "*Je vais me noyer dans la brume,*" ("I'm off to drown myself in the fog,") is almost a cheery greeting in the village.

It is not clear how Ste Agnès acquired her sainthood. One legend has it that she was a Roman empress who sought refuge from a storm in a local grotto and, in thanks, built a chapel on the spot. The more colourful version is that Haroun, a Saracen chief, raided the village and selected a Provençale for his harem. The chaste Agnès resisted her kidnapper until he converted to Christianity.

From the 12th century, the village was fought over by the Counts of Ventimiglia and Provence. In the 16th century the ancient **Château** was dismantled and its stones incorporated into existing houses. The ruins overlook an Italianate cemetery

A 300-year-old elm stands in the centre of Gorbio's main square. Its trunk measures nearly 6 metres (20 ft) in diameter.

BELOW: Ste-Agnès.
RIGHT: a chapel in the trees near Castillon, north of Castellar.

and pine forest. The walk up is especially pungent in spring: woodsmoke wafts through the cherry blossom, herbs and damp pine trees. At the top, if the fog has lifted, there are views towards the Alps, the coast and even Corsica.

A shrine to Ste-Agnès

Just below the chateau ruins is the village, clustered around the foot of a cliff. Place de la Mairie is lined with old buildings, including **Notre-Dame-des-Neiges**, the parish church. The honey and herb shops outside are a prelude to the main assault on **rue Longue**, where an army of enamelists and herbalists, soap-sellers and crystal-engravers, jewellers and dried-flower designers ply their trade. With its neat stone steps, flower-hung archways and well-restored houses, Ste-Agnès is almost too perfect.

Rue Longue leads to **square Ste-Agnès**, perched on the edge of a ravine. This is where the original chapel was carved into the rock. All that now remains is a small shrine and a pretty statue of the saint. The chapel was destroyed during the construction of a wartime fortification system along the border. From 1930, the Italian threat was ever-present, so an extension to the Maginot line was created from the coast to the mountains beyond Sospel. Designed as an updated model of a Vauban fortress, **Fort-Maginot de Ste-Agnès** remains an impressive defensive system, only accessible via a narrow drawbridge (open July–Sept daily, Oct–June Sat and Sun pm only; admission charge).

Villagers whimsically attribute their wartime escape to the spirit of Ste Agnès, still lurking in her grotto within the military fort. On 21 January, her saint's day, a procession to Notre-Dame-des-Neiges is followed by a concert.

Just a few paces away from the fort is the **Le Righi** restaurant, an ideal place to stop and savour the local cuisine, like the spinach ravioli and home-made desserts, while admiring the breathtaking views over the coastline.

Rue des Comtes Léotardi leads out of the village, past covered passage-

Map on page 220

Stop by a friendly bar or restaurant for refreshment after a walking tour of the perched villages.

BELOW: isolated houses dot the mountainous landscape.

ways and medieval ramparts. Along here is the Vieille Auberge, with its promise of *raviolis maison, daube* and panoramic views. If you're not leaving Ste-Agnès over-fed or laden with pine-scented cologne and Saracen jewels, then consider a walk along mule tracks to Gorbio. The Chemin du Pierre Rochard is named after the wartime parish priest who regularly walked to Menton to bring back rations.

A good place for lunch

Castellar , just east of Ste-Agnès, is perched on a hillside covered with orchards and olives. The village is an acquired taste, historically richer than Ste-Agnès yet somewhat neglected. Entirely lacking in arts and crafts, Castellar is guileless, a traditional hilltop village not swarming in tourists. To the Niçois, its sole function is to serve Sunday lunch in a rural setting.

The rectangular village was laid out with military precision by the Lascaris Seigneurs. It remained in their hands until the Revolution, with peasants continuing to pay such feudal dues as a shoulder of pork for a day's grazing rights. Not until 1792 did Castellar become part of France, an event celebrated by *l'arbre de la liberté* (freedom tree) in the **place de la Mairie**.

From here, the formal grid-pattern is clear: three parallel streets, linked by covered passageways, lead to the church at the end of the village. Two encircling paths trace the outline of the former city walls. **Rue de la République** is lined with sombre medieval houses, each with a roughly hewn stone staircase. *Fougasse*, biscuits made from almonds and pine kernels, can be bought at the grocery.

Equally pleasant aromas waft from La Tour Lascaris, a rustic restaurant housed in the **Palais Lascaris**, the Counts' former residence. Although the *salle d'armes* has lost its frescos, it retains an austere charm in keeping with the cuisine. Favourites on the menu include *tourte de courge*, a courgette-and-aubergine pie, and *Barba Juan, crêpes* stuffed with mushrooms, cheese and rice. Food is simple and

There is a small Musée de Vieux Metiers on narrow rue Arson, Castellar. The museum, which highlights the work of local artisans and craftsmen is worth a look only if you happen to be exploring that part of the village. Opening hours can vary.

BELOW:
locals preparing for a village fiesta.

vegetable-based, a reflection of Castellar's peasant roots.

At the end of rue de la République is **St-Pierre**, a restored baroque church with an onion-domed bell tower and pinkish façade. From here, rue Général Sarrail leads back to the Mairie. The first house on the left was a medieval prison but has been converted into a crafts workshop. Opposite is the **Chapelle des Pénitents Blancs**, a baroque chapel hemmed in by medieval houses which can only be viewed from the outside. Further along is the **Chapelle des Pénitents Noirs**, sadly in need of restoration.

Covered passageways on the right lead to **rue Arson**, the prettiest part of the village, bordering the countryside. A circular medieval tower backs on to the ramparts and, close to the church, is an olive-processing mill and an old wash-house. The village is keen to attract visitors but not at the expense of peace and quiet. In short, scruffy Castellar will not succumb to the prettified Ste-Agnès effect, and is arguably more interesting for it.

Into the mountains

Heading north instead of northeast from Nice, the route towards St-Martin-Vésubie takes in more perched villages as well as the spectacular Gorge de la Vésubie.

Leave Nice on the N202 and take the D414 to Colomars, where it becomes the ridge road to **Aspremont ❽**, a charming village of concentric picturesque lanes with lots of little winding alleys leading from them. At the foot of the village stands the chapel of St-Claude, built in 1632 to guard the inhabitants against the plague. The church of St-Jacques has an unusual 13th-century Gothic nave, contrasting in style with the other village buildings. A castle once stood at the top of the village, but now only the solid ramparts remain.

Follow the rue des Remparts around the top of the village to reach the place Léandre Astraudo, a small square with a fountain; on one side is the highest remaining section of castle wall, with corbels and blocked-up windows. There is a stairway to a little playground with a

Map on page 220

The village festivals are family affairs, but visitors are welcome too.

BELOW: time to talk in Aspremont.

superb view of the mountains and a grove of trees marking the position of the castle keep.

Near by, **Castagniers** is a tiny village, largely rebuilt in the 19th century. There is a wonderful view of the Var Valley from the small square in front of the 1817 church.

If you continue up the Var Valley, you will come to **St-Martin-du-Var** ❾, just off the main road. The old village is a small tangle of lanes tucked behind the huge main square. **La Roquette-sur-Var**, high on its hill, was built at a strategic position on the old international frontier with Italy, and at the summit of the village there are the vestiges of a castle. The church of St-Pierre was completed in 1682.

Continuing north on the N202, you come to Plan-du-Var, the last stop for pizza and cold drinks before the **Gorges de la Vésubie** ❿, which lacks any kind of roadside refreshment. The gorge is stunning, its steep sides plummeting to the river below, the road winding and tunnelling through the rock. In a car it can be difficult to stop to admire the view; cycling or rambling is a much better way to appreciate it all.

On the salt route

At **St-Jean-la-Rivière**, the deep gorge is spanned by a dramatic bridge and the houses are built on top of each other either side of the river. This is where the Vésubie canal, much of which is underground, begins. From here, you can take the steep, winding road to **Utelle** ⓫, one of the villages on the original *route du sel* (salt route) from the salt flats of Hyères to the Southern Alps, a route which was abandoned in the late 18th century.

Utelle is a very pleasant little town, dependent mainly on olive cultivation. It is built like a star on a rocky outcrop, originally the crossroads of a number of mule paths over the mountains. The hillsides, covered in wild lavender and fragrant herbs, are perfect for walking and picnics.

The 16th-century **Eglise St-Véran** replaced an earlier one destroyed by the earthquake of 1452. It is a curious mixture of

architectural styles, with Romanesque columns and capitals, 18th-century baroque decoration, a Gothic loggia and 16th-century high altar. Don't miss the primitive altarpiece of the *Annunciation* in the north aisle or the doors with their 12 panels carved with dragons. The village has some intriguing door lintels; near the post office there is one at knee level, carved with esoteric alchemical symbols.

The mountain road continues beyond the village, climbing higher and higher with hair-raising views of the valleys below, until you reach a magnificent wind blown plateau and the sanctuary of **Madone d'Utelle**. According to legend, it was founded by sailors who were guided to safety during a tempest by a mysterious light on the mountain and founded the sanctuary in gratitude. The chapel, which is usually open, was restored in the mid-1970s, and the building next to it is used as a retreat.

There is a viewing platform with a spectacular 360-degree panorama of mountain peaks and valleys and beyond to the distant sea; on a clear day you can see as far as Cap d'Antibes and even Corsica.

Further up the valley

The main road, the D2565, continues towards Lantosque, climbing all the way. The gorge widens into meadows and pastures; this is an area of pony rides, horses, camping and caravanning.

There can be few things more pleasurable than sitting beneath a parasol at one of the cafés in the lively little square at **Lantosque ⑫**, with a distant view of the village of La Bollène-Vésubie clinging to its hilltop further up the valley. Lantosque itself is built on the rocky spine of the hill up which the streets climb in a series of staircases. There is an Italianate influence in the architecture, with open loggias on the top floors of many of the older houses.

A little further on is **La Bollène-Vésubie**, a charming town with big, shady lime trees lining the wider streets. At the top of the village is a pretty baroque church dated 1525. There are no architectural highlights

Map on page 220

The high vaulted ceiling and ornate altar in the Eglise St-Véran, Utelle.

BELOW: alpine view from Utelle.

in the village; it is the ensemble that makes it so delightful.

The D2565 road leads on through trout-fishing country to **Roquebillière** , an ancient village partially destroyed by a landslide in 1926. A bridge leads over to the new town, built after the disaster, with uniform red-tiled roofs. High on the mountain, overlooking them both, is **Belvédère**, a hill town with a rather good clock and sundial on the bell tower and a large barn-like church. The houses are many-storeyed, with balconies and top-floor loggias in the mountain tradition. Lavender and jasmine grow everywhere, and the views are wonderful.

End of the road

Once beyond Roquebillière, the architecture becomes noticeably Alpine, with large overhanging roofs and balconies in the Swiss chalet style. Not for nothing is this area known as the "Suisse Niçoise".

The principal town in this region is **St-Martin-Vésubie** , a gateway to the Parc National du Mercantour. It is a mountaineering centre and summer retreat, popular with the people of Nice, but even in high season it's a sleepy kind of place. The main shopping and restaurant street is the rue du Docteur Cagnoli, which stretches the full length of the town. It has a fast-flowing gutter running down the middle and is lined with Gothic houses with corbels and balconies, the oldest of which are at the bottom, near the church. There is quite a mix of architectural styles, blending Swiss-style chalet roofs and wooden balconies with Italian loggias, Gothic doors and jettied roofs.

At No. 25 is the **Maison Gothique** of the Counts of Gubernatis, a national monument. It has a jettied first floor, ornamental frieze and arched ground floor. On one side of the street the buildings lean out over the river, and the restaurants have tree-shaded dining terraces at the back. Near the 18th-century **Chapelle des Pénitents Blancs**, which has an interesting bulb cupola, is a tiny marketplace. The baroque church is 17th-century, but possesses a 13th-century Virgin

Every December Lucéram's streets are awash with Nativity scenes in what is known as the Circuit des Crèches. *Everyone and anyone can take part, and Nativities can range from just a few toys put together to life-sized statues and a living crib with real animals.*

BELOW: St-Martin-Vésubie, popular in the summer.

which is carried in procession on the last Saturday in June to the high mountain sanctuary of Madone de Fenestre, where she remains until the end of September.

From the terrace in front of the church door there is a view looking south to the perched village of Venanson. Behind the east end of the church, to the right, is the place de la Frairie, a terrace looking out over the Madone de Fenestre river, which has its origins in the Lac de Fenestre in the mountains to the east on the Italian border. The steep river valley can be followed for 13 km (8 miles) along the D94, ending at the Madone de Fenestre chapel.

Back towards the coast

A variety of return routes to the coast are possible. You might go via **Peïra-Cava** , originally a military camp but now a winter-sports and holiday resort. The view from the Pierre Plate, a 10-minute walk or drive from the centre of the village, is superb. There is parking near the top.

Lucéram , further south, is situated at the crossroads of ancient paths, in particular the salt route from the coast. Until recently, it depended on mountain farming for survival, mainly olive and lavender cultivation. Today, the fortified village, with tall stacked houses in pastel colours and sombre vaulted alleys, depends almost entirely on tourism. It is noted particularly for the church treasures in the 15th-century **Eglise Ste-Marguerite** (open Tues–Thur and Sun pm only; Fri and Sat on request; call the tourist office on 04 93 74 46 50), which include a silver reliquary and retables attributed to Niçois artist Louis Bréa.

Finally, **Coaraze** is worth a detour – a restored medieval perched village with concentric lanes, arches, covered passages and public gardens. The church is 17th-century in the *baroque-rustique* style, and there are various modern sundials (one by Jean Cocteau) in the square outside. Visit the cemetery, which uses cement boxes for burials because the rock is too hard to dig. At the summit of the village is the place du Château, site of the now demolished castle. ❑

In the Alps visitors can explore medieval villages in the summer, or head to one of the mountain ski resorts, such as Utelle or Peïra-Cava, in winter.

RESTAURANTS

Coaraze

Auberge du Soleil
5 chemin de la Bégude. Tel: 04 93 79 08 11. Open L & D Mar–Nov. €–€
A popular but quiet restaurant serving up good and tasty country cooking in front of the most spectacular view.

Falicon

Le Parcours Live
1 place Marcel Eusebi. Tel: 04 93 84 94 57. Open L Sat–Sun only, D daily July–mid-Sept; closed Sun pm, Mon & Tues midday. €€

www.parcour?liverestaurant.com
This restaurant stands in the central square of this colourful town. The chef proposes an original, innovative, quality cuisine and the sommelier (one of the best in Europe) an interesting choice of wines.

Gorbio

Beau-Séjour
Main square. Tel: 04 93 41 46 15. Open L & D Thur–Tues; closed Nov–Mar. €€

A colourful yellow restaurant with green shutters serving delicious Provençal dishes. the terrace overlooks the central square and a 300-year-old elm tree.

Peillon

Auberge de la Madone
2 place Auguste Arnulf. Tel: 04 93 79 91 17. Open L & D Thur–Tues; closed Thur L, closed Jan & Nov–24 Dec. €€€
A wonderful Provençal inn offering excellent regional cuisine and lovely mountain views.

St-Martin Vésubie

La Treille
68–70 rue Cagnoli. Tel: 04 93 03 30 85. Open L & D, L only Wed; closed Thur, closed Mon Jul–Aug. €
This popular restaurant has an elegant dining room and terrace, as well as delicious regional cuisine, including seasonal game and mushroom dishes.

● ● ● ● ● ● ● ● ● ● ● ● ●

Prices for a three-course meal without wine.
€€€ €40 and over, €€ €25–40, € under €25.

BORDER COUNTRY

The Italian influence is everywhere in the towns and villages of the Riviera's mountainous hinterland, many of them clinging on to the sides of gorges. Once only linked by the salt route along the high ridges, this magnificent region still has a feel of isolation and adventure

The **Haut-Pays** resembles Piedmont rather than Provence and, in accent, sounds Italian rather than French. The Italian influence colours the architecture: loggias, arcaded squares and onion-topped bell towers abound. A love of decoration is present in such flourishes as carved lintels, elegant balconies and madonnas in niches. The dreamy Italianate villages strive after colour, with painted façades, *trompe l'œil* decoration and glinting fish-scale roofs. Sospel and the **Bévéra Valley** mark the transition from the outward-looking Mediterranean world to the inward-looking mountain world. Here olives, lavender and lemons give way to pine, oak, mountain laurel and carpets of vivid blue gentians.

The **Haute Roya Valley** begins just northeast of Sospel, and from Breil-sur-Roya the mountain atmosphere becomes more pronounced. The rural architecture acquires an Alpine sturdiness, with drystone barns and *cazouns*, the shepherds' primitive shelters.

Sleepy town

The natural gateway to the mountainous hinterland is **Sospel** ⑱, sprawling along the Bévéra Valley. As a great advocate of green tourism, Sospel offers a wide range of walks through classic hill country (the GR 52 long distance footpath runs through here). As well as for walking, it's popular with the Mentonnais for a day out and for hunting in autumn. Tourism is low-key and has not changed the character of this sleepy medieval town.

Sospel was an independent commune by the 11th century and an important trading post on the old salt route linking Piedmont with France. Medieval Sospel depended, in turn, on the Counts of Ventimiglia,

Map on page 220

LEFT: Eglise St-Michel, Sospel. **BELOW:** viewing the mountains.

Cyclists enjoy the twists and turns of the mountain roads and the Alps are also the location of several cycle races including the Roc d'Azur.

Provence and Savoy, but retained a degree of autonomy. This was partly due to the presence of charitable confraternities which played a major role in city life. By the 17th century, Sospel was a noted artistic and intellectual centre, but fell into a gradual decline, not reversed by the town's return to France in 1860.

The town did, however, experience brief glory, and much suffering, during World War II. In 1944–5 there were fierce battles in the area, and the German forces only withdrew in April 1945. By then, many Resistance workers had been executed and other Sospellois had been deported to Italy. In recognition of Sospel's sacrifices, the town was awarded the Croix de Guerre.

The focal point of the town is the **Pont Vieux**, the 11th-century tollgate and bridge spanning the River Bévéra. It is the oldest tollgate in the Alpes-Maritimes and was still in use in the 18th century, levying tax on goods carried over the bridge. Carriages from Nice transported salt, fish, citrus fruits, porcelain and silk towards Piedmont. In the opposite direction came rice, flax, muslin, lace and dry white wine. Today it contains the tourist office.

Although the bridge was partly blown up in 1944, the stones were fished out of the river, and the Pont Vieux was restored in 1953. The left bank of the river, originally outside the city walls, is lined with attractive pastel-coloured buildings.

Beside the old bridge is a small square with an arcaded medieval building and fountain. This faded apricot-coloured building was the **Palais Communal** until 1810, housing both the town council and religious tribunals. Place Garibaldi, the adjoining square, has a series of medieval arcades incorporated into later buildings.

The riverside quarter, stretching from place Garibaldi to place Ste-Croix, consists of austere 14th-century houses, once home to Sospel's prosperous merchant class. The houses in rue de la République contain vast interconnecting wine cellars. In the same street is the Maison de Toia, a sculpted Romanesque *hôtel particulier*.

Medieval Sospel had five confraternities offering hospitality to pilgrims and loans to impoverished peasants. While most Franciscan confraternities were egalitarian, Sospel's were hierarchical: the Pénitents Noirs served the nobility while the Rouges only welcomed local dignitaries; the Blancs were for the bourgeoisie, the Bleus for the young and the Gris for the poor. The **Chapelle Ste-Croix**, which dates back to 1518, is still the headquarters of the Pénitents Blancs, who continue to serve charitable purposes.

A beautiful square

From place Ste-Croix it is a short stroll across the river to the main street, avenue Jean Médecin, and place St-Pierre, a marketplace overlooking plantain trees. Rue St-Pierre, a medieval street leading to **Cathédral St-Michel**, is lined with dilapidated houses, including the Romanesque Maison Domérégo. This dingy passage astonishingly opens on to **place St-Michel**, the most theatrical square in the region.

Tucked into a graceful Romanesque clock tower is the cathedral's peaches-and-cream façade: frothy stucco and kitsch gladiatorial figures adorn the exterior.

Opposite the cathedral is the **Foyer Rural**, also subject to the *trompe l'œil* effect. This cultural centre used to be the town hall, until an earthquake shattered the building in 1887. Next door is the **Palais Ricci**, an arcaded Romanesque mansion which in 1809 welcomed Pope Pius VII on his journey to Tuscany. Curiously, this baroque square echoes Pienza, the Tuscan Renaissance town built by Pius II.

Sospel's cathedral is in its element during a sudden summer thunderstorm. It is also a magical building in the late evening, when the bells are chiming and a sliver of moon is visible between the tower and the baroque façade.

The majestic interior is well-preserved and full of light. The highlight is a 15th-century *Madonna* by François Bréa, the renowned Niçois artist. The Virgin, dressed in a gold embroidered dress, stands in front of

 TIP

The Ligurian Bréa family produced three artists in the second half of the 15th century, born in Nice. Their frescos and friezes can be seen in many churches and cathedrals in and around the border towns. For information on the route des Bréa, visit www.cerclebrea.com, or call 04 93 27 27 01.

BELOW: enter Sospel by Vieux Pont.

*A façade detail
on Ste-Catherine
Church, Breil-
sur-Roya.*

BELOW: restored mill
by the Roya River.

a Mediterranean coastal scene. Facing Bréa's work is a 15th-century depiction of *The Virgin and Christ*. The composition features the Pénitents Blancs, who commissioned the work. The painting, awkward and less idealised than Bréa's work, is also more moving.

War and resistance

From place St-Michel, the Montée de Louis Saramito leads up to the ruined castle and abbey. From Sospel, a signposted walk leads all the way through Provençal countryside to Olivetta in Italy. Longer hikes lead south to Castellar, or north to Moulinet and L'Authion, mountainous terrain where the Germans made their last stand at the Battle of Sospel.

War memorials are on every hill, but **Fort St-Roch** (tel: 04 93 04 00 70; open July–Aug daily pm only, Sept–Oct and Apr–Jun Sat and Sun pm only; admission charge; call ahead for a tour) is the most impressive and now houses a museum dedicated to the local resistance. Just south of Sospel, St-Roch was built

in 1930 against the threat of an Italian invasion. It is virtually an underground village, protected by anti-tank defences where 250 soldiers, with artillery and equipment, could survive for at least three months.

Local fears of an invasion were well founded and, although Sospel held out against superior Italian forces, occupation was inevitable, by the Italians in 1940 and the Germans in 1943. By September 1944, the Germans had lost Nice and Menton but were hanging on to Sospel, despite an Allied advance to the north.

Just 5 km (3 miles) south of Menton, the Allies were told to stay put and wait for the advance across northern Europe. As a result, Sospel suffered even longer in German hands and was exposed to American artillery attacks. In October, the Germans retreated northwards and Hawaiians were the first Allies to enter Sospel. Cries of *"Vive Sospel! Vive la IVème République!"* were short-lived, however, as the battle continued until April 1945.

The Roya Valley

Compared with the Vallée de la Bévéra, the **Roya Valley** is wilder, poorer and more rugged. In the past, routes didn't follow the valley floor because of fears of flooding or landfalls in narrow gorges. Instead, paths were carved along the side of the mountains and through high mountain passes. The Roya's medieval villages, often perched beside fearsome gorges, were linked only by the old salt route.

Until the 19th century, this route was the only way through the region; the Roya Valley did not open up until 1860 when Napoleon III, newly in control of the Comté de Nice, wished to increase trade with Piedmont. The Italian influence, along with a troubled history and terrible communications, have all

helped to preserve the Roya Valley in its splendid isolation.

Breil-sur-Roya makes an arresting first impression, particularly if reached by rail or via the precarious Col de Brouis. The train from Sospel emerges from a long mountain tunnel and suddenly there is a fish-shaped pattern of pastel houses clinging to a bend in the River Roya. The mountains bank steeply behind the red-tiled houses. A golden angel blows a trumpet from a chapel rooftop.

Breil likes to call itself the "French gateway to the Roya", since until 50 years ago the Italian border ran just north of the village. However, France is only skin-deep. *Ciao* is a normal greeting; the *cuisine provençale* tastes of Piedmont, and Italy lies only a few miles to the east.

Breil was ruled by the Counts of Provence, Ventimiglia and Genoa before becoming part of the House of Savoy until 1860. Unlike Sospel, Breil depended almost entirely upon olive-growing and farming. The lower slopes are still given over to olives, and 300 tonnes are harvested each year. As for farming, the village still operates traditional grazing rights: from October to April more than 4,000 Breil sheep and goats graze on communal land. It was a dispute about this issue that led to an 18th-century revolt against the feudal lords. The event is re-enacted every four years in Stacada, complete with mock battles and a show trial. The next re-enactment is in 2009.

A church beside the river

A gentle walk along the river leads to place Briançon in the heart of the medieval village. Open to the river on one side, the square is dominated by an apricot-coloured church, **Sancta Maria in Albis**. Its 18th-century baroque façade is echoed by a flamboyant Italianate interior, with a vivid Bréa panel-painting and a fine organ. The church, like many others in the Roya Valley, has a glittering multicoloured onion dome.

Although many Breillois are civil servants or coastal commuters, the village is enough of a retirement haven to radiate relaxation. Residents

Map on page 220

Breil is well-worn hiking country; signed walks lead to medieval watchtowers, such as La Cruella, or to isolated chapels to the west of the village. Longer hikes lead to Sospel or La Vésubie further west.

BELOW: bridge over the Roya in Breil.

A fountain in the fortified old town of Saorge.

BELOW: rugged mountain terrain.

include poets, local historians and the food writer Mademoiselle Sassi, whose book *Recettes Breilloises* provides an excellent guide to traditional Breil cuisine.

Breil is in many ways untypical of the Roya Valley. The vegetation is lushly Mediterranean and blurs the impact of the brooding mountains. Relative prosperity and an influx of outsiders have diluted its Italian atmosphere. In the Haute Roya, however, the transition to mountainous terrain is complete. The dramatic **Gorges de Saorge**, immediately north of Breil, announce serious terrain, with high waterfalls, deep forests, wind-blown Alpine pastures and mauve-grey canyons.

Roya history

Italian sentiments are not muted in the Haute Roya. From medieval times, the effects of epidemics and wars forced local *seigneurs* to recruit labour from further afield, particularly from Piedmont, Lombardy and Liguria. This Italian influx continued until the 1950s and

has left its mark on the language, culture and architecture.

In 1860, unlike the rest of the Comté de Nice, the Upper Roya remained with the House of Savoy, rulers since medieval times. La Brigue, Tende and the other villages in the Upper Roya were in an anomalous position. In the 1860 plebiscite they voted to rejoin France rather than remain with Piedmont, but were refused permission by Cavour, Victor Emmanuel's astute Prime Minister. Cavour's subterfuge was to claim that the region, bordering the game-rich Mercantour, formed part of the King's *terrains de chasse*. The reality had nothing to do with retaining hunting grounds and everything to do with controlling the vital mountain passes.

It was not until a 1947 plebiscite that the Haute Roya was incorporated into France. The head rather than the heart determined this political allegiance: trading links were with the French coast, and the French standard of living was far higher. So, while Niçois rightly claim that they were never Italian but merely Piedmontese, the same cannot be said of the distinctly Italian Roya Valley. Since becoming French, there have been no great social changes to this self-sufficient mountain community. Although mainly spoken now by the older generation, the dialects remain resolutely *piémontais*, as do the local crafts and traditions.

Shimmering tiles

The most spectacularly sited of all Roya villages is **Saorge ⓴**. At first sight, it appears suspended between a hazy mountain sky and the lush valley floor. The village forms a vast amphitheatre around a sheer cliff. Down below flows the Roya river, and on the other side of the canyon lie olive groves rising to terraced Alpine pastures.

Saorge looks like a traditional *village perché*: it is perched on high for defensive reasons and favours a south-facing slope, both as winter shelter and summer suntrap. The painted Venetian façades and the bell towers covered in a mosaic of shimmering tiles are also typical of Roya hilltop villages. But the height of the narrow medieval houses, the disparity of street levels and the complexity of the interlinking passages mark Saorge out as a perfect example of a *village empilé*, a "stacked village".

Saorge is set at right angles to the slope, so that the equivalent of a 30-storey tower separates the foundations of the lowest house from the roof of the highest one. Each house can be up to 10 storeys high, with entrances at five different street levels. The heights are so varied that some streets are merely corridors linking individual apartments rather than houses. This resembles a medieval version of the complex walkways found nowadays in modern shopping malls.

As a fortified village controlling the Col de Tende, Saorge seemed impregnable, but was finally captured by the French in 1794. Though it later returned to Piedmont, this former capital of the Roya never regained its prestige. The building of a valley road in the 19th century

Map on page 220

The Nice-Turin railway line through the Roya has 39 viaducts and is considered to be the most acrobatic line in Europe. In some of the mountain tunnels, the track does a loop so that the train emerges from the tunnel just above its entry point.

BELOW: the vast amphitheatre of Saorge.

Vallée des Merveilles

Cradled in a majestic circle of Alps, the Vallée des Merveilles is aptly named. The valley is a vast open-air museum of prehistory. It is also a Wagnerian landscape of rock-strewn valleys, jagged peaks and eerie lakes. Thanks to the presence of minerals, the lakes are green, turquoise and even black.

Just west of the Lac des Mèsches is the Minière de la Vallaure, an abandoned mine quarried from pre-Roman times to the 1930s. Prospectors came in search of gold and silver but had to settle for copper, zinc, iron and lead. The Romans were beaten to the valley by Bronze Age settlers who carved mysterious symbols on the polished rock, ice-smoothed by glaciation. These carvings were first recorded in the 17th century but investigated only from 1879, by Clarence Bicknell, an English naturalist. He made it his life's work to chart the carvings, and died in a valley refuge in 1918.

The rock carvings are similar to ones found in northern Italy, notably those in the Camerino Valley near Bergamo. However, the French carvings are exceptional in that they depict a race of shepherds rather than hunters. The scarcity of wild game in the region forced the Bronze Age tribes to turn to agriculture and cattle-raising. Carvings of yokes, harnesses and tools depict a pastoral civilisation, and these primitive inscriptions may have served as territorial markers for the tribes in the area.

However, the drawings are also open to less earthbound interpretations. Anthropomorphic figures represent not only domestic animals and chief tribesmen but also dancers, devils, sorcerers and gods. Such magical totems are in keeping with Mont Bégo's reputation as a sacred spot. Given the bleak terrain, it is not surprising that the early shepherds looked heavenwards for help. Now as then, animals graze by the lower lakes. However, the abandoned stone farms and shepherds' bothies attest to the unprofitability of mountain farming.

The Vallée des Merveilles is accessible only by four-wheel drive or on foot, and now, due to vandalism, you can visit areas where there are engravings only with an official guide. Given the mountain conditions, the drawings are only visible between the end of June and September. It is an 8-km (5-mile) drive west from St-Dalmas to the Lac des Mèsches. Then follows a 10-km (6-mile) trek through the woods to Lac Long and the rock-carving zone. In the nearby town of Tende, the tourist office (tel: 04 93 04 73 71) offers information on trips and guides (or visit www.tendemerveilles.com; French only), and you can also visit the fascinating Musée des Merveilles *(see page 246)*.

The Vallée des Merveilles is part of the Parc National du Mercantour, a vast conservation area worth visiting in its own right. Roughly 90 by 30 km (56 by 19 miles), Mercantour is a wilderness of pine forests, gorges and pastures. There are no permanent residents, just a few hamlets occupied by summer visitors. It is ideal rambling country with an amazing variety of flora and fauna. Wild geraniums, gentian violets and forest fruits are common on the lower slopes, while orchids, edelweiss and rare saxifrage grow higher up.

The park is also a game reserve, with ibex, wild boar and mountain goats. The only problem is poaching – mainly for venison. ❑

LEFT: a rock carving at the Vallée des Merveilles.

turned the village into a backwater – only valleys prospered. In 1806, a visiting tax-collector complained of "a road riddled with wolves and bandits, crossed in peril of one's life". The dangers have gone but the isolation remains.

Saorge is a remarkable composition, making it difficult to single out individual attractions. The rough slate roofs, a feature of the Roya Valley, add a severe touch to the 15th-century houses below. The façades are tinted pink, ochre and russet, bathing the village in a warm Ligurian glow at odds with the stark setting. The deepest alleys never see any sunlight.

In the 1960s, at the height of the exodus from the countryside down to the coastal towns, houses in Saorge sold for 2,000 francs; now the average price of a property is 150 times that, a true sign that many have been snapped up as *résidences secondaires*. The population, a mere 400 in winter, swells to 1,200 in summer. In winter the shutters are closed, and the village only stirs on market day.

Exploring Saorge

At the entrance to the village is a panoramic view of the valley below. On the square itself is a group of peach-coloured buildings, including a chapel and a Mairie crushed against the cliff. From here, rue Ste-Jeanne d'Arc winds upwards through covered passageways.

At the top is **St-Sauveur**, the 15th-century parish church. The forbidding exterior is not misleading; inside is a damp, mauve-tinged interior and a chilly atmosphere not redeemed by a fine Italian organ. Virtually next door is a cheerful restaurant, Lou Pontin, a chance to sample *quiques*, a local variant on spinach fettuccini.

Cobbled streets lead up to a **Franciscan monastery** set among cypresses and olives (tel: 04 93 04 55 55; open Wed–Mon; admission charge). The sunny terrace is a place for contemplation, with telescopic views of Saorge below and of barren mountains beyond. The monastery is essentially baroque, although built around a Romanesque church.

A former mule track leads from

Map on page 220

The names of streets in Saorge are often confusing, since most have three names, usually after rival leaders of the Resistance.

BELOW:
the village of Saorge.

Botanists now believe that more than half of the 4,000 or so species of wild flower found in France grow in the Mercantour, including 63 varieties of orchid.

BELOW: crossing the River Roya on the way to La Brigue.

the monastery to the **Madone del Poggio**, an isolated Romanesque church topped by an octagonal tower. This graceful sliver of a tower is supported by a honeycomb apse, all that remains of the original abbey. The church and surrounding estate have been in the Davio family for years, so the vivid frescos in the crypt cannot be seen. The view of Saorge at sunset is one consolation: the light shifts across the terraced crescent, colouring the façades sienna and casting deep shadows over the onion-domed towers.

Despite the wonderful scenery, the inhabitants are a disparate, warring group. The core of the winter community consists of doddering *vieux du pays*, a few hippies, young professionals and weekenders. The *vieux* are quite content to let run-down shepherds' shacks and outlying farms to the hippies, who want to lead a pioneer lifestyle, bee-keeping, weaving and tilling the soil. It is subsistence farming – the pastures are known locally as "Siberia" because they receive no sun for four months of the year.

More gorges

Between Saorge and La Brigue the landscape is ravaged by a series of gorges. The building of the Nice–Turin railway brought much-needed work to the Roya villages. Although the line was begun in 1910, work stopped in 1914 and the track was destroyed during World War II. Finally finished in 1972, the result is a spectacular feat of engineering.

A little before La Brigue is **St-Dalmas** station, an overbearing piece of Fascist architecture, which served as a communications centre in Mussolini's time. Despite its baroque church and sturdy architecture, St-Dalmas itself is an unremarkable village. It is best-known as a base for excursions into the **Vallée des Merveilles ㉑** *(see page 240)*. This remote valley lies in the heart of a huge national park known as the **Parc National du Mercantour** (www.parc-mercantour.com). Created in 1979, the park joins up with the Parco Naturale Alpi Marittime around the Argentera Massif in Italy. It consists of two zones: the highly protected, largely uninhabited central zone, and the peripheral zone where the villages are situated.

Alpine pastures

La Brigue ㉒ is at once the richest and simplest of Roya villages. Set amidst Alpine pastures, La Brigue has always been a remote place, wholly dependent on the wool trade. Until the late 19th century, three-quarters of the population reared the sure-footed breed of sheep known as the Brigasque. After spending the summer in La Brigue, local shepherds took their flocks to winter pastures in Breil, Eze and Menton. The itinerant La Brigue shepherd, dressed in red velvet cap and green corduroy, has entered French folklore as a born storyteller.

The wealth created by the wool trade attracted Jewish merchants,

Map on page 220

money-lenders and goldsmiths to set up shop in the quarter known as Rû (rue) Ghetto. By the 15th century, wool merchants and notables could afford to indulge in artistic patronage. Italian craftsmen were commissioned to build new chapels and to adorn bourgeois homes with engraved lintels. The village was deeply influenced by the Italian Renaissance: the local architecture was enriched by arcaded streets and sculpted columns. Italian frescos replaced traditional Niçois murals.

As late as the 19th century, there was a flourishing crafts tradition in the village. However, La Brigue's return to France in 1947 divided the commune with scant regard for history. The "low" village of La Brigue became part of France while the "high" village, Briga Alta, remained Italian, along with virtually all the neighbouring hamlets. The population of La Brigue dropped from a peak of 4,000 to a mere 600, making it about the same size as it was in the 12th century.

Still, there are compensations for such depopulation. With the excep-tion of one ugly square, there has been little recent development. The remoteness of the location has deterred potential buyers of second homes, as has the impenetrable local dialect and the sense of a closed community. After the War, the villagers may have diversified into cattle-rearing, but agriculture is the mainstay. Today's farmers are horse-breeders, cheese-makers and bee-keepers, not to mention amateur fly-fishermen. The River Levense is rich in both rainbow trout and the speckled local variety.

The streets of La Brigue

La Brigue, lying along the Levense river, is dwarfed by snowcapped mountains, including the majestic Mont Bégo. The oldest quarter fans out from Rû (rue) Sec, but the nat-ural introduction to the village is place St-Martin, an Italianate square.

A 17th-century chapel, with a leaning campanile, looms against the mauve canyon walls. This is **L'Assuntà**, once the home of the Pénitents Blancs, a chapel which

TIP

If you are partial to ultra fresh trout, choose one of the restaurants bordering place St-Martin in La Brigue and the fast-flowing river. Apart from *truites vivantes* in their tanks, the rustic restaurants offer gnocchi, lasagne and *tartifauluza* (leek tart).

BELOW: a square in La Brigue.

TIP

Each August, the Festival International des Orgues Historiques gives the chance to hear the historic organs housed in many of the churches of the Roya and Bévéra Valleys. (Tel: 04 93 04 92 05; www.royabevera.com)

BELOW: walking through the old quarter in La Brigue.

answered to Rome. Decorative Tuscan pillars adorn the façade, creating a purity of line which is not reflected in the interior.

Next door, bordering a more intimate square, is the **Collégiale St-Martin**, the village church. The Romanesque bell tower surmounts a mellow, stone structure. St Martin is said to have preached here before settling in the Loire Valley as bishop of Tours. The interior is the richest in the region, boasting Tuscan decor and striking 16th-century paintings. The ceiling, with its starry blue sky, is reminiscent of Siena Cathedral. Equally Italianate are the frescos of angels in flight, the vaulted arches and the altar screen.

The works of art, including two attributed to Louis Bréa, are individualistic and memorable. Bréa's *Nativité* portrays a luminous Virgin and Child against a dark, craggy background resembling La Brigue. Like his *Assomption*, also in the church, the painting is a sober yet knowing work. The expressive faces and the delicate handling of drapery are typical of Bréa's artistic gifts.

A baroque venue

In summer, concert-lovers wallow in baroque waves of emotion as the church echoes to the sound of Boccherini and Respighi *(see also Tip, left)*. The organs in La Brigue have been made by such masters as the Lingiardi brothers. Standard church organs weren't able to play baroque music and opera, still less Piedmontese airs and ballets. However, the church organs in the Roya were all adapted to respond to the 19th-century vogue for *Bel Canto*. Sometimes shepherds' folk songs about love and war are played.

On the far side of the church is another fine Pénitents Blancs chapel, **L'Annonciade**, which contains a collection of religious art. It has a lovely carved baroque façade, also built of the warm local stone. From here, all alleys lead inwards, towards the medieval heart of the village. The cobbled streets are confusingly named in local dialect with Frenchified equivalents, so Rio Secco is also Rû Sec, a reference to the dry river bed that traces the arcaded street.

La Brigue has the greatest variety of decorative slate lintels in the Roya Valley. Made of green-and-black stone, these lintels are the work of 15th- and 16th-century Italian stonemasons. The lintels usually link a biblical saying or a wise saw to a pictorial motif, such as a Renaissance dragon, cherubs, shepherds and lambs. Rue Filippi, rue de la République and rue Rusca are all good lintel-hunting grounds.

Gods and ghouls

Four kilometres (2 miles) east of La Brigue sits **Notre-Dame-des-Fontaines** ㉓ (tel: 04 93 79 09 34; visits arranged at La Brigue tourist office), arguably the most remarkable place of worship in the Riviera hinterland. This simple medieval chapel, overlooking a mountain

stream, has been a pilgrimage centre since the 14th century. The chapel is supposedly built over a temple to Diana. Legend has it that after a serious drought, the region was saved by a miraculous outpouring of water from this spot. *Jean de Florette* legends aside, the chapel is celebrated for its 15th-century frescos, which were painted by Ligurian artists Jean Baleison and Jean Canavesio.

Baleison's frescos, decorating the choir, are faded Marian images, painted as refined courtly figures. Jean Canavesio's frescos, however, are more satisfying compositions, painted around a central figure. What sets his work apart is the drama and intensity of the moral message, designed to make pilgrims repent of their sins. A grotesque *Judas Iscariot* shows the traitor's disembowelment, performed by a demonic monkey. There is a Hieronymus Bosch quality to the most tormented work.

Elsewhere, there are quieter scenes reflecting medieval daily life and landscapes. The *Garden of Gethsemane*, for instance, is full of lush Provençal plants. The artist's palette comes from the region, too: the green is crushed slate, the white is limestone and the black is burnt oak twigs.

From Notre-Dame-des-Fontaines, walkers can hunt for mushrooms, strawberries and blackcurrants in wooded glades. The enchanting walk back to La Brigue is via a medieval bridge and small orchards. A more strenuous hike leads to **Briga Alta**, the Italian village that once belonged to La Brigue. The villagers still meet during hunting and fishing competitions, when it is a time to celebrate their common heritage: trout, gnocchi and *salumeria*, Italian salami.

The head of the valley

Tende ㉔ is as strange as anywhere in the Roya Valley. Despite being a frontier post, it remains a musty, medieval town with heavy wooden doors closed to the world. But what it lacks in charm, it certainly makes up for in atmosphere.

Tende guards the **Col de Tende**,

Map on page 220

The chapel of Notre-Dame-des-Fontaines, near La Brigue, is a local place of pilgrimage, renowned for its vivid frescos, painted in 1492 by Canavesio of the Niçoise school

BELOW: frescos decorate Notre-Dame-des-Fontaines.

TIP

The **Musée des Merveilles** at the northern end of Tende is worth a visit for the insight it gives into the history and significance of the Vallée des Merveilles *(see page 240)* and its bizarre engravings (tel: 04 93 04 32 50; www.museedesmerveilles.com; open Sept–Jun Wed–Mon, Jul–Aug daily; admission charge).

BELOW: Lac du Basto, in the Parc National du Mercantour.

the old mountain pass connecting Piedmont and Provence. Now bypassed by a road tunnel, the pass was once a fearsome experience. Writer Tobias Smollett (*see page 25*), crossing it in 1765, was "speechless in front of this celebrated and perilous mountain". Along with fears of bandits and smugglers, the crossing was beset with difficulties: it took six manservants to cut the ice with pick-axes before Smollett could get through.

Approached from La Brigue, Tende is still an impressive sight. The newer part of town hugs the river; behind is stacked the medieval town, rising in tiers to an Italianate cemetery and a stunted tower. The 14th-century tower is all that remains of the feudal château built by the Lascaris dynasty. The town's fortunes are a familiar story of a powerful church and the oppressed, poverty-stricken peasants.

At the start of the 20th century, Tende's farmers and miners were still impoverished: travel was on foot or by mule; bread was a luxury and dried so that it lasted longer. Under Fascism, Tende became a garrison town with over 3,000 Italian soldiers. In 1947, the town, newly French, was deserted by the military, as well as by Italian civil servants and manual workers. The economic decline was only checked in the 1980s, with the opening of a new rail link and ski resorts. The Mercantour park and the Vallée des Merveilles *(see page 242)* have also helped to attract visitors to the area.

Blackened by time

The Vieille Ville is made of greyish-green schist, a type of slate still quarried near by. Blackened by time and traffic fumes, these sombre houses set the tone. The overhanging roofs are not decorative, as a glance at the snowy peaks will confirm. Nor is Tende ever hot: "*En été il y a toujours de l'air,*" as the hardy locals say. Only the orange-and-pink belfries, decorated in Ligurian colours, generate any warmth.

The late Gothic **cathedral**, tucked away down a dark alley, has

BORDER COUNTRY ◆ **247**

been restored and painted in ochre, red and touches of blue. The sculpted Renaissance façade is framed by pillars propped on stone lions, an unusual feature for a church.

Ancient walnut doors lead to a majestic interior, adorned with a starry Tuscan ceiling and a nave emblazoned with the Lascaris arms, a two-headed eagle. Medieval houses and confraternity chapels are clustered around the cathedral.

The gloomy, claustrophobic atmosphere is intensified by a walk through the Vieille Ville. Thick oak doors are adorned with medieval lintels representing the medieval guilds. **Rue Béatrice Lascaris** climbs through the medieval quarter to the Lascaris tower, ruined ramparts and Italianate cemetery. At the end of covered passageways are blind alleys with views of terraced allotments lined up beside a pretty stream.

Old habits

Out of season, Old Tende feels almost medieval. Locals collect firewood in hand-drawn carts; old men strip olive wood; chestnuts are roasted over open fires; dogs fight with each other in dark street corners. Day-to-day life is punctuated with the diverse sounds of sawing, chopping and howling, as it has done for centuries.

For a change of atmosphere, stroll down to place de la République. Here, the aromas vary from lasagne and pizza to trout soufflé and Piedmontese polenta. The stodgy polenta dishes are a reminder of Tende's humble origins: the poorest people once lived on chestnut and cabbage soup or on a pasta made from flour, oil and potatoes. On Sundays, this was supplemented by *une bonne sauce*, generally rabbit, as a treat.

Game, such as wild boar and deer, was caught in the woods and sold to wealthier citizens. Nowadays the local cuisine is on a par with Sospel's, but Tende still harbours hunters who stray into the Mercantour to catch the odd wild boar *(sanglier)* or deer. It is best not to question the provenance of game in local restaurants. ❏

Map on page 220

TIP

Several companies based in Tende and nearby villages offer guided 4WD excursions to the archaeological sites of the Vallée des Merveilles. You should still allow for about 3 hours' walking. www.tende merveilles.com

---

RESTAURANTS & BARS

Castel du Roy
Route de Tende. Tel: 04 93 04 43 66. Open L Sun & D daily; closed Nov–Mar. €€
Delightful riverside restaurant with tranquil, shaded terrace, serving specialities of the region.

La Brigue

Le Mirval
Rue St-Vincent Ferrier. Tel: 04 93 04 63 71. Open daily L & D, D only Fri; closed Nov–Mar. €

The most charming restaurant in La Brigue, situated outside the village, beside the river. Local specialities include trout, spinach ravioli and game.

Sospel

Sout'a Laupia
13 rue St-Pierre. Tel: 04 93 04 24 23. Open daily L & D. €
In the heart of this medieval village, Sout'a Laupia offers homemade regional dishes

using carefully selected produce. Try the rabbit with *c pes* followed by the succulent fig tart.

Tende

Le Prieuré
Rue Jean Médecin, St-Dalmas-de-Tende. Tel: 04 93 04 75 70. €
Scenic setting in a valley at the foot of the Bégo mountain. Specialities of *tourtons* and *daube*.

Cafés

Saorge

Librairie Café du Caïros
Place Ciapagne. Tel: 04 93

04 51 60. Open daily non-stop July–Aug, closes earlier rest of the year. Café with internet access doubling up as the local newsagent's and souvenir shop. It also has a good selection of regional guides selected by the owner, Lydia, a native of Saorge who knows the valley like the back of her hand and is happy to share information.

● ● ● ● ● ● ● ● ● ● ● ●
Prices for a three-course meal without wine.
€€€ €40 and over, €€ €25–40, € under €25.

TRANSPORT

GETTING THERE AND GETTING AROUND

GETTING THERE

By Air

British Airways and British Midland both offer direct flights to Nice from several British cities. **British Airways** flies direct from Heathrow, Gatwick and Manchester; **British Midland** flies direct to Nice from Heathrow and East Midlands, and via either of these two airports from Aberdeen, Belfast, Edinburgh, Glasgow, Leeds, Manchester and Dublin. **Air France** operates flights from Paris to Nice. There are no direct Air France flights to the Riviera from the UK.

From the US, most flights to the south of France involve a connection in a European city. **Delta** and **Air France**, however, have direct flights from New York to Nice.

There are a number of low-cost flights to the Riviera from the UK. Flights to Nice are operated by **easyJet** from Luton, Stansted, Gatwick, Liverpool, Newcastle, Bristol and Belfast; and by **bmibaby** from Heathrow and Birmingham. Ryanair flies from Stansted to Toulon.

The internet is an excellent place to look for attractively priced air fares. Some of the better-known ticketing sites include: www.travelocity.com and www.expedia.com (UK and US sites), www.cheapflights.com (UK) and www.cheaptickets.com (US). Two popular French sites to look at are www.lastminute.fr and www.anyway.com; www.opodo.com has sites for both France and the UK.

Specialist travel agencies cater to students and travellers under 26. Look for CTS Travel in the UK (www.ctstravel.co.uk), USIT (www.usitnow.com) in Ireland, and STA Travel (www.statravel.com) plus Student Universe (www.studentuniverse.com) in the US.

By Sea

Deciding which ferry to take depends on your starting point in the UK and how much driving you want to do in France. Since the opening of the Eurotunnel, ferry services have become much more competitive. It's worth shopping around for discounts and special offers.

The following companies operate across the English Channel to various ports. All carry cars as well as foot passengers.

Brittany Ferries offers sailings from Portsmouth to Caen,

AIRLINES

Air France: tel: 0870 142 4343 (UK); 800-237 2747 (US); 08 20 82 08 20 (France); www.airfrance.com
American Airlines: tel: 0845 778 9789 (UK); 800-433 7300 (US); 08 10 87 28 72 (France); www.aa.com
British Airways: tel: 0870 850 9850 (UK); 800-247 9297 (US); 08 25 82 54 00 (France); www.britishairways.com
British Midland: tel: 0870 607 0555 (UK); 800-788 0555 (US); 01 41 91 87 04 (France); www.flybmi.com
Delta: tel: 0800 414 767 (UK); 800-241 4141 (US); 08 11 64

00 05 (France); www.delta.com
United Airlines: tel: 0845 8444 777 (UK); 800-538 2929 (US); 08 10 72 72 72 (France); www.united.com

Budget Airlines
bmibaby: tel: 0870 264 2229 (UK); 800-788 0555 (US); 08 90 71 00 81 (France); www.bmibaby.com
easyJet: tel: 0905 821 0905 (UK); 08 99 70 00 41 (France); www.easyjet.com
Ryanair: tel: 0906 270 5656 (UK); 1530-787 787 (Ireland); 08 92 23 23 75 (France); www.ryanair.com

Cherbourg or St-Malo; from Plymouth to Roscoff; and, May–Oct only, from Poole to Cherbourg: The Brittany Centre, Wharf Road, Portsmouth PO2 8RU; tel: 0870 366 5333; www.brittany-ferries.com

P&O sails from Dover to Calais in 90 minutes: Channel House, Channel View Road, Dover CT17 9TJ; tel: 0870 598 0333; www.poferries.com

Norfolkline sails from Dover to Dunkerque in 1 hour 45 minutes (motor vehicles only): Norfolk House, Eastern Docks, Dover, CT16 1JA, Kent; tel: 0870 870 1020; www.norfolkline-ferries.com

By Train

From the UK, **Eurostar** trains run from London and Ashford to Calais, Lille and Paris Gare du Nord (tel: 0870 518 6186; www.eurostar.co.uk). Services for the south of France depart from the Gare de Lyon. The TGV high-speed train reaches Marseille in about 3 hours. From Paris Gare de Lyon, 10–15 trains a day depart for Marseille. Seven to nine TGVs per day depart for Nice (journey time approximately 6 hours). All of these stations connect with the local train network (for more information, visit www.voyages-sncf.com).

Alternatively, travellers can change trains at Lille, thus avoiding the considerable trek across Paris.

Sleepers

A comfortable way to get to the south is by overnight sleeper. The cheapest alternative is to take a night train with reclining seats (no extra charge). Another option is the *couchette*, which has six beds per carriage in second class (four in first) with an ad hoc mix of men, women and children (women-only *couchettes* are available on request). The *voiture-lit* is more private, with a cabin for up to two people. Reservations must be made well in advance.

ABOVE: rural transport.

Tickets

In the UK, tickets for journeys in France can be booked at the Rail Europe Travel Centre (178 Piccadilly, London W1; tel: 0870 837 1371) or book online at www.raileurope.co.uk. In the US, call Rail Europe at 888-382 7245 or book online at www.raileurope.com.

In France, buy tickets in any SNCF train station or by phone on 3635 (in France only), open 7am–10pm daily. You can also book, pay and find web discounts on www.voyages-sncf.com. Journeys on the TGV must always be booked in advance. Children under 4 go free if they don't have a seat, and those aged 4–12 are half price.

Remember that before you get on the train you must date-stamp your ticket in the *composteur* machine at the station, marked "*compostez votre billet*".

Bicycles

Most long-distance trains have special areas designated for bicycle transport. You must reserve in advance and pay a small fee. Alternatively, if you partially dismantle your bicycle and put it in a carrier (available at most bicycle shops) you can carry it on as luggage for no extra fee. Most regional trains also make provisions for bicycles, as does Eurostar. Ask

about bicycle transport when you are booking.

Eurotunnel

Eurotunnel carries cars and their passengers from Folkestone to Calais on a simple drive on drive-off system (journey time 35 minutes). Payment is made at toll booths (which accept cash, cheques or credit cards). It is best to book ahead, particularly during peak periods; you will pay less and save time. You can turn up half an hour before and wait for the next available service.

Eurotunnel runs 24 hours a day, all year round, with a service about three times per hour during the day, and every 2 hours from midnight to 8am.

Information and bookings from Eurotunnel, Customer Relations Department, PO Box 2000, Folkestone, Kent CT18 8XY; tel: 0870 535 3535; www.eurotunnel.com. In France, tel: 08 10 63 03 04.

By Bus

The cheapest way to get to the Riviera is by bus, though you need to be prepared for a long journey. **Eurolines** (tel: 0870 580 8080; www.eurolines.com) has regular services from London to

Avignon, Marseille and Nice. For local bus information *see* *page 251*.

By Car

Many drivers are daunted by the thought of a long drive (1,200 km/ 745 miles from London and over 900 km/560 miles from Paris) before even starting their holiday. Indeed, in high season the roads can become crowded. For those in a hurry, the *autoroute* (motorway) from Paris to Nice (A6, A7, A8) takes about 8 hours, but toll fees can add up along the way. For travellers driving from Calais, it is possible to travel all the way to the Riviera by motorway (Calais–Marseille is 1,060 km/ 660 miles).

However, if you intend to make the drive part of your holiday, take the back N and D roads, which can be empty. You will discover parts of France you never knew existed. Weekends between 14 July and the end of August, and particularly the public holiday on 15 August are the worst times to travel, so avoid them if you can. Traffic bulletins on Radio Traffic (107.7) are useful; in summer they have hourly bulletins in English.

Most *autoroutes* have *péages*, or tollbooths, where payment can be made by cash or credit card. For information on the motorways, including toll estimates, weather conditions and route-planning, see www.autoroutes.fr.

Another option is to drive to Paris and drive on to the train. The SNCF has an "*Auto/Train*" service from Paris to Marseille,

Toulon, and Fréjus/St-Raphaël. You travel in a comfortable TGV compartment while your car rides behind in a special wagon. Visit www.voyages-sncf.com/autotrain for information and schedules. One-way fares for the vehicle only in high season are around €200.

GETTING AROUND

From the Airports

The main gateway to the French Riviera is the Nice-Côte d'Azur airport (www.nice.aeroport.fr). The 20-minute taxi ride to the centre of town can be expensive (€20–30); the bus is a better option. The express bus (No. 98) from Terminal 2 takes 20–30 minutes to get to the town centre and costs only a few euros. If the next leg of your travel is by train, take the No. 99 bus direct to the SNCF station (*gare*).

If your flight arrives in Marseille (Marseille Provence airport, www.marseille.aeroport.fr), an express bus to Marseille Gare St-Charles railway station takes 25 minutes and costs under €10. The only other alternative is a taxi at €40–50.

Toulon (Toulon-Hyères airport, www.toulon-hyeres.aeroport.fr) is another convenient arrival point, particularly for St-Tropez. Bus line No. 102 takes 40 minutes from the airport to the main bus station and costs under €2, but there are only five per day; visit www.reseaumistral.com for a schedule. Otherwise, a taxi to the centre of town takes around 25 minutes and costs around €45 during the day and €55 at night.

DISCOUNTS AND PASSES

A variety of passes and discounts are available for travel to and within France, many of which can be purchased at Rail Europe (www.raileurope.com). For travel exclusively within France, visit the website of the national railway, the SNCF (www.voyages-sncf.com).

• A **Eurodomino** pass (only for EU citizens) allows unlimited travel on France's rail network for 3–8 days' duration within one month, but this must be bought before travelling to France. Discounted rates are available to children aged 4–11, or young people aged 12–25.

• European and North African citizens are eligible for the **InterRail** pass (www.interrail.com), which permits unlimited second-class travel in up to 28 European and North African countries.

• Non-Europeans and non-North Africans can buy a **Eurailpass** (www.eurail.com) which allows unlimited first- or second-class travel throughout France and 18

other participating countries. Eurail also offers **Flexi** and **Select** passes for more limited travel. These must be purchased before your arrival in Europe.

• You can save on train fares by purchasing special discount cards in France. The **Carte 12/25** gives 12 to 25-year-olds a 25–50 percent reduction. Pensioners benefit from similar terms with a **Carte Senior**. A **Carte Enfant +** entitles a child under 12 and up to four accompanying adults to travel at a 25–50 percent reduction.

• Discounts are also available for weekend round trips (**Découverte Séjour**), as well as for a round trip for two people (**Découverte à 2**). Ask when making reservations, or consult the SNCF website for more information on "*Découverte*" discounts.

• The SNCF also posts special offers and promotional packages on its website, so keep a regular check on it.

Public Transport

Public transport within towns and cities on the Côte d'Azur is fairly efficient and avoids the problem of trying to find a parking space, which can be a time consuming activity. If you are going to be staying in one or two different

ABOVE: the TGV on the Corniche d'Estérel.

towns during your trip, a car is not really necessary, as there are plenty of trains and buses to get you from one place to another. But if you will be touring, or you are planning to stay out in the country, a car is essential.

By Bus

Within towns and cities For details of timetables and routes for buses, check with the local tourist office *(see page 277)* or ask at your hotel. When boarding, tickets should be punched in the machine next to the driver, and passes should be shown.

Between towns and cities For travel in the area between **Cagnes** and **Menton** (including Nice and the surrounding area) contact Ligne d'Azur, Le Grand Hôtel, 10 avenue Félix Faure,

BUS STATIONS

Below are telephone numbers for the main bus station *(gare routière)* in some of the larger towns on the French Riviera:
Cannes 04 93 45 20 08
Grasse 04 93 36 37 37
Menton 04 93 35 93 60
Monaco 377 97 70 22 22
Nice 08 92 70 12 06

Nice; tel: 08 10 06 10 06; www.lignedazur.com. Réseaumistral rules the roads between **Toulon** and **Hyères** (720 avenue Colonel Picot, Toulon; tel: 04 94 03 87 03; www.reseaumistral.com).

In the *département* of the Var (including St-Tropez and St-Raphaël), call the departmental office; tel. 08 25 00 06 50, or better still, visit their website www.transports.var.fr, which has times and itineraries for all the bus lines in the *département*. Here again, local tourist offices can be very helpful, as is contacting the bus stations directly *(see box below)*.

By Train

Reservations and information between towns and cities The TER regional rail network links all the coastal towns, and smaller, local lines run inland. For tickets and schedules, go to the closest SNCF office or any railway station, call 3635 (in France only), or visit the SNCF website at www.voyages-sncf.com.

Two scenic mountain lines depart from Nice: the Roya Valley line via Sospel, and the privately operated Train des Pignes which runs up the Var Valley to Digne-les-Bains. Remember to have

your ticket validated at one of the machines in the stations before boarding the train. These are marked *"compostez votre billet"*.

By Taxi

Within towns and cities Taxis can be hailed in the street or at a taxi stand (look for the blue sign) in most of the larger cities, like Nice and Cannes, but they are expensive: an average trip across Nice is around €20. In smaller cities and towns, contact the local tourist office *(see page 277)* or ask at your hotel for a list of taxi numbers and call ahead.

Between towns and cities This is prohibitively expensive. If at all possible, consider renting a car.

By Car

Within towns and cities Driving in towns is to be avoided at all costs, especially during high season. Larger cities have ample public transport; smaller ones are crossable on foot.

In the main resorts, **parking** is costly; once again, time is of the essence, because the cheaper spots on the street get snapped up early. Parking meters have been replaced by *horodateurs* (pay-and display machines),

TRANSPORT

ACCOMMODATION

ACTIVITIES

A – Z

which take coins and/or special parking cards that can be bought at any tobacconist *(tabac)*.

Between towns and cities Roads to and around the main resorts get very choked up during July and August, and you can spend as much time getting to the beach as you spend on it. Try to avoid weekends, mid- to late mornings (when everyone's going to the beach) and late afternoons (when everyone's going home). Lunchtime is usually a good bet, as is taking the *autoroutes* for longer distances.

Driving Documents

British, US, Canadian and Australian driving licences are all valid in France, though it is a good idea to carry an international driving licence as well. You should always carry your car's registration document and insurance (third-party is the absolute minimum, but it is advisable to ask your insurance company to provide added cover).

Additional insurance cover, which can include a get-you-home service, is offered by a number of organisations, including the British **Automobile Association**, tel: 0800 107 0567; www.theaa.com; and **Europ-Assistance**; tel: 0870 737 5720; www.europ-assistance.co.uk

Car Hire

Hiring a car is quite expensive in France, partly because of the high VAT (TVA) rate of 19.6 percent. Some airlines have partnerships with car-hire companies; for example, if you fly with Air France you'll get discounts at Hertz. The SNCF, the French national railway, offers discounts with train-plus-car hire packages under its *Voyage Alacarte* scheme (www.voyages-sncf.com). Weekly rates are often better than daily hire, and it can be cheaper to arrange before leaving home. Major car-hire companies in France are listed below:
Avis, tel: 08 20 05 05 05; www.avis.com

Budget, tel: 08 25 00 35 64; www.budget.com
Europcar, tel: 08 25 358 358; www.europcar.com
Hertz, tel: 01 39 38 38 38; www.hertz.com
Rent-a-Car, tel: 08 91 700 200; www.rentacar.fr
Thrifty, tel: 01 34 29 86 76; www.thrifty.com

Rules of the Road

The use of seat belts (front and rear if fitted) and crash helmets for motorcyclists is compulsory. Children under 10 are not permitted to ride in the front seat unless the car has no rear seat.
Priorité à droite An important rule to remember is that priority on French roads is always given to vehicles approaching from the right, except where otherwise indicated. In practice, on main roads the major road will normally have priority, with traffic being halted on minor approach roads with any one of the following signs:
• STOP
• *Cédez le passage* – give way
• *Vous n'avez pas la priorité* – you do not have right of way
  Particular care should be taken in towns, where you may wrongly assume you are on the major road, and in rural areas, where there may not be any road markings (keep an eye out for farm vehicles).

In general, traffic signs conform to the icons and signage of most EU countries. Non-EU visitors would be well advised to study European road signs and symbols before driving off.

At a roundabout, drivers already on the roundabout always have priority over those entering it.
Toll roads Nearly all motorways *(autoroutes)* are toll roads, so you will need to have some cash on you (especially small change) for the *péages* (tollbooths) if you intend to use them, although you can pay by credit card. There is always a manned booth.

Autoroutes are designated "A" roads and national highways "N"

roads. "D" *(départemental)* roads are usually well maintained, while "C" or local roads may not always be so.
Speed limits are 130 kph (80 mph) on toll motorways, 110 kph (68 mph) on dual carriageways, 90 kph (56 mph) on other roads except in towns where the limit is 50 kph (30 mph) and, in some areas, 30 kph (19 mph). There is now a minimum speed limit of 80 kph (50 mph) on the outside lane of motorways during daylight with good visibility and on level ground. Speed limits are reduced in wet weather as follows: toll motorways 110 kph (68 mph), dual carriageways 100 kph (62 mph), other roads 80kph (50 mph).

On-the-spot **fines** can be levied for speeding. On toll roads, the time is printed on the ticket you take at your entry point; your average speed can thus be calculated and a fine imposed on exit. Radars have recently been installed in many urban areas and on major roads.
Accidents and breakdowns It is strongly recommended that you carry a red triangle to place at least 30 metres (100 ft) behind the car in case of a breakdown or accident. In the event of an accident or emergency, call the police (dial 17) or use the free emergency telephones (every 2 km/1 mile) on motorways. A European Accident Statement Form (obtainable from your insurance company) will help to simplify matters in the case of an accident.
Petrol/gas Unleaded petrol *(essence sans plomb)* is the norm in France: leaded petrol is no longer available, and has been replaced by a substitute unleaded petrol for leaded-fuel vehicles. If in doubt, a map showing the location of filling stations is available from main tourist offices.

For information about current road conditions on motorways, listen to Radio Traffic (107.7) or contact the Association des

ABOVE: hit the open road.

Sociétés Françaises d'Autoroutes (ASFA), tel: 08 92 68 10 77; www.autoroutes.fr. In the Alps you may need snow chains on your car in winter, which can be bought at hypermarkets or service stations.

Routes of Interest

Following a tourist circuit or route is a sure way of getting to see the major sights of a region. Local tourist offices (see page 277) will often help with suggestions. Some of the major routes are:

Route des Hauts Lieux de Provence: this covers an extensive area in the west of the region, from Toulon to Fréjus and as far north as Draguignan. It takes in, among other sites, the Cité Episcopale de Fréjus and the Roman Arenas, the Château de Grimaud, the Château d'Entrecasteaux and the Palais des Comtes de Provence à Brignoles. For a route map and detailed guide (in French), visit www.tourismevar.com/Provence_cote_a zur/routes_themes/hautslieux.htm.

Côtes de Provence Wine Route: much of this route takes in the same area as the Route des Hauts Lieux de Provence. For details of vineyards

open to the public and offering tastings and direct wine purchase, contact the Syndicat des Vins Côtes de Provence, 83460 Les Arcs-sur-Argens; tel. 04 94 99 50 20.

Route du Mimosa: this road starts in Bormes-les-Mimosas and follows the trail of the delicate yellow flower along the coast to Mandelieu-La Napoule and inland through the Mimosa forests of the Tanneron Massif. The route ends for both the flower and the driver at the perfume factories of Grasse. For more information, visit www.bormeslesmimosas.com/village/routedumimosa.htm

By Bicycle

Bicycles are readily available for hire; contact tourist offices (see page 277) for rental listings. Bicycles are carried free of charge on buses and on some trains; on other, faster services you will have to pay (check before you travel – some services have high charges for carrying cycles).

Travelling by a combination of bicycle and bus or train can be an excellent way of touring and viewing the region, if you are fit enough to do it.

Hitch-hiking

Hitch-hiking can be a risky way to travel, and therefore is best organised through an agency, such as Allostop France Covoiturage, 30 rue Pierre Sémard, 75009 Paris; tel: 01 53 20 42 42; www.allostop.net

The agency fee is usually around €35 for 10 trips, or €7 for one trip (€3 for one trip under 150 km/90 miles); then a participation (contribution) is given directly to the driver, anywhere from €4 for under 150 km (90 miles) on local roads to €90 for 3,000 km (1,860 miles) on a motorway. Contact the agency well in advance to arrange a convenient lift. Avignon, Marseille and Nice are all popular destinations in the warmer months.

In the Air

Tourist flights in helicopters are offered by:
Héli Sécurité (St-Tropez), tel: 04 94 555 999; www.helicopter-saint-tropez.com
Héli Air Monaco, tel: +377-92 05 00 50; www.heliairmonaco.com
Héli Riviera (Cannes), tel: 04 93 90 53 00; www.heliriviera.com

ACCOMMODATION

SOME THINGS TO CONSIDER BEFORE YOU BOOK THE ROOM

Choosing a Hotel

Accommodation on the French Riviera includes grand city hotels or seafront palaces, country villas or *gîtes*, campsites and a range of small town hotels, country *auberges* (inns) and *chambres d'hôte* (bed & breakfast). During the summer it is advisable to book, especially along the coast, but outside the peak holiday period (July and August) it should be easier to find accommodation. Some hotels may close between November and February, and most campsites will be closed in winter.

Hotels

All hotels in France conform to national standards and carry star-ratings, set down by the Ministry of Tourism, according to their degree of comfort and amenities. Prices (which are charged per room, rather than per person) on the Riviera range from as little as €35 for a double room in an unclassified hotel (i.e. its standards are not sufficient to warrant a star, but it could well be clean, cheap and cheerful) in low season, to around €200 for the cheapest double room in a 4-star luxury hotel in high season. Hotels are required to display their menus outside, and room

prices should be visible either outside or in reception, as well as on the back of bedroom doors. Don't rely on the star system – the ratings are more about quantity (size of rooms, presence of hairdryers, etc.) than quality.

When booking a room you should normally be shown it before agreeing to take it; don't hesitate to ask. Supplements may be charged for an additional bed or a cot *(lit bébé)*. You may be asked when booking if you wish to dine, particularly if the hotel is busy – and you should confirm that the hotel's restaurant is open (many are closed out of season on Sunday or Monday evenings).

Lists of hotels can be obtained from the French Government Tourist Office in your country or from regional or local tourist offices in France *(see page 277)*.

If you just want an overnight stop to break a journey, you may find clean, modern, basic chains like Fasthôtel and Ibis handy.

Bed & Breakfast

Bed and breakfast *(chambre d'hôte)* accommodation is widely available in private houses, sometimes on working farms, whose owners are often members of the Fédération Nationale des Gîtes de France. Bookings can be made for

an overnight stop or a longer stay. Breakfast is included in the price, and evening meals – usually made with local produce and good value – are often available.

Gîtes de France has very strict standards for its members, and you can generally count on cleanliness and quality. For bookings contact:
Gîtes de France, 59 rue St-Lazare, 75439 Paris Cedex 09; tel: 01 49 70 75 75; fax: 01 42 81 28 53; www.gites-de-france.fr
Bed and Breakfast in France lists B&Bs, including chateaux. UK booking service, tel: 0871 781 0834; www.bedbreak.com
Fleurs de Soleil (www.fleurs-soleil.tm.fr), offers B&Bs only.

If you do not wish to book in advance, look out for signs along the road (usually in the country) offering *chambres d'hôte*. You will be taking pot luck, but will probably find a bed off-season and may be delighted by the value of the simple farm food and accommodation on offer.

Gîtes

Rural *gîtes* (holiday cottages) are a good way to appreciate a holiday in the south, though most will be found in rural areas away from the coast. Accommodation can range from converted barns to grand chateaux.

There are several national networks of *gîtes*, the largest of which is **Gîtes de France** *(see page 254)*, whose members are regularly inspected by the Relais Départemental (the regional office of the national federation) and rated; the number of "*épis*" (ears of corn) indicates the level of quality.

Other networks include **Clévacances** (www.clevacances.com), which has furnished apartments, cottages and B&Bs. Prices in popular areas on the Riviera average €375–600 per week in August for a 2–4 person *gîte*, less in the back country.

Gîtes are self-catering, and it's important to check exactly what you need to supply, such as bed linen or towels. Often they are in remote locations, and you will need your own transport. *Gîte* owners will be able to advise about shopping, local sights and activities. Some *gîtes* are equipped for guests with disabilities; check the websites or contact the network office.

Brittany Ferries is the UK agent for Gîtes de France; bookings can be made through The Brittany Centre, Wharf Road, Portsmouth PO2 8RU; tel: 0870 5360 360; www.brittany-ferries.co.uk. The Brittany Ferries brochure includes a selection of *gîtes* available; the website has more.

Various UK-based tour operators also offer a range of self-catering accommodation as part of a package holiday. Try the following:
French Life, 0870 444 8877; www.frenchlife.co.uk
Individual Travellers, 0870 078 0189; www.indiv-travellers.com
Chez Nous, 0870 191 7740; http://cheznous.com

Gîtes d'Etape

Gîtes d'étape offer very basic shelter for walkers or cyclists, often in remote mountain areas; expect communal accommodation, bunk beds and shared bathrooms. Make

reservations, especially in busy periods. *Gîtes de neige, gîtes de pêche* and *gîtes équestres* (for winter, fishing and riding holidays) offer similar facilities.

Mountain refuges *(réfuges)* offer communal accommodation, too, and may also provide meals. They range from large and solid stone houses to very basic huts. Many are open only June–Sept; they should be booked in advance. Prices vary between €8 and €15 per person.

Youth Hostels

To stay in many hostels *(auberges de jeunesse)* you need to be a member of the Youth Hostels Association (YHA), or join the Fédération Unie des Auberges de Jeunesse. Contact the following for more information:
Fédération Unie des Auberges de Jeunesse (FUAJ), 27 rue Pajol, 75018 Paris; tel: 01 44 89 87 27; fax: 01 44 89 87 49; www.fuaj.org. The federation is affiliated to the International Youth Hostel Federation.
Hostelling International USA, 8401 Colesville Road, Suite 600, Silver Springs, MD 20910; tel: 301-495 1240; fax: 301 495 6697; www.hiusa.org
International Youth Hostel Federation, 2nd Floor, Gate House, Fretherne Road, Welwyn Garden City, Herts AL8 6RD; tel: 01707 324 170; fax: 01707 323 980; www.hihostels.com

Camping

French campsites *(les campings)*, often run by local councils, can be comfortable and well appointed. Prices on the Riviera range from €14 to around €30 per night for two people, with car, caravan or tent. Coastal campsites get crowded in high season; be sure to reserve early if you want to be near the beach. Camping rough *(camping sauvage)* is generally not permitted, though it may be worth asking the landowner. Fire is an ever-present

ABOVE: holiday cottages for rent.

risk in the region, so be careful when cooking.

Campsites are graded from one-star (minimal comfort, water points, showers and sinks) to four-star status, which allow more space for each pitch and above-average facilities, like swimming pools and launderettes. *Aire naturelle de camping* and *Camping à la ferme* tend to be cheaper, with minimal services.

The *Guide Officiel* of the **French Federation of Camping and Caravanning** (FFCC), available from French Government Tourist Offices as well as the FFCC website (www.ffcc.fr), lists 11,000 sites nationwide, and indicates those with facilities for disabled campers. The FFCC also runs another site, www.campingfrance.com which has an extensive listing of French campsites.
Avis Car Away (camping cars in France), tel: 01 47 49 80 40; www.aviscaraway.com
Canvas Holidays (UK), tel: 0870 192 1154; www.canvasholidays.co.uk
Select Site Reservations (UK), tel: 01873 859 876; www.select-site.com
Vancansoleil, tel: 0870 077 8779; www.vacansoleil.co.uk

Hotels by Region

This listing names the region's best-known hotels and suggests others that have a certain distinctive charm. Prices on the

TRANSPORT

ACCOMMODATION

ACTIVITIES

A – Z

LANGUAGE

Côte d'Azur tend to be higher than elsewhere in France, but it is still possible to find reasonably priced rooms. Opening and closing dates and room prices may vary. Note: hotels are listed in accordance with the order of the Places chapters.

Hotel Guides

Various guides can be obtained from the French Tourist Government Office. These include *Châteaux & Hotels de France* (mid- to high-end hotels, restaurants and stays in private chateaux; tel: 08 92 23 00 75; www.chateauxhotels.com) and *Relais du Silence* (mid- to high-end hotels "*de charme*", often in chateaux or grand houses in peaceful settings; 01 44 49 90 00; www.silencehotel.com).

Logis de France is France's biggest hotel federation, with over 3,000 private hotels. Most of these hotels are in the budget to mid-range category, and vary greatly in facilities, atmosphere and levels of service. Contact the **Fédération Nationale des Logis et Auberges de France**, 83 avenue d'Italie, 75013 Paris; tel: 01 45 84 70 00; www.logis-de-france.fr, or the French Government Tourist Office for a *Logis de France* handbook. They have a list of hotels accessible for disabled travellers.

HYERES AND THE MASSIF DES MAURES

Hyères

Hotel du Soleil
Rue des Remparts
Tel: 04 94 65 16 26
Fax: 04 94 35 46 00
www.hotel-du-soleil-hyeres.com
A friendly and peaceful hotel close to the Parc St-Bernard. Breakfast is included in the price of a room. 22 rooms.
€–€€

Bormes-les-Mimosas

Le Domaine du Mirage
38 rue de la Vue des Iles
Bormes-les-Mimosas
Tel: 04 94 05 32 60
Fax: 04 94 64 93 03
www.domainedumirage.com
On a marvellous site overlooking the Bay of Lavandou, the plush

rooms are decorated in bold Provençal colours, and many have balconies and views. There are two lovely pools on the terrace. 68 rooms. €€€

Le Lavandou

Azur Hôtel
Cavalière
Tel: 04 94 01 54 54
Fax: 04 94 01 54 55
www.lelavandou.com/azur-hotel
This hotel is located high on a hill overlooking Cavalière Bay, all of the basic but cheerful rooms have balconies and spectacular views. 24 rooms. €–€€
Beau Soleil
Aiguebelle
Tel: 04 94 05 84 55
Fax: 04 94 05 70 89
www.beausoleil-alcyons.com
Reasonably priced attractive hotel where all the rooms have balconies and you can dine under plane trees. *Demi-pension* in July and Aug. Closed Oct–Easter. 15 rooms. €€

Les Roches
1 avenue des Trois Dauphins
Tel: 04 94 71 05 07
Fax: 04 94 71 08 40
www.hotellesroches.com
Set on the cliffs with fabulous sea views, a luxurious modern hotel with tasteful decor. Private beach, freshwater swimming pool. Closed early Jan–early Mar. 39 rooms. €€€–€€€€

Ile de Porquerolles

Mas du Langoustier
Tel: 04 94 58 30 09
Fax: 04 94 58 36 02
www.langoustier.com
Luxurious establishment in an old Provençal *mas* (farmhouse) on the Ile de Porquerolles, surrounded by an exotic garden, with a fabulous restaurant. Closed mid-Oct–Apr. 50 rooms; half-board only. Free transport from the port to the hotel. €€€
L'Oustaou de Porquerolles
Place d'Armes
Tel: 04 94 58 30 13

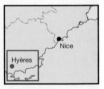

Fax: 04 94 58 34 93
www.oustaou.com
Simple but comfortable hotel in the centre of the village with a lively bar-restaurant. Several of the air-conditioned rooms have sea views. Closed Oct–mid-Feb. 7 rooms; breakfast included. €€–€€€

Ile de Port-Cros

Le Manoir
Tel: 04 94 05 90 52
Fax: 04 94 05 90 89
The only hotel on the no-smoking, no-car island of Port-Cros. Colonial-style family house with a large garden and a tropical feel. Comfortable rooms, some with balcony. Closed early Oct–Mar. 22 rooms. €€€

ST-TROPEZ AND ITS PENINSULA

Cogolin

La Croix-Valmer
Souleias
Plage de Gigaro
Tel: 04 94 55 10 55
Fax: 04 94 54 36 23
www.souleias.com
Modern hotel in large
grounds overlooking the
unspoilt beach of
Gigaro. Spacious
rooms, swimming pool,
tennis court, private
yacht. Closed Oct–mid-
Apr. 48 rooms. €€–€€€

La Maison du Monde
63 rue Carnot
Tel: 04 94 54 77 54
Fax: 04 94 54 77 55
www.lamaisondumonde.fr
A converted town house
and garden provide
serene lodgings with a
small pool and cosy
salons for reading and
relaxation. Closed early
Nov–late Dec and mid-
Jan–mid-Feb. 12 rooms.
€€–€€€

Grimaud

La Boulangerie
Route de Collobrières
Tel: 04 94 43 23 16
Fax: 04 94 43 38 27
www.hotel-laboulangerie.com
Simple yet elegant
rooms in a small,
friendly hotel situated in
the Maures hills. Pool
and tennis court.
Closed mid-Oct–early
Apr. 10 rooms. €€–€€€

Hostellerie du Coteau
Fleuri
Place des Pénitents
Tel: 04 94 43 20 17
Fax: 04 94 43 33 42
www.coteaufleuri.fr
An old hostelry on the
side of a hill with rustic
dining room and lush
garden. Closed Nov–15
Dec. 12 rooms. €€

Plan-de-la-Tour

Mas des Brugassières
1.5 km (1 mile) south of the
village, 10 km (6 miles) from
Ste-Maxime
Tel: 04 94 55 50 55
Fax: 04 94 55 50 51
www.masdesbrugassieres.com
In the Maures hills, this
intimate hotel was
modelled after a
Provençal mas
(farmhouse). The large
garden has a small
pool; many rooms open
on to a semi-private
terrace. Closed mid-
Oct–Mar. 14 rooms. €€

Ramatuelle

Le Baou
Avenue Gustave Etienne
Tel: 04 98 12 94 20
Fax: 04 98 12 94 21
www.alpazurhotels.com
Large hotel with stylish
modern rooms, many
with balconies and
views of the garden and
countryside. Closed
mid-Oct–mid-May. 39
rooms. €€€–€€€€

La Ferme d'Augustin
Plage de Tahiti
Tel: 04 94 55 97 00
Fax: 04 94 97 59 76
www.fermeaugustin.com
A comfortable hotel in
an excellent location
next to the Pampelonne
beach. Some rooms with
sea view. Closed mid-
Oct–Mar. 48 rooms. €€€

La Ferme d'Hermès
Route de l'Escalet
Tel: 04 94 79 27 80
Fax: 04 94 79 26 86
An old Provençal farm-
house in vineyards, with
terracotta tiles, a garden
with olive trees and
lavender. Small pool.
Closed mid-Oct–Mar. 9
rooms. €€–€€€

St-Tropez

B Lodge Hôtel
23 rue de l'Aïoli
Tel: 04 94 97 06 57
Fax: 04 94 97 58 72
www.hotel-b-lodge.com
Contemporary styling in
an old building at the
base of the Citadelle
gardens. English-style
pub on the ground floor.
Closed mid-Nov–mid-
Dec. 15 rooms €€–€€€

Bastide de St-Tropez
Route des Carles
Tel: 04 94 55 82 55
Fax: 04 94 97 21 71
www.bastide-saint-tropez.com
The height of luxury in
beautiful grounds.
Some rooms and suites
with private garden and
jacuzzi. Closed Jan–mid-
Feb. 26 rooms. €€€€

Hôtel Byblos
Avenue Paul Signac
Tel: 04 94 56 68 00
Fax: 04 94 56 68 01
www.byblos.com
Legendary glamorous
hotel still popular with
the Johnny Hallyday set.
97 rooms. €€€€

Lou Cagnard
18 avenue P. Roussel
Tel: 04 94 97 04 24
Fax: 04 94 97 09 44
www.hotel-lou-cagnard.com
Reasonably priced hotel
in town, near the port.
Eat breakfast in the
pretty courtyard under a
centuries-old fig tree.
Closed Nov–Dec.
19 rooms. €–€€

La Ponche
3 rue des Remparts
Tel: 04 94 97 02 53
Fax: 04 94 97 78 61
www.laponche.com
Once a favourite of
Picasso's, this hotel
was originally a row of
fishermen's cottages in
the old town. Excellent

restaurant. Closed
Nov–mid-Feb.
18 rooms. €€€–€€€€

Résidence de la Pinède
Plage de la Bouillabaisse
Tel: 04 94 55 91 00
Fax: 04 94 97 73 64
www.residencepinede.com
Luxurious hotel under
the pine trees on
Bouillabaisse beach.
Large, modern rooms
with sea views, private
beach and gourmet
restaurant. Closed
Oct–Apr. 39 rooms.
€€€€

Le Yaca
1 boulevard d'Aumale
Tel: 04 94 55 81 00
Fax: 04 94 97 58 50
www.hotel-le-yaca.fr
A beautiful old
Provençal residence in
town, refurbished with
taste. Accommodation
built around pool and
gardens. Closed 15
Oct–Mar. 28 rooms.
€€€€

Ste-Maxime

Hôtel Montfleuri
3 avenue de Montfleuri
Tel: 04 94 55 75 10
Fax: 04 94 49 25 07
www.montfleuri.com
On the edge of the
and 10 minutes fr
Ste-Maxime's be
this comfy hote
small pool, ga
some rooms
conies and
Closed No
and Jan–
30 roo

ST-RAPHAEL, FREJUS AND THE ARGENS VALLEY

Agay

Relais d'Agay
Boulevard de la Plage
Tel: 04 94 82 78 20
Fax: 04 94 82 78 33
There are two separate
hotels here: Les
Platanes, which is
basic, though clean and
tidy, and Les Acacias,
which has a little more
style. Both are right on
the water's edge on a
fine sand beach. Closed
mid-Oct–mid-Apr.
33 rooms. €€€

Les Arcs sur Argens

Le Logis du Guetteur
Place du Château
Tel: 04 94 99 51 10
Fax: 04 94 99 51 29
www.logisduguetteur.com
A cosy, modern hotel
built out of ancient
stone blocks just next
door to an 11th-century

fortress. Many of the
rooms have beautiful
views of the rooftops
and of the vineyards
below. Closed mid-
Feb–mid-Mar. 10
rooms. €€–€€€

Fréjus

Aréna
145 blvd Général de Gaulle
Tel: 04 94 17 09 40
Fax: 04 94 52 01 52
www.arena-hotel.com
Situated in the old town
with a swimming pool, a
garden and an excellent
restaurant serving
regional specialities.
Closed Dec–mid-Jan.
36 rooms. €€–€€€
Sable et Soleil
158 rue Paul Arène
Tel: 04 94 51 08 70
Fax: 04 94 53 49 12
www.hotelsableetsoleil.site.voila.fr
A 1950s building under
the pines with a pergola.
Plain but adequate

rooms at a reasonable
price. No restaurant.
Closed mid-Nov–mid-
Dec. 20 rooms. €

Les Issambres

Hôtel les Calanques
RN 98, rue du Nid au Soleil
Tel: 04 98 11 36 36
Fax: 04 98 11 36 37
www.french-riviera-hotel.com.
On the coastal highway
between Ste-Maxime
and St-Tropez, next to a
rocky cove with a small
beach. The rooms are
simple but colourful;
many have views of the
sea. Closed Nov–mid-
Mar. 12 rooms. €€–€€€

St-Raphaël

Ambassador Hôtel
89 rue Boetman
Tel: 04 98 11 82 00
Fax: 04 98 11 82 01
www.ambassador-saint-
raphael.com

In the centre of town
and just a short walk to
the beach. The simple
but spacious rooms
have high ceilings and
wrought-iron bedsteads.
20 rooms. €€
Golf de Valescure
Avenue Paul l'Hermite
Tel: 04 94 52 85 00
Fax: 04 94 82 41 88
www.valescure.com
A modern hotel built in
a traditional Provençal
style surrounded by
pine trees. Rooms have
terraces, some with
views over the well-
known golf course.
Restaurant and elegant
club house also on site.
40 rooms. €€–€€€

CANNES

3.14 Hôtel
5 rue François Einesy
Tel: 04 92 99 72 00
Fax: 04 92 99 72 12
www.3-14hotel.com
An eccentric yet
luxurious hotel with
unusual decor: rooms
are splashed in brilliant
colours, with modern
[ing]. Each of the
['s] five floors is
[...]d according to a
[...]nt. There is an
[...]us glass
[...] the lobby; a
[...]rooftop and
[...]t serves
[...]fluenced
[...]ms.

Carlton Intercontinental
58 La Croisette
Tel: 04 93 06 40 06
Fax: 04 93 06 40 25
www.intercontinental.com/cannes
Cannes's world-famous
waterfront palace hotel,
with splendid rooms
and lobby, a private
beach, and a 24-hour
health centre on the top
floor. 338 rooms. €€€€
Chalet de l'Isère
42 avenue de Grasse
Tel: 04 93 38 50 80
Fax: 04 93 68 73 22
http://perso.orange.fr/novel.hotel
Guy de Maupassant
once lived in this
charming little house
with a leafy garden, a

few minutes from the
beach. Rooms are basic
but functional; a good
restaurant. Closed Nov.
8 rooms. €–€€
Hôtel Martinez
73 La Croisette
Tel: 04 92 98 73 00
Fax: 04 93 39 67 82
www.hotel-martinez.com
A trendy Art Deco palace
(pictured on page 259)
where the stars love to
stay during the film
festival. Renovated
rooms including two vast
rooftop suites, a de luxe
spa, a private beach and
two restaurants, most
notably the Palme d'Or.
412 rooms. €€€€

Hôtel de Paris
34 boulevard d'Alsace
Tel: 04 97 06 98 88
Fax: 04 93 39 04 61
www.hotel-de-paris.com
Behind the old Victorian
façade lies a modern
hotel decorated in a
vaguely Louis XIII style.
An attractive pool
surrounded by a tropical
garden; just beyond the
hedges, though, lies a

busy boulevard. Comfort for a reasonable price. Closed 10–27 Dec and 7–17 Jan. 50 rooms. €€–€€€
Hôtel de Provence
9 rue Molière
Tel: 04 93 38 44 35
Fax: 04 93 39 63 14
www.hotel-de-provence.com
Comfortable, quaint lodgings 100 metres/yds from La Croisette. The small balconies on the front-facing rooms look out over a lush garden (and the back of the

Noga Hilton). Closed Dec. 30 rooms. €€
Hôtel Splendid
4–6 rue Félix Faure
Tel: 04 97 06 22 22
Fax: 04 93 99 55 02
www.splendid-hotel-cannes.fr
A white Belle Epoque-era hotel with an old-fashioned atmosphere and great views. Situated near the port and almost opposite the Palais des Festivals. Updated rooms retain their period features. 62 rooms. €€–€€€

ABOVE: the lobby of the Hôtel Martinez.

ANTIBES AND THE PLATEAU DE VALBONNE

Antibes

Bleu Marine
4 rue des Chemins
Tel: 04 93 74 84 84
Fax: 04 93 95 90 26
www.bleumarineantibes.com
Small hotel near the centre of town. Simple rooms, some with balconies that have sea and mountain views. 18 rooms. €–€€
Relais du Postillon
8 rue Championnet
Tel: 04 93 34 20 77
Fax: 04 93 34 61 24
www.relaisdupostillon.com
A pleasant hotel in the old town. Reasonable rates. Good restaurant. 15 rooms. €–€€

Biot

Hotel des Arcades
16 place des Arcades
Tel: 04 93 65 01 04
Fax: 04 93 65 01 05
A 15th-century mansion that combines antique furniture with modern convenience. The restaurant is also an art gallery and meals and rooms are reasonably priced. 12 rooms. €–€€

Cap d'Antibes

Grand Hotel du Cap-Eden Roc
Boulevard Kennedy
Tel: 04 93 61 39 01
Fax: 04 93 67 76 04
www.edenroc-hotel.fr
Exclusive hotel on the water's edge in wooded grounds. Luxurious rooms. Swimming pool, tennis courts. Closed mid-Oct–Mar. 124 rooms. €€€€
La Jabotte
13 avenue de Max Maurey
Tel: 04 93 61 45 89
Fax: 04 93 61 07 04
www.jabotte.com
Adorable and affordable lodgings in a residential area minutes from the beach. The original artwork is by one of the owners. Closed Nov and Christmas week. 10 rooms. €€

Juan-les-Pins

Belles-Rives
Boulevard Edouard Baudoin
Tel: 04 93 61 02 79
www.bellesrives.com
Close enough to town for the atmosphere, but far

enough from the crowds. This 1930s villa was home to Zelda and F. Scott Fitzgerald. Closed Nov, Jan–Feb. 43 rooms. €€€€
Garden Beach Hotel
15–17 boulevard Baudoin
Tel: 04 92 93 57 57
Fax: 04 92 93 57 56
www.juanlespins.lemeridien.com
On the site of the former casino, in the town centre. A terrace overlooks the bay. Closed Dec. 175 rooms. €€€
Juan Beach
5 rue de l'Oratoire
Tel: 04 93 61 02 89
Fax: 04 93 61 16 63
www.hoteljuanbeach.com
Old family house with simple rooms and summer dining in a flower garden. Good value. Closed Nov–Mar. 24 rooms. €€–€€€

Mougins

Le Moulin de Mougins
Notre-Dame-de-Vie
Tel: 04 93 75 78 24
Fax: 04 93 90 18 55
www.moulindemougins.com
Small gastronomic hotel

set in an old restored mill run by Alain Llorca. Three elegant rooms and four spacious suites overlook the garden. €€€
Les Muscadins
18 boulevard Courteline
Tel: 04 92 28 43 43
Fax: 04 92 28 43 40
www.les-muscadins.com
An attractive hotel on the edge of the village, with a view of the Bay of Cannes. The 11 spacious rooms are decorated in a different style. Closed Nov–Mar. €€€

PRICE CATEGORIES

Price categories are for an average double room in high season:
€ = under €80
€€ = €80–150
€€€ = €150–250
€€€€ = more than €250

GRASSE AND THE LOUP VALLEY

Grasse

La Bastide Saint-Antoine
48 avenue Henri Durant
Tel: 04 93 70 94 94
Fax: 04 93 70 94 95
www.jacques-chibois.com
Best known for its restaurant run by chef Jacques Chibois, this beautiful 18th-century *bastide* (country house) has 16 stark but chic modern rooms. €€€

Hotel de Patti
Place du Patti
Tel: 04 93 36 01 00
Fax: 04 93 36 36 40
www.hotelpatti.com
A large central hotel with standard modern rooms and *"Chambres de Charme"* in Provençal colours. View of the town from many rooms. One of the few Riviera hotels that does not have seasonal price swings. 73 rooms. €€

Hôtel des Parfums (Odalys)
Rue Eugène Charabot
Tel: 04 92 42 35 35
www.hoteldesparfums.com
Basic, moderately priced rooms with great views. Hammam and pool. €€

Tourrettes-sur-Loup

Auberge des Gorges du Loup
4 Pont du Loup

Tel: 04 93 59 38 01
Fax: 04 93 59 39 71
www.auberge-gorgesduloup.com
Small hotel on the edge of the river gorge. Lovely terrace restaurant. Closed Nov. 10 rooms. €

CAGNES, VENCE AND THE VAR VALLEY

Haute de Cagnes

Le Cagnard
45 rue Sous Bari
Tel: 04 93 20 73 22
Fax: 04 93 22 06 39
www.le-cagnard.com
Near Château Grimaldi, a charming hotel with a rustic atmosphere. 22 rooms. €€€

Roquefort-les-Pins

Auberge du Colombier
Tel: 04 92 60 33 00
Fax: 04 93 77 07 03
www.auberge-du-colombier.com
A small friendly hotel set in wooded grounds. Swimming pool and tennis courts. Closed

mid-Jan–mid-Feb. 20 rooms. €€–€€€

St-Paul-de-Vence

La Colombe d'Or
Place du Général de Gaulle
Tel: 04 93 32 80 02
Fax: 04 93 32 77 78
www.la-colombe-dor.com
A lovely old building once frequented by Picasso, Matisse, Miró and Léger, whose works adorn the walls. Private courtyard and swimming pool. Closed mid-Oct–mid-Dec. 16 rooms. €€€€
Mas d'Artigny
Route de la Colle
Tel: 04 93 32 84 54
Fax: 04 93 32 95 36

www.mas-artigny.com
Beautifully situated in the woods between St-Paul and La Colle with a 360° view of the sea and the mountains. 85 rooms. €€€–€€€€

Vence

Auberge des Seigneurs
Place du Frêne
Tel: 04 93 58 04 24
Fax: 04 93 24 08 01
A former tavern in a wing of the Château de Villeneuve. The white rooms come with dark-wood furniture, pretty rugs and a lot of space for the price. Closed Nov–Feb. 6 rooms. €€

Château du Domaine St-Martin
Route de Coursegoules
Tel: 04 93 58 02 02
Fax: 04 93 24 08 91
www.chateau-st-martin.com
True luxury set on the hills above Vence. All rooms (junior suites or suites) have balconies with views. Extensive grounds, swimming pool. Closed mid-Oct–Feb. 46 rooms. €€€€

NICE

Hôtel Aria
15 avenue Auber
Tel: 04 93 88 30 69
www.aria-nice.com
This completely renovated 19th-century hotel overlooks an attractive garden square amid the Belle

Epoque and Art Deco buildings of the new town. Rooms are light with high ceilings and decorated in sunny colours. Good value. 30 rooms. €€
Beau Rivage
24 rue St-François-de-Paule

Tel: 04 92 47 82 82
Fax: 04 92 47 82 83
www.nicebeaurivage.com
Stylish hotel with a private beach. Matisse had an apartment here, and Nietzsche and F. Scott Fitzgerald are among other famous

visitors. Renovated in a sleek modern style with internet access and plasma TVs in the rooms. In the old town. 118 rooms. €€€–€€€€

Grimaldi
15 rue Grimaldi
Tel: 04 93 16 00 24
Fax: 04 93 87 00 24
www.le-grimaldi.com
An *"Hôtel de Charme"* with rooms beautifully furnished and decorated with designer fabrics in rich colours. €€€

Hi-Hotel
3 avenue des Fleurs
Tel: 04 97 07 26 26
Fax: 04 97 07 26 27
www.hi-hotel.net
Ultra-modern hotel designed by Matali Crosset – a disciple of Philippe Starck. Themed rooms; no restaurant. 38 rooms. €€€–€€€€

Hôtel Negresco
37 promenade des Anglais
Tel: 04 93 16 64 00
Fax: 04 93 88 35 68
www.hotel-negresco-nice.com
The last vestige of Nice's golden age at the end of the 19th century, with its famous dome dominating the Baie des Anges. The hotel has period furniture from the 16th and 18th centuries, and priceless paintings and tapestries. 150 rooms. €€€€

La Pérouse
11 quai Rauba-Capéu
Tel: 04 93 62 34 63
Fax: 04 93 62 59 41
www.hotel-la-perouse.com
At the east end of the promenade des Anglais, conveniently situated between the old town and the port. The rooms have splendid views of

ABOVE: the lobby of the Hôtel Negresco.

the Baie des Anges. Swimming pool. 56 rooms. €€€–€€€€

Hotel Windsor
11 rue Dalpozzo
Tel: 04 93 88 59 35
Fax: 04 93 88 94 57
www.hotelwindsornice.com
A unique hotel with many rooms decorated by contemporary artists. One room is covered in

colourful writing; another is painted entirely in gold with a glowing white bed. An elevator with a space shuttle collage starts a countdown to blast-off when you push the button. The small swimming pool is surrounded by a tropical garden. 57 rooms. €€–€€€

CAP FERRAT AND THE GOLDEN TRIANGLE

Beaulieu-sur-Mer

La Réserve de Beaulieu
5 boulevard du Général Leclerc
Tel: 04 93 01 00 01
Fax: 04 93 01 28 99
www.reservebeaulieu.com
A luxurious late 19th-century villa, beautifully situated on the coast with private harbour. Swimming pool. Closed Nov–mid-Dec. 39 rooms. €€€€

Eze

Château Eza
Rue de la Pise
Tel: 04 93 41 12 24
Fax: 04 93 41 16 64
www.chateaueza.com
Perched high above the Mediterranean on a cliff, and accessible only on foot (your baggage is carried up by

a porter), this 400-year-old castle overlooks 260 km (160 miles) of coast. Rooms are decorated in beautiful fabrics and lush colours; the modern furniture has a period feel. Some rooms have a fireplace. Closed Nov–mid-Dec. 10 rooms. €€€–€€€€

St-Jean-Cap-Ferrat

Brise Marine
58 avenue Jean Mermoz
Tel: 04 93 76 04 36
Fax: 04 93 76 11 49
www.hotel-brisemarine.com
A warm welcome is given at this 19th-century Italian villa, which has an attractive terraced garden. Some of the comfortable rooms have a terrific

view of the bay, the coastline and, in the distance, the Alps. Closed Nov–Jan. 16 rooms. €€€

Clair Logis
12 avenue Centrale
Tel: 04 93 76 51 81
Fax: 04 93 76 51 82
www.hotel-clair-logis.fr
A lush garden surrounds this pleasant hotel, which is in a residential area about a 15-minute walk from town. Closed mid-Nov–mid-Dec, and Jan–mid-Feb. 16 rooms. €€–€€€

La Voile d'Or
Yachting Harbour
Tel: 04 93 01 13 13
Fax: 04 93 76 11 17
www.lavoiledor.fr
An exclusive hotel in a luxurious Italian villa with port-side views. It has lodged stars and

celebrities such as Roger Moore and Madonna. The property has a seawater pool and private beach. Closed Oct–Mar. 45 rooms. €€€€

PRICE CATEGORIES

Price categories are an average double room in high seas
€ = under €80
€€ = €80–150
€€€ = €150–
€€€€ = more

TRANSPORT

ACCOMMODATION

ACTIVITIES

A – Z

MONACO

Monte-Carlo

Alexandra
35 blvd Princesse Charlotte
Tel: 377-93 50 63 13
Fax: 377-92 16 06 48
www.monaco-hotel.com/
montecarlo/alexandra
In the centre of town, the
elaborate Belle Epoque
façade is a cover for
recently refurbished
lodgings. 56 rooms. €€€

Ambassador
10 avenue Prince Pierre
Tel: 377-97 97 96 96
Fax: 377-97 97 96 99
www.ambassadormonaco.com
Near the new high-tech
Port Hercule, a classic
modern hotel offering a
high level of comfort for

the price, considering
the location. Gourmet
Italian restaurant.
35 rooms. €€€

Columbus
23 avenue des Papalins,
Fontvieille
Tel: 377- 92 05 90 00
Fax: 377-92 05 91 67
www.columbushotels.com
A sleek, modern luxury
hotel with matching bar
and restaurant over-
looking the new harbour.
181 rooms. €€€€

Hôtel de France
6 rue de La Turbie
Tel: 377-93 30 24 64
Fax: 377-92 16 13 34
www.monte-carlo.mc/france
A cosy hotel near the
railway station in the

Condamine quarter, 10
minutes from palace and
casino. 26 rooms. €€

Hermitage
Place Beaumarchais
Tel: 377-98 06 48 12
Fax: 377-98 06 26 26
www.montecarloresort.com
Beautiful Edwardian
architecture, spacious,
luxurious rooms. Spa,
swimming pool and
fitness centre.
280 rooms. €€€€

Miramar
1 avenue J.F. Kennedy
Tel: 377-93 30 86 48
Fax: 377-93 30 26 33
www.hotel-miramar.mc
Sleek modern lodgings
with a subdued decor;
all 11 rooms have sea

views, 7 of them
balconies. €€–€€€

Hôtel de Paris
Place du Casino
Tel: 377-98 06 30 16
Fax: 377-98 06 25 25
www.montecarloresort.com
The most prestigious of
Monaco's luxury hotels,
with a Belle Epoque
façade. Alain Ducasse's
3-star restaurant, Louis
XV. A royal experience.
187 rooms. €€€€

MENTON AND ROQUEBRUNE-CAP-MARTIN

Menton

Hôtel Aiglon
7 avenue de la Madone
Tel: 04 93 57 55 55
Fax: 04 93 35 92 39
www.hotelaiglon.net
A 19th-century mansion
converted into an
atmospheric hotel with
beautiful architectural
details. The Belle
Epoque bar/salon is a
delight; rooms are less
elaborate, with an old-
fashioned look. Closed
mid-Nov–mid-Dec.
29 rooms. €€–€€€

Grand Hôtel des
Ambassadeurs
Je Partouneaux
04 93 28 75 75
4 93 35 62 32
bassadeurs-menton.com
Menton has a
hotel following
over of the ven-
assadeurs in
ntly baroque

style. Different floors
are dedicated to art,
literature, music and
cinema. Champagne
bar and restaurant.
Entirely non-smoking.
32 rooms. €€€€

Hôtel de Londres
15 avenue Carnot
Tel: 04 93 35 74 62
Fax: 04 93 41 77 78
www.hotel-de-londres.com
Small central hotel,
popular during the
lemon festival (see
page 206). Rooms are
basic, but they open out
on a garden courtyard
ideal for alfresco
breakfast. Closed
Nov–Dec. 27 rooms. €€

Hôtel Napoléon
29 port de France
Tel: 04 93 35 89 50
Fax: 04 93 35 49 22
www.napoleon-menton.com
Stylish lodgings with
contemporary flair right
on the edge of the Bay

of Garavan. Private
beach with restaurant,
as well as a small pool;
terrific value and com-
fort. 44 rooms. €€–€€€

Hôtel Royal
Westminster
1510 Promenade du Soleil
Tel: 04 93 28 69 69
www.vacancesbleues.com
A classic seafront hotel
evoking Menton's
dignified past. A garden
runs down to the
seaside promenade. 92
rooms and spacious
salons with restaurant
and piano bar. €€

Roquebrune-
Cap-Martin

Vista Palace Hotel
1551 route de la Grande
Corniche
Tel: 04 92 10 40 00
Fax: 04 93 35 18 94
www.vistapalace.com
A modern luxury hotel

that sits high above
Monaco with wonderful
views. Spacious rooms;
swimming pool and
fitness centre. Closed
Feb–mid-Mar.
68 rooms. €€€–€€€€

Westminster
14 avenue Louis Laurens
Tel: 04 93 35 00 68
Fax: 04 93 28 88 50
www.westminster06.com
This small family-run
hotel has lovely views
and terraced gardens.
Most of the simply
furnished rooms face
the sea. Closed first
3 weeks in Dec and
Jan–mid-Feb. 28 rooms.
€–€€

THE PERCHED VILLAGES

La Turbie

Hostellerie Jérôme
20 rue du Comte de Cessole
Tel: 04 92 41 51 51
Fax: 04 92 41 51 50
www.hostelleriejerome.com
Primarily known for its Michelin two-star restaurant, this tiny hotel has elegant rooms with furniture *à l'ancienne*, some of which have splendid views of the sea below the village. Closed Dec–Jan. 5 rooms. €€–€€€

Lantosque

Hostellerie de l'Ancienne Gendarmerie
Quartier Le Rivet
Tel: 04 93 03 00 65
Fax: 04 93 03 06 31
www.hotel-lantosque.com
Hotel in the former *gendarmerie* (police station). Eight spacious, simple rooms with beautiful views of the Massif of Mercantour. Garden restaurant and pool. Closed Nov–Feb. €€

Peillon

Auberge de la Madone
2 place Auguste Arnulf
Tel: 04 93 79 91 17
Fax: 04 93 79 99 36
www.auberge-madone-peillon.com
This smartened-up country *auberge* located at the gates of the village has a Michelin one-star restaurant. Rooms have splendid views of the hilltop village and the valley. Closed Nov–mid-Dec and Jan. 18 rooms. €€–€€€

Annexe Lou Pourtail
A less expensive but lovely alternative just across the street from the Auberge de la Madone; it is owned by the same proprietors. Same closing dates as the Auberge; 5 rooms. €

BORDER COUNTRY

Breil-sur-Roya

Hôtel Le Roya
Place Blanchéri
Tel: 04 93 04 48 10
A simple hotel next to the village car park (market here on Tuesdays) offering B&B for those on a budget. €

Sospel

Hôtel des Etrangers
7 boulevard de Verdun
Tel: 04 93 04 00 09
Fax: 04 93 04 12 31
www.sospel.net
Family-run hotel right next to the Bevera river; rooms have lovely views of mountains and forest. Swimming pool on site;

proprietor is expert on local history. Closed Nov–Mar. 25 rooms. €€

Hôtel de France
9 boulevard de Verdun
Tel: 04 93 04 00 01
Fax: 04 93 04 20 46
www.hoteldefrance-sospel.com
Simple rooms in a friendly environment – owned by two welcoming Belgian couples. The terrace overlooks the river. 10 rooms. €

Tende

Le Chamois d'Or
Hameau de Casterino
Tel: 04 93 04 66 66
Fax: 04 93 04 66 68
www.hotelchamoisdor.net
A traditional mountain chalet at the gates of the Vallée des Merveilles. The large rooms are furnished in a contemporary "*montagnard*" style – lots of light wood and muted colours. Regional cuisine. 22 rooms. €€–€€€

Le Prieuré
St-Dalmas-de-Tende
Tel: 04 93 04 75 70
Fax: 04 93 04 71 58
www.leprieure.org
At the foot of Mont Bego, this unpretentious inn offers comfortable, colourful rooms and a good family-style restaurant. In a lovely setting with fishing, skiing and kayaking all in the

immediate area. Organises summer trips to the Vallée des Merveilles. Closed Christmas week. 24 rooms. €

BELOW: hilltop window dressing.

ACTIVITIES

THE ARTS, FESTIVALS, NIGHTLIFE, SHOPPING AND SPORT

THE ARTS

Culture

The Riviera has a wealth of cultural events, especially in the summertime. There are a number of important art museums in Nice, St-Paul-de-Vence, St-Tropez and Antibes, and many smaller museums and galleries offering a huge variety of art and crafts. In larger towns you will find opera, theatre and cinema venues.

Theatre, Music and Dance

Monaco

Entertainment centres around the Casino, where the **Monte-Carlo Opéra** (tel: 377-98 06 28 28; www.opera.mc) is based in the magnificent opera house. The Casino is also the home of the **Monte-Carlo Philharmonic** (tel: 377-98 06 28 28; www.opmc.mc) and the **Monte-Carlo Ballet** (377-92 16 24 20; www.balletsdemonte-carlo.com), as well as **Le Cabaret du Casino** (tel: 377-92 16 36 36). In the summer, the **Théâtre du Fort Saint-Antoine** (avenue de la Quarantaine; tel: 377-93 25 66 12) hosts outdoor theatre and concerts.

Nice

The **Opéra de Nice** (4 rue St-François-de-Paule; tel: 04 92 17 40 00; www.opera-nice.org) offers symphony, ballet and opera. A smaller theatre and concert venue is the **Théâtre Lino Ventura** (168 boulevard de l'Ariane; tel: 04 97 00 10 70). For theatre classics and contemporary work, try **Théâtre de Nice** on the promenade des Arts (tel: 04 93 13 90 90). The **Cinémathèque** (Acropolis, 3 esplanade Kennedy; tel: 04 92 04 06 66; www.cinematheque-nice.com) presents recent releases, old classics, and obscure art-house films in their original version with subtitles.

Cannes

The **Regional Orchestra of Cannes, Provence and the Côte d'Azur** (tel: 04 93 48 61 10; www.orchestre-cannes.com) performs at concert halls all over the region.

Menton

The Palais de l'Europe (avenue Boyer) is the main venue for plays and concerts. Its **Théâtre Francis-Palmero** (tel: 04 92 41 76 95) stages productions several times a year. The **Lavoir-Théâtre** (63 boulevard du Fossan, tel: 04 93 41 41 55) is a more intimate theatre space. During the summer, open-air concerts are held at the Annonciade Monastery.

FESTIVALS

Diary of Events

January

Cannes: MIDEM (International Disc and Music Publishing Market)
Monaco: Monte-Carlo Rally; International Circus Festival
Valbonne: Festival St-Blaise – wine and local products

February

Bormes-Les-Mimosas: *Corso Fleuri* flower parade
Menton: Lemon Festival
Nice: Carnival

March

Antibes: *La Colombe d'Or* – magic festival
Tourrettes-sur-Loup: Violet Festival

April

Bar-sur-Loup: Orange Blossom Festival – orange-wine tasting; folklore
Cannes: MIP-TV – international TV festival
Juan-les-Pins: Jazz à Juan Révélations – jazz talent showcase
Monaco: Monte-Carlo Tennis Masters Series; Monte-Carlo Spring Arts Festival
Roquebrune-Cap-Martin: Good Friday costumed procession

Vence: Folklore and Flower Parade (Easter Sunday and Monday)

May

Cannes: Film Festival
Grasse: Expo Rose – international rose show
Monaco: Formula One Grand Prix
Nice: May Festival – folklore, picnics, dance concerts
St-Tropez: The Bravades festival in honour of the Roman soldier Torpes from whom St-Tropez takes its name

June

Antibes: Les Voiles d'Antibes – yacht regatta
Fréjus: Féria de la Côte d'Azur – bullfights, folklore
Menton: Mois des Jardins – guided garden tours during the entire month
Monaco: Fires of St Jean folk festival
Nice: Sacred Music Festival
Whole country: Fête de la Musique (21 June)

July

Antibes: Musiques au Cœur - opera festival
Fréjus: Los Nuits Auréliennes – theatre festival (through August)
Golfe-Juan: Jean Marais Festival – theatre and music
Juan-les-Pins: International Jazz Festival – Jazz à Juan
Monaco: Concerts in the Palais du Prince courtyard; Fireworks Festival and Monaco carnival
Nice: Grande Parade du Jazz – Nice's famous jazz festival
Vence: Les Nuits du Sud – world music festival.

Villefranche-sur-Mer: Moments Musicaux – open-air concerts in the Citadel
Whole region: Bastille Day (14 July, all France) – fireworks and celebrations

August

Antibes: International Fireworks Festival
Breil-sur-Roya and nearby towns: International Organ Festival in Alpine chapels
Fréjus: Fête du Raisin – wine-tasting and feasting
Grasse: Festival of Jasmine
Menton: Chamber Music Festival
Ramatuelle: Festival de Ramatuelle – theatre festival
Tendo: Shepherds' Festival – sheep parade, folklore groups, local products
Vallauris: Pottery Festival

September

Fréjus: Giant Omelette Festival
Nice: International Festival of Military Music (every 2 or 3 years)
Whole region: Journées du Patrimoine – historic monuments and official buildings open free to the public

October

La Garde-Freinet: Chestnut Festival
Monte-Carlo: Season of Symphony Concerts
Nice: Blues Festival; Festival of Underwater Images

November

Monaco: National Holiday (19 November) – parades, ceremonies and spectacles (fire-works the previous evening)
St-Tropez: Piano Festival

December

Fréjus: Foire aux Santons – Provençal craftsmen exhibit *santons* (small clay figures of saints).

NIGHTLIFE

Bars and Nightclubs

Below is a list of nightclubs, as well as cafés/restaurants where you can be entertained as you dine. Many of the luxury hotels also have piano bars. You will need a healthy bank account for most of them.

Antibes

La Siesta, route du Bord de Mer; tel: 04 93 33 31 31. Huge seaside restaurant, bar, casino and nightclub.

Cannes

L'Amiral, 73 La Croisette; tel: 04 92 98 73 00. Chic cocktail lounge at the Hôtel Martinez.
Au Bureau, 49 rue Félix Faure; tel: 04 93 68 56 36. Bar and dance club with themed parties and not too much attitude.
Le Milk, avenue Georges Gallice, Juan-les-Pins; tel: 04 93 67 22 74. Dance until dawn.
Morrisons, 10 rue Tessière; tel: 04 92 98 16 17. Friendly, boisterous Irish bar with live music.
Whisky à Gogo, La Pinède; tel: 04 93 61 26 40. Happening bar and discotheque.
Zanzi Bar, 85 rue Félix Faure, Juan-les-Pins; tel: 04 93 39 30 75. Well-established gay bar and club.

Monaco

Jimmy'z, avenue Princess Grace; tel: 377-92 16 22 77. Smart but expensive nightclub.
Monte-Carlo Sporting Club, avenue Princess Grace, tel: 377-92 16 22 44. Fashionable Euro-trash rendezvous.
La Rascasse, quai Antoine; tel:

TRANSPORT ACCOMMODATION ACTIVITIES A – Z

WHAT'S ON AND WHERE TO BUY TICKETS

The regional tourist office (Comité Régional du Tourisme Riviera Côte d'Azur) has a website with a good listing of cultural events at www.guide riviera.com. The Union Départe-mentale des Offices de Tourisme et Syndicats d'Initia-tive (UDOSTI) has a huge listing of cultural events and festivals at

www.cotedazur-en-fete.com (tel: 04 92 47 75 15).
You can pick up tickets for theatre, concerts, and other events at: Fnac, tel: 08 92 68 36 22; www.fnac.fr
Virgin Megastore, tel: 08 92 39 01 00; www.ticketnet.fr
France Billet, tel: 08 92 69 21 92; www.francebillet.com

377-93 25 56 90. All-night pub, with live music, plus restaurant.

Nice

Le Bar des Oiseaux, 5 rue St-Vincent; tel: 04 93 80 27 33. Friendly bar with live jazz and French *chanson*.
Blue Boy Enterprise, 9 rue Spinetta; tel: 04 93 44 68 24. An all-night gay club with drag shows.
Le Relais, 37 promenade des Anglais; tel: 04 93 16 64 00. A stunning 19th-century bar in the Hôtel Negresco.

Ste-Maxime

Café de France, place Victor Hugo; tel: 04 94 96 18 16. Classic bar with people-watching terrace.

St-Tropez

Bar du Port, 7 quai Suffren; tel: 04 94 97 00 54. Retro-style bar.
Café de Paris, 15 quai Suffren; tel: 04 94 97 00 56. Old bar, redesigned by Philippe Starck to attract a trendy crowd.
Les Caves du Roy, Hôtel Byblos; tel: 04 94 97 16 02. Legendary club in Hôtel Byblos.
L'Esquinade, 2 rue du Four; tel: 04 94 97 87 44. One of the originals.
Le Papagayo, Résidence du Port; tel: 04 94 54 82 89. The place to spot famous faces.
Le Pigeonnier, 13 rue de la Ponche, tel: 04 94 97 84 26. Popular gay club.
Le VIP Room, Résidences du Nouveau Port; tel: 04 94 97 14 70. One of St-Tropez's most fashionable nightclubs.

Casinos

Entrance to most casinos is around €12–20 (although some are free) and restricted to those aged over 21. Many require you to show your passport.

Antibes

La Siesta, Route du Bord de Mer; tel: 04 93 33 31 31. Casino open June–Sept, bar and restaurant all year. Huge nightclub and casino. www.lasiesta.fr

Cannes

Casino Barrière de Cannes Croisette, Palais des Festivals; tel: 04 92 98 78 00; www.lucien barriere.com. Open daily 10am–3am. Huge, swanky establishment in the Palais des Festivals.
Casino Barrière Les Princes, 14 La Croisette; tel: 04 97 06 18 50; www.lucienbarriere.com. Open daily 1pm–4am. Modern casino.
Palm Beach Casino, place Franklin Roosevelt; tel: 04 97 06 36 90; www.lepalmbeach.com. Open daily 11am–4am, in summer until 5am. Also has restaurants, lounge bar and disco.

Monte-Carlo

Casino de Monte-Carlo, place du Casino; tel: 377-92 16 23 00. Formal dress is required. Open daily, during the week from 2pm and weekends from noon; there is no closing hour. The casino has a separate cabaret venue and several restaurants. www.casino montecarlo.com.
Café de Paris, place du Casino; tel: 377-92 16 20 20. Roulette, craps and blackjack. Open daily 10am–2am.

Nice

Casino Ruhl de Nice, 1 promenade des Anglais; tel: 04 97 03 12 22. Open daily, weekdays 5pm–5am, weekends 10am–4am. Also has a restaurant, disco and cabaret.
Palais de la Méditerranée, 15 promenade des Anglais; tel: 04 92 14 68 00. Open daily, week-days 10am–4am, weekends 10am–5am. With a 4-star hotel.

SHOPPING

Where to Buy

Nice

The pedestrianised Masséna quarter has chic boutiques and department stores. For smaller stores and regional products, visit the old town around the cours Saleya.

Agnès B.
17 rue des Ponchettes
Tel: 04 93 62 32 39
High-end, hip casual wear.
Alziari
14 rue St-François-de-Paule
Tel: 04 93 85 76 92
www.alziari.com.fr
Selection of gourmet olive oils pressed on site.
Confiserie Florian
Quai Papacino
Tel: 04 93 55 43 50
www.confiserieflorian.com
Chocolates, candied fruits and flowers.
Escale en Provence
7 rue du Marché
Tel: 04 93 85 23 90
Herbs, vinegars and *tapenade*.
Les Olivades
8 avenue de Verdun
Tel: 04 93 88 75 70
www.lesolivades.fr
Gorgeous Provençal prints.
Oliviera
8 bis rue de Collet
Tel: 04 93 13 06 45
www.oliviera.com
Olive oils and Provençal spreads.

Cannes

Most of the glamorous stores are on La Croisette. Rue d'Antibes and the nearby pedestrian streets have a wider range of prices and products. Rue Meynadier, which is also pedestrianised, has clothing, food and regional specialities.
Benito et Fils
9 rue d'Antibes
Tel: 04 93 38 54 06
Fabergé, Chistofle, and other elegant top-grade brands.
Cannolive
16–20 rue Venizelos
Tel: 04 93 39 08 19
Olive oils, herbs and dried fruits.
Christian Lacroix
14 boulevard de la Croisette
Tel: 04 93 68 06 06
www.christian-lacroix.fr
Cutting-edge designer fashions.
Louis Julian & Fils
71 rue d'Antibes
Tel: 04 93 39 30 68
www.bijouterie-julian.com
High-end jewellery.

Maiffret
31 rue d'Antibes
Tel: 04 93 39 08 29
Candied fruits and chocolates.

Grasse
Famous for its perfume, which
can be bought at the boutiques
within the perfume factories.
Fragonard
20 boulevard Fragonard
Tel: 04 93 36 44 65
www.fragonard.com
Galimard
73 route de Cannes
Tel: 04 93 09 20 00
www.galimard.com
Molinard
60 boulevard Victor Hugo
Tel: 04 92 42 33 11
www.molinard.com

Monaco
The Cercle d'Or in Monte-Carlo,
bordered by avenue Monte-Carlo,
avenue des Beaux-Arts and allées
Lumières, specialises in luxury
shops and designer boutiques.
The Condamine has a large
shopping centre with around 200
boutiques; the Princesse Caroline
pedestrian zone is another
boutique-filled area.
Dior
Avenue des Beaux-Arts
Tel: 377-93 30 79 78
Prêt-à-porter, jewellery, shoes and
accessories.
Hermès
11–15 avenue de Monte-Carlo
Tel: 377-93 50 64 89
Scarves, accessories and leather
goods.
Repossi
Square Beaumarchais
Tel: 377-93 50 89 59
www.repossi.mc
Official jeweller of Prince Albert.

Biot
Well known for its glassworks,
which produces a beautiful,
bubble-filled product.
Verrerie de Biot
Chemin des Combes
Tel: 04 93 65 03 00
www.verreriebiot.com
There is a museum as well as a
boutique at this glassworks.

Tourrettes-sur-Loup
Violets grow in the hills over the
gorges, and some are turned into
confectionery, sold with fruit
confits and chocolates at the
Confiserie Florian Factory.
Confiserie Florian
Le Pont du Loup
Tel: 04 93 59 32 91
www.confiserieflorian.com

Markets
In many towns, there is a daily
market, except on Monday. They
mostly start early in the morning
and close at midday. Some of the
best general daily food markets
are in Nice (cours Saleya),
Antibes (cours Masséna covered
market), Cannes (Marché Forville,
also the flower market, rue Félix
Faure – not Monday), Vence
(place Clémenceau), Menton
(covered market), Monte-Carlo
(place d'Armes), Ste-Maxime
(covered market, rue Fenand
Bessy, open all day in summer).
Other markets which are worth
a visit, but not held daily are
(mornings): St-Tropez (Tues, Sat);
Fréjus (Wed, Sat; place Formigé),
also Fréjus-Plage (Tues, Fri; place
de la République), Hyères (Tues,
place de la République; Sat,
avenue Gambetta), Le Lavandou
(Thur), Draguignan (Wed, Sat), Ste-
Maxime (Thur, old town; Mon,
Marché du Capet, avenue
Georges Pompidou).
The specialist markets are

good too. All the above have flower
stalls, but Nice flower market
(open all day), and Cannes flower
market are especially colourful.
Antiques and second-hand
(brocante) markets are held
regularly and are open all day
unless otherwise indicated.
Antibes: Place Audiberti, Sat;
also cours Masséna for bric-à-
brac, Tues and Fri afternoons.
Cannes: Allées de la Liberté, Sat.
Menton: Place aux Herbes,
second Sun of month.
Nice: Cours Saleya, Mon; on rues
A. Gauthier/C. Ségurane/E.
Philibert, plus the flea market on
place Robilante, both daily except
Sun; philatelists' market,
square Durandy, rue Pastorelli,
Sun morning.
Ste-Maxime: Marché des
Artisans (craft market), every
evening in summer.
La Seyne-sur-Mer: City Hall
annexe parking lot, avenue Pierre
Mendes-France; flea market,
second Sun of month.
Vence: Place des Grands Jardins,
Wed.
Villefranche-sur-Mer: Place A.
Pollonais, Sun; Jardin Binon, Sun.
There are also craft fairs and
marchés exceptionnels. Check
with the tourist office.

Opening Times
Food shops, especially bakers,
tend to open early; boutiques and
department stores open from

BELOW: perfume makes an ideal souvenir from Grasse.

9–10am. Many city-centre stores, particularly department stores, stay open all day, but some small shops close from noon until 2pm. Most shops close at 7pm. Hypermarkets are usually open until 8 or 9pm. Most shops are closed on Sunday, and many are closed Monday morning. If you want a picnic lunch, buy everything you need before midday. Good delicatessens *(traiteurs)* have a selection of prepared dishes.

Buying Wine Direct

Many wine-producers invite you to taste their wines (look for *dégustations)* and other produce with the aim of making a sale. This is a good way to try before you buy and may include a visit to a wine cellar. Also, the wine should be cheaper here than in the supermarket. Try:
Maison des Vins, route Nationale 7, Les Arcs-sur-Argens; tel: 04 94 99 50 20.
Petit Village, La Foux junction, 4 km (2 miles) west of St-Tropez; tel: 04 94 56 40 17.

Reading Wine Labels

The best wines produced within the region are from the Côtes de Provence *appellation*, especially the rosés of the Massif des Maures. To the west of the Riviera, the lower Rhône Valley produces some even better wines, in particular the famous Châteauneuf-du-Pape.
  Wines are graded according to quality, and this must be shown on the label. The grades are:
• **Vin de table**: usually inexpensive table wine; quality can vary.
• **Vin de pays**: local wine.
• **VDQS** *(vin délimité de qualité supérieure)*: wine from a specific area; better than *vin de table*.
• **AOC** *(appellation d'origine contrôlée)*: good-quality wine from a specific area or chateau where strict controls are imposed on the amount of wine produced.
Other important phrases:
• *Mis en bouteille au château*: ▪ottled at the vineyard. Also

TAX

The price of most items includes Value Added Tax (called TVA in French), which is 19.6 percent. Non-EU visitors can get a refund *(détaxe)* if they spend over €175 in the same shop. The shop will supply a *détaxe* form, which you will need to fill in, sign and have stamped by customs when you leave the country (you can do this at the airport). Once home, send a copy back to the shop, which will refund the tax, either by bank transfer or by crediting your credit card. *Détaxe* does not cover food, drink, antiques or works of art.

indicated by the words *récoltant* or *producteur* around the cap.
• *Négociant*: a wine that has been bought by a dealer and usually not bottled on the estate. However, this is not necessarily to the detriment of the wine; there are many excellent *négociants*.

Complaints

If you have a complaint about any purchase, return it to the shop as soon as possible. In the case of any serious dispute, contact the Direction Départementale de la Concurrence et de la Consommation et de la Répression des Fraudes, tel: 3939 (in France only); www.finances.gouv.fr/dgccrf

SPORT

Participant Sports

Antibes and Cannes are major watersports centres, and the Iles de Lérins and Iles d'Hyères offer some of the best diving in the Med. For detailed listings pick up the *Watersports Côte d'Azur* brochure from main tourist offices or go to www.france-nautisme.com.
  The sea is usually warm enough for swimming from June

to September, and almost every town has a municipal pool, though it may only be open in school holidays. Even small villages have a tennis court, though you may have to become a temporary member to use it – enquire at the local tourist office or *mairie* (town hall).
  Mountains and river valleys offer walking, riding, cycling and climbing, river-rafting and canoeing, and skiing in winter.

Watersports

Only 70 percent of beaches are open to the public; the remaining 150 are privately owned and charge an entrance fee. Most private beaches have windsurfing, dinghies, catamarans, water skiing and parascending.
  To hire a boat or yacht for a day or longer, stroll around the resort and ask or call the tourist office.
Ligue de Voile Côte d'Azur, Espace Antibes, 2208 route de Grasse, 06600 Antibes; tel: 04 93 74 77 05; www.voilecotedazur. com. Sailing and windsurfing.
Fédération Française d'Etudes et de Sports Sous-Marins, 24 quai de Rive-Neuve, 13007 Marseille; tel: 04 91 33 99 31; fax: 04 91 54 77 43; www.ffessm.fr. Scuba diving.
Fédération Française de Canoe-Kayak, 87 quai de la Marne, 94340 Joinville-le-Pont; tel: 01 45 11 08 50; fax: 01 48 86 13 25; www.ffcanoe.asso.fr. Canoeing and kayaking.

Fishing

The fishing season opens around the second Saturday in March. For freshwater fishing you need to be affiliated to an association. For information and addresses of local fishing associations, contact:
Conseil Supérieur de la Pêche, 55 chemin du Mas de Matour, Grabels; tel: 04 67 10 76 76; fax: 04 67 03 14 12; www.csp.ecologie.gouv.fr

Climbing

For general information contact:
Club Alpin Français des Alpes-

Maritimes, 14 avenue Mirabeau, Nice; tel: 04 93 62 59 99; www.cafnice.org.

Cycling

You can rent cycles locally from bicycle shops or youth hostels, or see page 253 for advice on transporting your own bicycle. You might also consider a package cycling holiday, with accommodation and your luggage transported for you. The IGN 906 Cycling France map gives details of routes, cycling clubs and places to stay. More details are available from: **Cyclists Touring Club**, CTC Parklands, Railton Road, Guildford, Surrey GU2 9JX; tel: 0870 873 0060; www.ctc.org.uk. Their service to members includes cycle and travel insurance, touring itineraries and information sheets about France.

The club's French counterpart, **Fédération Française de Cyclotourisme** is at 12 rue Louis Bertrand, 94207 Ivry-sur-Seine Cedex; tel: 01 56 20 88 88; fax: 01 56 20 88 99; www.ffct.org

Golf

Most clubs provide lessons with resident experts.
Fédération Française de Golf, 68 rue Anatole France, Levallois-Perret; tel: 01 41 49 77 00; fax: 01 41 49 77 01; www.ffgolf.org
Golf de la Grande Bastide, Châteauneuf de Grasse; tel: 04 93 77 70 08. 18 holes, open all year.
Golf Opio-Valbonne, Opio; tel: 04 93 12 00 08. 18 holes, open all year round.
Golf de Valescure, avenue Paul l'Hermite, St-Raphaël; tel: 04 94 82 40 46; fax: 04 94 82 41 42. 18 holes, open all year.

Skiing

The Alpes-Maritimes are popular for skiing, and there are several large resorts only a few hours from the coast.
Fédération Française de Ski, 50 rue des Marquisats, 74011 Annecy Cedex; tel: 04 50 51 40 34; www.ffs.fr
Auron: Office du Tourisme; tel: 04 93 23 02 66; www.auron.com

Isola 2000: Office du Tourisme; tel: 04 93 23 15 15; www.isola2000.com

Walking

Walking is a popular way to enjoy the less trammelled parts of the Riviera, especially inland in the mountains. Ensure you are suitably equipped with water, warm clothing and good boots. There is an excellent network of signposted footpaths.

The hinterland behind the coast, the Massifs of Maures and Esterel, and the Mercantour national park are ideal for walkers. There are also coastal paths, including the **Sentier du Littoral**, which hugs the coast for some 200 km (125 miles). All main footpaths in France are part of a national network of long-distance footpaths (Sentiers de Grandes Randonnées or GR).

Note that both the Parc National du Mercantour and the Vallée des Merveilles enforce a code of country behaviour, and it is forbidden to enter many of the sites in the latter without a guide. Tourist offices or ramblers' organisations may organise guided walks. The French Ramblers' Association, **Fédération Française de la Randonnée Pédestre** (FFRP, www.ffrandonnee.fr) publishes Topo-guides (guide books with IGN 1:50,000-scale maps) to all France's footpaths, in French. However, there is also a series of guidebooks in English published by Robertson-McCarta called Footpaths of Europe that include the IGN maps.

IGN's Série Bleue maps at a scale of 1:25,000 and their Top 25 are ideal for walkers, and they publish maps of the national parks, too. IGN's walking maps are also available on CD-ROM.

The **Comité Départemental de Randonnée Pédestre Alpes-Maritimes** (tel: 04 93 20 74 93; www.cdrp06.org) organises a variety of activities during the year such as **guided walks** that take a day, a weekend or more, as well as themed walks on flora or wildlife.

Walking holidays with accommodation either in hotels or under canvas are available through package operators in the UK, or through organisations such as **Terres d'Aventure**, a specialist in walking holidays (tel: 08 25 84 78 00; www.terdav.com).

Spectator Sports

Probably the most famous event in the region is the **Monte-Carlo Car Rally**, held in January. A lesser-known rally is held in October at St-Tropez – the **Porsche Rally**. The other big motoring event is the **Monaco Grand Prix** in May.

April is the time for the international **tennis** championships in Monte-Carlo, the **Monte-Carlo Open**, which is complemented by the **Golf Tournament** in early July. Another golfing event is the **International Pro-Am** at Mougins (Cannes), in October.

The major **horse-racing** venue is the **Côte d'Azur Hippodrome** at Cagnes-sur-Mer where meetings are held during the day from December to March and in the evenings in July and August. Hyères is popular for racing, and meetings are held at the **Hippodrome du Var** during the spring and autumn. There is also an international **show-jumping** competition in Cannes during May. St-Tropez hosts the **International Polo Cup** in July.

There are all kinds of **sailing** and other **watersports** events, with most of the major competitions taking place at Mandelieu-la-Napoule, west of Cannes, including the **Grand Prix de la Corniche d'Or** (April) and the **International Rowing Regatta** (August) and the **Grand Prix de la Ville** (October). Other events are the **International Semi-Marathon** on the Baie des Anges, Nice, in April and the **Royal Regattas** in September in Cannes, coincide with the **International Pleasur Boat Festival**; there is also th **Généraliste** sailing race at Beaulieu-sur-Mer in June.

A–Z

A HANDY SUMMARY OF PRACTICAL INFORMATION, ARRANGED ALPHABETICALLY

A dmission Charges

The entrance fees for visiting museums and galleries generally fall between €4–9 per adult, with free admission for children – check on the qualifying age, for some places it is under 18 and others under 12 or 7 years old. Look out for special rates for students, over 60s and families of five or more. Usually admission is free every other Sunday and often during public holidays.

There are also passes available in the major towns which can be bought at a local tourist office or the museums themselves. The **Carte Musées Côte d'Azur**, which can be purchased at any of the sites, is valid for one (€10), three (€17) or ~~even~~ (€27) days and provides

unlimited access to all museums and monuments from Thoronet to Menton. In the Var there is a **Pass Sites** valid for 24 sites and one year. You pay for the first admission, the second site visited is then free.

B udgeting for Your Trip

Mid-range hotels generally range from around €70 for a double in a small family hotel in low season to upwards of €175 for nicer lodgings at the busiest time. Seasons are key: prices can triple during the highest season, which is generally mid-July to the end of August. Hotels in the country, even just a few kilometres from the beach, tend to be much less expensive.

A three-course dinner with

wine in a small family-style restaurant will cost around €20–30; the same in a more stylish establishment will cost €40–50. Once again, if you opt for luxury, the sky is the limit. Prices increase as you get closer to the beach.

Transport by train: a full fare return ticket on the TGV Paris to Nice costs around €200–250, and local fares, for example, single Marseille to Nice costs around €30. Ask about special passes and rates at the ticket office.

Travelling by coach is less expensive: for example, TAM bus services have a single ticket costing €1.30 for any one-way destination. Car hire varies according to the type of car and the rental period, but on average runs to about €30 per day.

Business Hours

Office workers normally start at around 9am and don't leave for the day until 6pm or later. While some banks and public offices still honour the traditional 2-hour lunch (starting at noon or 12.30pm), most offices have cut back to an hour for lunch. Many shops still close from noon to 2pm, though the larger ones tend to stay open. Most businesses close on Sunday (although some food shops open in the morning) and many on Monday as well, though in tourist areas Monday closings are less common. Bureaux de change open at weekends. Banks are normally open 8.30am–noon and 2–4.30pm, Mon–Fri, and Sat am.

Business Travellers

The Chamber of Commerce of Nice-Côte d'Azur runs a website, www.businessriviera.com, which offers loads of information on regional commerce, economics and business tourism.

Most major banks can refer you to lawyers, accountants and tax consultants; some provide specific expatriate services.

On the Côte d'Azur, business tourism has developed alongside its tourist industry. Nice, Cannes and Monte-Carlo all attract visitors to annual trade fairs. The larger hotels depend on the conference trade for a large part of their business. The international airport at Nice has direct flights to Europe and the US.

Cannes, Nice and Monte-Carlo all have huge, modern convention centres in very attractive locations. Most larger hotels also have conference facilities.

BFM on 96.4 FM is a French-language business radio station (www.radiobfm.com). **Les Echos** gives stock quotes on the website www.lesechos.fr. Business directories *Kompass France* and *Kompass Régional* give company details and detailed French market profiles on www.kompass.fr.

C hildren

The Riviera is the kind of place that attracts adults to its beaches and nightlife rather than a family resort, and young families would be well advised to stay away from the crowds (and high prices) of the high season. The coastal resorts to the west are more easily approached by car and a little less crowded. To get to the beaches of Nice or Cannes in August could be a nightmare with young children, as parking is so difficult. However, the private beaches of the Riviera do cater for children, and have beachclubs with amusements (for a fee). Some public beaches have similar facilities (expect to pay for the morning/afternoon session).

In France, generally, children are treated as people, not just nuisances. French children, being accustomed to eating out from an early age, are on the whole well behaved in restaurants, so it helps if one's own offspring understand that they can't run wild.

Many restaurants offer a children's menu; otherwise, they will often split a *prix-fixe* menu between two children. If travelling with very young children, you may find it practical to order nothing specific but request an extra plate and give them morsels from your own dish.

Most hotels have family rooms and a cot (*lit bébé*) will usually be provided for a small supplement. Check availability if booking in advance. Some of the hotels offer a baby-listening or child-minding service.

The following listing includes some fun places to take the kids:

Jardin d'Oiseaux Tropicaux
D559, La Londe-les-Maures
Tel: 04 94 35 02 15
www.jotropico.org
A unique collection of exotic birds and rare plants in landscaped woodland. Open daily.

Le Village des Tortues
Gonfaron
Tel: 04 94 78 26 41
www.villagetortues.com
"Tortoise Village" is a refuge and

study centre. Open Mar–Nov daily, closed Dec–Feb.

Aqualand
RN98, Fréjus
Tel: 04 94 51 82 51
www.aqualand.fr
A huge water park. Open June–Aug daily (weather permitting). A second park in Ste-Maxime on route de Plan de la Tour; tel: 04 94 55 54 54.

Parc Zoologique de Fréjus
Le Capitou, Fréjus
Tel: 04 98 11 37 37
www.zoo-frejus.com
An eco-friendly zoo. Open daily.

Base Nature
Fréjus
Tel: 04 94 51 91 10
Large seafront park with beaches, a nature reserve, and varied sport and leisure activities. Open daily.

Marineland
RN7, 4 km (2 miles) north of Antibes
Tel: 04 93 33 49 49
www.marineland.fr
Marine park/entertainment complex with water slides. Open daily.

Museum of Oceanography
(Musée Océanographique de Monaco)
Avenue St-Martin, Monaco
Tel: 377-93 15 36 00
www.oceano.mc
A fascinating aquarium with impressive displays of whale skeletons and stuffed marine fauna. Open daily.

CLIMATE CHART

☐ Maximum temperature
■ Minimum temperature
— Rainfall

Climate & Clothing

The Côte d'Azur enjoys around 2,700 hours of sunshine a year, but the heat is never unbearable (unless you are inland) because of the sea breezes (nights can be cool). The highest temperatures are in July and August – often over 30°C (86°F). Winter is mild and sunny – frost is a rarity.

There is snow on the mountains, but the heat of the sun means that it is often possible to ski in a T-shirt. The wettest period is the autumn, but then the rain comes in short, heavy downpours followed by bright sunshine. Spring, too, can have some wet spells when the sky becomes heavy and overcast. The mistral, a strong northerly wind that can blow in any season, is the worst aspect of the weather and particularly affects the Rhône Valley and Marseille. This fearsome wind, said to be able to "blow the ears off a donkey", causes considerable damage, and some claim that it has a depressing effect on the local population.

Weather Information

Tel: 3250. For local forecasts dial 08 92 68 02 followed by the two-digit *département* number (e.g. 06 for Alpes-Maritimes); www.meteo123.com

Crime & Security

Sensible precautions regarding personal possessions are all that should be necessary. Be aware of pickpockets in cities, and be careful on trains, especially when travelling at night – make sure doors are securely locked.

Customs

You are permitted to take any quantity of goods into France from another EU country as long as it is for personal use and tax has been paid on items in the country of origin. Customs can still question visitors.

Quantities accepted as being for personal use are:
• up to 3,200 cigarettes, 400 small cigars, 200 cigars or 1 kg loose tobacco
• 10 litres of spirits (over 22 percent alcohol), 90 litres of wine (under 22 percent alcohol) or 110 litres of beer

From outside the EU you can bring in:
• 200 cigarettes, 100 small cigars, 50 cigars or 250g loose tobacco
• 1 litre of spirits (over 22 percent alcohol) and 2 litres of wine and beer (under 22 percent alcohol)
• 50g perfume

Visitors can also carry up to $7,600 in currency.

D isabled Travellers

Travel

Disabled travellers on **Eurotunnel** (UK tel: 0870 535 3535; www.euro tunnel.com) get priority boarding. **Eurostar** trains (UK special requests, tel: 0870 518 6186; www.eurostar.co.uk) give wheelchair passengers and their companion first-class one-way travel for only £59. Most **ferry** companies offer facilities if contacted beforehand.

Vehicles fitted to accommodate disabled people pay reduced tolls on *autoroutes*. A motorway *(autoroute)* guide for disabled travellers *(Guides des Autoroutes à l'Usage des Personnes à Mobilité Réduite)* is available free from Sociétés Françaises d'Autoroutes et d'Ouvrages à Péages (ASFA), 3 rue Edmond Valentin, 75007 Paris; tel: 01 47 53 63 26. You can also find out about accessible rest stops and other info at www.autoroutes.fr.

If you are disabled, a French **taxi** driver cannot refuse to take you. He or she must help you into the vehicle and is obliged to transport a guide dog for a blind passenger.

Parking is usually available and indicated with a blue wheelchair sign. The international

orange disabled parking disc scheme is recognised in France (don't forget to bring the disc with you).

Holidays and Accommodation

The **Gîtes de France** guides to *gîtes* and B&Bs list accommodation that is accessible to disabled travellers. The guide is available in most French book stores; you can also find it online at www.gites-de-france.com. The **Fédération Française de Camping et de Caravaning** (French Federation of Camping and Caravanning) guide indicates which campsites have facilities for disabled campers. Available from most French bookshops or at www.ffcc.fr.

The *Michelin Guide: Camping France* lists sites with facilities for the disabled (www.michelin.co.uk).

The **Association des Paralysés de France** (13 place de Rungis, Paris 75013; tel: 01 53 80 92 97; www.apf.asso.fr) publishes a *Guide Vacances* which also lists suitable accommodation.

Access

Even if museums, hotels, etc claim to have access for disabled people, it's always wise to check beforehand exactly what they mean. They may be able to accommodate wheelchair-users but not have accessible toilets, for example. Small villages with steep streets and inaccessible clifftop castles can be difficult to negotiate with a wheelchair or by someone with limited mobility. Bigger cities can be better equipped, but don't bank on it. Check out your route in advance.

To hire a wheelchair or other equipment, enquire at a pharmacy.

E mbassies & Consulates

You can find a list of embassies and consulates in the *Pages Jaunes* under *Ambassades et Consulats*. For general enquiries or problems with passports or visas, try the local consulate

ELECTRICITY

The standard voltage in France is 220/230 volts. Round-pin plugs are used everywhere, so pack an adaptor (available at any shop selling travel items). Visitors from the US will also need a transformer for the higher voltage or they will destroy their electrical appliances.

first. They will advise whether you need to consult the embassy in Paris, or a local honorary consul. Phone first, in case you need to make an appointment. Otherwise, the answerphone should provide an emergency number.

Consulates on the French Riviera

UK
24 avenue Prado, 13006 Marseille; tel: 04 91 15 72 10; fax: 04 01 37 47 06; www.british embassy.gov.uk. Open Mon–Fri 9am–noon and 2pm–4pm.
US
7 avenue Gustave V, 06000 Nice; tel: 04 93 88 89 55; www.amb-usa.fr/marseille/nice
Canada
10 rue Lamartine, 06000 Nice; tel: 04 93 92 93 22; www.international.gc.ca
Ireland
152 boulevard J.F. Kennedy, 06160 Cap d'Antibes; tel: 06 77 69 14 36; http://foreignaffairs.gov.ie

Emergencies

Ambulance (SAMU) – dial 15
Police – dial 17
Fire *(sapeurs-pompiers)* – dial 18
In the case of a serious accident or medical emergency, call the *Service d'Aide Médicale d'Urgence* (SAMU), or alternatively, the police or fire department. Though primarily a fire brigade, the *sapeurs-pompiers* are trained paramedics, and both they and the police have medical back-up and work in close contact with the SAMU.

Entry Regulations

EU citizens require only a valid passport. Citizens of the US, Canada, Australia and New Zealand do not need a visa for visits of up to three months. For longer stays, contact your nearest French consulate to apply in advance for a visa.

Other nationalities should apply to the French consulate in their home country before travelling. The French government website, www.diplomatie.gouv.fr, provides guidance on visa requirements.

Animal Quarantine

It is possible for pets to re-enter Britain from France without quarantine. Conditions are stringent, however, with tough health requirements and restricted points of entry.

For information on bringing pets into and out of the UK via the **Pet Travel Scheme**, visit www.defra.gov.uk.

Travelling between countries other than Britain and the Continent requires the **European Pet Passport**, which is available from most veterinarians. For more information visit http://europa.eu/abc/travel/pets.

G ay Riviera

General information is available from **Radio FG** (98.2 MHz), www.radiofg.com and national magazines *Têtu* and *Lesbia*. Local listings magazines include *L'Excès* and *XTRA*. A good web resource for bars, clubs and associations is the **Queer Resource Directory-France**, www.qrd.france.org; **Voyager-en-France.com** also has good gay listings (bars, clubs, beaches). For help or more information call the Paris-based **Centre Gai et Lesbien**, 3 rue Keller, 75011 Paris; tel: 01 43 57 75 95; www.cglparis.org. Gay and lesbian bars and clubs include:
Cannes
Le Queen, 48 boulevard de la République; tel: 04 93 68 13 13

Cannes's version of the famous Parisian nightclub.
Zanzi Bar, 85 rue Félix Faure; tel: 04 93 39 30 75
One of the Riviera's oldest gay bars. An institution.
Nice
Blue Boy Enterprise, 9 rue Spinetta; tel: 04 93 44 68 24.
Nice's best gay club; everyone welcome; floorshows.
Le Morgan, 3 rue Claudia; tel: 04 39 86 86 08. Friendly bar with go-go dancers on Friday nights.
St-Tropez
Le Pigeonnier, 13 rue de la Ponche; tel: 04 94 97 84 26.
Famous gay club in the heart of the town.

H ealth Care & Services

The **International Association for Medical Assistance to Travellers** (IAMAT) is a non-profit-making organisation which anyone can join free of charge (a donation is requested). Benefits include a membership card (entitling the bearer to services at fixed IAMAT rates by participating physicians) and a traveller clinical record (a passport-sized record completed by the member's own doctor prior to travel). A directory of English-speaking IAMAT doctors on call 24 hours a day is published for members.

EU nationals staying in France are entitled to use the French Social Security system, which refunds up to 70 percent of medical expenses (but sometimes less, e.g. for dental treatment).

To get reduced-cost and free medical treatment, British nationals should obtain the **European Health Insurance Card** (EHIC) before leaving the UK. These are available online at www.dh.gov.uk or from post offices. The card is open-ended; you don't need a new one every time you travel. However, the card does not necessarily cover all the treatments you would be entitled to at home; if you have serious ongoing medical problems, travel insurance can be a better option.

TRANSPORT ACCOMMODATION ACTIVITIES A – Z

If you have treatment while in France, the doctor will give you a prescription and a *feuille de soins* (statement of treatment). The medication will carry *vignettes* (little stickers), which you must stick on to your *feuille de soins*. Send the prescription and a copy of your European Health Insurance Card to the local *Caisse Primaire d'Assurance Maladie* (in the phone book under *Sécurité Sociale*). Refunds can sometimes take over a month to come through.

Even though health costs can be substantially less than in some non-EU countries, nationals of non-EU countries should consider taking out travel and medical insurance before leaving home. Medical consultations and prescriptions have to be paid for in full at the time of treatment; the average visit to a doctor can cost €20–40.

To contact IAMAT:
US: 1623 Military Road, Suite 279, Niagara Falls, NY 14304; tel: 716-754 4883.
Canada: 1287 St Claire Avenue West, Toronto, Ontario M6E 1B8; tel: 416-652 0137; or 40 Regal Road, Guelph, Ontario N1K 1B5; tel: 519-836 0102; www.iamat.org

Pharmacies

Pharmacies in France are good, and medicines are not expensive. However, many toiletries sold in pharmacies are cheaper in the supermarket. Staff are usually well qualified and able to advise on many minor ailments – they may be able to help with minor wounds and other basic medical services. All pharmacies can be identified by a neon green cross outside. Most open from 9am or 10am to 7pm or 8pm and almost all are closed on Sunday.

If the pharmacy is closed there will be a notice indicating the nearest *pharmacie de garde*, which will also offer a night service. If you can't find a pharmacy, consult the *gendarmerie*.

L ost Property

To report a crime or loss of belongings, visit the local *gendarmerie* or *commissariat de police*. Telephone numbers are given at the front of local directories, or in an emergency, dial 17. If you lose a passport, report it first to the police, then to the nearest consulate. If you have the misfortune to be detained by the police for any reason, ask to telephone the nearest consulate for a member of staff to assist you.

In case of **credit-card loss** or theft, call the following 24-hour services, which have English-speaking staff:
American Express: 01 47 77 72 00
Diners Club: 01 49 06 17 76
MasterCard: 08 00 90 23 90
Visa: 08 92 705 705

M aps

Maps are found in stationery stores, large news-stands, or service stations. Tourist offices usually provide free city maps.

Maps from the **Institut Géographique National** (IGN) are excellent. Those covering the Riviera are listed below:
Red Series (or *Cartes Régionales*, 1:250,000, 1 cm to 2.5 km) sheet R18 covers the region at a good scale for touring.
Cartes Départementales (1:125,000, 1 cm to 1.25 km) cover individual *départements*; sheet D06 covers the Alpes-Maritimes (the eastern half of the Riviera), and sheet D83 covers the Var (the western half).
Blue Series (1:100,000, 1 cm to 1 km) are more detailed; sheets 61 and 68 cover most of the region; for the far north, sheet 60 may be necessary.
The Top 25 and Orange Series are highly detailed maps that are good for walkers and mountain bikers. For planning your route IGN 901 covers the whole of France at a scale of 1 cm to 10 km and is regularly updated. You

can order maps from the IGN website (www.ign.fr).

Good mountain maps for walkers and winter sports are also produced by Didier Richard, mostly at a scale of 1:50,000, but a few at the more detailed 1:25,000 scale.

Stockists in London include:
Stanfords, 12–14 Long Acre, London WC2E 9LP; tel: 020 7836 1321; www.stanfords.co.uk
The Travel Bookshop, 13 Blenheim Crescent, London W11 2EE; tel: 020 7229 5260; www.thetravelbookshop.com
IGN maps are also available from their agent in the UK:
World Leisure Marketing, Navigator Maps, 41a Kilbourne Road, Belper, Derbyshire DE56 1HA; tel: 01773 822447; www.navimaps.co.uk

Media

Newspapers

Regional newspapers, with national and international as well as local news, are often read in preference to national dailies. British and American dailies, notably *The Times* and the *International Herald Tribune*, are widely available, as are local English-language publications for tourists and the expatriate community.

Look out for the *Riviera Reporter*, which gives an irreverent, insider's view of the region in English; www.riviera-reporter.com

Radio

France Inter is the main national radio station (FM 87.8 MHz) with in-depth news and talk shows.
Radio International (100.5, 100.9, and 101.0 FM) is an English-language station that broadcasts music and BBC World Service bulletins. On motorways, **Radio Traffic** (107.7) has bulletins in English in summer.

Another all-English station is Monte-Carlo's **Riviera Radio** (106.3 and 106.5 FM), which has

24 hours of world news, regional broadcasts and small ads.

Television

The main TV stations are **TF1** (features, movies, game shows, dubbed soaps, audience debates, and news), **France 2** (news, game shows, documentaries and cultural chat shows), **France 3** (news, sports, wildlife documentaries and late-night movies), **Arte** (a Franco-German hybrid, specialising in intelligent arts coverage and films in the original language), and **M6** (dubbed US television series, variety shows and "tele-reality" shows like *Star Academy* and *Survivor*). **Canal+** offers a roster of satellite and cable subscription channels with recent movies (sometimes original language), exclusive sport and late night porn. CNN and BBC news are often available in hotels.

Money

The unit of currency in France (and in most of the EU) is the euro (€). There are 100 cents in a euro. Banknotes are €5, €10, €20, €50, €100, €200 and €500. Coins are 1, 2, 5, 10 and 20 cents, and €1 and €2.

Since the introduction of the euro, fewer and fewer banks will change foreign currency (you will need to produce your passport in any transaction). Those that do usually have better exchange rates than hotels or independent bureaux de change, but you will get the best rate if you use your debit or credit (ATM) card.

Most major credit cards are accepted, though American Express is sometimes refused due to high charges to the retailer.

Credit Cards and Cash Machines

Credit and debit cards issued from many European banks that use the chip and pin system can be used as payment in many

shops and restaurants. Most establishments have card readers that accept foreign credit and debit cards with a valid PIN number. Check with your bank before leaving home that your card will operate abroad, and how much you will be charged for each transaction.

You can withdraw money from bank and post office cash machines (ATMs) using a PIN number, as long as the card and machine show either a Visa or Cirrus symbol. Occasionally, there are problems when presenting cards issued by UK or US banks with magnetic strips, but problems can usually be rectified with a call to the card issuer.

Tipping

You do not usually need to add a service charge to a restaurant bill in France, as 10 percent service is included in the price of your meal. (If in doubt, ask "*Est-ce que le service est compris?*" Is the service included?) If you want to show your appreciation, leaving a euro or two on the table after a meal is quite acceptable.

Taxis generally expect a 10 percent tip. It is also usual to tip doorman, guides and hairdressers about €1.50.

Note that in bars and cafés you pay less at the counter than if you sit at a table.

P ostal Services

Post offices (*la Poste*) are generally open Mon–Fri 9am–6pm, Sat 9am–noon. In small towns, they often close noon–2pm, and in tiny villages they may only be open for a short time in the morning.

Before you start queuing check that you are at the right counter; in larger post offices, some counters have specific services. If you only want stamps, look for the sign "*Timbres*". Standard-weight letters within France require a €0.54 stamp; other EU countries require a €0.60 stamp, and any

PUBLIC HOLIDAYS

It is common practice, if a public holiday falls on a Thursday or Tuesday for French business to *faire le pont* (bridge the gap) and have the Friday or Monday as a holiday, too. Details of closures should be posted outside banks, etc, a few days before the event, but it is easy to be caught out, especially on Assumption Day (15 August), which is not a holiday in the UK.

New Year's Day: 1 January
Easter Monday (but not Good Friday)
Labour Day: Monday closest to 1 May
Ascension Day: 8 May (commemorates the end of World War II)
Whit Monday (Pentecost)
Bastille Day: 14 July
Assumption Day: 15 August
All Saints' Day – Toussaint: 1 November
Armistice Day: 11 November
National Holiday in Monaco: 19 November
Christmas Day: 25 December

country in the rest of the world is a €0.85 stamp.

You can also buy stamps at tobacconists (*le tabac*) and some shops selling postcards. Large post offices and *maisons de presse* (newsagents) also offer fax and photocopying services; many supermarkets have coin-operated photocopiers.

Mail can be kept poste restante at a post office, addressed to Poste Restante, Poste Centrale (for the main post office), then the town postcode and name. A small fee will be charged and you will need to show your passport to collect your mail. Mail is kept for 15 days.

Urgent post can be sent via the Chronopost system, which is fast but expensive. However, packages up to 25g can be guaranteed delivery within 24 hours.

S tudent Travellers

Student & Youth Discounts

To qualify for reduced entry prices to museums, cinemas and theatres you need an **International Student Identity Card** (ISIC) from CROUS *(see below)* or from travel agents specialising in student travel. ISIC cards are only valid in France if you are under 26. Under 26s can also get up to 50 percent discounts on certain trains with the **Carte 12/25** *(see page 250)*.

Studying in France

Foreign students in France can get information on courses, grants and accommodation from the **Centre Régional des Oeuvres Universitaires et Scolaires** (CROUS), 39 avenue Georges Bernanos, 75231 Paris Cedex 05; tel: 01 40 51 55 55; www.crous-paris.fr. The Nice branch is at 18 avenue des Fleurs, 06050 Nice Cedex 1; tel: 01 92 15 50 50; www.crous-nice.fr

The **Socrates-Erasmus Programme** is a scheme that enables EU students with a reasonable level of French to spend a year of their degree following appropriate courses in the French university system. The UK office publishes a brochure and helps with general enquiries.
In Britain: UK Socrates-Erasmus Council, Rothford, Giles Lane, Canterbury, Kent CT2 7LR; tel: 01227 762712; www.erasmus.ac.uk
In France: Agence Socrates-Leonardo da Vinci, 25 quai des Chartons, F-33080 Bordeaux Cedex; tel: 05 56 00 94 00; www.socrates-leonardo.fr

Other useful organisations include:
Alliance Française, 101 boulevard Raspail, 75270 Paris Cedex 06; tel: 01 42 84 90 00; www.alliancefr.org
Non-profit, highly regarded French language school, with beginners' and specialist courses.
Centre des Echanges

Internationaux, 1 rue Gozlin, Paris 75006; tel: 01 40 51 11 71; www.cei4vents.com
Sporting and cultural holidays and educational tours for 12–30-year-olds. Non-profit-making.
Souffle, Espace Charlotte, 83260 La Crau; tel: 04 94 00 94 65; www.souffle.asso.fr
An umbrella organisation for courses in French.

Local language courses
Actilangue, 2 rue Alexis Mossa, 06000 Nice; tel: 04 93 96 33 84; fax: 04 93 44 37 16; www.actilangue.com

French courses
Azurlingua, 47 rue Hérold, 06000 Nice; tel: 04 97 03 07 00; fax: 04 97 03 07 03; www.azurlingua.com
Centre International d'Antibes, 38 boulevard d'Aguillon, 06600 Antibes; tel: 08 70 40 74 34; www.cia-france.com
Language holidays.
Institut d'Enseignement de la Langue Française sur la Côte d'Azur (ELFCA), 66 avenue de Toulon, 83400 Hyères; tel: 04 94 65 03 31; fax: 04 94 65 81 22; www.elfca.com
Language holidays.
Institut de Français, 23 avenue Général Leclerc; 06230 Villefranche-sur-Mer; tel: 04 93 01 88 44; fax: 04 93 76 92 17; www.institutdefrancais.com
Intensive immersion courses for adults in lovely surroundings.

T elephones

Standard French telephone numbers are all 10 digits, always written – and spoken – in sets of two-digits, e.g. 01 23 45 67 89. When dialling from outside the country omit the first zero and add the country code (33) before the number. If you want numbers to be given singly rather than in pairs, ask for them "*chiffre par chiffre*". Four-digit numbers (such as 3635 for the SNCF) can only be dialled from within France.

Note that the country code for Monaco is 377. When phoning a Monégasque number from outside

the principality – including France – you must dial the code. To phone abroad – including France – from Monaco, dial 00 then the country code (33 for France).

The international access codes for US phonecards are as follows: **AT&T:** 0800 99 00 11. **MCI:** 0800 99 00 19. **Sprint:** 0800 99 00 87.

Public Phones

You should be able to find telephone boxes *(cabines publiques)* in every sizeable village. Most take only phonecards *(carte téléphonique)*, available from post offices, stationers, railway stations, some cafés and *bureaux de tabac*.

Be sure to specify: a *carte à puce* (works only in telephone boxes) or a *carte à code* (works from any phone). The *cartes à code* tend to have better international rates, and are handy for calls abroad from a hotel phone.

Phone Directories

Phone directories *(annuaires)* are found in all post offices and in most cafés. The *Pages Blanches* (White Pages) lists names of people and businesses alphabetically. The *Pages Jaunes* (Yellow Pages) lists businesses and services by category. Both are also now available on the internet at: www.pagesjaunes.fr; www.pagesblanches.fr

A single **directory enquiries** number has been replaced with over 20 operating companies. The numbers all start 118, for example:
Le Numéro 118 218
France Télécom 118 711
Pages Jaunes 118 008

International Calls

The international code for France is 00 33. For Monaco, tel: 00 377 plus an eight-figure number.

To make an international call dial 00 followed by the country code. This is found in the front of the *Pages Jaunes* section of the phone directory or on the information panel in a telephone box.

TRANSPORT

ACCOMMODATION

ACTIVITIES

A – Z

TIME ZONE

France is always one hour ahead of the UK (i.e. Greenwich Mean Time +1 in winter, and GMT+2 in summer).

Reverse-Charge Calls

You cannot make a **reverse charges call** (call collect) within France, but you can to countries which will accept such calls (called PCV, "pay say vay"). To do so, dial 3006 and then the number you wish to contact.

Free Calls

Numéros verts are **free numbers**, usually beginning with 0800; 08 numbers – 0800, 0803, 0804 and 0805 – are all toll-free, 0810 and 0811 are charged as local calls, but all other 08 numbers are toll calls, which are increasingly common and expensive.

Internet

Good hotels usually have Internet access, as do many libraries and post offices. Internet cafés are popular in main towns.
Cannes: Cyber Internet, 32 rue Jean Jaurès; tel: 04 93 38 85 63.
Nice: Panini and Web, 25 promenade des Anglais; tel: 04 93 88 72 75.

Tourist Information

The **office de tourisme** is sometimes still called the *syndicat d'initiative* in small villages. Where there is no tourist office the *mairie* (town hall) can provide local information on places to stay, sights to see, local festivals, etc. Tourist offices can provide a wide variety of information and will often book hotels and supply local maps free of charge.

Regional Tourist Offices

Comité Régional du Tourisme de Provence-Alpes-Côte d'Azur, 10 place Joliette, Les Docks, Atrium 10.5, BP 46214–13567, Marseille Cedex 02; tel: 04 91 56 47 00; fax: 04 91 56 47 01; www.crt-paca.fr
Comité Régional du Tourisme Riviera Côte d'Azur, 400 promenade des Anglais, BP 3126 06203 Nice Cedex 3; tel: 04 93 37 78 78; fax: 04 93 86 01 06; www.guideriviera.com
Direction de Tourisme et de Congrès de la Principauté de Monaco, 2a boulevard des Moulins, Monte-Carlo, MC 98030, Monaco Cedex; www.visitmonaco.com

Tourist Offices Abroad

You can log on to the French Government Tourist Office website at www.franceguide.com. They have offices in the following countries:
UK: 178 Piccadilly, London W1J 9AL; tel: 09068 244 123 (premium rate); fax: 020 7493 6594
USA: 444 Madison Avenue, New York, NY 10022; tel: 514-288 1904; fax: 212-838 7855
Canada: 1800 Avenue McGill Collège, Suite 1010, H3A 3J6 Montreal, Quebec; tel: 514-288 2026; fax: 514-845 4868
Australia: Level 13, 25 Bligh Street, Sydney, NSW 2000; tel: 02 9231 5244; fax: 02 9221 8682

W ebsites

www.provenceweb.fr Listing of villages, hotels, restaurants with links to all main towns and cities.
www.provencebeyond.com English-language website covering Provence and the Riviera with lots of information, including lesser-known places, towns and sites.
www.riviera-reporter.com Local English-language magazine site with archive of articles on a variety of practical and political subjects and links to other relevant government/advice sites.
www.gulderiviera.com Regional government tourist site with information on sights, travel and accommodation.
www.angloinfo.com English-language site with a huge directory of services.
www.sncf.fr French national railway network.
www.eurostar.co.uk Eurostar information, rates, schedules.

www.raileurope.com Rail passes and information on most European rail networks.
www.chateauxhotels.com Chateaux and independent hotels network.
www.fuaj.org Youth hostel association.
www.relaischateaux.fr Luxury hotels and chateaux.
www.campingfrance.com Campsite listings and information.
www.gites-de-france.fr B&Bs and gîtes.
www.bottingourmand.com Online guidebook.
www.gayot.com *Guide Gayot* online.
www.guides-gaultmillau.fr Selections from the Gault Millau guide.
www.meteo.fr Weather.
www.meteo123.com Weather.

What to Bring

You should be able to buy anything you need in France. There will be plenty of things you will want to take home, so leave space in your suitcase or pack another cup in bag.

Pharmacies have a wide range of medical supplies and toiletries, and expert advice, but you should bring any prescription drugs you need, as well as the prescription, in case you need refills. Spare spectacles or contact lenses are a good idea.

Sunscreen and anti-mosquito products are advisable in summer. If you bring electrical equipment you will need adaptors. Electrical appliances from the US will require a voltage transformer.

Clothing will depend on your destination and when you travel; you will only need to dress up for big-city restaurants or casinos. Summer wear is casual, although be prepared to dress up for dinner. Dress appropriately for visiting churches; a scarf or shirt is always useful as a cover-up.

Most sports equipment can be hired, but you should bring personal equipment such as walking boots with you.

LANGUAGE

UNDERSTANDING FRENCH

About French

French is an official language in 60 countries and spoken fluently by some 200 million people around the world. It is a Romance language descended from the Vulgar Latin spoken by the Roman conquerors of Gaul. If you make an effort to speak their language, the French will usually be helpful and may try to respond in English. Some French people, especially the young, speak a little English, but don't assume that everyone does. There are many French words in the English vocabulary, and travellers will recognise helpful words such as *hôtel, café* and *bagages*. But be aware of some misleading "false friends" *(see opposite)*.

Basic Rules

Even if you speak no French at all, it is worth trying to master a few simple phrases. The fact that you have made an effort is likely to get you a better response. Some French people like practising their English on visitors, especially waiters/waitresses and young people. Pronunciation is the key; they really will not understand if you get it very wrong. The stress is often on the second syllable in

French, as opposed to the first in English; confusing the stress can render some words unrecognisable. As a rule, do not pronounce the last consonant of a word (this includes the plural "s") and always drop your "h"s.

When addressing someone you don't know very well, use the more formal "*vous*", and "*tu*" for children, relatives and friends. However, young people tend to use "*tu*" even with strangers (of their own age). It is important to be polite; always address people as *Madame* or *Monsieur* and use their surnames until you are confident first names are acceptable. When entering a shop or restaurant say, "*Bonjour Monsieur/Madame*," and "*Merci, au revoir*," when leaving.

THE ALPHABET

Learning the pronunciation of the French alphabet is a good idea. In particular, learn how to spell out your name.
a = ah, **b** = bay, **c** = say, **d** = day, **e** = euh, **f** = ef, **g** = zhay, **h** = ash, **i** = ee, **j** = zhee, **k** = ka, **l** = el, **m** = em, **n** = en, **o** = oh, **p** = pay, **q** = kew, **r** = ehr, **s** = ess, **t** = tay, **u** = ew, **v** = vay, **w** = dooblah vay, **x** = eex, **y** = ee grek, **z** = zed.

Words & Phrases

hello *bonjour* ("*allo*" on telephone)
goodbye *au revoir*
good evening *bonsoir*
yes/no *oui/non*
please *s'il vous plaît*
thank you (very much) *merci (beaucoup)*
you're welcome *de rien*
OK *d'accord*
excuse me *excusez-moi*
here *ici*
there *là*
today *aujourd'hui*
yesterday *hier*
tomorrow *demain*
now *maintenant*
later *plus tard*
this morning *ce matin*
this afternoon *cet après-midi*
this evening *ce soir*
What is your name? *Comment vous appelez-vous?*
My name is... *Je m'appelle...*
Do you speak English? *Parlez-vous anglais?*
I am English/American *Je suis anglais/américain*
I don't understand *Je ne comprends pas*
Please speak more slowly *Parlez plus lentement, s'il vous plaît*
Can you help me? *Pouvez-vous m'aider?*
Where is...? *Où est...?*
I'm sorry *Excusez-moi/Pardon*
I don't know *Je ne sais pas*

TRANSPORT

NUMBERS

0	zéro	11	onze	30	trente
1	un, une	12	douze	40	quarante
2	deux	13	treize	50	cinquante
3	trois	14	quatorze	60	soixante
4	quatre	15	quinze	70	soixante-dix
5	cinq	16	seize	80	quatre-vingts
6	six	17	dix-sept	90	quatre-vingt-dix
7	sept	18	dix-huit	100	cent
8	huit	19	dix-neuf	1000	mille
9	neuf	20	vingt	1,000,000	un million
10	dix	21	vingt-et-un		

Have a good day! *Bonne journée!*
That's it *C'est ça*
Here it is *Voici*
There it is *Voilà*
Let's go *On y va/Allons-y*
See you tomorrow *A demain*
See you soon *A bientôt*

On Arrival

I want to get off at...
Je voudrais descendre à...
What street is this? *A quelle rue*
sommes-nous?
How far is...?
A quelle distance se trouve...?
Validate your ticket
Compostez votre billet
airport *l'aéroport*
railway station *la gare*
bus station *la gare routière*
bus *l'autobus, le car*
bus stop *l'arrêt*
platform *le quai*
ticket *le billet*
return ticket *aller-retour*
hitch-hiking *l'autostop*
toilets *les toilettes*
This is the hotel address
C'est l'adresse de l'hôtel
I'd like a (single/double) room...
Je voudrais une chambre (pour
une/deux personne/s) ...
....with shower *avec douche*
....with a bath *avec bain*
Does that include breakfast?
Le prix comprend-il le petit
déjeuner?
May I see the room? *Est-ce que*
je peux voir la chambre?
bed *le lit*
key *la clé*
lift (elevator) *l'ascenseur*
air conditioned *climatisé*

On the Road

Where is the nearest garage?
Où est le garage le plus proche?
Our car has broken down *Notre*
voiture est en panne
I want to have my car repaired
Je veux faire réparer ma voiture
**I think I must have put diesel in
the car by mistake** *Je crois que*
j'ai mis du gazole dans la voiture
par erreur
the road to... *la route pour...*
left *gauche*
right *droite*
straight on *tout droit*
far *loin*
near *près d'ici*
opposite *en face*
beside *à côté de*
car park *parking*
over there *là-bas*
at the end *au bout*
on foot *à pied*
by car *en voiture*
town map *le plan*
road map *la carte*
street *la rue*
square *la place*
give way (US: yield) *céder le*
passage
dead end *impasse*
no parking *stationnement interdit*
motorway *l'autoroute*
toll booth *le péage*
speed limit *la limitation de*
vitesse
petrol *l'essence*
unleaded *sans plomb*
diesel *le gazole*
water/oil *l'eau/l'huile*
puncture *un pneu crevé*
bulb *l'ampoule*
wipers *les essuie-glace*

Shopping

**Where is the nearest bank/post
office?** *Où est la banque/Poste*
la plus proche?
I'd like to buy *Je voudrais*
acheter
How much is it? *C'est combien?*
Do you take credit cards? *Est-ce*
que vous acceptez les cartes de
crédit?
I'm just looking *Je regarde*
seulement
Have you got...? *Avez-vous...?*
I'll take it *Je le prends*
I'll take this one/that one *Je*
prends celui-ci/celui-là
What size is it? *C'est quelle*
taille?
Anything else? *Avec ça?*
size (clothes) *la taille*
size (shoes) *la pointure*
cheap *bon marché*
expensive *cher*
enough *assez*
too much *trop*
a piece *un morceau de*
each *la pièce (e.g. ananas, €2*
la pièce)
bill *la note*
delicatessen *la charcuterie/*
le traiteur
market *le marché*
tobacconist *tabac*

FALSE FRIENDS

False friends are words that
look like English words but
mean something different.
le car coach, also railway
carriage
le conducteur bus driver
la monnaie change (coins)
l'argent money/silver
ça marche can sometimes
mean walk, but is usually used
to mean working (the TV, the
car, etc.) or going well
actuel "present time"
(*la situation actuelle* the
present situation)
rester to stay
location hiring/renting;
box office
personne person or nobo
according to context
le médecin doctor

ACCOMMODATION

ACTIVITIES

A – Z

EMERGENCIES

Help! *Au secours!*
Stop! *Arrêtez!*
Call a doctor *Appelez un médecin*
Call an ambulance *Appelez les SAMU*
Call the police *Appelez la police*
Call the fire brigade *Appelez les pompiers*
Where is the nearest telephone? *Où est le téléphone le plus proche?*
Where is the nearest hospital? *Où est l'hôpital le plus proche?*
I am ill/sick *Je suis malade*
I have lost my passport/purse *J'ai perdu mon passeport/porte-monnaie*

Dining Out

table d'hôte **one set menu served at a fixed price**
le menu/la formule **fixed-price menu**
à la carte **dishes from the menu are charged separately**
breakfast *le petit déjeuner*
lunch *le déjeuner*
dinner *le dîner*
meal *le repas*
first course *l'entrée*
main course *le plat principal*
drink included *boisson comprise*
wine list *la carte des vins*
the bill *l'addition*
fork *la fourchette*
knife *le couteau*
spoon *la cuillère*
plate *l'assiette*
glass *le verre*
ashtray *le cendrier*

Breakfast and Snacks

baguette **long thin loaf**
ain **bread**
tits pains **rolls**
rre **butter**
e **pepper**
alt
sugar
e jam
gs
ue **boiled eggs**

...au bacon **bacon and eggs**
...au jambon **ham and eggs**
...sur le plat **fried eggs**
...brouillés **scrambled eggs**
tartine **bread with butter**
crêpe **pancake**
croque-monsieur **ham and cheese toasted sandwich**
croque-madame **...with a fried egg on top**
galette **type of pancake**
pan bagna **bread roll stuffed with salade niçoise**

L'Entrée (Starters)

anchoïade **sauce of olive oil, anchovies and garlic, served with raw vegetables**
assiette anglaise **cold meats**
potage **soup**
rillettes **rich fatty paste of shredded duck, rabbit or pork**
tapenade **spread of olives**
pissaladière **Provençal pizza with onions, olives and anchovies**

Viande (Meat)

bleu **very rare**
à point **medium**
bien cuit **well done**
grillé **grilled**
agneau **lamb**
andouille/andouillette **tripe sausage**
bifteck **steak**
boudin blanc **white pudding (chicken or veal)**
boudin noir **black pudding**
blanquette **a veal stew with a creamy egg sauce**
à la bordelaise **cooked with red wine and shallots**
à la bourguignonne **cooked with red wine, onions and mushrooms**
brochette **kebab**
caille **quail**
canard **duck**
carré d'agneau **rack of lamb**
cassoulet **stew of beans, sausages, pork and duck, from southwest France**
chateaubriand **thick steak**
choucroute **Alsace dish of sauerkraut, pork and sausages**
confit **duck or goose preserved in its own fat**
contre-filet **cut of sirloin steak**
coq au vin **chicken in red wine**
côte d'agneau **lamb chop**

daube **beef stew with red wine**
dinde **turkey**
entrecôte **beef rib steak**
escargot **snail**
faisan **pheasant**
farci **stuffed**
faux-filet **sirloin**
foie **liver**
foie de veau **calf's liver**
foie gras **fatty goose or duck liver pâté**
grillade **grilled meat**
hachis **minced meat**
jambon **ham**
lapin **rabbit**
lardons **small pieces of bacon**
magret de canard **breast of duck**
médaillon **rolled meat/medallion**
moelle **beef bone marrow**
navarin **stew of lamb with onions, carrots and turnips**
oie **goose**
perdrix **partridge**
pintade **guinea fowl**
porc **pork**
pot-au-feu **casserole of beef and vegetables**
poulet **chicken**
poussin **young chicken**
rognons **kidneys**
sanglier **wild boar**
saucisse **fresh sausage**
saucisson **dry sausage**
veau **veal**

Poissons (Fish)

à l'armoricaine **with white wine, tomatoes, butter and cognac**
anchois **anchovies**
anguille **eel**
bar (or loup) **sea bass**
barbue **brill**
belon **Brittany oyster**
bigorneau **sea snail**
Bercy **sauce of fish stock, butter, white wine and shallots**
bouillabaisse **fish soup, served with grated cheese, garlic croutons and rouille (spicy sauce)**
cabillaud **cod**
calmar **squid**
colin **hake**
coquillage **shellfish**
coquilles St-Jacques **scallops**
crevette **shrimp**
daurade **sea bream**
flétan **halibut**
fruits de mer **seafood**
homard **lobster**

huître **oyster**
langoustine **large prawn**
limande **lemon sole**
lotte **monkfish**
morue **salt cod**
moule **mussel**
moules marinières **mussels in white wine and onions**
raie **skate**
saumon **salmon**
thon **tuna**
truite **trout**

Vegetables

ail **garlic**
artichaut **artichoke**
asperge **asparagus**
avocat **avocado**
champignon **mushroom**
cornichon **gherkin**
cru **raw**
crudités **chopped or shredded raw vegetables**
frites **chips, French fries**
haricots **dried beans**
haricots verts **green beans**
lentilles **lentils**
mesclun **mixed-leaf salad**
noisette **hazelnut**
noix **nut, walnut**
oignon **onion**
poireau **leek**
pois **peas**
poivron **bell pepper**
pomme de terre **potato**
ratatouille **Provençal vegetable stew in olive oil**
roquette **rocket, arugula**
salade niçoise **egg, tuna, olives, onions and tomato salad**
salade verte **green salad**

Fruit

ananas **pineapple**
cerise **cherry**
citron **lemon**
citron vert **lime**
figue **fig**
fraise **strawberry**
framboise **raspberry**
groseille **redcurrant**
mirabelle **small yellow plum**
pamplemousse **grapefruit**
pêche **peach**
poire **pear**
pomme **apple**
prune **plum**
pruneau **prune**
raisin **grape**

Sauces

ailloli **garlic mayonnaise**
béarnaise **egg, butter, wine and herbs**
forestière **mushrooms and bacon**
hollandaise **egg, butter and lemon sauce**
lyonnaise **onions**
meunière **butter, lemon and parsley sauce (for fish)**
meurette **red wine**
Mornay **cream, egg and cheese**
paysan **rustic-style, ingredients depend on the region**
pistou **Provençal sauce of basil, garlic and olive oil; vegetable soup with the sauce**
provençale **tomatoes, garlic and olive oil**
papillotte **cooked in paper**

Desserts

Belle Hélène **fruit with ice cream and chocolate sauce**
chèvre **goat's cheese**
clafoutis **baked pudding of batter and cherries**
coulis **purée of fruit or vegetables**
crème anglaise **custard**
crème caramel **caramelised egg custard**
crème Chantilly **whipped cream**
fromage **cheese**
île flottante **whisked egg whites in custard sauce**
pêche melba **peaches with ice cream and raspberry sauce**
tarte tatin **upside-down tart of caramelised apples**

In the Café

If you sit or stand at the bar (le zinc), drinks will be cheaper than at a table. Settle the bill when you leave; the waiter may leave a slip of paper on the table to keep track of the bill.

drinks les boissons
coffee café
...with milk or cream au lait or crème
...decaffeinated déca/décaféiné
...black/espresso express/noir
tea thé
...herb infusion infusion/tisane
hot chocolate chocolat chaud
milk lait
... full-cream entier

... semi-skimmed demi-écrémé
... skimmed écrémé
mineral water eau minérale
... fizzy gazeuse/pétillante
... non-fizzy non-gazeuse/plate
fizzy lemonade limonade
fresh lemon juice served with sugar citron pressé
fresh squeezed orange juice orange pressée
fresh or cold frais, fraîche
beer bière
...bottled en bouteille
...on tap à la pression
pre-dinner drink apéritif
white wine with cassis, blackcurrant liqueur kir
kir with champagne kir royal
with ice avec des glaçons
neat sec
red rouge
white blanc
rose rosé
dry brut
sweet doux
sparkling wine crémant
house wine vin de maison
local wine vin de pays
pitcher carafe/pichet
...of water/wine d'eau/de vin
half-litre demi-carafe
quarter-litre quart
mixed panaché
after-dinner drink digestif
cheers! santé!

TABLE TALK

I am a vegetarian Je suis végétarien (végétarienne if female)
I am on a diet Je suis au régime
What do you recommend? Qu'est-ce que vous recommandez?
Do you have some local specialities? Avez-vous des spécialités locales?
I'd like to order Je voudrais commander
That is not what I ordered Ce n'est pas ce que j'ai commandé
Is service included? Est-ce que le service est compris?
May I have more wine? Encore du vin, s'il vous plaît?
Enjoy your meal Bon appétit!

TRANSPORT   ACCOMMODATION   ACTIVITIES   A – Z

FURTHER READING

History and Culture

France in the New Century, by John Ardagh. Peter Smith. Weighty tome on modern France.
Côte d'Azur: Inventing the French Riviera, by Mary Blume. Thames and Hudson. Excellent account of émigré Riviera.
The Identity of France, by Fernand Braudel. HarperCollins. Hard to put down analysis in two volumes, weaving major events with everyday life, by one of France's best historians.
A Traveller's History of France, by Robert Cole. Interlink. Background reading.
France on the Brink: a Great Civilization Faces the New Century, by Jonathan Fenby. Arcade. Detailed account of French politics and society.
When the Riviera was Ours, by Patrick Howarth. Pimlico. The development of the Riviera as a tourist resort.
Travels in the South of France, by Stendhal. John Calder. Record of a journey made by the author in 1838.
The French, by Theodore Zeldin. Harvill Press. Analysis of contemporary French society.

Fiction

The Rock Pool, by Cyril Connolly. Persea Books. Satirical novel set in 1930s Riviera.
Tender is the Night, by F. Scott Fitzgerald. Penguin. Tale of wealth and decadence originally published in 1933.
Collected Short Stories, by Katherine Mansfield. Penguin. Mansfield wrote some of her best stories during her stay on the Riviera in 1920.
Bonjour Tristesse, by Françoise

Sagan. Penguin. Hugely successful novel written by Sagan in 1955 when she was 18 years old.
Perfume, by Patrick Süskind. Penguin. Unusual bestseller set in the perfumed world of 18th-century Grasse.

FEEDBACK

We do our best to ensure the information in our books is as accurate and up-to-date as possible. The books are updated on a regular basis, using local contacts, who painstakingly add, amend and correct as required. However, some mistakes and omissions are inevitable and we are ultimately reliant on our readers to put us in the picture.
We would welcome your feedback on any details related to your experiences using the book "on the road". Maybe we recommended a hotel that you liked (or another that you didn't), as well as interesting new attractions, or facts and figures you have found out about the country itself. The more details you can give us (particularly with regard to addresses, e-mails and telephone numbers), the better. We will acknowledge all contributions, and we'll offer an Insight Guide to the best letters received.

Please write to us at:
Insight Guides
PO Box 7910
London SE1 1WE
United Kingdom
Or send e-mail to:
insight@apaguide.co.uk

Food and Art

A Table in Provence, by Leslie Forbes. Penguin. Recipes.
A Life of Picasso, Vols I, II and III, by John Richardson. Jonathan Cape.
France: A History in Art, by Bradley Smith. Weidenfeld & Nicolson. The history of France seen through the eyes of artists.
The Unknown Matisse, by Hilary Spurling. University of California Press.

Other Insight Guides

Insight Guides to France include *Southwest France*, *Provence* and *Paris* among other regions.

Insight Pocket Guides, which contain route-based itineraries and a large fold-out map, cover *Paris*, *Provence* and *other regions of France*.

Insight Compact Guides and the new *Insight Smart Guides*, fact-packed easy-reference guides, cover a number of French regions. *Insight Fleximaps*. Durable maps with essential information. French regions include Provence.

ART & PHOTO CREDITS

Agence Images/Alamy 6T, 75, 240
Jean-Pierre Amet/BelOmbra/Corbis 111T
Ingo Arndt/NPL 77
Jon Arnold Images/Alamy 55
Art Archive/Culver Pictures 42
Aslan-Macault/epa/Corbis 38
Ian Badley/Alamy 12/13, 159BL
Pete Bennett/APA 4CL
Bettmann/Corbis 44R, 45
Peter Bowater/Alamy 62
The Bridgeman Art Library 47, 48
Courtesy of Cannes Tourism 246
Herve Champollion/akg-images 157
Douglas Corrance 87T, 95, 98, 109L, 155, 161, 191, 237, 238, 239, 243
Douglas Dickens 228
Directphoto.org/Alamy 165
Mary Evans Picture Library 28, 40
Pascal Guyot/Pool/Getty Images 190T
George W Hales/Getty Images 39
Nick Hanna/Alamy 76BL
Hulton Archive/Getty Images 124
Michael Jenner/Alamy 68BR
Jtb Photo/Photolibrary 171
Wolfgang Kaehler/Alamy 135L
János Kalmár 197
Catherine Karnow 3BR, 36, 56, 57, 67, 73, 86T, 130, 131, 134, 178, 179, 181, 196, 198BR, 199, 205, 209, 221, 229, 233
Charles & Josette Lenars/Corbis 7CL, 136T
Ken Lewis/Images France 8BR, 242T
Ludovic Maisant/Corbis 174BL
Clive Mason/Getty Images 200
Barry Miles 132, 223
Gail Mooney/Corbis 9BR, 111, 135R
Nègre 21, 23, 27
Pictor International 175, 214
Profimedia International s.r.o./Alamy 54
Roy Rainford/Robert Harding Picture Library 164
Rex Features 31, 33
Roger-Viollet/Topfoto 29, 35, 43
Eric Ryan/Getty Images 129T
Pascal Le Segretain/Getty Images 110, 190BR

Sygma 37
Time & Life Pictures/Getty Images 46
Topham Picturepoint 41, 44L
David C Tomlinson/Getty Images 206T
UPP/TopFoto 49
Bill Wassman 3TL, 17, 34, 69, 123T, 154, 160, 175T, 195T, 224R, 234T
Gregory Wrona/APA 1, 2/3, 4T, 5BR, 6BL, 6BR, 7TR, 7BR, 8TR, 8BL, 9TR, 9CL, 10/11, 14, 16, 18, 19, 52, 53, 58/59, 60/61, 66, 68T, 69T, 70, 70T, 71, 74, 75T, 76BR, 76T, 77T, 78L, 78R, 78T, 80, 81, 82T, 83BL, 84BR, 84T, 85, 86, 87, 88BL, 88T, 89, 89T, 90BR, 91, 91T, 92, 94, 96T, 97, 97T, 99L, 99R, 100, 101, 101T, 102, 103, 104, 104T, 105, 106, 107, 108T, 109R, 112, 112T, 113, 113T, 114, 114T, 115, 116, 117, 121, 122, 123, 125, 126, 127, 128, 129, 133, 133T, 134T, 136, 138, 139, 140BR, 140T, 141, 141T, 142, 142T, 143, 143T, 144, 144T, 145T, 148, 149, 150L, 150R, 151, 151T, 152, 153L, 153R, 153T, 154T, 155T, 156, 157T, 158, 158T, 159T, 161T, 162L, 162R, 163, 167, 167T, 168, 169, 170, 172, 173, 174T, 176, 177, 182, 183, 183T, 184, 185, 185T, 186, 188, 189, 191T, 192, 192T, 193, 194, 196T, 199T, 201, 204, 207, 208T, 210, 211, 212, 212T, 213, 214T, 215, 216, 217, 218, 219, 222L, 222R, 223T, 224L, 225, 225T, 226, 227, 227T, 229T, 231T, 232, 234, 235, 236, 236T, 238T, 241, 242, 244, 245, 245T, 249, 251, 253, 255, 259, 261, 263, 267

PICTURE SPREADS

50/51: The Art Archive/Musée d'Orsay Paris/Dagli Orti 50CR; The Art Archive/Museo Picasso Barcelona/Dagli Orti 51BC; Robert Capa/Magnum 51TR; DACS/Galerie Daniel Malingue, Paris, France/ The Bridgeman Art Library 50/51;

DACS/Giraudon, Kunstmuseum, Basel, Switzerland/The Bridgeman Art Library/ 51CL; DACS/Lucien Herve, Private Collection/The Bridgeman Art Library 50BL; Catherine Karnow 50TL; Gregory Wrona/APA 51BR

118/119: ABACA/Empics 118BR; Agence images/Alamy 119BR; Andanson James/Corbis Sygma 119CL; Pascal Guyot/AFP/Getty 118/119; Hemis/Alamy 118CR; PA/Empics 118TL; Eric Ryan/Getty 118BL; Ian Walton/Getty 119TR

146/147: Agence Images/Alamy 146/147; Robert Harding/Getty 147TR; Gregory Wrona/APA 146TL, 146CR, 146BL, 146BR, 147CL, 147BR

202/203: Dave Bartruff/Corbis 202/203; Hervé Champollion/akg-images 203BR; Robert Harding/Alamy 203TR; Chris Hellier/Corbis 202TL, 202BR; Chris Lisle/Corbis 202BL; Barry Mason/Alamy 202CR, 203BL

Permissions
The Pigeons, 1957 by Pablo Picasso
©Succession Picasso/DACS, London 2006
Cannes, 1947 by Pierre Bonnard
©ADAGP, Paris and DACS, London 2006
The Bay of Angels, Nice, 1929 by Raoul Dufy
©ADAGP, Paris and DACS, London 2006

Touring Map: Bill Wassman/APA cover; **Pete Bennett/APA** wine basket; **Gregory Wrona/APA** all other images

Map Production: Phoenix Map and Neal Jordan-Caws

©2007 Apa Publications GmbH Verlag KG, Singapore Branch

Production: Linton Dona

GENERAL INDEX

Register with
HotelClub.com
and get £15!

At **HotelClub.com**, we reward our Members with discounts and free stays in their favourite hotels. As a Member, every booking made by you through **HotelClub.com** will earn you Member Dollars.

When you register, we will credit your account with **£15** which you can use for your next booking! The equivalent of **£15** will be credited in US$ to your Member account (as **HotelClub Member Dollars**). All you need to do is log on to **www.HotelClub.com/cityguides**. Complete your details, including the Membership Number and Password located on the back of the **HotelClub.com** card.

Over 2.2 million Members already use Member Dollars to pay for all or part of their hotel bookings. Join now and start spending Member Dollars whenever and wherever you want – you are not restricted to specific hotels or dates!

With great savings of up to 60% on over 20,000 hotels across 97 countries, you are sure to find the perfect location for business or pleasure. Happy travels from **HotelClub.com!**

www.insightguides.com

HotelClub.com